May '06

To Lou, thanks #4
for a great time!
Vx

SCARS OF
SWEET PARADISE

D0609088

ALSO BY ALICE ECHOLS

Daring to Be Bad:
Radical Feminism in America,
1967–1975

(photograph courtesy of Baron Wolman)

SCARS OF
SWEET PARADISE

THE LIFE AND TIMES OF

JANIS
JOPLIN

ALICE ECHOLS

A *Virago* Book

Published by Virago Press 2001
First published by Virago Press 2000

First published by Metropolitan Books, an imprint of
Henry Holt and Company, Inc 1999

A CIP catalogue record for this book is
available from the British Library

ISBN 1 86049 729 2

Printed and bound in Great Britain
by Clays Ltd, St Ives plc

Virago Press
A Division of
Little, Brown and Company (UK)
Brettenham House
Lancaster Place
London WC2E 7EN

For my mother
and in memory
of my father

If you don't believe there's a price
For this sweet paradise
Just remind me to show you the scars.

BOB DYLAN
"Where Are You Tonight?"

Contents

Introduction

When Janis Joplin was a small child her mother found her one night outside on the sidewalk sleepwalking away from their house. "Janis, what are you doing?" she shouted after her daughter. "Where are you going?" Her question was one the Joplins would surely want to ask their wayward daughter many times in the future, but then Janis simply said, "I'm going home. I'm going home." Even as a child, Janis seemed to know it was a bad match, that her home just couldn't be the oil refinery town of Port Arthur, Texas.

Janis stopped sleepwalking, but she never stopped moving. The small child setting out for home alone in the middle of the night—there couldn't be a more poignant and true image of the singer whose life and music were defined by restlessness. You can hear the restlessness in her incredible wall-of-sound voice. Janis wasn't content merely to hit a note right; she trained her voice to sound as if she were singing two notes simultaneously. And while most white blues musicians played respectful and faithful renditions of the classics, Janis's blues were slash-and-burn assaults, screeches and screams of bewilderment and despair at life's many injustices, among them her own terrible loneliness. In the end, home was a place Janis glimpsed but never really found, remaining instead curiously unanchored throughout her life. One close friend called her "the most obvious, best-publicized homeless person of the sixties," so palpable was her loneliness.

But Janis's alienation was more than a personal estrangement—it was the experience of a generation. "She went through all the changes we did," said Jerry Garcia when she died. "She went on all the same trips. She was just like the rest of us—fucked up, strung out, in weird places." Garcia may have been exaggerating the similarities, but certainly Janis's journey was not hers alone. Along with many other wannabe beatniks, Janis spent years on the road emulating Jack Kerouac, paving the way for the counterculture. Crisscrossing the country, bohemian kids lived like nomads, "sailing," as Tom Wolfe observed, "like gypsies along the Service-center fringes" of America.

When they did settle for a while, it was in America's crumbling inner-city neighborhoods, San Francisco's Haight-Ashbury, for example, where Janis landed in the midsixties. While her parents had participated in the largest migration of American history—the post–World War II urban exodus—Janis and her drop-out friends pioneered a reverse migration back to the cities their parents had abandoned. In contrast to the generations of immigrants forced to live in ghettoes as they pursued the American Dream, the hippies "came to the ghetto fleeing America." For them, as for the Beats before them, constant motion and identification with the downtrodden served to fend off the blandness, conventionality, and hyperdomesticity of the fifties. Theirs was a way of life underwritten by America's extraordinary affluence but predicated on the conviction that wealth and comfort bred spiritual and emotional impoverishment and strangled all authenticity and soulfulness. "Money doesn't talk, it swears," sneered Bob Dylan.

Rootless, unattached, and defiant, Janis was the quintessential "nobody's girl," a position that was both liberating and painful. She craved motion; it was such an exhilarating distraction—from herself and from the hurts that plagued her, from her agonizing coming of age in Port Arthur.

And stardom brought Janis all kinds of motion, but it also intensified her loneliness as life became a blur of hotel rooms, dressing rooms, airports, and bars; dressed outrageously, her wild mane bedecked with pink and blue feathers, her arms loaded with bracelets that jangled away noisily, Janis was set apart, frequently an object of admiration but often of ridicule and scorn. Although she thumbed her nose at straight society, Janis still desperately wanted to be liked, even by those she despised. If she bristled at having her independence compromised by intimate relationships, she nevertheless despaired at belonging to no one. Like other rebels of her time, Janis rejected rigid categories of identity; in her world, racial and sometimes even sexual categories were disdained as straitjackets. Janis, however, took experimentation further than most, pursuing sex with men and women, proclaiming herself the "first white-black person," and drinking and carousing like one of the boys. There was wild pleasure in all her freedom, but there were costs as well. Janis tried to shield herself from the abuse that followed her rebelliousness by projecting a tough-girl ballsiness, but the put-downs and insults hit home nevertheless.

Much of Janis's pain stemmed from her desire to be somebody at a time when girls were supposed to be satisfied nabbing Mr. Right. Janis wanted to nab Mr. Right, too, but she wanted something else as well. On more than one occasion she admitted "no guy ever made me feel as good as an audience." But hers was an uncharted path and she moved down it unsteadily. Janis may have been a rebel (the first girl at the University of Texas to go braless, or so legend has it), but she was never able to break fully with the orthodoxies of the fifties. And in truth, virtually no one—not even the most determined rebels—escaped the fifties unscathed. What makes Janis's rebelliousness particularly remarkable is that she was so far ahead of her time, refusing to be a good girl long before the revival of modern feminism legitimized such refusal. In 1967, when Janis began commanding headlines, the first women's liberation groups had not yet formed, and career and family still seemed utterly unreconcilable for women. And when it came to relations between men and women, even the counterculture wasn't really counter. Janis's struggle would have been hard enough had she just set out to be a successful pop singer, but she was also trying to carve out a space for herself in a culture where the only sanctioned role for a woman was as her man's "old lady."

Janis may have been nobody's girl, but she didn't die a nobody. In the end, the "pig" of Port Arthur became rock's first female superstar—a reversal of fortune that Janis always relished. Indeed, like her idol Bessie Smith, Janis was the very embodiment of the "dynamic of reversal" so central to blues music—the making of nobodies into somebodies. In a reflective moment Janis once pondered "what strange, weird events" had brought her "to this place." As usual, she minimized her talent, suggesting that "every fucking conceivable thing brought it all together to make this strange person, this chick who was good at this one thing, man, just this one fucking thing." She had "lost a lot along the way," she said, adding, "I may never get it back." But she never gave up. "I know I ain't quittin'," she insisted. Janis suffered tremendous losses, but neither those nor the tragedy of her death can dwarf her achievements or her spirit, which was nothing if not resilient.

Before Janis Joplin, there was another Janis, Janis Martin. In 1956, fifteen-year-old Janis Martin scored a top-ten hit for RCA with "Will You, Willyum." Just months before signing Martin, who'd been performing since she was eleven, RCA had paid Sun Records the unprecedented sum of $25,000 for Elvis Presley's contract. Within weeks, someone at RCA had the bright idea of capitalizing on Elvis's success by billing Martin the "female Elvis," a moniker approved by both Elvis and his manager, Colonel Tom Parker. At first the formula seemed to work, as Martin broke into the Top 10 again with the rockabilly tune "My Boy Elvis." But Martin never really found a niche. Country audiences were often put off by rock 'n' roll moves they'd found adorable in her when she was a child but deemed vulgar and unseemly in a young lady. Martin claims that despite her love of R & B and rock 'n' roll, she was pushed toward country. Her RCA promo shot, however, offers some more-likely clues about why her career as a rock 'n' roller faltered. One look at the earnest, guitar-strumming Martin, and it's obvious that if there could have been a female Elvis, she wasn't it. While everything about Elvis, from his sneer and his long, pomaded, dyed black hair to his pumping pelvis, signaled he was a boy from the wrong side of the tracks, Martin evoked the wholesomeness of the girl next door. In truth, the effort to market her as the female analogue to Elvis was bound to fail. Fifties girls—black or white—could never have achieved stardom by staking out the same sexually transgressive territory that Elvis had so effortlessly claimed. After all, this was postwar America, where girls were supposed to be sexy, not sexual. How fitting, then, that RCA dropped Martin in 1958 on learning she'd been secretly married at fifteen and was now pregnant.

In the 1950s rock 'n' roll was a boys' club. *Grace of My Heart,* the film based loosely on the life of Carole King, shows the young singer-songwriter being turned down by yet another talent scout, who lets her in on an industry secret—not only does each label already have its one female singer, it's devising ways to dump her. And so it was until King and other New York songwriters began turning out hits for girl groups. Although the girl-group phenomenon began as a novelty with the Chantels' "Maybe" (a song Janis covered ten years later), by the early sixties girl groups had established a beachhead for women in rock 'n' roll. But if their songs were wildly popular, the singers themselves (with the exception of Diana Ross) remained anonymous—nameless and faceless to their listeners because record companies treated them like so many interchangeable cogs in a musical assembly line. Folksingers Joan Baez, Odetta, and Mary Travers of Peter, Paul and Mary also provided an opening wedge for women. Because of its simplicity—"Folk music was so easy," Joni Mitchell joked, "I was a professional in six months"—and its promotion of expressiveness over virtuosity, folk music, like punk of the seventies, encouraged women to grab a guitar, a ukelele, or an autoharp and climb up onstage. Of course, folk wasn't "music for the neck downwards," as Keith Richards once dubbed rock 'n' roll. Baez and other female folkies projected intelligence and sincerity, but they generated very little sexual heat. By contrast, black R & B singers like Etta James and Tina Turner (who now blames her ex-husband, Ike, for all those simulated blow jobs she gave microphones across America) sizzled with sexual energy, but most white Americans were completely unaware of them.

The white rock world had never seen or heard anything like Janis when she stormed the stage with Big Brother and the Holding Company at the Monterey Pop Festival in 1967. Grace Slick, the lead singer with the Jefferson Airplane, recalls that "Janis was *so* powerful and *so* different, all the emotions right out there." After a set that left the audience breathless,

Janis was on her way. The rock critic Robert Christgau raved about her performance, hyping her as perhaps the best rock singer since Ray Charles. But he was equally moved by her left nipple, "erect under her knit pantsuit, looking hard enough to put out your eye." Janis, said Christgau, "rocked and stomped and threatened any moment to break the microphone, or swallow it." A year later, when Columbia released Big Brother's album *Cheap Thrills*, Janis was already one of rock's reigning superstars. Her incredible rise signaled America's move away from the rigid categories of postwar culture, but it also, and above all, testified to her extraordinary talent and ambition. She was simply a force of nature. In a nation coming out of the fifties, Janis's unapologetic sexuality proved irresistible, especially to the reporters whom she supplied with an endless stream of outrageous copy. Janis likened performance to orgasm, swore like a sailor, and dressed like a psychedelicized hooker. Forget beachheads— Janis was like an invading army, seizing that rock 'n' roll land of desire in a way no white woman ever had.

It would be wonderful to imagine that Janis utterly remade the world of rock 'n' roll, but she didn't—its stubborn sexism persisted. Given the current popularity of female musicians it's easy to forget that rock 'n' roll has only recently become a more congenial place for women. That Janis didn't single-handedly close rock's gender gap isn't so odd; what is strange is that, unlike Jimi Hendrix and Jim Morrison, whose music remained staples of FM rock, Janis disappeared from the airwaves soon after her death. But while she was curiously absent, her style was absorbed, without credit and in a way that obscured her influence. Indeed, the singer Debbie Harry observes that "people do [Janis] even when they don't know they're doing her." In fact, more often than not, Harry points out, the people "doing" Janis are guys in heavy-metal hair bands, which may explain the amnesia surrounding the debt. Led Zeppelin's Robert Plant, the man most responsible for the Joplinesque quality of heavy-metal vocalizing, has to the best of my knowledge never cited her as an influence. Female rockers, on the other hand, have mostly stayed away from Janis's style; perhaps they have felt apprehensive or uneasy about the pain and masochism driving her performances.

Despite its intractability, the rock world did feel the effects of her powerful influence, as did the larger culture. Janis expanded notions of beauty for white women, as had Bessie Smith for black women forty years earlier. While Jimi Hendrix gave "bad hair" a good name among blacks, Janis made fashionable the frizzy, electric hair many white teenaged girls had struggled daily to iron into modish straightness. Janis, who achieved the look by sticking her wet mop in a heated oven, can take substantial credit for liberating American women from the tyranny of weekly beauty salon visits. And, as a sixties rock critic, Lillian Roxon, remembers, from girdles and bras as well. "You could walk around a concert or a festival anywhere in America and see them, the daughters of Janis, their tough and battered little faces defiantly free of make-up and other synthetic improvements; their hair positively triangular in its electricity; their clothes long, loose, and nomadic; and, look ma, no pantygirdles and better even than that, nipples."

Like Elvis, Janis refused to honor the borders she'd been raised to respect. In their appropriations of black style, both Janis and Elvis undermined the color line by subverting notions of white sexual restraint and black promiscuity. Just as Elvis made available to white boys a renegade masculinity, so Janis broadened the range of possibilities for white girls with her sexually provocative style. Etta James, whose blistering vocals so influenced Janis, said that Janis was "like an angel who came and paved a road white chicks hadn't walked down before." Of course, as whites Janis and Elvis also profited from their race bending. This is just about the oldest story in American show business, stretching back to blackface minstrelsy of the nineteenth century, but Janis handled her indebtedness to African Americans very differently from Elvis. While Elvis reportedly said that blacks could buy his records and shine his shoes, Janis promoted black artists and even put up money to finance a tombstone for Bessie Smith, who Janis said "showed me the air and taught me how to fill it."

Janis was by no means the only musician refusing to honor the color line in the 1960s. As Janis was trying to get down Etta James, Motown artist Marvin Gaye dreamed of becoming Frank Sinatra. Jimi Hendrix, Michael Bloomfield, Stevie Wonder, Paul Butterfield, the Rolling Stones, and Sly Stone are just a few of the artists whose music deliberately defied racial categorization. Nor was the transracial identification that characterized the sixties limited to the world of music. Civil rights activists struggled to forge a "beloved community" of blacks and whites. Even the founders of the Black Panther Party, Huey Newton and Bobby Seale, listened to Bob Dylan's "Ballad of a Thin Man" rather than to Aretha Franklin or Otis Redding as they composed their group's ten-point program. This extraordinary musical cross-fertilization was short-lived; by decade's end, racial boundaries—both political and cultural—were being shored up in ways that would narrow Janis's musical options.

The culmination of five years' worth of intensive interviewing and research, *Scars of Sweet Paradise* is both a biography of Janis Joplin and a cultural history of the time in which she lived. In contrast to other of her biographers, I don't pathologize or normalize Janis or make her over into a true lesbian. Rather than treat her life as an object lesson about the excesses of those times, I've tried to explore why for so many of us the sixties presented such stark choices: the quiet desperation of suburbia held in check by TV and all manner of material goodies or the full-tilt drive to "lay life" with desperate abandon. *Scars of Sweet Paradise* is my attempt to rethink this period we seem in danger of never getting over. Even after almost forty years the sixties remain mired in myth, reduced to a set of clichés that seem to function as a defense against true remembering. The sixties were "sex, drugs, and rock 'n' roll," or, to quote the Grateful Dead, a "long, strange trip." And, as Robin Williams put it, "If you can remember the sixties, you weren't really there." In other words, the sixties were so weird and trippy they defy understanding. It was "like a flying saucer landed," is Bob Dylan's recollection. Many still prefer to view the decade as the time when, out of the blue, America was abducted or went haywire in the grip of a collective hallucination.

Although the larger culture resists remembering, scholars of the sixties have made the period the subject of lively and contentious debate. But it's the world of radical politics that interests most scholars. Their books tend to portray young radicals as clean-cut, patriotic, and optimistic, at least until disillusionment sets in. But, as Paul Buhle, a former activist, points out, not all the rebels were nice boys and nice girls. Buhle, for one, did what Janis and so many other youthful nonconformists did: in the early sixties he headed for San Francisco, where he hung out in a "post-Beat, bohemian experimenting underground" marked by considerable cynicism and self-destructiveness. This was Janis's world, in Texas and San Francisco, a subculture peopled by the disenfranchised and the desperadoes, kids fleeing "the emotional dust bowl of their families, their schools, their hometowns, and their jobs."

Scars of Sweet Paradise is about that other world, the drop-out underground of sex, drugs, and rock 'n' roll—not the caricatured version to which we've become accustomed but something less familiar. This book is not a blow-by-blow account of Janis's every fuck and fix. It is, though, about rock 'n' roll: its dynamic relationship to race and gender; the merging of art and commerce that followed from Bob Dylan's electric turn and the cheeky pop of the Beatles; the shift toward corporatism, especially in the aftermath of Woodstock; the blues revival and the relationship of white blues musicians such as Janis and Michael Bloomfield to their black elders and to black culture. Finally, this book challenges the conventional view that remembers sex, drugs, and rock 'n' roll as one big, happy bash. Bob Seidemann, the photographer and Haight Street scenester who took the picture that made Janis America's first hippie pinup, says about those times, "It wasn't a party, man. The media liked to view it as a party and we were having fun and a lot of laughs, but it was very intense and people were dying among us and all around us." He remembers "fucking and sucking and getting it while we could. It was exciting to be there because you were literally on the cutting edge, but you *were* the edge of the sword doing the cutting. You were the fucking cannon fodder. That's what the people in the counterculture were. We all laid our bodies on the line."

"Put your body on the line" was a slogan sixties radicals often invoked to inspire themselves and their followers to greater acts of resistance. "There's a time when the operation of the machine becomes so odious, makes you so sick at heart, that you can't take part," declared Mario Savio of Berkeley's Free Speech Movement in 1964. "And you've got to put your bodies upon the gears and upon the wheels, upon the levers, upon all the apparatus and you've got to make it stop." Hippies and activists occupied different worlds but they were all involved in high-risk experimentation, often with the self the site of experimentation. To Ken Kesey and the Merry Pranksters, whose acid tests helped ignite the counterculture, the goal was simply "Furthur," as their Day-Glo bus proclaimed. Or as one survivor put it, "the feeling then was, if you've got a light, burn it out." No one did this more determinedly than Janis, who was fond of saying, "I'd rather have 10 years of superhypermost than live to be 70 by sitting in some goddamn chair watching TV." In the end, *Scars of Sweet Paradise* is about my generation's restless and sometimes reckless excursions to the edge, excursions from which Janis and many others never came back. It's about the longing, desperation, and alienation that fueled our self-experimentation, and the pleasure as well as the pain that followed from it.

Scars of Sweet Paradise is based largely on interviews—just over 150. Obtaining these interviews was far from easy. Although most people I contacted eventually agreed to speak to me and were often quite generous, they usually required considerable coaxing. Early on I began to see that mine was a phone call they were dreading. Even if they'd been thinking that no one else could possibly turn up to write another book about Janis, her friends and lovers all knew that one day some new writer would come along and dredge it all up again. And here I was, maybe not their nightmare but close to it. Their wariness was understandable, given the less than respectful biographical bottom-feeding Janis's life has sometimes inspired. In any case, each phone call began pretty much the same way, that is, uncomfortably. When I would explain the reason for my call, I'd be greeted by a sigh or a long silence. Milan Melvin, who'd been a San Francisco deejay and Janis's on-again, off-again boyfriend for two years, expressed what most everyone felt: "trepidation about walking with you on this trail."

So when I dialed Patti Skaff, one of Janis's closest friends from her days in Port Arthur, and she rejected my request for an interview, I was disappointed but hardly surprised. After reading a few of my articles, though, Patti finally agreed to talk with me. She told me about the despair she and Janis had felt about being stuck in east Texas, how they'd felt "screwed" by the "phony culture" all around them. Patti loved Janis, and to illustrate the intensity of her affection and loyalty, she told me about a strange, powerful incident.

In the seventies, Patti was living in New York City and working for a sculptor, Mark di Suvero. When the artist Neal Williams died, his friends arranged a memorial service at the Socrates Sculpture Park, where Patti worked as director. All the glitterati, including Andy Warhol and his entourage, showed up for the service. As befits a seventies art world event, there was a full bar, lots of food, and major attitude. Throughout the evening a bonfire burned. Eventually, the minimalist artist Larry Bell gave a eulogy for his friend. Bell and Williams had been among the many artists and musicians who made the hip bar Max's Kansas City their second home, and Bell regaled the crowd with a story about the night at Max's when Williams had gotten into a drunken argument with Janis that culminated in his actually kicking her under the table. While people chuckled and guffawed, Patti found herself growing angrier and angrier. After the eulogy, she walked over to Williams's friends and asked what they planned to do with his ashes, which were in a sealed urn. She remembers, "They were like, 'Whatever.'" Maybe their vagueness gave her the idea, or maybe just the time she needed. Patti went back to her apartment and grabbed a can opener. Returning to the park, she walked straight over to the urn, pried it open, and dumped Williams's ashes into the bonfire as his friends looked on in horror. "I was doing it for her," Patti explained. "I just felt, this guy's going back into the fire. People were very pissed at me, but I couldn't walk away from it. I really loved her and I still do. I defended her then and I'll defend her today. Janis was a victim and I always felt like a big sister to her."

Patti's rage that night came from feeling that Janis had been violated one too many times. It was an anger that many of her closest friends initially felt toward me, the new biographer. In telling me the story, Patti was demonstrating the lengths she would go to in order to protect Janis, from me as much as anyone else. Milan Melvin was more direct when he promised to do what he could for me and Janis, but he said, "If you misquote me or grossly switch the context, Janis will haunt you until I can get my hands on you."

Although I don't view Janis precisely as a victim, I understand why some people do—she was vilified, scorned, laughed at, and trivialized. Here's another story: Not long after Janis died, a little-known rock journalist published an especially spiteful article about her. It was the night of her New York debut and she had leveled the place, bewitching the city's notoriously hard-boiled critics. After the show, the guys in the band went out with some pretty young girls, and Janis, left alone, wandered off to a bar. It should have been a triumphant evening for her, but when the writer spotted Janis she was sitting by herself in a Lower East Side dive.

He joined her at the bar, but before long he began to find her "tiresome." Oblivious to him, Janis talked on and on about herself, her career, and her band. It must have made him furious, because, as he sat there half listening to her, he fantasized shutting her up with the ultimate put-down: "You forget you have acne." This is what her detractors couldn't forgive her: here she was, an acne-scarred, frizzy-haired woman who refused to cede center stage either to the guys or to the pretty girls. "Who does she think she is?" was one response she frequently provoked. But for me, Janis's refusal to abide by the rules of the game, her insistence on taking up space—lots of it—both on- and offstage, make her something other than a victim. As much as her singing, it was Janis's chutzpah, her refusal to knuckle under, that to this day awes so many of us.

Scars of Sweet Paradise won't please all the friends and lovers Janis left behind. After all, Janis was sometimes part of a rather down-and-dirty scene, which I cover in all its sordid detail. And while I can appreciate the social significance of Janis's assault on good-girl femininity, I'm sure it was sometimes more appealing in theory than in practice. Janis was nothing if not complicated, and so it's not surprising that she provoked in me a complicated response—annoyance, frustration, delight, and deep sadness. In the end, though, I trust readers will see that this book was written out of appreciation and profound regard for the not-so-pretty, scruffy singer from Texas who wailed, "No, it just can't be," and in the process made the world a different place for us all.

SCARS OF
SWEET PARADISE

1

The Great Nowhere

What's happening never happens there" was how Janis summed up life in her hometown. Port Arthur was so suffocating it felt as if it might suck the life right out of you, especially if you were a smart and curious girl like Janis. Dwarfed by oil refineries, chemical plants, and row after row of huge, squat oil-storage tanks, the town seemed like an afterthought to this vast industrial sprawl. At night when the burning flares from the refineries turned the sky "an eerie doomsday red" the place even looked like hell on earth. Then there was the smell, what some residents called "the smell of money." The whole "Golden Tri-angle" of Port Arthur, Orange, and Beaumont stank like a rotten egg. There was no way to avoid the fumes; in those days the plants simply blew all the gas out into the open air. At Lamar Tech, where Janis began college, the fumes from a nearby sulfur plant could become so noxious they'd melt the girls' nylons. After a day on campus, "you'd end up feeling like you'd eaten a book of matches." To Janis and her friends, the Golden Triangle was a smelly, stultifying, mosquito-ridden swamp—"a foot fungus" growing along the Texas-Louisiana border, wrote Molly Ivins. Even that organ of Establishment-think *Business Week* named Port Arthur one of the "ten ugliest towns on the planet."

Still, that wasn't the worst of it. The town that boasted "it oiled the world" seemed a cultural and intellectual wasteland to Janis and her friends. Port Arthur may have been in the technology forefront, but in every other respect it was as barren as its landscape was flat—"all drive-in movies and Coke stands," groused Janis. Its only bookstore was a Christian one. The place offered so little in the way of diversion that Janis's father would take the kids on outings to the post office to look at the latest Most Wanted posters. "There was simply nowhere to go," sighs Janis's high school friend Dave Moriaty.

Patti Skaff blames the cultural drought on middle-class Port Arthurans who "didn't really have much of an idea of what to do except to buy a new car every other year." After all, she says, "look where they built their first country club—directly below a refinery." Moriaty has a different explanation. Most residents, he points out, moved there to work in the refineries. It was one of the few places that people, even MIT-educated engineers, could find work during the Great Depression. "It went from nothing," says Moriaty, "to the fifth-largest city in Texas in 1940." Yet few people, he argues, thought about making it a congenial place for the children of all the professionals hired by the refineries. "Intellectual and cultural achievement didn't give you any advantage," recalls Moriaty. "Nobody cared that we were smart and talented." Harry Britt, a gay activist who grew up in Port Arthur, says it's pretty clear why Janis and her hometown weren't a match. "Port Arthur is not a Janis Joplin town. Port Arthur would see country western star Tex Ritter, who was born in nearby Nederland, as its own, not Janis Joplin."

The dissonance Britt identifies was real. It also provided journalists with a ready-made hook: Janis Joplin, red-hot hippie mama from redneck Bible-banging Port Arthur. Journalists loved the implausibility of her story. Port Arthurans, for their part, were happy to disown her. And Janis enjoyed nothing so much as nurturing her own outsized legend as the Lone Star State's most famous misfit rebel, a canny move in the years after

President Kennedy's assassination, when Texas became the state it was okay to hate. Janis and her friends certainly were out of place, and they did feel cheated growing up there. The childhood reminiscences of her friends, though, begin to solve the mystery of how Janis Joplin could have emerged from Port Arthur.

First of all, Janis's hometown wasn't a typical Bible Belt backwater. Unlike many southern towns, Port Arthur boasted one of the best white school systems in Texas because the oil companies pumped money into it. And if Port Arthur's solid citizens seemed overly concerned with piety and propriety, it may well have been because their downtown was funkier than just about any other in the South, outside of New Orleans. Port Arthur was a real-life Sin City, a "wide-open town with whorehouses, casinos, slot machines—the whole thing." Its thirty-two brothels offered a cornucopia of red-light-district delights. (None of this was lost on Janis and her teenage pals, who kept count of the town's brothels.) The whole show was run by a New Orleans mob family who made a fortune off transient sailors stuck in Port Arthur for a night or two. The police looked the other way until the late fifties, when an investigating committee from the Texas legislature came to town and shut it all down. Curious teenagers, aware of the sexual underground thriving in their midst, could hardly help being struck by the hypocrisy and "phoniness" of the townspeople. They certainly understood that not all the men slipping off to visit prostitutes were sailors passing through town and that the same cops who talked law and order were in bed with the mob. One of Janis's friends remembers watching the town's sheriff trying to explain on TV how "those envelopes of cash would magically end up on the front seat of his car while he was in a café grabbing a cup of coffee."

Graft, gambling, and prostitution were not Port Arthur's only distinguishing features. A city of uprooted people, Port Arthur lacked the entrenched class structure that characterized most southern cities. There were tensions, for sure, between the educated "Yankee" professionals and the backwoods east Texan and Louisianan laborers, but their kids attended the same high school. Class distinctions were also muted because Port Arthur was a union town—the only one in all of Texas. Blue-collar refinery workers, like autoworkers of that period, were fairly well paid. "Lots of working-class boys' dads bought them new cars," says Moriaty. In fact, blue-collar workers with seniority sometimes made more money than the town's professionals. As a result, working-class and middle-class kids didn't inhabit entirely separate worlds, especially if, like Janis, they were bent on confounding social mores. Port Arthur's relatively porous class lines help explain why Janis, who was raised middle class, sometimes came off as working class.

Blue-collar and white-collar workers and their families may have mingled, but blacks and whites in Port Arthur lived strictly separate lives. In the fifties, Port Arthur was 40 percent black, with significant numbers of Cajuns and Mexican Americans, too. Segregation was the rule; indeed, to avoid integrating the high school, the town built another one outside city limits. Racism was so much a part of the town's fabric that "nigger knocking"—where whites would hang out of speeding cars wielding wooden boards and take aim at black pedestrians—was a favorite pastime among white teens. Those who tried to breach the color line found few opportunities to do so. When one of Janis's friends got involved in an impromptu game of touch football with some black kids, the police promptly broke it up. Racial containment was pursued all the more vigorously in the South in these years when the civil rights movement—and rock 'n' roll—were upending the logic and practice of segregation. Rock 'n' roll concerts and dances promoted the very mixing of races and cultural styles segregationists feared would lead to the "mongrelization" of America. In the spring of 1956, the segregationist Asa Carter led a campaign to have rock 'n' roll records removed from all jukeboxes in Birmingham and Anniston, Alabama. That same year, San Antonio, Texas, banned rock 'n' roll from the jukeboxes at its public swimming pools. To many segregationists, rock 'n' roll was nothing less than an NAACP plot to pull white men "down to the level of the Negro."

Though Port Arthur had white and black schools, churches, water fountains, and everything else, whites still had to go through the black section of town to get to the refineries or the ocean. On those drives, white kids like Janis could see the hypocrisy of "equality" firsthand; they also encountered something more vital than the depleted culture in which they felt trapped. And though Cajuns hadn't yet acquired the cultural capital they have today, the area's Cajun community also seemed alive and dynamic: Cajuns "had passion," Patti Skaff felt; "they had music, they had bars, dances, and fights with each other." Once Janis and her friends were able to pass for eighteen, they'd cross over to Cajun Louisiana—just a few minutes from Port Arthur over the Rainbow Bridge—and haunt its dives.

Port Arthur was stultifying, but it was a city on the make. With nearby Beaumont, it boasted the largest petroleum seaport in the world. There was no reason to think the town wouldn't just continue to flourish. However, with the downsizing of the oil refineries, a process that began in the 1970s, Port Arthur lost thousands of jobs. Today, it's just "a poor, beat-up remnant of a town," as Moriaty puts it. "Malled out of existence," Port Arthur is a virtual ghost town, so desolate it rivals Rust Belt cities like Flint, Michigan. Go downtown and you'll find no hardware stores, pharmacies, or department stores, only a few scattered businesses: a nail salon, a bar, and a chemotherapy clinic—the legacy of all that smelly air. Even the bus station is shuttered. Port Arthur's finest hotel, the elegant twelve-story Goodhue, the site of Janis's high school reunion, is gone, torn down. Small wonder, then, that what's left of the "Yankee elite" congregates at the Port Arthur Club, a windowless building where members can while away the hours reminiscing about the good old days without having to look out at the boarded-up storefronts all around.

Once controlled by whites, Port Arthur is now predominantly black, with a smaller but significant Vietnamese population. In the late seventies, whites began moving to nearby Port Neches, Groves, and Nederland, some say to avoid school integration. Like many other towns facing economic ruination, Port Arthur has tried to put a good face on its troubles by erecting a tribute to itself, the Museum of the Gulf Coast. It's perhaps the most telling sign of the town's desperation that Janis is prominently featured there. Some things, however, never change. When an elderly white volunteer learns why I've stopped in, she can't resist telling me that she has never approved of Janis, thereby allowing me to glimpse, if only for a moment, what it was like being Janis Joplin in Port Arthur.

Janis's parents, Seth Joplin and Dorothy East, met in the Texas panhandle town of Amarillo. Dorothy grew up on a farm in Nebraska and a ranch in Oklahoma. After her father's hog-farming venture failed, he moved the family to Amarillo and embarked on a career selling real estate. Dorothy's

mother, a dour woman whose mood wasn't helped by her husband's wom-
anizing and drinking, fled the family several times. Dorothy witnessed terrible shouting matches between her parents and vowed that when she was
married she would always "make things work." Seth, too, grew up knowing something about hardship and pain. His father managed the stock-
yards in Amarillo, but the family was far from financially comfortable. To
make ends meet the Joplins took in boarders. Lots of poorer Americans
did this, but most didn't split up their own families. The Joplins, however,
felt they had to protect their children from the rough-and-tumble stock-
yard workers moving in and so they settled their daughter in town and
installed Seth in a small cabin behind the house.

Dorothy had a powerful soprano voice, but Amarillo afforded her few
opportunities for showing it off. Her voice did land her a college scholarship at Texas Christian University. Dissatisfied with the college's singing
program, she returned to Amarillo, where she found a temporary job as a
sales clerk at Montgomery Ward. Although there were limits to how far a
woman could go in those years, Dorothy went pretty far. In no time she'd
displaced the vacationing worker, and shortly thereafter she was named
department head. But while Dorothy was a dynamo, Seth seems to have
been something of a slacker, nearly flunking out of the engineering program at Texas A&M. He said it was the Depression rather than poor
grades that forced him to drop out during his final semester. Though only
a term short of graduating, Seth never completed his degree. Returning to
Amarillo in 1932, he found work pumping gasoline at a service station.
After hours he was reputed to be something of a "playboy."

Seth met Dorothy on a blind date. In 1935, about three years into their
courtship, one of Seth's college friends recommended him for a job in
Port Arthur at Texas Company, which would later be renamed Texaco.
Dorothy's boss offered to double her salary if she would stay, but she
chose to go to Port Arthur instead. Seth worked at a Texaco plant that
made petroleum containers, a job that doesn't seem to have involved any
actual engineering work, although it did exempt him from military service
during World War II. Family legend has it that even with the new job he
and Dorothy were so poor they couldn't afford to get married right away.
When they finally wed in 1936, it was a spartan affair without a single relative in attendance. Before long, however, Dorothy's mother, now sepa-
rated, showed up on their doorstep with her youngest daughter, Mimi, in

tow. Their arrival pushed Seth and Dorothy to buy their first house. When the Joplins weren't working, they were partying across the Sabine River in the bars of Vinton, Louisiana, the same town where Janis and her pals would drink and carouse. When Dorothy became pregnant, six years after they were married, their hijinks across the border came to an abrupt end.

Janis Lyn was born on the morning of January 19, 1943. She remained an only child until she was six and, for those years at least, she was the undisputed star of the Joplin family. She also shone outside the home, doing so well at school she skipped the second grade. Up through the ninth grade, Janis was a popular girl; she even had a boyfriend, Jack Smith. Their relationship was "real tame," according to him, amounting to nothing more than going to a few church outings and movies together and playing bridge with her parents. He also accompanied the Joplins to church, where Janis was getting a reputation for her singing. Jack reports that Janis was among the featured soloists in the church choir. She only sang solo on a verse here and there, but it was a big deal for Janis, who corralled Jack and others into going to church to hear her. Janis never mentioned this part of her teenage years to the press, preferring to tell apocryphal stories about stealing hubcaps. But contrary to her legend, Janis didn't start out feeling like a nobody in Port Arthur. Far from it, contends Jack. "She was already a little star." She was also, he says, "the apple of her mother's eye."

Janis's beautiful soprano voice must have pleased her mother—but it also pained her. Just before Janis's sixth birthday Dorothy had bought her a secondhand upright piano and had taught her how to play nursery tunes. Janis loved pounding away at the piano, but it didn't stay in the Joplin house for long. Seth got rid of it when Dorothy's crystalline singing voice was destroyed by a thyroid operation that damaged her vocal chords. Unable to sing, Dorothy found it too painful listening to Janis, and Seth had always disliked the nightly cacophony anyway. One wonders how Janis absorbed their justifications for the piano's removal.

Around the time Janis lost her piano she gained a sister. Shortly after Laura's birth, the Joplins moved to the fringes of Griffing Park, a wealthier area of Port Arthur. Though their home was still modest by any standards, it signaled their arrival in the middle class, even if only on its lower rungs. Four years after Laura's birth, when Janis was ten, Michael was born. The Joplins had high hopes for their three children, whom they encouraged to read and study diligently. Self-improvement was the rule in the Joplin household. Dorothy arranged private art lessons for Janis, who loved to draw from an early age. In contrast to many of their peers, Janis, Laura, and Michael did not spend hours pasted in front of the family television set. "The biggest thing in our house was when you learnt to write your name," recalled Janis. "You got to go and get your library card." Janis considered her father, who refused to get a TV, "a secret intellectual, a book reader, a talker, a thinker." He was also an inveterate tinkerer, putting his creative energy into building unusual playground contraptions that delighted—and, on occasion, injured—neighborhood kids. Dorothy was the parent who tried to instill discipline and the value of perseverance in the children. Although Laura writes with great affection about her mother, calling her the "best teacher" she ever had, she says Dorothy always "monitored" their lives, pushing them to excel, suggesting how they might improve on whatever they were doing, even if they were only playing.

To most Port Arthurans, the Joplins seemed like the proverbial nice family. Like so many other Americans who lived through the dislocations and deprivations of the Great Depression and the Second World War, Seth and Dorothy Joplin wanted nothing so much as a "normal" home. What was understood as normal in the postwar years, however, was qualitatively different from anything that had preceded it. As historian Elaine Tyler May points out, the legendary nuclear family of the fifties was not, as is commonly believed, the "last gasp of 'traditional' family life" but rather the "first wholehearted effort to create a home that would fulfill virtually all its members' personal needs." According to the new gospel of family togetherness, parents were supposed to be friends with their children, and husbands and wives each other's closest companion. Unfortunately, the harshness of their own early years put the Joplins at a disadvantage as they set out to raise a normal "fifties" family of their own. They tried to be good parents, but they had each grown up in families with little intimacy or emotional warmth. Asked if Janis had received much affection growing up, Dorothy Joplin tellingly replied, "Well, she got her share." It's an unsettling response but hardly surprising, given Dorothy's own lifelong feelings of deprivation; well into her seventies she continued to complain "half-bitterly" about having been fed plain oatmeal for breakfast every morning of her life until she went off to college.

Dorothy Joplin was an attentive mother—she read Dr. Spock faithfully—but she was hardly warm or affectionate. Bernard Giarratano, a social worker who counseled Janis when she was in her early twenties, describes Dorothy as "very straight, very staid, very somber. If she had passion, it was in the dark of night somewhere." Jim Langdon, one of Janis's closest friends from Texas, agrees. Dorothy was "very straitlaced, critical, rigid, and cool—not a warm person." Another friend remembers her as very forceful and extraordinarily controlling—destructively so. And though Seth could not be accused of being domineering, he too was emotionally distant and may well have been an alcoholic. An intensely private man who likened himself to a monk, Seth was "kind of in the background," which usually meant in the garage, the only place Dorothy would permit him to drink. Seth apparently spent hours in the garage tinkering and drinking, away from the rest of the family. He was a discreet drinker, never a sloppy, public drunk. In fact, it seems only Dorothy knew that he drank; it must have pained her that he preferred solitude and the bottle to her company. And as a Sunday school teacher at Port Arthur's First Christian Church, she could hardly have been pleased that her husband was a nonbeliever.

Despite their differences, Seth and Dorothy didn't fight, probably because Seth made himself scarce. Once, when Janis was still a young child, Dorothy upbraided him for regaling Janis with stories of his college days making bathtub gin. Seth didn't take Dorothy on; he simply put an end to his nightly afterwork chats with his daughter. This was his way of getting along, and as he retreated further into himself, he increasingly came to view life as a big cheat. "The Great Saturday Night Swindle" he called it. As an adult, Janis spoke proudly of her father's cynical philosophy, as if it revealed how cool he was rather than how unhappy.

Janis's own chronic unhappiness is such a large part of her legend that biographers have scrambled desperately to explain what went wrong. But as hard as they've looked, they've found nothing to suggest her family was uniquely pathological. The Joplins had their share of problems, but they were not spectacularly dysfunctional in the ways Americans have come to expect of their celebrity families. This is not to say that Janis fabricated stories of a painful childhood or that everything was just fine. But whatever the discontents and dissatisfactions within the Joplin household, they remained subterranean until Janis became a teenager.

Janis viewed her life as rent by a "geologic fault." She saw her early years as idyllic. "Then the whole world turned. It just turned on me!" she said. In interview after interview, Janis placed the fault line at age fourteen, the age she lost her looks. "She'd been cute and all of a sudden she was ugly," reported one classmate. Years later, Janis half jokingly attributed her high school troubles to the fact that she "didn't have any tits at fourteen." Most of her classmates were older and that didn't help, but Janis's flat chest was the least of her problems. At fourteen Janis started to put on weight and her face began breaking out in what her sister calls "a never-ending series of painful bright red pimples." Janis's acne was so bad her mother took her to a local dermatologist, who applied dry ice to the worst outbreaks—one of several ineffective treatments at the time—and blamed Janis when her skin failed to clear up.

Her transformation couldn't have come at a worse time—just as she entered senior high in 1957. As her high school friend Grant Lyons argues, "once you turned fourteen in Port Arthur, Texas, you were in a kind of sexual race if you were a girl. And if you didn't have the goods, well, then, you fell behind. The girls who were popular were good-looking, and Janis wasn't." Janis's metamorphosis must have played a role in her failure to be selected to the Red Huzzars, her school's elite drum and bugle corps. Thomas Jefferson High was a perennial football powerhouse and much of the school's culture revolved around sports. The Red Huzzars (or "Red Huzzies," as Janis called them) performed at the Cotton Bowl, and it was considered quite a feat to earn a position on the squad. Janis began high school certain she'd be chosen: after all, she'd always been popular. The rejection devastated her. Janis was supposed to be a star, not a runner-up, a loser. To Janis, her physical transformation must have seemed a terrible betrayal.

Of course, there were plenty of other homely teenage girls in Port Arthur and they were largely ignored. Janis could have chosen to be inconspicuous, but she decided to fight what other girls accepted as fate. As a precocious only child for the first six years of her life, Janis hadn't grown up feeling like the other girls of Port Arthur, anyway. She was extremely bright, very inquisitive, and headstrong—not the sort of child to accept the prevailing wisdom about much of anything. When she set about getting people's attention again, she not only made a point of her difference but embellished it. Better negative attention than no attention at all. Janis began high school in regulation fifties dress—demure skirts and white shirts, bobby sox and loafers, but within a year she'd abandoned it all for skirts cut daringly above the knee or, even more risqué, tights—sometimes black, sometimes purple—which she'd wear with a man's white shirt and a black belt. She remade herself into a beatnik girl—the only one in all of Port Arthur. Janis was bent on becoming an eyesore, an affront to everything the townspeople believed in. She worked up a special cackle and tried it out on her friend Karleen Bennett. "Was it loud enough, Karleen? Was it irritating enough?" she'd ask. It was a risky strategy, but it ensured she wouldn't be invisible. They might revile her, but they couldn't ignore her.

Seth and Dorothy were completely mystified by Janis's determination to flout as many social conventions as she could. "Our parents were in a sad situation," Bob Dylan would later observe of the emerging generation gap. Predictably, the person most aggravated by Janis's bad-girl drag was her mother. Dorothy may have wanted Janis to be assertive, as Laura contends, but she would never have encouraged her daughter to be sexually forward. "She just changed totally, overnight," claimed Dorothy. "A complete turnabout from her former self." Dorothy wasn't exaggerating. Janis *had* been a good little girl. Years later Dorothy would describe Janis's early childhood as perfect. "I even worried about it a little," she recalled, because Janis "never did anything for me to correct!"

Faced with the new Janis, Dorothy said, she didn't know what to do. But if she felt confused, she acted decisively. "Think before you speak," she'd lecture Janis. "Learn how to behave yourself." Everything became a fight between Janis and her mother. Laura felt so "emotionally terrorized" by all the turmoil that she "started going to church and prayed for everyone," a move that undoubtedly further solidified her position as the good daughter. For Dorothy, the tumult must have evoked memories of the fighting that had ravaged her own family. As a woman who had scrambled to get a toehold in the middle class and understood the iron-clad connection between sexual propriety and social position for women, Dorothy probably felt that her own reputation was at stake, that Janis's provocative behavior reflected badly on her and the whole family. One night, angry that Janis had stayed out with Karleen past midnight, she accosted her at the front door and screamed, "You're ruining your life. People will think you're cheap!" On another occasion, Dorothy called Janis a harlot. "We had to look it up," Karleen remembers with a laugh. "But Janis couldn't believe that's what she was calling her, because she hadn't done anything to deserve it."

Janis made no secret of her rift with her mother. Her home life in Port Arthur had been a "drag, a big drag," she told reporters once she became famous. "I was one of the girls who always wanted to do things that my mother said I couldn't because only boys get to do those things." By contrast, Janis talked fondly of her father. "He was very important to me, because he made me think," she told one journalist. "He's the reason I am like I am, I guess." Eventually, though, Seth pulled away from Janis, a move that baffled her all her life. "He used to talk to me and then he turned right around from that when I was fourteen—maybe he wanted a smart son or something like that—I can't figure that out." Despite his withdrawal, she seemed more mystified than angry at her father. Janis's friends all say she adored Seth, who, they claim, remained fairly tolerant of her behavior. To Patti, who felt her own father ran his family as if it were Du Pont, Seth seemed ideal, "one of those Henry Fonda–type dads." But one of Janis's college friends was struck by the disjuncture between Janis's description of her father as warm and open and the emotionally distant man he met. In truth, Seth wasn't necessarily more tolerant than Dorothy, he just "didn't want to be the bad guy, which forced Dorothy further into that role," according to social worker Giarratano. You'd never know it from Janis's rosy retrospective portrait of Seth, but Janis and her father "clashed a great deal," just less noisily than she and Dorothy.

Seth and Dorothy used different strategies in dealing with Janis. Seth tried reasoning with her whereas Dorothy argued on the basis of what was right—a category Janis was always eager to challenge. Her mother implored her to "be like everybody else." Janis did go through the motions, for a while at least. At school she joined the sorts of "good groups" Dorothy would approve of—the Future Nurses of America, the Future Teachers of America, the Art Club, and Slide Rule Club. But Janis continued to misbehave, and Dorothy's dreams of a "good family" seemed dashed forever, as the Joplins took on the appearance of one of those troubled families whose every misfortune becomes grist for the town's gossip mill.

Though Janis fought with both her parents, Dorothy's relentless criticism seems to have scarred her more deeply, solidifying her feeling that everything about her was wrong. One friend insists there was nothing Janis could have done to make her mother accept her. "She could never win her mother's approval," she says. And by this point, even had Janis stopped acting like a bad girl, she would never have occupied center stage again. She wasn't pretty and she wasn't a malleable child any longer. Her sister, Laura, had now become the perfect daughter. Of course, none of this would stop Janis from trying to undo the rejection. It would be her life's project.

Years later, Janis told reporters that her mother threw her out of the house when she was fourteen. While it's unlikely Dorothy Joplin literally kicked her out, Janis did suddenly feel like an outsider. She began spending more and more time at Karleen's house. "My parents were a lot more lenient than hers were," says Karleen. "And they liked Janis. I mean, Janis was part of the family. The only time I ever remember my parents being rude to *anybody* was years later when Janis was on *The Ed Sullivan Show* and somebody was at the house and was making derogatory remarks about her, and my parents asked him to leave. 'She's our second daughter and you're not gonna talk like that at our house,' they said." Janis became so much a part of their family that Karleen's grandmother once asked, "Don't you ever leave her at home?" They rarely did; Janis even went to temple with the Bennetts. Janis's two closest friends in high school—Karleen and Arlene Elster—were both Jewish, a coincidence that may not have been entirely random. Port Arthur was overwhelmingly Baptist and Catholic, and the town's very few Jewish families were outsiders of sorts, too. For that matter, anyone not a good white Christian would feel like an outsider in Port Arthur. Janis seemed to find solace in the company of others whose difference likewise caused them pain. She also became close to the African American woman who worked as a domestic for the Joplins. This woman, who was "kind of plump and sang and was very soulful," was a fixture in the Joplin household. According to Patti, "she taught Janis secret things, mysterious things you didn't get from white culture. It was solely between them." Through her, Janis glimpsed another world, apart from what Patti calls Port Arthur's "nonsense environment."

Port Arthur's dos and don'ts may have seemed like nonsense to

Janis and her friends, but in fact, everyone knew the rules. Appearance was everything. Nowhere was this truer than at Thomas Jefferson High School. All high schools have a pecking order, but TJ High was particularly "vicious," contends Patti. "Once you got singled out, that was it," remembers Karleen's younger brother Herman Bennett. "You were a target. There were winners and losers and a definite caste system." He fared better than some, but he learned all about TJ's caste system when he woke up one morning to find a swastika burned into his family's lawn—the football team's way of retaliating for his dating a girl who'd broken up with one of them. At least Karleen's brother wasn't the effeminate boy who was nominated Homecoming Queen. Mary Karr, the author of *The Liars' Club*, her memoir of life in the Golden Triangle, claims that in her hometown you knew what to expect: "Your greatest weakness will get picked at in the crudest local parlance. In fact, the worse an event is for you, the more brutally clear will be the talk about it. In this way, guys down there born with shriveled legs get nicknamed Gimpy, girls with acne Pizzaface." Herman Bennett reflects, "If people weren't already traumatized enough for being different, I'm certain the constant antagonism from these people made life pretty miserable." For a girl like Janis, says her friend Grant Lyons, it was "absolute poison."

TJ High was huge, as big as most community colleges. Vocational education was its strong suit; the school had a completely equipped print shop and metal shop and offered welding, architectural and mechanical drafting, and a carpentry program in which seniors actually built a house. It was one thing to excel in carpentry, however, and quite another to do well in English or mathematics. "In Port Arthur, man, if you were an academic-award winner you'd be just as happy if no one knew about it," recalls Dave Moriaty. "That would open you up to being beaten. So you didn't let on you read books. It was a cultural minus if you read anything." Janis not only read books; she even, at her mother's urging, took a class in mechanical drawing, thinking it might help her with her art. The lone girl, Janis was relentlessly harassed by her classmates. Then there was the time in another class when Janis spoke out in favor of integration. Karleen agreed with Janis but kept quiet because she knew she'd be ostracized. "It didn't so much turn people against her," recalls Karleen, "as make people think she was crazy."

But what really sealed Janis's fate as a social untouchable was her growing reputation as the school slut. At some point in her junior year, Janis felt compelled to appear promiscuous. Among her friends there is no consensus on how Janis came by her new role. It may have developed because word had it that Janis was sleeping around and she simply decided that, if people were going to call her a slut, she might as well act like one or because Janis was tired of being ignored and threw herself into the one activity that was sure to get a Port Arthur girl talked about. Whatever the reason, Janis certainly knew it wouldn't take much to earn a bad reputation at TJ High. By her senior year, the rumors were flying that Janis Joplin read pornography and was making it with guys right and left. At TJ, like so many other American high schools, "you could do it one time and everyone in the whole school would know and say they'd slept with you," says Patti. Once the kids started calling Janis a whore, Patti figures Janis might have said, "Oh fuck, I'll just go ahead and do it." Other friends suspect Janis did go all the way but not nearly as often as many other girls who simply had the sense to keep quiet about their sex lives. And yet several good friends contend that, while Janis did everything in her power to suggest she was loose, she never really "put out." Grant Lyons thinks "it's possible Janis could have played the make-out queen without actually having intercourse." Karleen insists Janis remained a virgin until after graduation. So does her classmate and friend Tary Owens, despite the fact that to this day "every guy down there says they slept with her." As for the porn, Karleen says, "You want to know what it was? Mickey Spillane novels." Whether or not Janis lost her virginity in high school matters less in the end than the lengths to which she went to appear loose.

As Janis's reputation grew, so did the ostracism. Every year the local country club threw a dance for high school seniors. Karleen belonged to the club, but her classmates excluded her from their planning meeting because of her friendship with Janis. "I found out later that I had not been invited because they said I would invite Janis to the dance and that would just totally ruin it." A decade later, Janis would complain about the "country club" girls in the pricey front-row seats—often the only girls she could really see at her concerts. "Sometimes they think they're gonna like you. And then you get out there and you really damage and offend their femininity. You know, 'No chick is supposed to stand like that.' I mean, crouching down in front of the guitar player goin' 'uuuuhhhn!' You know, lettin' your tits shake around, and your hair's stringy, and you have no makeup on, and sweat running down your face, you're coming up to the fuckin' microphone, man, and at one point their heads just go 'click,' and they go, 'Oooh, no!' . . . and the expressions on their faces are of absolute *horror*. The girls are going, 'Oh, my God, she may be able to sing, but she doesn't have to act like that!' "

It seems almost inconceivable that Janis would have embarked on this strategy of deliberate provocation had she known how vicious the backlash would be. Students spat on her and threw pennies at her in the hallways. Tary Owens recalls that their senior year "it got really bad because there was a group of guys—future fraternity guys—who made up stories about her and called her a pig. Of course, most of them now say they loved her and she was just wonderful." One reason the harassment was so relentless, Owens says, was that the guys wanted to "get a rise out of her, get her to say, 'Fuck you'—and she often took the bait." After these confrontations, he says, Janis would "be hurt and she'd show it through anger mostly." She'd also seek solace with a group of kids who were as disaffected as she was.

Janis's entree to this world came through Grant Lyons, whose mother ran Port Arthur's Little Theater. Lyons's family came from back East; his mother, especially, was determined to introduce some culture into the local scene. Janis was one of several kids who took part in the theater. She painted sets and even played an ingenue in a musical called *Sunday Costs Five Pesos*. Lyons was a football star, but that's where his resemblance to TJ's most popular boys ended. At first, he says, he didn't have "any friends at all, either jocks or non-jocks. I wasn't dating. My social life was nil." Gradually, five smart rebel boys—Grant Lyons, Dave Moriaty, Adrian Haston, Jim Langdon, and Randy Tennant—began hanging out together, drawn to one another by their love of jazz and folk music and their exasperation with the town's parochialism and blandness. "We were saboteurs," claimed Jim Langdon.

Like many other sixties rebels in the making, they were drawn to the Beats. Mass-circulation magazine stories about beatniks invariably vilified or ridiculed them, often calling into question the masculinity of the men. These articles may have scared off most Americans, but they also alerted all those kids who felt like mutants in fifties America to an alternative existence. Maybe they could escape the awful gray dullness looming before them. Janis first learned about the Beats in *Time* magazine. Years later, after she was already a star, she made fun of her teeny-beatnik past. "Port Arthur people thought I was a beatnik, and they didn't like beatniks, though they'd never seen one and neither had I." Janis had never seen one in the flesh, but the piece in *Time* was enough—she was entranced.

Like the Beats they admired, Port Arthur's tiny gang of beatniks was a male fraternity. Janis was the only girl who managed to insinuate herself into their ranks. Four of the five boys had girlfriends, but the girlfriends weren't part of their group; girls, and femininity in general, were synonymous with conventionality and domesticity. But Janis wasn't your typical teenage girl. She came into the group not as one of the guys' girlfriends "but as somebody who'd be there to party, go across the river to the bars, those sorts of things," Lyons says. Unlike other girls, Janis "wore pretty much what we wore, and no makeup," and she was "extremely expressive," which was "part of what made her such fun," he adds.

Patti thinks there were lots of reasons Janis and the guys got on so well. They were all outsiders, she says, and "emotionally destitute." And then there was Janis's high-voltage energy. "She would enter a room of people and say, 'Hey, baby, what's happening?' in this loud, ballsy voice, and get immediate attention." Sometimes the group would use Janis as a "secret weapon" in situations where people were putting on airs. Jim Langdon remembers a party given by a "Beaumont socialite" where Janis cruised in with a bottle of booze under each arm and said, "Cut this bullshit." People were incredulous, says Langdon; the punch was so much more powerful coming from a woman than from a man. And Janis delighted in shocking people.

Still, it wasn't easy muscling in on the guys, especially because at TJ High hanging out with Janis, says Dave Moriaty, got you "weirdness by association." She was also a grade behind the others. At first, "the gang didn't make space for Janis, she shoehorned her way into the group," according to Moriaty. "She'd call us up and say, 'Where are you going? Come pick me up.'" And they would, because they were polite. "I mean, she was whining and pouting and demanding to be included and so we'd take her along." But Moriaty admits Janis also got her way because "she was fun, you know, and very smart and very talented." Lyons never felt

Janis wheedled her way into their group, but he acknowledges she may have had to go to extra lengths. "Obviously she was a girl, and we were boys, and that took some doing, but she did it." Janis did it by coming across as one of the guys—probably the *only* way in for a girl. She put on a great act, says Jack Smith, who wasn't at this point a part of the beatnik crowd. Janis never allowed Jack to curse and joke with her the way Moriaty and the other guys did. "She was a chameleon," Jack contends. She acted tough with the rebel boys because "she'd just figured out what that group was after."

Being one of the guys meant not having a boyfriend, of course, and Janis was conspicuously without a boyfriend throughout high school, though both Jack Smith and Tary Owens say they had a crush on her. "She was not perceived by us as a potential sexual partner," says Lyons. "I know it must sound odd," he adds, "given the sexual persona she developed." Moriaty used to call Janis a "good old girl," which she hated. "She always used to say, 'Goddamnit, don't call me a good old girl.' She thought it was patronizing and condescending," he recalls. It certainly was a term that underscored the boys' lack of sexual interest in her. "Patching" herself into their group would be good practice for crashing the boys' club of rock 'n' roll, but it left her with a sense of being sexually nullified. Lyons thinks that feeling was "permanent," one she was "always trying to work through or away."

When Janis wasn't hanging out with the gang, she was often holed up somewhere painting. She loved painting nudes, but her parents found her choice of subject "inappropriate," yet another of Janis's sexual provocations. "Her parents thought a lot of art was pornography," explains Karleen. They tried steering her toward landscapes and seascapes. Laura remembers her father driving her and Janis out to Pleasure Pier so Janis could paint ocean scenes. But Janis persisted in painting nudes. Things came to a head when she painted one on the inside panel of her bedroom closet door. Her parents, determined to protect their other children from being "exposed to such visions," forced her to paint over the offending image. For the work of a teenager stuck in the Golden Triangle, Janis's paintings are remarkably strong, but her passion for art counted as a deficit in Port Arthur, where it only made her seem more peculiar to the kids outside her gang. "The rumor was that she went to an old abandoned drive-in near the high school, . . . set up her easel and did artwork there," remembered a classmate. "She was wild and strange and unusual." For her parents and almost all her classmates, her artistic expressiveness confirmed her sexual precocity.

Music, too, became a passion for Janis and her fellow rebels. Music wasn't just background noise; it was a declaration of difference. Listening to late-night radio or combing the bins at the local record store, they searched out music they'd never hear at a TJ sock hop—in particular, folk, jazz, and the blues. To them, this was renegade music, untainted by commercialism. By contrast, rock 'n' roll in the late fifties and early sixties—its Frankie Avalon years—seemed hopelessly commercial, just so much mass-produced dreck. "It seemed so shallow, all oop-boop," explained Janis years later. "It had *nothing*."

At their parties or as they drove between Port Arthur, Orange, and Beaumont—"making the triangle," they called it—the gang would sing folk songs. Like other young folkies and white blues aficionados, they idolized Huddie Ledbetter, better known as Leadbelly, who had grown up just across the state line in Louisiana. "This is the thing," was Bob Dylan's reaction on first hearing Leadbelly. Grant Lyons brought a Leadbelly record to a party, where Janis heard it. She later said his music was "like a flash. It *mattered* to me." An ex-con, pardoned twice (once for murder) by southern governors, Leadbelly was irresistible to disaffected young white kids, a lightning rod for their sense of marginality and alienation. Discovered by a musicologist, John Lomax, on one of his song-collecting trips to southern prisons and penitentiaries, Leadbelly became the darling of white lefty intellectuals in the thirties. He made his professional debut, amazingly enough, at the tweedy Modern Language Association convention, where literature professors and graduate students gather each year. Leadbelly died of Lou Gehrig's disease in 1949, but his voice was so powerful—like "the force of a sledgehammer hitting steel"—that it helped spark the folk music revival of the late fifties and early sixties.

Janis claimed the first record she ever bought was a Leadbelly, but the first singer she tried imitating was Odetta. Before Joan Baez came along, Odetta was the queen of folk music. Born in Los Angeles, Odetta was, with Richie Havens, Len Chandler, and Jackie Washington, one of a handful of younger African American folksingers of the sixties. Legend has it that Janis discovered she could sing when she mastered an Odetta song. Although people disagree about their whereabouts that day, they all remember the moment Janis "did" Odetta. Tired of listening to her friends butcher an Odetta song, Janis suddenly broke out in a voice that sounded like she'd conjured her up. The guys fell silent from the shock, "dumbfounded," recalls Moriaty. "She just burst out and sounded exactly like Odetta. That showed us up. We used to sing folk songs on our way driving anywhere. Well, after that, we still did, but it wasn't the same. We weren't all in the same class anymore." Tary Owens remembers Janis declaring, "Hey, I think I have a voice." Janis probably did say this, but she already had a hunch she could sing, even if the guys didn't. Maybe what she discovered was that singing allowed her to express herself, not just sound pretty for the benefit of others.

The gang's passions were folk, blues, and jazz, but they also spent many a night across the line in the Cajun town of Vinton, Louisiana, where Jim Langdon began getting gigs playing trombone in rock 'n' roll bands. Vinton was the sort of place where, "if you were old enough to look over the bar, they'd sell it to you," claims one of Janis's friends. While Port Arthur bars had only beer and wine licenses, Louisiana bars could serve hard liquor. On the Louisiana side of the state border the road was lined with bars—Lou Ann's, Busters, the Big Oak, and Shady Rest were favorite spots. Lots of girls, not just "bad" girls, crossed the line, but they didn't go to the really raunchy bars like Busters and Shady Rest that Janis and the guys preferred. (Karleen, for example, never went on these excursions.) There the gang would hear white soul bands like the Boogie Kings and Jerry LaCroix and the Counts. At Lou Ann's they might hear black musicians cranking out what Janis called "great Jimmy Reed down-home funky blues music." Some accounts rave about the "swamp rock" they'd hear in the bars, but Patti says the music was "loud, hard, beating rhythmic music, rock-around-the-clock music. It was just the beat. And you could go there at eleven in the morning or eleven at night and it would be pretty much the same. It was just bad, bad music, but to us it was Disneyland."

Of course, lots of white kids (including some of the musicians with whom Janis would later play) were crossing over to catch glimpses of cultures that seemed more "authentic" than their own. Future blues musicians like Michael Bloomfield, Nick Gravenites, and Paul Butterfield were hanging out in South Side Chicago blues joints. Big Brother drummer Dave Getz had been among the thousands of kids to catch deejay Alan Freed's first rock 'n' roll show at the Brooklyn Paramount. And other teenagers, including James Gurley and Peter Albin of Big Brother, were haunting jazz clubs like the Black Hawk or Jimbo's Bop City in San Francisco. Despite the best efforts of their parents, middle-class white teenagers were fascinated with those on the margins of American society—truck drivers like Elvis Presley and dishwashers like Little Richard who became the stars of early rock 'n' roll. Since the 1920s, this process of "prestige from below" had been at work among a tiny minority of jazz-loving white kids, but with the rise of rock 'n' roll in the fifties and sixties it threatened to become a mass phenomenon.

When it came to music or the struggle for justice—and the two were linked—white America in the fifties was definitely "drawing its juice" from blacks. The power of black culture was first transmitted to white teens by two groups of white men whose paths rarely crossed—radio deejays and Beat writers. In the forties, radio programmers had to scramble to fill up all the air space left empty when programs like *I Love Lucy* or *Amos and Andy* deserted radio for TV. They began targeting black audiences, among others, and white kids were the unintended beneficiaries, hearing music rawer and wilder than the usual AM fare. The repercussions were immense. Michael Bloomfield was just one of many teenagers whose lives were irrevocably changed by radio. With his tiny portable AM transistor radio pressed to his ear he'd stay up late listening to hometown stations, to Nashville's megawatt WLAC and to XERB in Mexico. It was "another realm," like a "jungle in the city," he recalled. Janis and her friends tuned in to some of the same stations, although they also listened to locals such as Beaumont's Big Bopper of "Chantilly Lace" fame.

It was Alan Freed, sensing the huge market for this music among white teens, who first applied the term *rock 'n' roll* to the R & B sounds he and others were playing on the radio. White deejays like Freed, John "R" Richbourg and Gene Nobles in Nashville, and George "Hound Dog" Lorenz in Buffalo were race rebels of sorts, playing records by black artists rather than white cover versions and often affecting a "black" speaking style on the air. Jive-talking John R and Gene Nobles of WLAC had many in their audience—black and white alike—believing they were black. Like a number of other young white men in early rock 'n' roll—the songwriters Jerry Leiber and Mike Stoller, for example—they were enamored of black culture, going so far as to engage in a kind of racial drag, and occasionally something much more meaningful. Johnny Otis, an R & B musician and impresario, married a black woman, lived in the black community, and carried on a life-long struggle against racial discrimination.

A jazz aficionado, Jack Kerouac wasn't especially interested in rock 'n' roll, but he, too, was drawn to black culture, writing in *On the Road* of wanting to "exchange worlds with the happy, true-hearted, ecstatic Negroes of America." No one captured white Beats' and hipsters' infatuation with blackness better than Norman Mailer in his controversial 1957 essay, "The White Negro." For Mailer, "the Negro (all exceptions admitted) could rarely afford the sophisticated inhibitions of civilization and so he kept for his survival the art of the primitive, he lived in the enormous present, he subsisted for his Saturday night kicks, relinquishing the pleasures of the mind for the more obligatory pleasures of the body." Mailer's essay was so rife with racial objectification that it raised quite a few eyebrows even at the time. The poet Kenneth Rexroth, the "Daddy-O of the Beat Generation," denounced white hipsters like Mailer for believing "the Negro is born with a sax in his mouth and a hypodermic in his arms. . . . In Jazz circles it's what they call Crow Jimism." In "The Black Boy Looks at the White Boy," James Baldwin accused white men of seeing the black man as "a kind of walking phallic symbol." For all their efforts to break free, the next generation of white kids trying to cross America's color line absorbed uncritically this fetishizing of blackness.

Janis and the gang drew much of their inspiration from black culture, but they weren't living in New York or San Francisco, frequenting clubs and cafés where whites and blacks mixed. Port Arthur's one coffeehouse closed after six months; Janis and her pals were its only customers. They were in segregated east Texas, where hanging out on the margins meant hanging out in rough redneck joints in Louisiana. "You didn't have to mess with anyone to get into trouble there," recalls Dave Moriaty. "All you had to do was to go in and act funny and you'd get into plenty of trouble." Fashioning themselves as outlaws, he and the others became familiar with the hard-living working class that frequented the Vinton bars. As Dave Getz of Big Brother points out, Janis had a real ease with that world "even though her family was definitely not white trash. Janis had this southern, trashy thing she was drawn to. It was the thing in her personality that made her comfortable with bikers, even though her friends were educated and so was she. In that part of the world where she grew up there were a lot of people like that and that's where you went if you didn't walk the straight and narrow. And she didn't walk the straight and narrow." Of course, affiliating with that "white trash" world was one sure way Janis could declare herself different from her parents, who had left that world behind in the great postwar class shift.

In fact, by the time Janis was a senior in high school she was doing everything she could to show her parents she would never become the Port Arthur schoolteacher of their dreams. She began drinking. "My mother fixed Janis the first drink she ever had," Karleen says. "My mother said, 'If you're gonna drink, you're gonna do it at home.' She fixed us a whiskey sour, which was really sophisticated. We drank it and that was it." Except it wasn't for Janis, who refused to confine her drinking to home. "Then," says Karleen, "Janis started going across the river." One weekend Janis went even farther than Vinton. She lied to her parents, telling them she was driving her father's work car for an overnight stay at Karleen's. Instead she drove with Jim Langdon and two other male friends to New Orleans to listen to music. Had they not had a minor accident she might have gotten away with it. But when the Louisiana police looked at their papers and noticed they had three overage boys with one underage girl—all from Texas—things turned scary. Jim Langdon says, "They were talking the Mann Act, statutory rape, and the trip was all her idea!" When the police called the Joplins in Port Arthur, Dorothy pretended nothing out of the ordinary had happened, but Laura reports that Janis's behavior "was so bad, our parents didn't know what to say about it."

If transgressions were met with silence in the Joplin home, they weren't at school, where rumors of Janis's promiscuity abounded. Janis was even called into the school counselor's office to answer charges of "drinking and improper behavior." She denied the accusations, but she later told Karleen she'd had to be real careful about how she put her purse down on the floor in the counselor's office because she had a wine bottle concealed in it. The Joplins felt so helpless in the face of her wildness they sent her to a psychologist—a highly unusual step for parents to take in the fifties, especially in Port Arthur, where seeing a psychologist was tantamount to admitting mental illness. Janis managed to graduate without incident. Prom night she spent cruising around Port Arthur with Karleen, whose boyfriend was in the air force and stationed in Biloxi, Mississippi. The night's highlight occurred when they picked up two guys looking for a ride to nearby Port Neches, drove them there, and dropped them off. That was it.

In 1970, at the age of twenty-seven, Janis said, "I've been this chick for twelve, thirteen years now. I was younger then, more inexperienced, but I was the same person with the same drives and the same balls and the same style." The mythic Janis Joplin—the tough, raw, trashy broad—was a creature Janis began crafting as a teenager. It gave her a version of control. She could say it wasn't her they were rejecting, it was the cackle she'd devised, or her swearing, or her drinking, or her cheapness. Perhaps she imagined the facade she so skillfully constructed could take all those blows while her core would remain untouched. Her ballsy chick impersonation also got her lots of attention, even if it was negative. Jim Langdon acted tough as well. "Port Arthur was hostile. . . . I wouldn't stand for being victimized by the Neanderthals of the world. Being tough worked." But it didn't work very well for Janis, whose toughness only seemed to invite further abuse.

Elvis had been a misfit in high school, too, but the experience didn't haunt him. He made Memphis his home and built a mansion there, while Janis would flee Port Arthur. Being an unpopular boy was no cakewalk, but popularity wasn't absolutely demanded of boys. For girls, popularity was the whole show, and Janis inhabited the most despised category among fifties teens, the girl who couldn't get a date. A decade after she'd graduated from high school, Janis was still locked in battle with her hometown, complaining on national TV that she'd been "laughed out of class, out of town, and out of the state." As David Dalton, a reporter, observes, "It just seemed like every time something went wrong, that big, ugly, sprawling oil town would loom up and say, 'We know you, and we'll always be the truth about you.' " Years later, Janis said, "Anyone with ambitions like me leaves [Port Arthur] as soon as they can or they're taken over, repressed, and put down." Janis made it sound easy, a matter of simple resolve. But when it came time for her to go to college Janis found herself still living in what writer Mary Karr calls "the great Nowhere."

You didn't escape Port Arthur by going to Lamar," explains Dave Moriaty. "This was the disappointed choice; there was no dividing line between graduating from high school and going across the street to Lamar." Lamar State College of Technology, though not literally across the street but one town over in Beaumont, was nonetheless like an extension of TJ High. "You take all those high schools," says Grant Lyons, "roll a lasso around them, pull it tight and you have Lamar Tech." The idea of attending Lamar for even two years was a "horror" to him. Luckily, he received a reprieve in the form of a football scholarship to Tulane. TJ students who did well in the classroom or on the playing field usually went elsewhere if their parents could afford it. The son of an electrical engineer, Dave Moriaty enrolled at the University of Texas in Austin, where most of the "creative, off-the-wall people went." But of their group, Jim Langdon, Adrian Haston, Tary Owens, and Janis weren't so lucky. Janis's high school grades had been good, but it's doubtful that either Janis or her parents imagined her going anywhere but Lamar.

For kids in the Golden Triangle, Lamar was cheap because they could save money by living at home. Janis, though, lived in the girls' dormitory, despite her parents' tight finances. Perhaps Seth and Dorothy wanted her out of the house, away from their other children. Or maybe Janis insisted on leaving and her parents capitulated. In any case, Janis was so thrilled to be away from home that when her family helped her move the last box into her dorm room, Laura recalls, Janis practically "hurried us out with promises of 'See you soon.' "

Lamar was certainly an improvement over high school. For one thing, Janis didn't feel like quite such a freak, because the Port Arthur renegades banded together with rebel kids from everywhere else in east Texas. Fifty strong, they staked out their own area of the student union, where they made a point of keeping to themselves. They were still, however, very much in the minority. Moreover, some of the students at the surrounding tables were the same people Janis had unintentionally "entertained" at TJ High. Sorority girls gossiped about what a slut she was and even tried talking her roommate into dumping her. Some students undoubtedly believed the gossip and stayed away, not wanting to put their own reputations on the line. For Janis, Lamar bore an uncanny resemblance to TJ High in another respect as well. Classes were usually boring, and Janis responded by cutting them. Laura claims her sister was a serious studio art major, but Tary Owens says no one in their crowd was serious about school. Janis's transcript reveals she managed to accumulate only three hours of transferable credit from Lamar, for an English composition course in which she received a B. Even Janis's interest in painting waned when she met a boy from Beaumont named Tommy Stopher and decided he was the better painter. Janis couldn't tolerate being second best at something she loved, says Tary.

Like many other boho students across America, Janis was perfecting "the fine art of hanging out." Patti recalls that she and Janis would "go and sit in bars in Beaumont when we were supposed to be in class at the college. We'd just drink and talk and drink and talk. Who knows what we talked about." The "kids seeking engineering degrees were just in and out," while Janis and her crowd spent their time partying. Compared with the girls pursuing their MRS. degrees and "the country boys with slide rules" in training to become oil refinery engineers and technicians, they were models of laid-backness. They pulled all-nighters not to finish schoolwork but to have intense, boozy discussions of Leadbelly's music or Sartre's *No Exit*, Ferlinghetti's *A Coney Island of the Mind*, or anything by Faulkner and Hemingway. Occasionally they tried playing music, but for the most part they just listened to records. At this point, "Janis couldn't play worth anything, and the rest of them were just as bad," claims Patti Skaff. "If you can imagine a trombone, a bad guitar, and a harmonica—there wasn't much to it."

At the heart of their group were Janis, Patti Skaff, and Dave McQueen. Dave had grown up knowing about life on the fringes, because when his dad wasn't working as an itinerant oil worker he was in prison. To survive what Dave calls a "dank and lonely" childhood, he lost himself in books. When he was fourteen, his mother moved the family to Port Arthur, where she found a job as a waitress. "A voracious reader," by his senior year at TJ he was hanging out with some Lamar students who introduced him to the Beat writers. "I started reading everything by those guys that I could get a hold of. I read all of Kerouac, including all the really boring stuff." At Lamar he began dating Patti, who had managed to "drink her way out of UT." Patti was an art student who sometimes modeled for studio art classes, though always in a bathing suit—this was Lamar, after all. Patti's parents belonged to the Port Arthur Country Club, but she was drawn to the other side of the tracks. As soon as Patti and Janis met they connected, and they were soon driving each other to ever-greater feats of outrageousness. "One of us would say, 'I'll do *this*,' and the other would say, 'Well, I'll do *that*.'" Growing up in Port Arthur, Patti didn't expect much. As she puts it, "Meeting somebody who was at all interesting was a huge exception."

And Janis was a huge exception. Dave McQueen first heard about Janis from Tary Owens, who told him about "this woman we really ought to get to know because she was clearly one of us. So one afternoon we went to the Luby's cafeteria right up the road from the Joplins' house and we all sat around and drank coffee and talked all afternoon. I thought she was out-of-sight. She was clearly one of us. We were just book-reading, rebellious, and hell-raising, and we all eventually wanted to go to North Beach." Soon Patti, Dave, and Janis formed a "kind of family" in Beaumont. "We were constantly together and we related to each other very intensely," says Dave. Janis even went to New Orleans with Dave and Patti on their honeymoon. Before they were married, Dave and Janis had made love once in the backseat of a car. "I always thought she was pretty, and we found ourselves sitting next to each other and went from there," he says. Emulating the Beats meant sexual experimentation: "We felt like outlaws and renegades in that culture and we were trying very hard to be hip."

Like most other commuter schools, Lamar had little campus life. This being the early sixties, before campus rebellions undid archaic in loco parentis policies, restrictive curfews made female students virtual prisoners of their dorms at night. And Lamar was particularly watchful of its female students. One of Janis's classmates, a twenty-four-year-old divorcée, not only was forced to live in a dormitory but was expelled for wearing a bikini on her dorm's terrace. The Lamar rebels simply circumvented the rules by partying off-campus, which they could do because male students were not required to live in dorms. Janis apparently devised a simple strategy for partying all night—she'd sneak out *after* the curfew check. At their off-campus parties Janis and her friends drank "prodigious amounts," especially beer, which they could buy by the gallon from the Paragon, a drive-in restaurant where the customer supplied the container. Janis's group broke other taboos, too—there were sometimes black kids at their parties as well as white. Although they didn't see themselves as political, they were consciously integrationist; the group even participated in efforts to integrate the local Walgreens lunch counter.

Janis liked the partying, but by the end of the fall semester she decided she'd had enough of school. Lacking any means of support, she moved back in with her family. Her parents prevailed on her to take some classes in keypunch operating and typing at Port Arthur College, where Dorothy had been hired as a typing instructor two years earlier. (Always extremely capable, Dorothy had enrolled in a typing class, which she ended up teaching before the term was over. Soon she was appointed college registrar.) Janis missed enough classes (twenty days over a four-month period) to suggest she wasn't thrilled about becoming a secretary. The deal she'd struck with her parents, however, required that she pass her secretarial proficiency exam before moving to a city.

When she wasn't in class she was off with Patti, hanging out downtown, especially in the local record store, where they'd hole up in listening booths absorbing everything from down-home country blues to jazz and country. Sometimes they'd go over to the Skaffs', where Patti would use her dad's expensive Webcor reel-to-reel tape deck to record Janis singing. Janis wasn't yet performing, but seeing her Lamar Tech friend Frances Vincent onstage that spring with the Beaumont Community Players may have rekindled memories of the pleasure she'd felt as a little girl soloing in church. Frances was appearing in a musical comedy, *The Boyfriend*. "I had one of the good roles, and Janis came down to a rehearsal. When we got through and I came down, she said, 'I wanna do what *you* do!' She said it passionately. I think she wanted to be the center of attention. She was very emotional about it. I was a little flabbergasted, but I told her, 'Well, you can do it.' Little did I know. When I look back on it now, I think, Hoo hah!" It would be a little over a year before Janis started performing in earnest.

In the summer of 1961, Janis passed her secretarial exam and her parents sent her to Los Angeles. Putting thousands of miles between her and the Golden Triangle's boho fringe seemed to them the only way to get her on the straight and narrow. In L.A. they would still be able to "keep tabs" on her through Dorothy's two sisters, who'd moved there. "My impression," says Jim Langdon, "was that Janis didn't like the setup as far as going to live with the aunts, but she wanted to get out of the house and she wanted to go to California." Her friend Randy Tennant agrees Janis didn't like the idea of being chaperoned by her aunts, though he recalls she was fond of them. But what really struck him was that Janis felt "as if she were being banished." Janis wanted out of Port Arthur, but she didn't want to feel as if she were being sent away. The visit began less than auspiciously. Her aunts, who met her at the bus station, were not pleased to find their niece standing by her shiny new luggage with a young black man whom she proudly introduced as her companion for the ride. When they complimented her on the luggage, Janis emphasized it hadn't been her idea. "Mother insisted on buying it for me. I didn't want it. I was all set to stuff my things in an old bag, but she insisted."

Janis first moved in with her aunt Mimi, who lived in Brentwood and let Janis stay in the "artist shack" in back where her husband painted. Janis's parents insisted she get a job, and with the help of her aunts she found work as a keypunch operator at the telephone company. It wasn't exactly the big-city boho life she'd envisioned. Stuck in a huge room with hundreds of other women, trying to concentrate despite the deafening clatter and the mind-numbing routine, Janis must have hated it. One friend recalls Janis later getting "a lot of mileage" out of a question a co-worker asked her after her first day. " 'Well, honey,' this old lady asks me, 'how do you like punchin' for a livin'?' That just cracked Janis up, and she told it endlessly."

After camping out with her aunt Mimi, Janis moved into an apartment that her other aunt, Barbara, a real estate agent, helped her find. Unable to pay the rent, she then moved into the two-bedroom apartment Barbara shared with her daughter. Janis felt closer to this aunt, who not only had a checkered past but an unconventional present as well. Barbara Irwin had been married twice and had a close relationship with her boss. Uninterested in upholding the notions of female respectability Dorothy tried so hard to enforce, she must have seemed like a dream aunt, beginning her day at 10:00 A.M. drinking martinis with her employer and repeating the ritual six hours later. They even allowed Janis to join them.

This arrangement might have worked had it not been for Barbara's daughter, who felt displaced by Janis in her mother's affections. The situation grew so tense that Janis moved out and rented an apartment in a sleazy part of Venice. The neighborhood was bad and the apartment was worse. A huge steel barrel filled with trash dominated the living room, and Janis's sole attempt at interior decorating consisted of a collage she'd constructed out of a "dried-up pot of split pea soup with a ham bone" all hanging from "an old rope." Appalled by the squalor, Barbara yelled at her, "You weren't raised to live like this." They fell into a shouting match, which ended with her aunt vowing she'd never visit her there again.

In Venice, Janis found cheap rents and some remnants of the Beat scene Lawrence Lipton had made briefly notorious in his 1959 book, *The Holy Barbarians*. There were the coffeehouses, which featured informal hootenannies where anyone could sing or play. Janis sang at the Gas House a couple of times. There were minor boho celebrities like Eric Nord, the former owner of San Francisco's Co-Existence Bagel Shop, who was among those featured in *Look* magazine's August 1958 article, "The Bored, the Bearded and the Beat." But on the whole, by the summer of 1961, when Janis showed up, Venice had become a lifeless and tacky tourist trap. Janis decided to hitchhike up the coast to the North Beach of her dreams and check out the scene. Her aunts offered her bus fare, but she rebuffed them: "I don't want your money. I want to go and go *my* way." She wrote Jim Langdon of her plan to hitchhike to San Francisco, and he and Randy Tennant hitched and rode the freight trains from Port Arthur, intending to meet her there. Arrested at the California border, they never made it. Janis did, though, and apparently stayed a couple of months. There she met another southern rebel, Sally Lee, who hitchhiked with her back down to L.A. to retrieve her stuff from her aunt's. Somewhere along the line she acquired a World War II bomber jacket with sheepskin lining, which she wore inside out day after day when she returned to Port Arthur around Christmas.

Janis arrived home unannounced, surprising everyone as she bounded out of a taxicab, stumbling over her stuff. She'd ditched the nice suitcases her mother had given her and replaced them with shoe boxes she'd strung together. Laura reports that her parents were happy to see their prodigal daughter and that she and Michael were thrilled. But very soon the problem of what Janis was going to do with her life once again dominated the household. She reenrolled at Lamar, this time living at home, where her parents let her come and go as she pleased as long as she went to church and did her work. Her dad even offered to put up half the money for a used car if she paid the rest. So Janis started working as a waitress at a bowling alley. Laura claims Janis enjoyed the independence, but Patti says it was a "wretched job" that entailed wearing a hair net—the true mark of a bad waitressing job.

Life at home, too, fell into familiar patterns. Laura remembers her parents drew "an invisible line between Janis and Michael and me, tolerating things in her behavior but ruling them out for us." Still, Janis couldn't resist provoking her parents by encouraging her siblings to "adopt her ways." Now that Janis actually knew something about being a beatnik, her "ways" were more threatening. She had smoked marijuana and had stowed some in one of those shoe boxes. One night after she'd returned to town, Tommy Stopher's brother, Wali, recalls, "a few of us were hanging out, and Jim Langdon starts in on Janis, saying, 'We know you've got some marijuana and we want to try some. You've been out there, you must have some.' And she says, 'There's just enough for me, man.' Finally she reluctantly rolled a skinny little joint and we took a couple of hits." Janis's parents probably didn't know about the dope, but they must have fretted about all the bad habits Janis could pass on to the younger children.

Janis began spending more of her time with Patti. After Janis's shift ended at midnight the two of them would go out and share a six-pack and the "pain and the badness" of being stuck in east Texas. Sometimes their affection for each other surprised even them, as it did one night at one of their many drunken parties. "I don't know what brought it on," says Patti. "We went into this embrace and kissed each other at a party and all hell broke loose after that." According to most accounts, Dave McQueen, Patti's husband, arrived shortly thereafter and was so upset when he heard of their kiss that he hurled a beer bottle at Patti. The bottle narrowly missed her, smashing instead into Jack Smith, who lost several front teeth. As Janis, visibly distressed, helped Jack out of the house and into her car to go to the hospital, she mumbled over and over, "This wasn't supposed to happen. This is horrible. Why did this happen?"

According to Dave McQueen, it happened because of his allergy pills. Plagued by serious chronic allergies from living in Port Arthur, Dave lived on allergy medicine, which could make him pretty "weird" at times, he says. "I was a speed freak and didn't even know it." Patti herself is not so sure their kiss didn't bother him: "Well, maybe it didn't upset him, but maybe it did." The kiss "meant something" to Patti: "We did it. We meant it. We weren't just fucking with people's heads. Oh, we might have been a little bit." If they were, it may be because neither they nor the gang were entirely comfortable with the intensity of their feelings for each other. During a New Year's Eve blowout, somebody suggested Janis and Patti beat each other up. "I think it was probably the same energy," says Patti, comparing the kiss to their fake fight. "It's just an animal thing caused by large quantities of beer and youth," she says laughingly. "But I really did love her very deeply. And she loved me."

For all their intimacy, Janis and Patti never became lovers, but around this period Janis did have sex with a woman, probably for the first time, says Jack Smith. They were partying as usual, and Janis had been drinking quite a lot. At some point, she went off with a woman and apparently made it with her in a car parked behind a hedge. Jack was supposed to give Janis a ride home and was looking for her when she suddenly reappeared. Jack recalls her asking him, "So, how do you feel about me now? Do you think this makes me a bad person?" She also said, "Alcohol makes you do funny things." Jack assured her his feelings for her hadn't changed. "It just seemed perfectly natural for Janis to be so adventuresome." He does say he thinks it was "situational and circumstantial. I kind of think everything about Janis was like that." Though it's unlikely that anyone in the group gave Janis a hard time about her sexual experiments, that doesn't mean there was any real support for her same-sex adventures.

The group may have been "deliberately trying to be on the cutting edge," as Dave McQueen says, but homosexuality wasn't really cool. Dave had told no one, not even Patti, about his few sexual experiences with men. And Janis was uncharacteristically reticent about her nonheterosexual encounters. In fact, she was so upset by the kiss and the commotion it caused, she started seeing a therapist. After all, this was almost a decade before gay liberation, and homophobia was pervasive. No one was entirely outside its reach, not even Janis.

Patti thinks they "fed each other just enough to keep going," but Janis longed for something more; she wanted to break out of Port Arthur. Having gone solo to the West Coast once before, however, she wasn't eager to do it again. She wanted company this time. "Why is everyone a pair except me?" she'd ask. One night Jim Langdon remembers Janis saying, "There's Jack and Nova, there's Jim and Rae, there's this one and that one, but there's always just Janis." Even though Patti was married, Janis asked her to hitchhike with her to California. "Janis asked me to go down this road with her," recalls Patti, "and I just couldn't do it." Janis became briefly infatuated with a fellow Lamar student and Leadbelly devotee, Frank Davis, who played guitar. Perhaps she thought he was her way out of Texas, a boyfriend with whom she could play music.

Maybe it was her loneliness, her conviction that she'd always be alone and the rest of the world smugly coupled, that accounts for her behavior one night with Dave McQueen. "Once Janis and another guy and I took off late in the morning and drove to Galveston," Dave recalls. "We bought some six-packs and sat around on the beach drinking and talking all day. And in the early evening as we were driving home Janis was in the backseat, and just apropos of nothing, she suddenly began sobbing and just completely fell apart. It was like nothing I'd ever seen before. We had to stop the car. She got out and she walked up and down the side of the road for a while, wringing her hands and just sobbing. I tried to comfort her, but she didn't want to be touched. After a few minutes, almost as suddenly, she pulled herself together and got back in the car and off we drove, wisecracking as always." It was the only time Dave ever saw "the depth of her vulnerability."

Janis's friends felt that her tough-chick act often exacerbated her loneliness. "Janis wanted to be loved so much, but she'd make sure you'd have quite a trip to make if you were gonna touch this soft side," says Frank Davis. "The more rejected she felt, the angrier she got, the uglier she got, and the meaner she got." And, inevitably, the more rejected she was. When Frances Vincent first met Janis at Lamar, she found her hard to take. "The aura that came off of her was such anger. But what I did understand fairly quickly was that she was not only *very* bright but really very fragile and vulnerable, also." "Janis could be adorable and incredibly lovable," says Frank Davis, "but she would swat you like a cat playing with a mouse to get you angry, even violent, so you'd be at her level of passion." Unwilling to live in perpetual struggle, he got out.

For a while, Janis turned to her junior high boyfriend, Jack Smith, for company and comfort. Jack remembers Janis putting him up against a wall and saying that it was the two of them, not he and Nova, his girlfriend, who belonged together. Nova was out of town attending college, and Jack and Janis did spend a lot of time with each other. But Janis acted as if she had more than hanging out on her mind; she even said she wanted to marry him. Jack didn't take her seriously. "I was just around and other people weren't," he says. In the end, he thinks "Janis was really happy with the way it was." After all, proposing marriage to Jack was safe—he was already taken. Janis may not have been happy being the odd girl out, but neither was she ready to settle down and get married.

After Janis became famous she liked to say that from the beginning all she ever wanted to do was "be a beatnik" and "get stoned, get laid, have a good time." But that's not the refrain Jack Smith heard. "Why can't I be the kind of person who wants the house with the white picket fence?" Janis often asked him at the time. It bothered her that her desires weren't conventional, especially given the alternatives. The jobs she held—waitress, keypunch operator—were the kinds of work available to a young woman without a college education in the early sixties. It wasn't as if she could look forward to supporting herself as a singer. And at this point being a singer was a distant dream rather than an aspiration. "I knew I had a good voice," Janis would later say, "and I could always get a couple of beers off of it." As it turned out, in east Texas a couple of beers was all her voice would earn her. Her few efforts to sing around Port Arthur came to nothing. Jim Langdon arranged for her to join a friend's jazz band for a few songs during a New Year's Eve party at a private club. His friend cut her off after only one number because he didn't want a chick singer who was going to steamroll her way through a song.

Meanwhile, the parties and the trips to the state-line bars in Vinton grew wilder. Janis and Patti had a routine where they'd come on to Cajun guys who'd not only pay their cover charge but would continue forking over cash for their drinks. Sometimes when the locals realized Janis and Patti had no intention of holding up their end of the bargain, they would get angry and the Texas boys would end up in a fight to bail the women out. "Janis and Patti used to get into these predicaments because the locals would come on to them and the girls would give them a rash of shit," says Tary Owens. Girls weren't supposed to behave like that, but as another friend puts it, "in those days even rednecks didn't beat up women they weren't at least engaged to." One night, Patti had been flirting a lot at the bar, much to Dave's consternation. In a brooding fury, Dave drove the group back home to Texas—at about 110 miles per hour. Some say that as he was rounding a curve he lost control and the car rolled over three times before ending up in a ditch. According to one account, disputed by others, someone whispered, "I hope we'll all be killed" as the car rolled over. Dave maintains the car didn't crash, much less roll, because his '55 Olds was a "tank" and far too heavy to roll over. The car did blow two tires as it went off the road, but that was the extent of it, he claims. No one was injured.

"We were creative, we were rebels, and we just didn't go for it," says Patti of their pranks. "So we'd go out and do crazy things. We'd drive around and drive around in whoever's parents' car had any gas in it that we could get a hold of. We were just these people who wouldn't give up. And I guess we were on the verge of being put in jail or institutionalized." They were never in serious trouble, but they did have several run-ins with the police. One night Janis bullied Jack Smith into stealing one of the portable lights at the base of the drawbridge to Pleasure Island. The police threw him in jail until Janis put up a fuss, claiming responsibility for the stunt, and they finally released him. Another time the group clambered up to the catwalk underneath the Rainbow Bridge to Louisiana; the police, alerted by a driver to a possible suicide attempt, descended on them with sirens screaming and lights flashing.

The Rainbow Bridge, the tallest in the South, was one of their favorite hangouts. Jim Langdon says it was a symbol for them. "None of us planned on staying in Port Arthur. Whatever lay ahead, it was 'out there' somewhere. From a couple hundred feet above the Neches River . . . you could see there actually was a far horizon to reach toward." In the spring of 1962, some of the group opted for marriage and others took the first steps toward that horizon and moved to Austin, Texas. When Jack Smith chided Janis for thinking she could just hang out in Port Arthur and party forever, she agreed. Sort of. Why end the party when she could join the one in Austin, where a lively folk music scene was emerging? "She set out to make an impression in Austin," says Jack. Janis had been a little star; now "she was going to get it back."

2

Magnetized into Music

Today Austin enjoys enormous cultural cachet as the hip music capital of the Southwest, but in the sixties the town was, in Jim Langdon's words, "the best-kept secret in America." The state capital and home to the University of Texas, Austin was so small back then that all traffic on Interstate 35 came to a standstill whenever a train came through. Still, to Langdon and other Port Arthurans who moved there, Austin with its lush rolling hills "seemed like Nirvana," a "little center of enlightenment" amid the "vast primitive wasteland of Texas." Starting around 1960, Austin experienced an invasion of sorts as all the college-age "oddballs, weirdos, characters, and artists migrated there from the rest of the state." Just about everyone who was part of Janis's Lamar crowd lived there for a while. Austin may have been "racist, redneck, and somnolent," but it was also "an oasis for anyone with a mind or a creative spark." To rebels like Janis who'd been stuck in places like Port Arthur, moving to Austin was "like being granted sanctuary."

Soon after Janis returned from California, she began hearing about the wonders of Austin, mostly from Jack Smith, who'd been there. He marveled at all the people who read books, like they did. "You could see people our own age who had apartments filled with books, and arguing passionately about things in the student union. I came back with this grand vision." Late one night while others were piling into cars to make the obligatory trip to a state-line bar in Vinton, Janis turned to Jack and said, "Let's go see this Austin you're always talking about." Driving Seth Joplin's car, they went straight to the epicenter of Austin's nascent counterculture, a ramshackle two-story cluster of barracks-style apartments on Nueces Street, known affectionately as the Ghetto. Arriving at around five-thirty in the morning, they found a few bleary-eyed revelers, including a folkie named John Clay, who was perched on top of a refrigerator with a bottle of wine nestled between his legs, strumming his banjo. "I think you're right," said Janis, beaming at Jack. "I'm gonna love it here."

The next day, back in Port Arthur, Janis had to deal with the consequences of having run off with her father's car—and not for the first time. Janis's unscheduled trips out of Port Arthur were routine by now as were the frustration and exasperation they provoked in her parents. Janis's latest screwup was one too many; desperate for any solution, the Joplins finally allowed Janis to leave the Golden Triangle and enroll at UT. Dorothy put her foot down, however, when Janis announced she wanted to live at the Ghetto; she hadn't helped her cause by showing it to her mother and sister when they accompanied her to Austin to find an apartment. In the end, there was no fight—the university required freshman and sophomore girls to live in dorms or university-approved boarding-houses presided over by watchful house mothers. Janis lived in a boardinghouse, but her house mother couldn't have been too vigilant, because the Ghetto quickly became her hangout.

For all its burgeoning culture of dissent, in the summer of 1962 the UT campus was still ruled by jocks, frat rats, and "bubbleheads" (sorority girls with bouffant hairdos). As a consequence, Janis and her friends didn't have to look very hard to find one another. Fredda Slote arrived at UT from a New England boarding school with "straight hair down to my hips and little wire-rim glasses." Her first day on campus she wore a denim dress she'd had specially made and leather sandals that laced all the way up to her knees. She'd bought them in Greenwich Village, of course. "I didn't look like your average University of Texanite. And as I was standing in line to sign up for a class a young woman came up to me and tapped me on the shoulder and said, 'Come with me, I'm going to introduce you to the people you're going to spend the next four years with.' And she took me over to the student union and she introduced me to Powell St. John [her future boyfriend] and all his friends. And she was right, those people have stayed my close friends to this day."

Fredda Slote might have found more boho students at Brandeis or Berkeley, but for the most part college campuses in the early sixties were "monoliths of conventionality." Indeed, college students of the era seemed so conformist that most observers predicted a resurgence of conservatism on America's campuses. Reflecting on those years a decade later, John Clay argued there was undeniably a "generation gap" at UT, "but not like the one they talk about today. People like Janis and me were rejecting the standards of our *own* generation." Most UT students supported segregation, for example, while Janis's crowd took part in civil rights demonstrations. The few African American students admitted to the university had to put up with the humiliation of "white" and "colored" bathrooms and byzantine dormitory visitation rules. As late as 1961, the only black men allowed in white women's dormitories were messengers and delivery personnel, and they were restricted to the lobby. Black female visitors were permitted to venture beyond the lobby but were barred from using the restrooms or drinking fountains. If a black girl visited a white girl's room, the door was to be kept shut—an odd reversal of the universal college rule about keeping doors open when men came to visit. These demeaning regulations aroused almost no controversy among UT's white students; largely apathetic, they reserved their passion for Longhorn football, rivalries within the Greek system of fraternities and sororities, and beauty contests. Every month there seemed to be a new beauty contest—the University Sweetheart Contest, the Varsity Queen Contest, the Miss Campus Chest Contest—not to mention the annual cheerleader competition.

If all the oddball students were tyrannized by campus culture, UT held particular terror for the girls. Janis's friend Pepi Plowman remembers a science class in which she was "more afraid" of her lab partner than of anything else. "She had this bouffant hairdo and everything about her was *absolutely perfect*," recalls Pepi. "Here we were trying to some extent to be ourselves and look ourselves as opposed to what was expected of us—at least the girls were." In a climate so conformist, their efforts were bound to cause a stir. No one was more provocative than Janis, whose uniform still consisted of a man's white dress shirt, now worn with khaki pants or blue jeans and either white tennis shoes or moccasins. She didn't bother with a bra or makeup or tease her hair into "a great lacquered helmet" to achieve the perfect bubblehead look. All this in 1962, when "most women never left the bedroom without a girdle and full makeup." As in the past, Janis's rebellion went far beyond clothing. Back then, "women never passed gas, much less said 'shit' in public," making Janis's refusal to act like a lady "positively revolutionary," according to her friend Ramsey Wiggins, a graduate student in English. But then, Janis had set out to make an impression in Austin, according to Jack Smith.

Janis got the attention she wanted. After she'd been on campus only a few months, the *Daily Texan* devoted an entire article to her. "She Dares to Be Different!" screamed the headline, a point underscored by the accompanying picture of a plain but fierce-looking girl strumming an autoharp and singing. Without makeup or a proper do, Janis could not have looked more different from the belles who usually graced the pages of the campus newspaper. "She goes barefooted when she feels like it, wears Levi's to class because they're more comfortable, and carries her Autoharp with her everywhere she goes so that in case she gets the urge to break out into song it will be handy." It was her singing that brought Janis to the notice of Pat Sharpe of the *Daily Texan*, though Sharpe devoted lots of ink to Janis's look and jive lingo and to her Ghetto compatriots. Sharpe says she liked Janis, but she admits she was taken aback when Janis showed up for their interview at the student union with her own booze—behavior that could have gotten her expelled. It was the first—but hardly the last—time Janis would try to shock a reporter.

Janis worked at being the most outrageous figure on campus, but she had some competition. "Everybody had an attitude and they were all trying to figure out what people were wearing in Greenwich Village," recalls a friend. "We had the same sort of clothes—berets, turtleneck sweaters—trying to be Beat." Not surprisingly, Janis's group of friends became the nucleus of the sixties counterculture in Austin. Quite a few of them—

the self-described Texas mafia—later moved to San Francisco, where they helped shape the emerging culture of the Haight. In addition to Janis, Pepi, and Fredda, there was Gilbert Shelton, an art student and folkie who was editor of the *Texas Ranger*, an award-winning student humor magazine and "the stronghold of the counterculture" on campus. Shelton created Wonder Warthog comics for the *Ranger* and then in 1966 started a strip called *The Furry Freak Brothers* that earned him "a living as well as counterculture fame in San Francisco."

Shelton worked with Jack Jackson, whose *God Nose* is often credited as the very first underground comic book; Jackson would later handle the sale of psychedelic posters at Chet Helms's Avalon Ballroom in San Francisco. When Chet, a UT dropout and former Young Republican, wasn't hitchhiking across the country, he was part of the group, too. Although a future pooh-bah of San Francisco rock 'n' roll, at the time he was simply the "skinny kid high on peyote at their Wednesday afternoon drunks." Then there was Stephanie Chernikowski, an English major who had grown up in Beaumont and gone to the same state-line bars as Janis. As a teenager she'd worshiped Elvis, but at UT she was into folk music and walked around campus with a "battered paperback copy of *On the Road* in the rear pocket of [her] Levi's." Dave Moriaty, Janis's fellow Port Arthuran, who was already living at the Ghetto when Janis arrived, would go on to found San Francisco's Rip Off Press. Fredda Slote's boyfriend, Powell St. John, lived downstairs from Moriaty and Jackson. He had a passion for the harmonica, which he would play in two bands, Austin's own Conqueroo and San Francisco's Mother Earth. Powell was joined in the Conqueroo by Bob Brown, a precocious Austin high schooler who hung out with the Ghetto crowd. Also part of the group were Travis Rivers, who later managed the *Oracle*, Haight-Ashbury's psychedelic newspaper, and Ramsey Wiggins and his brother Lanny, whose "vast repertoire of songs" and ability to play a five-string banjo made him something of a "guru" among local folk musicians.

There was Julie Paul, a folkie who, like Janis, refused to dress like a proper coed. Julie was overweight and also wore a man's white shirt with the sleeves rolled up and the tail hanging out over jeans and loafers. The adopted daughter of a lobbyist for the railroads, Julie had grown up in Austin. She "drank a lot and misbehaved when she did," recalls Ramsey

Wiggins. "And she usually had a Marlboro hanging out of the side of her mouth." She raced around town in her red TR3, often after boozing it up. "She was a good ol' girl," according to Fredda Slote. "She used to say, 'If I'm too drunk to walk, just sit me in my car and I can drive.' And, enlightened fools that we were, we would do it, and ride with her." Julie has frequently been compared to Janis because her surface toughness never totally concealed her vulnerability and sweetness. Both of them, notes a friend, were "ballsy but insecure," but there was a key difference: Julie didn't seem perpetually about to boil over; she wasn't angry like Janis.

Finally, there were the Stopher brothers from Beaumont. Wali Stopher, who had transferred from Lamar, was a key figure in Austin's counterculture (the town's first head shop was named for him). But, according to Ramsey Wiggins, it was Wali's handsome brother, Tommy, who "set the standard of personal freedom" that most of the group, Janis included, "tried to live up to, then and later in life." As the painter whose work convinced Janis she should find another outlet for her creativity, Tommy Stopher was at least indirectly responsible for Janis's interest in pursuing singing. He was also the first person Wiggins and the others had ever met "who proclaimed himself an Artist." Stopher's "personal hero" was Janis's favorite painter, Modigliani. Stopher loved talking about the artist, "how he balanced his short life between two mistresses, his easel, and the ever-present bottle of wine, all in the same studio in Paris." Tommy thought this was the life, recalls Wiggins. "And awed by such worldliness, we found it fitting that Modigliani's mistress killed herself and their child by jumping out the window after he finally died of his excesses." Janis no doubt shared Tommy's conviction that true artists led beautifully doomed lives.

"Between the folksing people, the art students, and the *Ranger* crowd, you had a veritable mob of counterculture novitiates," says Bob Brown. Despite their differences, "this amazing group of disaffiliates" functioned "like a fraternity" and their frat house was the Ghetto. There were only four or five apartments at the Ghetto, but people were constantly coming and going, making it hard to determine who actually lived there at any given time. "It was a crash pad," says Jack Jackson of the place he shared with Dave Moriaty. "I mean, no one ever swept the floor." And so it was at the other $35-a-month apartments, none of which ever came up for rent because they were always passed from friend to friend. The Ghetto was "party central," and also the place couples went to have sex. Because the girls couldn't entertain in their dorms or boardinghouses, and many of the guys lived in dorms or rooms that afforded little privacy, the Ghetto— especially Tommy and Wali Stopher's apartment—became "a commonly held place of assignation." Their bedroom "was constantly in use by balling couples who didn't live there and it got to be something of a joke," recalls Ramsey Wiggins, "to the point that some wag lettered 'Main Ballroom' over the door and decorated the sign with a stylized drawing of a pair of testicles." By all accounts, Janis spent a lot of time in that bedroom.

Although they drank heavily, the UT gang also consumed lots of speed, marijuana, and peyote. Possession of even a single joint of marijuana carried a heavy prison sentence—up to ten years—but peyote, which was available at nearby Hudson's Cactus Gardens, was both legal and, at ten cents a plant, very cheap. Even so, peyote was still for the very few; everyone, on the other hand, used speed, even the straightest students. College health services routinely handed it out during midterms and finals. Although nobody was shooting up speed or trying heroin, Tary Owens says, "We were all experimenting with lots of different kinds of drugs and drinking all the time." Both Jack Jackson and Bob Brown are careful, however, to differentiate their experimentation with drugs from what followed, claiming that in the early years taking drugs grew out of their interest in mysticism and the writings of intellectuals and Beat poets. "People were reading Aldous Huxley long before anyone heard of Timothy Leary," Jackson explains. In their crowd, drugs were about altering consciousness, not just getting fucked up, although this distinction doubtless meant more to some than to others.

Certainly for Janis drugs were about getting fucked up; they served to obliterate consciousness, not heighten it. She craved drugs that took her out of reality. Because she so symbolizes the sixties counterculture, Janis is sometimes remembered as rock's acid queen. However, Janis's response to her first LSD trip was unequivocal: "Shit, man, that ain't dope!" Jack Jackson doesn't remember ever seeing Janis trip. "She was always there with her quart of beer in a paper bag. I think she was scared of acid, that she'd get out there and never come back. I didn't have enough sense to be scared of it." Another Ghetto habitué, David Martinez, claims he did peyote with her twice. "She didn't know what it was the first time. It was a big surprise." Janis didn't really enjoy hallucinogens, he says. "She didn't want to let go and she became panicky."

Drugs and drink aside, most of the beatnik crowd had come to UT with the intention of graduating; Janis, who attended UT from the summer of 1962 through December 1962, came to hang out at the Ghetto and play music. Although she enrolled as an art major, she took only one art class. The two Cs she earned in anthropology and psychology and her five withdrawals indicate that Janis was a slacker student even in a stimulating environment. She could be quite provocative, however. Robert Morrison, who was in her class on Western philosophy, remembers her as one of the few bright, outspoken students. She would sit in the back and stop the professor midstream. "Wait a minute, Jack," she'd say, "you can't get away with that." The young Ivy League–educated professor "loved it," says Morrison, because Janis "was *so* bright." According to Morrison, despite her mediocre record Janis was invited to take part in Plan II, an accelerated program for UT's brainy students.

In the end, Janis was uninterested in what UT had to teach; her real education was taking place elsewhere, at the campus folksings and at Threadgill's, a honky-tonk bar north of town. While other students crammed for exams, Janis and the gang stayed up late playing folk music and the blues. Like hundreds of other student folk music aficionados in Cambridge, Greenwich Village, Ann Arbor, and Berkeley, they made music the center of their lives. Bob Dylan, officially enrolled at the University of Minnesota, was really a student at the "University of Dinkytown," the bohemian enclave near campus. Other college folkies, like Eric von Schmidt and Jim Rooney, describe themselves as "foundering on the reefs of folk music." Janis was just one of many kids who were "magnetized into music," as Maria Muldaur of the Jim Kweskin Jug Band says of her own obsession. "It wasn't as if people were sitting around college dorms and said, 'How can we make a million?' " recalls Muldaur. "We just did it like crazies."

Art students were apparently the first to pick up instruments, and their parties "were rarely without guitars, banjos, fiddles, and harmonicas." But art students were not the only ones to get caught up in the folk craze. Among offbeat students, soon "everybody with $35 to his name had a

Harmony guitar and was picking 'Old Joe Clark,' or something by Woody Guthrie," claims Ramsey Wiggins. Although Janis had moved to Austin to be part of the music scene, at first she was too shy to join in. Wiggins had known her at least a month before he even knew she could sing. "I remember being in the Ghetto when I heard what I thought was a recording being played in the next room, a loud, strong, clear contralto. I was completely shocked when I went in to ask who was being played and discovered that it was Janis singing into a tape recorder. I also remember that when I expressed my approval, Janis was very self-deprecatory, even a little sullen." Wiggins wasted no time in telling his brother Lanny, the banjo player, about Janis's voice.

Wali Stopher was there the first time Janis sang with Lanny on banjo and Powell St. John on the harmonica and says they were both "blown away" by her voice. Wiggins and St. John had already been playing together as the Waller Creek Boys, doing songs like "Cripple Creek" and "Railroad Bill," but neither was much interested in singing. They immediately asked Janis to join their group, named after a polluted creek that ran through the university. (Even after she joined, they were usually called the Waller Creek Boys or the Waller Creek Boys Plus One. No matter, Janis had always been one of the guys anyway.) After that, Janis spent hours with Lanny and Powell in the backyard of the Ghetto playing bluegrass, blues, country, and folk music. "Anytime we had a party," recalls Fredda Slote, "you could guarantee that by the end of it the musicians would be in one corner practicing and playing and all of their significant others would be hanging around being widows together." Years later, Janis said they would "hang out and get drunk a lot, get in big fights, roll in the mud, drink beer, and sing, pick and sing, pick and sing."

The singing and picking was limited to parties until Stephanie Chernikowski put together the university folksings during the spring of 1962. The folksings weren't a lot more organized, but they marked the formal beginning of both the Austin music scene and Janis's career as a performer. Although Chernikowski dreamed up the folksing as a way for her musician friends to get together, it soon became a weekly event that brought together all the nonconformists, all the kids who felt like "displaced persons." At other campuses with a more established culture of dissent, such as the University of Chicago or Berkeley, folksings or hootenannies might attract hundreds, even thousands. The blues singer Nick Gravenites claims that when he was a student at the University of Chicago in the late fifties the hoots were attended by thousands of people. At UT, Chernikowski believes that thirty to forty people showed up, while others remember close to a hundred people crowded in the room.

Every Wednesday night the musicians would meet at the Chuckwagon area of the student union, where they'd push aside the ugly white Formica tables and orange plastic chairs. In any given week, the crowd might include political activists such as Jeff Shero Nightbyrd, David Martinez, and Roger Baker, art students like Tommy Stopher and Gilbert Shelton, the academic folklorists Americo Paredes and Roger Abrahams, the *Ranger* staff, and other assorted beatniks from the Ghetto. Sometimes a faculty member would take a few minutes to explore the roots and meanings of the music. In their egalitarianism, informality, and sense of community, the folksings mirrored the political movements of the sixties. The musicians didn't perform on a stage but rather sat around in a circle on the floor sharing instruments and taking turns singing. Bob Brown remembers the folksings were "entirely unmanaged or directed. There was a protocol, but no actual rules. When someone finished a song, you applauded, then someone else would just start playing. All it took was the nerve to jump in before the next guy."

Anywhere from ten to twenty-five people might perform on a given night, but few were as talented as the Waller Creek Boys. "Some of the players were truly awful," recalls Bob Brown, "though we stifled our groans and gave as much polite deference to the gosh-awful as to the truly entertaining." Everyone specialized in someone else, he says: "Woody Guthrie, the Carter Family, Bob Dylan, Elizabeth Cotten, Jimmie Rodgers, Pete Seeger, and so on. The Dylan imitator would slump in a corner, trying to look very jaded and Dylan-like with his harmonica brace around his neck. The first time I saw Janis, the thing that struck me wasn't her voice or her untidy hair. She was the first girl I'd ever seen who was not wearing a bra."

However Janis caught people's attention, it was her voice that kept them riveted. Everyone agrees that her tremendous talent was immediately apparent. "It took a couple of weeks to persuade her to sing," recalls Chernikowski. "But when she performed we were spellbound." For some of the men in their crowd, Janis's talent eclipsed what they considered her physical liabilities. "Almost everyone knew she was a monster in terms of talent," recalls one. "She could be ugly, pimply, with her tits hanging out, but she was so good." During the folksings Janis mostly sang in her gravelly Bessie Smith voice. On occasion, though, she'd display her natural voice, which was clear and pure. Robert Morrison remembers accosting Janis one day after he'd heard her use her "pretty" voice. "Joan Baez was really big then, and I got very excited and said, 'Janis, I had no idea you could sing that way. You could become a recording star!'" Janis wasn't interested. "Oh man, I don't want to sing that way," she said. Jack Smith, who knew Janis's natural voice from her church choir days, says she told him, "I'm never going to be able to compete with singers like Joan Baez and Judy Collins. And who wants to? That's saccharine pap, that's not me."

Janis developed a real seriousness about her music in Austin, reflecting perhaps the commitment of players like Powell St. John and Lanny Wiggins. In Austin, singing wasn't a way of whiling away the time as you made the triangle or drove over to Vinton. It was about studying and mastering a craft. According to Jack Jackson, "Janis and her friends were trying to learn about the blues and Appalachian mountain music. It really was an intellectual pursuit, though hardly anyone realizes it." Powell St. John claims Janis was a "real scholar. She knew music I never heard way back then. I'm continually running across stuff now and thinking, Oh, Janis heard that. She picked up things from all kinds of diverse sources. She acknowledged Bessie Smith, of course. But there were others, too. Leadbelly, Memphis Minnie, and country music."

Fredda Slote remembers how devoted they all were to playing music. "Janis didn't just happen to start singing folk music and be discovered by the media. She worked very hard at it. She studied and practiced it. She was interested in all different varieties of music. She was one of those people who'd practice long into the night to get one twist of phrase right or the transition from one chord to another. They were all fanatics. You have to be if you're going to be a musician. An artist is a fanatic by nature and that's what she was." Nevertheless, Janis had no time for formal training. When a friend suggested she take voice lessons, she said, "They'd only want me to sing differently."

Janis was excited by all the enthusiasm her singing generated, but it also made her anxious. She had finally managed to get people's attention back, and she wasn't about to lose it. In truth, Janis didn't have much competition in Austin, except for her friend Pepi Plowman. "Janis didn't like me to sing unless I was alone with her," Pepi remembers. "If she was at the folksing, I'd just bow out. If we were with other people and I'd say, 'Do you know this song?' and start singing, she'd say, 'I know that. I can sing it so much better than you.' She was so competitive." Success didn't ease Janis's insecurity, either. Later, after Janis had established her reputation at Monterey Pop, Pepi visited her in San Francisco. "Well, what's it like having a band?" Pepi asked her. Janis shot her a look and snapped, "What! Are you thinking of having a band?" Janis had reason to feel nervous: not only was Pepi a wonderful singer with a "big, bluesy voice," says Wali Stopher, she was a good guitarist, too. Janis, by contrast, never mastered the guitar. "She could barely play the autoharp," jokes Frank Davis, her guitarist friend from Lamar. No doubt Janis found Pepi's looks equally intimidating. "Pepi was really beautiful, with long, gorgeous curly blond hair and a tan," recalls Wali Stopher.

In the early sixties, the term *folk music* covered a much wider patch of musical territory than it does today, including unplugged blues and country music. In fact, until 1942, when *Billboard* magazine inaugurated its Harlem Hit Parade, "hillbilly" and "race" records were lumped together under the catchall designation *folk*. No one thought it odd that Bob Dylan, in his 1961 debut at Gerde's Folk City, New York's premier folk club, opened for bluesman John Lee Hooker.

For Janis and other hard-core Austin musicians, the genre was irrelevant as long as the music was "real." They venerated the authentic and disdained the commercial. "We weren't alone," Powell points out; "this was true on other campuses as well. Everyone wanted to get to the sources." For folkies, the "thing was to exhume an authentic folk song" as Dave Van Ronk had with "The House of the Rising Son" (which, ironically, became a top-ten hit for the British Invasion group the Animals a few years later). Like folk music aficionados in Cambridge, New York, and Berkeley, the Austin crowd was "snobbish about their music" says Pepi. "At the time, we looked down on Peter, Paul and Mary because they were commercial. The Kingston Trio was the same." Powell goes further, saying the Austin group was anti-"folksinger." They objected to the "whole button-down image" of mainstream folk music made popular by groups like the Kingston Trio. "Joan Baez barely made the grade," according to Powell, "and Peter, Paul and Mary were hopeless." Powell points out that Bob Dylan also mocked "button-down" folk music: "There's a line in a Dylan song where a club owner says, 'You sound like a hillbilly, we want folk singers here.'" Janis would occasionally make fun of Joan Baez, impersonating her "just to show she could," but her imitation of Jean Ritchie, a folksinger who specialized in Appalachian music, was sincere. That's because, Powell clarifies, "Jean Ritchie was cool."

Cool. Folkies were forever embroiled in arguments about who or what was the coolest, the hippest, and authenticity was the critical factor. Peter Albin, the bassist for Big Brother, remembers that the obsession with authenticity encouraged "a lot of one-upmanship" as musicians vied for the mantle of coolest by searching out the most ethnic and obscure songs, artists, and instruments. Peter recalls one Bay Area folkie boasting about his latest acquisition, a "volzither," which he claimed was a "very ethnic instrument played by the Croatians in the 1800s. When you'd ask, 'How do you play it, Bruce?' he'd say, 'I don't know yet, but I'm going to learn,' which he never did." Austinites were purists too, but their snobbery was Texas-inflected. Whether it was Jimmie Rodgers, Hank Williams, or Rose Maddox (one of Janis's favorites), country possessed real cultural capital at UT. It was "less Pete Seeger, more Hank Williams, though we listened to Seeger, of course," says Stephanie Chernikowski. And, always, Leadbelly—not to mention a growing roster of "cool" blues artists like Sonny Terry and Brownie McGhee, Jesse Fuller, Blind Lemon Jefferson, and Forest City Joe.

By 1962 folk music was becoming big business. The Kingston Trio, who scored a smash hit in 1958 with "Tom Dooley," had started the craze. With their clean-cut collegiate look and slick Vegas-style act, they made folk music, once the preserve of the left, safe for mainstream consumption. In the wake of their success, the Chad Mitchell Trio, the Limelighters, and countless others jumped on the bandwagon. The craze first hit Greenwich Village, which was soon overrun on weekend nights with tourists eager to hear Kingston Trio–like musicians. The streets were so thick with traffic the police were forced to put up barricades. By spring 1961 landlords, eager to capitalize on the fad, had converted "every available nook and cranny zoned for commercial use into a coffeehouse." By 1963 folk music was so hot that no fewer than eleven million viewers were tuning in each week to catch ABC's *Hootenanny*, a show featuring mainstream folk musicians.

No one watched the hyping of folk music with greater interest than Janis's future manager, Albert Grossman, who had quickly grasped the commercial potential of folk music. "The American public is like Sleeping Beauty waiting to be kissed awake by the prince of folk music," he told Robert Shelton of the *New York Times* in the late 1950s. Just a few years later, he was managing Odetta, Bob Dylan, and Peter, Paul and Mary—a group he put together from scratch ("Paul" was actually a stand-up comic named Noel Stookey; the group never played together until Grossman suggested they form a trio). For Grossman, there was just one hitch: "Some 'pure' folk singers act as if money were heroin." In truth, money wasn't the only obstacle. To serious folkies their music's lack of popularity was precisely the point—it signified their difference and defiance. In this environment, disdain for the commercial was obligatory, even when it wasn't heartfelt. Dave Van Ronk recalls how much his circle of Greenwich Village folkies loathed Peter Yarrow's piece of pop fluff, "Puff the Magic Dragon." "You *had* to hate that song even if you liked it!"

In their commitment to authenticity and egalitarianism, their rejection of the commercial, and their longing for community, the folksingers at UT and other colleges seem to us today indistinguishable from the student activists of the time. The students who gathered to sing and listen at folk-sings across the country were also rejecting the culture of apathy and conformity that prevailed on college campuses and throughout America. But while the two groups shared a great deal, folkies did not necessarily see themselves as cultural emissaries of the activists' movement. Folk music's connection to the left dates back to the Great Depression and the Popular Front, when the Communist Party enlisted folk music—"people's music"—to advance a homegrown, homespun kind of communism. A generation of musicians—Paul Robeson, Cisco Houston, Leadbelly, and Woody Guthrie—sang songs articulating the grievances of the downtrodden. Guthrie painted "This Machine Kills Fascists" on the body of his guitar. In fact, the hootenanny came into being in July 1940 when Seattle Democrats launched fund-raising parties with folk songs. Pete Seeger and

Woody Guthrie attended those hoots and brought the concept, as well as the term, back East. Seeger and the Almanac Singers, and later the blacklisted Weavers, maintained folk music's connection to the left through the forties and the fifties. Some of the new generation of folksingers, most notably Phil Ochs and Joan Baez, explicitly identified with sixties political movements. Bob Dylan, at first just one of many Woody Guthrie clones, was also busy cranking out one protest song after another—songs he'd later dismiss as so much "finger-pointing."

For the most part, though, the folkies' activism was implicit, limited to distrusting authority and championing the rights of the underdog, which meant they opposed segregation and, once it escalated, the Vietnam War. Tary Owens, Lanny and Ramsey Wiggins, and Powell St. John were among the folkies who participated in the "stand-ins" to desegregate Austin's movie theaters. A few years later, Bob Brown penned an antiwar song because he knew "hating the war was a popular sentiment among my new college friends." Jeff Shero Nightbyrd, a UT activist, contends that the "alienated and rebel groups were all in alliance in those days, the integrationist groups, the motorcycle riders, the folk singers and the cave explorers." Most folksingers, however, including Mr. Finger-Pointer himself, Bob Dylan, were not joiners. "We were outsiders, not activists," maintains Stephanie Chernikowski. "And as outsiders we took a dim view of organizations." The divide between cultural and political radicals continued to grow. Toward the end of the decade, Wali Stopher says, the politicos "thought we were apolitical weed smokers, and we thought they were obnoxious, irritating, shouting people."

Former Austin folkies tend to agree that the Ghetto crowd was basically "apolitical," but that fact obscures the challenge they posed to business-as-usual. In their dress, drug use, disregard for materialism, and, perhaps most of all, their interracialism, they were suggesting transgressive alternatives to other young people. Certainly to UT administrators, the Ghetto group was a hotbed of subversion undermining Longhorn tradition. In 1962, the university's Office of the Dean of Student Life began keeping tabs on the group, or the "cell," as the investigators termed it. They were as interested in the group's drug use and freewheeling sexuality as in the few lefty political connections they could dig up. Sixty-eight people—including the novelist Billy Lee Brammer, several maverick professors, and Ghetto regulars like Powell, Pepi, and Janis—were targeted.

"We all suspected it," says Tary Owens, who found out about the list years later. Travis Rivers agrees. "I used to say, 'The eyes of Texas are upon you—at all times.'"

In more-urban places like Cambridge, Berkeley, and Greenwich Village the search for authenticity led folk music mavens to seek out obscure records and songbooks. But in Austin authenticity was considerably less hard to come by. Texas was a region still alive with "real" music, including country and western. "It was less academic for us," says Chernikowski, "because we were living in the past." In fact, authenticity could be found every Wednesday night at a beer joint called Threadgill's, a converted gas station on the northernmost edge of Austin. Once a week Janis and her friends would drive out to Threadgill's to play music with old-time blue-grass and country players. The bar's owner, Kenneth Threadgill, had been a bootlegger during Prohibition and is said to have acquired the first beer license in Travis County after its repeal. He was also a Jimmie Rodgers enthusiast whose jukebox was stocked with old 78s—every last one a Jimmie Rodgers record. Known as the father of hillbilly, or country and western, Rodgers began his career performing in blackface and was often paired with Frank Stokes, a black Memphis songster from whom he sup-posedly learned much of his repertoire. Rodgers developed a falsetto yodel that in turn influenced countless singers from famous bluesman Howlin' Wolf (whose nickname, he said, derived from his failed efforts to sound like Rodgers) to an amateur like Threadgill, who'd seen him per-form in 1928.

Threadgill had purchased the gas station in the midthirties, and by the midforties he was selling soda pop and beer out of some old coolers while his friends played guitar and fiddle and sang hillbilly music. By the midfifties a group of local amateur musicians were showing up every week to play, and Threadgill would pay them with two rounds of free beer. There were few regulars, mostly "cedar choppers," day laborers, and mechanics—rednecks, in other words. In 1959 a group of UT graduate students with a love of bluegrass music discovered the honky-tonk and began to join in the music making. For the next year or so, nothing much changed, because the students played the same music as the old-timers and the audience remained tiny.

Once the folksing students got wind of Threadgill's, however, everything changed. Driving out to Threadgill's became a postfolksing ritual for the Waller Creek Boys and other campus folkies. Their Wednesday-night gatherings became raucous affairs that drove away most of Threadgill's redneck regulars. Bluegrass and C & W remained the music of choice, but the younger students added blues and jug band music. Whereas the old-timers had played without amplification, the crowds jamming into the joint required that Threadgill set up "a microphone and a small, old amplifier to render the singer audible." There was no stage at Threadgill's. Instead, the performers played right in the middle of the customers. "We all sat around a big oak table reserved for musicians," recalls Tary Owens, "and there was a microphone and a little amp and someone would sing a song and then pass the mike to the next person." Over time, though, as the bar became more crowded, "the musicians had to move to the back rooms to wait their turns at the mikes and sound system Threadgill had installed." Some nights there was such a crush that Threadgill's son, who often helped out at the bar, did little more than open beer bottles, pass them out over people's heads, and accept money when it was passed back to him. Threadgill sold so much beer on these nights that Lone Star Beer donated T-shirts to the regular players, who started going by the name the Hootenanny Hoots. Eventually even frat boys started coming to Threadgill's to catch the action, the first intimation in Austin of that sixties sea change—the transformation of the weird and eccentric into the hip and the cool.

Janis was the star attraction at Threadgill's, the reason it was packed every Wednesday night. "Oh yeah, the Waller Creek Boys were the best," recalls Pepi Plowman. "They were only a little acoustic trio, but Janis put on a big show. At the end of the night, she'd sing stuff like 'Sal's Got a Wooden Leg' and jump around." Jack Smith remembers the first time it hit Janis that people were driving out to Threadgill's just to hear her. "She thought the world had come to an absolute end. There's never been a wider grin or bigger eyes." Stan Alexander, one of the original UT students who discovered the bar, remembers the excitement swirling around Janis, even though she had not yet developed her own style. She was still carrying around her autoharp and singing Joan Baez and Judy Collins songs, Alexander remembers. "Her range and power were just beginning to come into play with songs like Bessie Smith's 'Black Mountain Blues,' and a piece or two she did in conscious imitation of Odetta." But there was the palpable thrill of something new happening at Threadgill's. Today we might call it energy, says Alexander, and most of it was focused on Janis.

"That girl's really good," Threadgill said when he first heard Janis sing. Both he and his wife, Mildred, took a real shine to Janis. Jack Jackson thought it odd because Janis was indisputably the weirdest and wildest student of them all. "She was sad, dirty, and unwashed, with a bad complexion and matted hair. She looked as if she'd been wearing the same clothes for weeks, even sleeping in them. And she had these coonskin caps, ratty old things—God knows where she got them. It's just bizarre that Threadgill would have done this Daddy thing with her." To most of the folkies, however, there was nothing mysterious about Threadgill's fondness for her. "Janis was obviously troubled, and he had a soft spot and a fatherly attitude toward her. He was a grand old guy," says Powell St. John. "Of course he loved her," says Stephanie Chernikowski. "Everybody adored her. She was very charismatic. And she could turn on the charm like all performers." And then there was her voice, which was so strong she didn't need a microphone. In fact, on the few occasions the Waller Creek Boys performed on other stages, Janis had to stand about five or six feet back from the microphone because her voice drowned out Lanny's banjo and Powell's harmonica. Whatever his reasons, Threadgill showed Janis "a kind of hick-genteel admiration and grace she never asked for or got from anyone else," observes Stan Alexander.

Indeed, Janis really cared for Threadgill, too. "He surpassed them all," Janis said later. "He was old, a great big man with a beer belly and white hair combed back on top of his head. He'd be dishin' out Polish sausages and hard-boiled eggs and Grand Prizes and Lone Stars." Every Wednesday night, after some coaxing, Mr. Threadgill, as the students called him, would sing Jimmie Rodgers's "T for Texas" or "Waitin' for a Train." "Someone would say, 'Mr. Threadgill, Mr. Threadgill, come out and do us a tune,'" Janis remembered. "And he'd say, 'No, I don't think so,' and they'd say, 'Come on, come on,' and he'd say, 'All right.' He'd close the bar down, and then he'd walk out front, and he'd lay his hands across his big fat belly, which was covered with a bar apron. . . . He'd come out like that and lean his head back and sing, just like a bird. . . . God was he fantastic!" When Threadgill yodeled, a hush fell upon the room.

The folksing crew was nothing if not a "bunch of weird kids," but either out of genuine openness or business calculation, Kenneth Threadgill, a Texas good ol' boy, welcomed them. Dave Moriaty thinks Threadgill "put up with" the folksing people to make money. Powell St. John, who remembers feeling nervous about going to the bar until he met Mr. Threadgill, disagrees: "We were light years away from where Threadgill was, but he was open to us." Jack Jackson says he's often wondered why Threadgill tolerated them, because "his customers were the kind of working-class people who had no use for longhairs." Jackson recalls little tension in the bar, although sometimes "you'd see this redneck guy come in and get this disgusted look on his face and leave." According to Jackson, "the parking lot was kind of scary, but I can't remember any nasty incidents, though we did always go in groups. This was how people hit Threadgill's—in a caravan, a wave." Others insist that Threadgill's regulars were a "pretty tame bunch of middle-aged rednecks," nothing like the ones who hung out at the Broken Spoke, a local cowboy bar. Of course, Janis and her Golden Triangle cronies had been haunting redneck Cajun bars for years. It was less a Beat affectation than a search for the genuine and the real. "The experience a lot of us were searching for was the folk experience, and Mr. Threadgill was unquestionably of the people," explains Ramsey Wiggins.

While Threadgill and his regulars were willing to overlook the students' scruffiness, they were not color-blind. Indeed, virtually all of Austin was segregated at the time, and it's unlikely that any black people would have wanted to set foot inside the place before the folksing crowd began hanging out there. Race did not seem to be an issue at the bar until Ed Guinn, a biracial UT student and folksinger, expressed an interest in playing with his friends at Threadgill's. His fellow folkie John Clay approached Threadgill, who made it clear that Guinn wasn't welcome. Fearing Guinn's presence would be "too disruptive," Clay dissuaded him from showing up.

Over thirty years later, people are still testy about the issue. Dave Moriaty claims the bar lost its allure for the folksing crowd when Threadgill excluded Guinn—which happened after Janis left town. Others say they knew nothing about it. But they must have noticed the bar was segregated. "I knew and everyone knew that black folks didn't come to Threadgill's," Powell St. John admits. Moreover, Tary Owens notes, "there was some of what we would now call racist material up on the walls at Threadgill's." A halfhearted protest was attempted when Joan Baez came to town. After her UT concert, Baez was set on going out to Threadgill's. When she learned it was segregated she and some others staged a protest outside the bar, but it quickly fizzled out.

"Looking back on it," says Powell, "it's clear that Threadgill's was a segregated venue because it always had been a segregated venue. I never figured Threadgill for a racist, he was just born into that world." Ramsey recalls Threadgill's saying that he had to be mindful of his regular customers. The UT folkies were "just a once-a-week aberration," and he was "fearful of losing business, even of violence, if he integrated before the law required it." As for the folkies, "we had all done our share of marching in the previous several years," says Ramsey, "and quite a few people were pissed about it. At the same time, the cooler heads among us realized the bind Mr. Threadgill was in and felt that the law that would resolve this temporary embarrassment was probably just months away. And we were right." Wiggins's keen sense of moral dilemma accurately expresses the tough spot the Austinites found themselves in. Folkies elsewhere could worship white country-and-western musicians at a distance; that those idols held sometimes less-than-enlightened political views was something they didn't need to confront. The Austin group, however, was on the scene and was truly in a quandary.

In the end, Texas bluesman Mance Lipscomb integrated Threadgill's. The first night Lipscomb was scheduled to play the bar in 1966, Threadgill reportedly told his regulars, "There's a black man coming here tonight, and we don't want any trouble." And there wasn't. "The place was absolutely packed," recalls Powell. He believes Lipscomb succeeded in breaking the color line at Threadgill's because he was a "consummate musician" and such a "nice, nonthreatening old gentleman." Nor did it hurt that Threadgill's idol, Jimmie Rodgers, had many years earlier asked Lipscomb to tour with him, an offer he'd declined.

Threadgill and his buddies were in awe of Lipscomb's musicianship, but the college kids idolized Lipscomb. "If I'd had my choice of grandfathers he would have been it," says Powell. Lipscomb would "indulge" his young fans, says Bob Brown, "allowing himself to be dragged off to parties after the show." "He'd tell us about how things were," says Powell, "and not just the music, either. Here we were these young kids who needed some guidance. He had insights about everything and he didn't hesitate to let us know."

It wasn't just in Austin that folkies were kneeling at the feet of masters like Lipscomb. Toni Brown, who played in a bluegrass band in Berkeley, remembers listening to Lipscomb, Elizabeth Cotten, and other old-timers at folk music parties there. But she stresses the nearly insuperable barriers separating the white kids from their idols. Lipscomb was a tenant farmer in Navasota, Texas; Elizabeth Cotten had been Pete Seeger's family's maid. The relations between privileged young white students and impoverished elderly black musicians were bound to be problematic. "Black players didn't come to parties to talk to white people but rather because this was their chance to move into a scene that had the potential for making them some bucks. So right away there wasn't just a race line, there was a class line, too."

The veneration of long-forgotten blues musicians from the back-woods South, and the blues revival that sparked it, certainly challenged the devaluation of black culture, even if it did not transform social relations. Phil Spiro, a Cambridge folkie who was instrumental in locating the Mississippi-born bluesman Son House, claims most white blues enthusiasts didn't seem to care that these elderly musicians "were *still* living on the wrong side of this poverty line." With few exceptions, "the rediscoverers didn't see the old guys as real, breathing, feeling, intelligent people," he contends. "In general, we were collectors of people, who we tended to treat as if they were the very rarest of records—only one copy known to exist."

Perhaps, paradoxically, the rift was less extreme in Austin. For one thing, the stakes were low: Austin was far off the beaten trail; no one's career was going to get revived or jump-started there. For another, as Powell points out, they were all—young and old, black and white—southerners. Powell feels confident that Lipscomb, for example, "understood that we loved music and that we were white boys who weren't racists. I think he respected that and liked our musicianship. He complimented me once on my harmonica playing and it was the most important compliment I ever got." Janis, though, was the one who received his highest praise. After seeing her perform in Austin, Lipscomb told her, "If I had yo voice, an I had my fangers, I'd be all right." Janis never forgot his words and reminded Lipscomb of them years later when she was performing at a birthday bash for Threadgill.

During the Austin period, Janis emerged as a formidable talent, and her voice was acclaimed unequivocally; her personality, however, elicited a more ambivalent response. "She could be so abrasive," Pepi says. "Janis pretty much took no shit off anyone," remembers Ramsey Wiggins. And David Martinez agrees that Janis could be harsh. "If she found someone boring she didn't hesitate to cut the person off." While Martinez admired her directness and intelligence, another Ghetto regular, Roger Baker, thought Janis was "a horse's ass. She could be real mean." Her put-downs, he says, were like "pre-emptive strikes." Explaining Janis's defensiveness, Pepi says, "She had a hard time accepting that anyone really loved her. And she always tended to think people had some ulterior motive. She'd say, 'Are you trying to put me down?'" Some of the guys in the Ghetto crowd would poke fun at Janis. Pepi remembers Lanny Wiggins taunting her. "'Yeah, yeah,'" he'd say, "'you can sing, but so what? You're a weirdo.'" And Janis would get into "huge fights" with John Clay. "If some of the guys were mean to her," Pepi insists, it was because "she was so defensive and nasty to them. She'd come into a room and make a cutting comment."

Janis was by no means the only one in the group to insult people. The Ghetto was the home of the clever put-down, often a last refuge for smart misfits. "There was constant quipping in that crowd," says Pepi. "Janis did it all the time and everybody had their own way of dealing with her, having a comeback ready or saying something to her before she got a chance to say something to them. It was like repartee, but sometimes it wasn't so funny." Wali Stopher says, "Coming from Port Arthur and Beaumont, that was our style. We all were defensive because we felt the whole Golden Triangle hated us."

The others may have rivaled Janis at the quick retort, but no one behaved as outrageously as she did. Even at the Ghetto, where there was a premium put on outrageousness, Janis's drunken performances were legendary, as was her language. "I sometimes think she may have been personally responsible for the explosion in the use of the word *fuck*," says Ramsey Wiggins. "Janis got us all peppering our conversation with 'Far fucking out!' 'In fucking credible!' and 'Big fucking deal!' I suspect she was no less successful in spreading the habit in San Francisco."

Janis's flamboyance extended well beyond the Ghetto. Travis Rivers recalls the time he accompanied Janis to a party thrown by UT's "Young Turk professors"—John Silber, Bill Arrowsmith, and Roger Shattuck. "For some reason Janis had been invited, maybe because of the hoots. She and I liked to dance, and she knew a kind of close-contact rock 'n' roll dancing and so did I." Appalled by their dirty dancing, one of the professors' wives asked them to leave. On another occasion, Janis and some of her Austin friends drove all the way to one of her old haunts in Vinton, Louisiana. At some point in the evening a local asked Janis to dance and she refused— no great breach of etiquette. But then Janis and Pepi began dancing together and acting provocatively, which Pepi says "pissed them all off." A huge brawl ensued that left one of the guys in their crowd with a smashed jaw. "Man, we were lucky to get out with our lives," recalls Travis. They were lucky not to end up dead another time too, this one on a Texas highway, when Ramsey Wiggins had the good sense not to be intimidated by Janis's bullying backseat driving. Stuck behind a slow car as they went up a blind hill, Janis yelled at Ramsey, "C'mon, chickenshit! Pass him! Pass him." Twenty-five yards from the crest of the hill a semitrailer "came barreling over the top" in the opposing lane. "That's when I first realized," says Wiggins, "that Janis could get you into trouble."

Stephanie Chernikowski argues that what gets lost in all the tales of Janis's outrageous behavior is her sweet, feminine side. "I remember her asking to borrow my compact to powder her nose," Stephanie says. Pepi, too, thinks Janis was a "real cream puff inside." "Janis had an external persona," Fredda Slote says. "And it wasn't a lie. She was that person partly. But only partly." One night the folkies were all out at Threadgill's when they discovered it was Janis's birthday. Fredda and a friend drove to a grocery store to buy a cake. "And there were very few choices about what we could put on this cake because it was late at night and it was a premade birthday cake. So we bought a plastic pink elephant to put on it because she always ordered this mixed drink called a pink elephant. We came back to the bar and had a big ceremony, and she said, 'Aww, man, a pink elephant.' She was just thrilled." Unfortunately, Janis's don't-mess-with-me armor left most people feeling exasperated rather than support-ive or affirming. "Janis was her own worst enemy," observes her Lamar friend Frances Vincent. "She fucked things up for herself right and left."

Janis's sexuality was yet another way she thumbed her nose at conven-tion. "Janis was always putting the make on people," claims Pepi. "She'd announce, 'I'm going to put the make on so-and-so.' Whether or not it panned out, who knows." UT wasn't high school, and Janis's "sexual flu-ency," as one friend puts it, certainly won her a lot of points. Even her more hesitant sexual interest in women seems to have raised few eye-brows among the Ghetto crowd, who incorrectly saw this less confident aspect of her desire as further confirmation of her outrageousness. Maybe her friends did find what they now call her "bisexuality" cool then, or maybe this is revisionism fueled by the fear that disclosures of past homo-phobia might be taken for current prejudice. In any case, everyone agrees Janis's sexuality was expansive, big enough to include both men and women. Janis's main girlfriend in this period was Julie Paul. Fredda remembers Julie as very butch. "She took care of Janis and treated her like a boy would treat her." But then, Janis tended to get involved with what Fredda calls "male-action girlfriends." Pepi remembers Janis telling her, "I didn't put the make on Julie, she did on me. I'm not gay, but I'm not averse." Although Janis did not hide their relationship, she didn't advertise it either. When asked if people knew about Janis's relationship with Julie, Stephanie's answer is "yes and no."

"Julie was a butch dyke *and* one of the sweetest people I ever met," says Powell. "It wasn't uncommon in those days to find lesbians who weren't sophisticated enough to know what they were. But Julie knew." There was plenty of drama in her relationship with Janis. Powell recalls them fighting all the time and then being "lovey-dovey." Julie was extremely possessive and jealous, especially when she'd been drinking, which was constantly. One night when Julie got wasted, she started chas-ing Janis around the Ghetto, accusing her of being unfaithful. "The absur-dity of anyone's getting upset about Janis taking a new lover was generally agreed upon," Ramsey Wiggins says. "My brother, who was probably just as drunk as everyone else, settled the dispute by tossing Julie down the stairs. No mean accomplishment, considering that Lanny weighed about

130 pounds soaking wet and Julie was built like a fullback." Pepi remembers Julie screaming upstairs at Janis, " 'Come down here and fight like a man.' It was really pretty funny."

Janis was a trying lover for Julie because "she went through men like Kleenex." Her months in Austin were the first time Janis actually slept with lots of men. Other girls in her crowd were more attractive, but Ramsey claims that once Tommy Stopher gave her his stamp of approval the rest of the guys became interested. "Tommy's approval made Janis a lover in whom we took pride, despite her lack of conventional beauty." Not everyone, however, needed Stopher's imprimatur. Powell St. John went to bed with Janis early on. He remembers their two-week affair as "intense and unforgettable, really something." It ended when Janis went off with someone else. "I loved Janis," says Powell. "I always did and I always will." But there was no chance of their relationship's going anywhere, he contends. "She wasn't ready for any kind of commitment and neither was I."

In addition to Powell, Janis was also briefly involved with an editor of the *Ranger*, Bill Killeen, who supposedly "kept her in line," and with Travis Rivers. "Women had been a source of confusion for me," says Travis, "but when Janis spoke I could clearly hear her. I wasn't looking around every corner for meaning. I was amazed." Travis felt that being with Janis was "like talking with myself." He, too, had survived a hellish adolescence, and he shared Janis's fondness for booze, drinking almost a quart a day. Nor was he put off by her unkempt style. "I didn't wash my clothes either. It was a style. We were angry. 'Accept us as we are. It's not about what we look like.' " There was one problem: Travis was already married. Janis was only the second woman he'd ever made love to, and after they'd finished, Travis was overcome with guilt. When he told Janis it had to be a one-night stand, she was furious, "flailing about" hitting him. Rejected and humiliated, she refused to talk to him for several months.

Her easy affair with Ramsey was more typical. "Janis liked to fuck," Ramsey says. "She enjoyed it, wouldn't do it if she didn't feel like it, would—and did on at least one occasion—get up and leave if she'd had enough before her partner did, and wasn't insulted by an invitation couched in the most basic terms: 'Hey, Janis, wanna ball?' That alone, her refusal of guilt and shame about fucking, was enough to endear her to me forever." Janis's sexual openness and availability might well have been rooted in a welcome absence of shame, but they were also a way of ensuring that men would pay attention to her. After she was famous, Janis told a reporter that her " 'Hi ya, boys' style" was something she'd affected so as to get laid. "Janis *was* easy with guys," says Peggy Caserta, a woman with whom Janis was later involved. "Because she felt so mistreated and thought she wasn't pretty, she always felt lucky if someone would fuck her."

Janis may have appeared a model of sexual openness to many of the guys, but she would sometimes fake orgasm or put up with bad sex to appear sexually liberated and perhaps to spare the egos of her male partners. Fredda Slote tells this story: "One of the guys said to me once, 'Well, it's great being with her because she comes in thirty seconds so you don't ever feel like you've let her down.' But when I talked with Janis about him, she said, 'Aw, man, you want to stay away from him. He's a thirty-second wonder.' " Another time, Janis warned Fredda off someone else whose uninspired and mechanical sexual performance she hadn't walked away from. "Janis said, 'It's a *slow* process with him. He goes on for hours and hours and hours.' And this was the same guy who came into the cafeteria and was saying, 'Man, do you ever tap out eight-eleven time?' And Powell said, 'No, why would I try to tap out eight-eleven time?' And he says, 'Well, you gotta do something to keep yourself occupied while you're fucking.' "

Ramsey Wiggins was aware of Janis's romantic side, but he insists, "If I'd told Janis that I loved her, that I wanted to get married and settle down with her, she would've been upset, possibly even felt betrayed. We were both committed to life outside the mainstream." Apparently not that committed, because Ramsey got married not long thereafter. If Janis did want a loving relationship, she seems to have kept it to herself, preferring to come off as if she were just looking for a fuck. Most probably that was her way of deflecting the sexual rejection she imagined was always waiting right around the corner. Travis Rivers feels sure she wanted a long-term relationship, but most men took her at face value, assuming her ballsiness signaled her lack of interest in anything more romantic and enduring. She was, they figured, like them.

Janis may have tried modeling her sexuality on men's, but emulating men didn't quite work for her. After all, the double standard was alive and well despite Janis's best efforts to dismantle it. While the guys' promiscuity didn't rule them out as potential mates, Janis's sexual availability dampened men's interest in having anything more than sex with her. Ramsey says, "There were two kinds of relationships with Janis: sexual, which was earthy, unsweetened, predatory, and volatile, and friendship, which was more durable." Like most men in their crowd, he chose friendship. "For us at least, sex was fooling around." And so it was with most of the men she slept with at UT. In the eight or nine months she was in Austin, Janis developed no sustained relationship with a man. "Janis was constantly searching for love," says Fredda. "She'd get involved with a three-eyed dog for affection, it did not matter. I have no idea about Janis's mother, but it made you wonder."

If Janis's relations with others in her crowd were sometimes tense, the situation was, predictably, much worse with the frat boys and bubbleheads. They hated Janis for her notoriety and her refusal to slink away from their taunts. She'd walk down the street, says Powell, and guys would "drive by and hoot and yell things at her. It just blew all over her." But Janis would sling it right back, which didn't go over well with the frat boys, who swore she'd pay for her uppityness. And in October 1962, they succeeded in getting back at her. In one frat-sponsored contest, female "beauties" competed for the title of Miss Campus Chest and male "beasts" for the title of Ugly Man. Male candidates, representing the different fraternities, tried to win votes by dressing up in gross costumes and parading around campus. The candidates' names were posted on a big board in the middle of campus, and the campaigning lasted for several days, lavishly reported by the *Daily Texan*. When the names of the nominees for Ugly Man went up on the board, Janis discovered that hers was among them.

Some claim Janis's nomination was a *Ranger* prank. Jack Smith insists Janis put her own name forward as a joke. Most of her friends, however, think her nomination was retaliatory, payback for the time Janis came on to a frat rat and then walked out on him. Whatever the joke's genesis, Jack Jackson doubts Janis was affected by it: "She probably wouldn't have been terribly concerned about what frat boys thought of her." Others, though, maintain she felt humiliated. "Of course she was upset," says Pepi. "She joked about it, but I knew better." Powell recalls seeing her in tears afterward. "That was enough for her. I couldn't really feel her pain, because it was so absurd to me. I just thumbed my nose at those people, but she couldn't ever really do that, even though she held them in contempt. They didn't like her and it hurt." Fredda says, "I started laughing about it and she looked as if I was hurting her feelings. I said, 'Janis, look, you're a pretty woman, but you would be a really ugly man.' But it didn't help. Janis's feelings were always close to the surface. It was very easy to hurt her." Janis didn't win the contest, but so many of her friends think she did that it seems likely she was the source of the misinformation. Later, Janis never mentioned the Ugly Man incident to the press. Instead she said she'd been laughed out of the state.

About three months after the contest, Janis's classmate Robert Morrison ran into her on the main drag during "dead week," the week before finals. "Hey, man, I'm going to San Francisco tomorrow," Janis called out to him. "You wanna come?" Morrison couldn't believe his ears. When he asked her about finals, she said, "Oh man, forget finals. Blow 'em off." They'd get Fs, he protested, but Janis acted like it was no big deal: "Oh man, none of that matters. I'm going to go out there and make it big." Morrison remembers "looking at her like, 'You poor deluded thing, you don't know what you're talking about.' " When he said there was no way he could go along, Janis patted him on the cheek and gave him a sweet look that seemed to say, Oh, you poor sucker. In fact, Janis wasn't quite as casual about school as she let on, because she earned Ws, not Fs, indicating that she had arranged to withdraw officially.

Powell believes that the Ugly Man incident was "the final nail in the coffin" for Janis, that "it strengthened her resolve to get out of Texas." Wali Stopher thinks Janis just felt she couldn't live in Texas anymore: "Of course she was singled out, because she was pushing so hard." Altogether, Texas began to feel less livable. Around the time of the Ugly Man contest, Tary Owens was beaten up badly by some high school kids as he was hitchhiking around Beaumont. Also, the Austin police had begun making its presence felt around the Ghetto. There were barely two hundred rebels on a campus of twenty thousand, but to UT administrators and the local police the number was still menacing, especially as the signs of rebellion grew. In the early sixties, the Austin authorities were under the impression that they could stop the cultural shift under way, that, in Powell's words, "they could round up all the people and stop it." The police made no effort to hide their activities. "Gilbert Shelton told me stories," says Powell, "about seeing a car parked down the street with a guy wearing headphones, pointing something at the house. So they'd get a book and go 'wham' with it, and watch through binoculars as he'd scream."

Apart from the town's repressive culture, Austin's biggest drawback for Janis was that she could never make it there as a folksinger. Indeed, Janis didn't leave until January 1963, some three months after the Ugly Man contest, when Chet Helms, the sometime member of her group, showed up and persuaded her to hitchhike with him to San Francisco, where, he claimed, her gutsy singing would be a huge hit. Tary Owens is convinced Janis left because she saw the opportunity to sing. "By that time, the Waller Creek Boys had done a couple of semiprofessional gigs and she'd decided to be a singer. She tried to get Powell and Lanny to move out to San Francisco with her." Janis had discovered the exhilaration of stopping an audience dead in its tracks; she had felt the thrill of capturing center stage. For all the distractions that she sought, it was performing, above all, that could banish the pain and elicit Janis's extraordinary giggle. For Jack Smith, those moments are unforgettable. "At the end of that giggle was the world's biggest grin. Her eyes would open wide, and she'd just spread out her arms and say, 'God, Jack, isn't it wonderful?'"

Now Janis had her eye on making it. She was shrewd enough to tell the campus newspaper that although her first love was the blues her ambition was to become a folksinger. That's where the money was in 1962. But in Austin, singing was something to do at Threadgill's, the folksings, or a Saturday-night party; it was not a "career move." In Cambridge and New York, a person could begin to think about making a living playing folk music; Austin, though, was rarely a stop on the "cross-country party" of traveling folk musicians. Janis knew what she was up against. She wasn't pretty, sexy, and diminutive like Maria Muldaur of the Jim Kweskin Jug Band. In fact, when Muldaur and the band came to town, Janis stayed in the background at a postconcert party, believing she'd lose in any kind of competition. "Janis had a tremendous desire to make it," as Pepi says. "She just wanted to *be* somebody because she was always viewed with such disdain."

Making it was one way to get back at all those people who had sneered at her for so long. In the age of the angry young man, Janis was an angry young woman. There was an assaultive quality to her. In her Austin months, Janis was pushing hard, perfecting what she would later call "living on the outer limits of probability." There were the barroom brawls, the close calls on the road, the endless boozing, and the experimentations with drugs and sex. It was high-risk living and it wasn't simply the result of some abstract commitment to adventuresomeness.

In a culture of containment, Janis and her friends refused to be contained. While other young people marched and picketed, they drank, played music, and drove like maniacs. This was their dissent, their way of refusing the compromises of their parents and the quiescence of the mainstream. They pursued their disaffection with recklessness and in ways that were frequently self-destructive. But not suicidal: Janis's recklessness wasn't about giving up but about not giving in, not capitulating. Wali Stopher remembers a story about his brother Tommy and Janis hitchhiking in Houston. "They looked outrageous," and as they passed a bar the customers started to harass them. Rather than ignore their taunts, Janis snarled back, "Fuck you. I ain't scared of you." And they left her alone. Janis would say, "A lot of people challenge you once to see if you've got the balls to look like that. And, you know, if you go, 'Oooh, I'm sorry' . . . you're shot down already." What's left out of these stories is the heavy price Janis paid—but it's there, as always, in her singing.

The night Janis packed up and left Austin she stopped by Julie Paul's place and left her a tape of a song she'd written for her. "So Sad to Be Alone" is a revelation because Janis sounds nothing like she does on any other recording. In a Joan Baez–like voice, Janis sings of looking "at other people through your tears" and feeling bereft, without friends or family. There's no big voice, no ballsy whiskey tenor or salty lyrics disguising her sadness and vulnerability. In contrast to everything else she ever recorded, Janis sounds little from beginning to end. The tape was her last gesture before she hit the road for what she hoped would be her big break. It's as if Janis knew what lay ahead, as if she'd glimpsed her future and the intractability of her pain and loneliness. It's fitting that Julie, who was Janis's twin in so many ways, was the one person with whom Janis let down her guard and discarded her tough-girl posing before leaving Texas and putting it on once again.

3

On the Edges of America

It was January 1963 when Janis and Chet set out to hitchhike to San Francisco, but the innocence and ignorance that defined the fifties still held sway. The "sixties," with their seismic transformations, hadn't yet arrived: political assassinations were still tragedies that only happened in other countries; white college kids hadn't yet begun chanting "Hey, hey, LBJ, how many kids have you killed today?" and blacks hadn't started torching the inner-city neighborhoods meant to contain them. The Beatles' American invasion was still a year away; Bob Dylan had not yet gone electric, and taking a trip still meant going somewhere by train, airplane, bus, or car.

In retrospect, though, it is clear that the first stirrings of the sixties occurred in the midfifties, when Rosa Parks defied segregation in Montgomery, Alabama, and Elvis Presley, Chuck Berry, and Little Richard struck a blow against the Jim Crow music industry by proving there was a market for something other than punchless white pop. By the midfifties, America was stumbling into Vietnam and Allen Ginsberg was writing "Howl," a poem whose nightmarish vision of America would be confirmed by the country's coming war. Desperate and defiant, "Howl" went beyond the beatnik celebration of the road to rage at the materialism, bureaucratic rationality, and joylessness of American culture, which is why the poem was so reviled. Thirty years later, Norman Podhoretz, the neoconservative editor, was still fulminating against "its glorification of madness, drugs, and homosexuality, and its general contempt and hatred for anything healthy, normal, or decent." According to Podhoretz, the poem "simultaneously foreshadowed and helped to propagate the values of the youth culture of the 1960s." He was right. "Howl" not only prefigured the sea change that was the sixties, it also created a sense of possibility for those who felt out of step or at odds with American culture. The poet Michael McClure recalls that after witnessing Ginsberg's impassioned reading of it in October 1955, "none of us wanted to go back to the gray, chill, militaristic silence, to the intellectual void—to the land without poetry—to the spiritual drabness." For New York Beat poet Diane Di Prima, "Howl" meant that at last all those who had "hidden and skulked" could "say their piece."

But it wasn't that easy. The spirit of the fifties hardly died the night Ginsberg read "Howl" at San Francisco's 6 Gallery or the day Parks refused to relinquish her seat to a white bus rider. The Beats, now remembered as cool cats in khaki, were pilloried in the press and targeted by the police. In 1958, Lawrence Ferlinghetti, the owner of City Lights Bookstore and the publisher of "Howl," was busted on obscenity charges. When approached shortly thereafter about publishing William Burroughs's *Naked Lunch*, Ferlinghetti declined, citing the censorial climate. The same year, San Francisco cops made their presence felt at the art openings, poetry readings, and jazz clubs beatniks frequented. The newspaper columnist Herb Caen helped spark the crackdown, complaining that North Beach, the Italian neighborhood that had become home to the Beats, reeked more of marijuana than of garlic. Responding to the hysteria about drug use in North Beach, the police decided to make an example of Jack Kerouac's road buddy, Neal Cassady, arresting him for the possession and sale of several joints. The judge, determined to stamp out the beatnik blight, sentenced Cassady to the draconian term of five years to life. Speaking at the 1960 Republican National Convention, America's highest law enforcement official, J. Edgar Hoover, chief of the FBI, declared "communists, beatniks and eggheads" the most dangerous groups in America. The point is that the fifties didn't give up without a fight in Austin, or even San Francisco. Of course, once the decade started to unravel it did so with dizzying speed, revealing, as Ginsberg noted, that America, which had seemed "as solid as the Empire State Building," wasn't "solid at all."

In 1963, North Beach was still home to City Lights Bookstore and the Coffee Gallery, but there were many more tourist bars and topless clubs than beatnik hangouts. Nor were Jack Kerouac, Allen Ginsberg, or William Burroughs just sitting around in the cafés and bars. The world of Beat writers and artists wasn't easy to penetrate. Carl Solomon, the writer to whom Ginsberg dedicated "Howl," was shocked when a friend spoke of the Beats as a movement. Like most other Beats (Ginsberg being the major exception), Solomon had an "aversion to movements." In *Memoirs of a Beatnik*, Diane Di Prima recalls thinking there were no more than forty or fifty people in New York "who knew what we knew: who raced about in Levi's and work shirts, made art, smoked dope, dug the new jazz, and spoke a bastardization of the black argot. We surmised there might be another fifty living in San Francisco. . . . But our isolation was total and inpenetrable, and we did not try to communicate with even the small handful of our confreres. Our chief concern was to keep our integrity . . . and to keep our cool." In truth, Di Prima and her friends published literary magazines like the *Floating Bear*, which would suggest they weren't completely isolated or insular. Opening their ranks to unfocused, troubled kids like Janis, however, probably wasn't what they had in mind.

In any case, for the kids who came looking to live the Beat life in 1963, North Beach fell far short of its reputation. Though Bob Kaufman, cofounder, with Ginsberg, of the journal *Beatitude*—who coined the term *beatnik* and memorably opined that "way-out people know the way out"— was once San Francisco's best-known Beat poet, he was in bad shape by then. A former speed freak who'd done time in prison and undergone shock therapy, he'd hang out in bars ranting and raving to anyone who would listen. Neal Cassady was around as well, having served two years in San Quentin; prison, the road, and speed had taken their toll on him too.

Linda Gravenites, a college dropout who had moved to North Beach in 1959, found it "a very depressing scene" even then. Most of the Beats had moved out of North Beach, and "all that was left were speed freaks." George Hunter, widely credited with starting the San Francisco rock scene in the midsixties, moved to the city "to be part of the Beat Generation," only to discover that the Beats had all gone.

Instead, North Beach was filling up with the scruffy children of the Beats, junior hipsters like Janis, Chet Helms, Hunter, and three women with whom Janis became close—Linda Gottfried, Linda Gravenites, and Sunshine. All three had been raised in or near L.A. and, like the protagonist of Kerouac's *The Dharma Bums*, felt that the "only thing to do was to get out of L.A." The adopted daughter of wealthy Republicans, Linda Gravenites had grown up in nearby Banning. She'd attended Richard Nixon's alma mater, Whittier College, where she'd staged her "own little civil rights movement" by dating a black guy and signing up to room with a black girlfriend. She was eventually kicked out for turning up at her dorm drunk one night. Forced to live at home and attend San Bernardino Valley College, she ran off to San Francisco with nothing but the proverbial clothes on her back and moved into a North Beach house full of Art Institute students for whom she modeled.

Sunshine, who is half Menominee Indian, grew up as Pat Nichols in Pasadena. As a child, she spent several summers with relatives on a Wisconsin reservation and remembers going into town and seeing signs that read "No Indians Allowed." The discrimination and prejudice she witnessed there influenced her decision "to stay out of the mainstream," as she puts it. At thirteen, she became pregnant and was relentlessly hassled by classmates until she left school to have the baby, who was given up for adoption. An A student despite her sporadic attendance, she made the beatnik turn and during her last two years of high school wore nothing but "black tights, a black leotard, a brown suede skirt, and sandals." Sunshine dated black guys and her best friend was black. Her crowd also included a drag queen and several artists, who all haunted hip Hollywood coffeehouses like Mother Neptune's, the Fifth Estate, and the Third Eye. She'd been to San Francisco a few times and felt something different was happening there. Arriving in North Beach in 1964, she waitressed first at Thelma's Soul Food and then at the Coffee Gallery, where she became its first female bartender in 1972 after California's passage of the ERA allowed women to work behind the bar.

Linda Gottfried was Janis's best friend in those early years in San Francisco. Linda's family, Jewish refugees from Eastern Europe, had come to the U.S. and settled in a Levittown-like community in L.A. On the surface, her household "seemed like the 1950s," according to Linda, "but behind closed doors it was the Second World War. There were a lot of us in a tiny little house and it was rare that somebody wasn't home, so I just tried to spend as little time there as I could." Like Janis and many of her friends, Linda felt very different from her family. Until she moved north to San Francisco in February 1963, Linda led an isolated and lonely life. "I was really such an alien. I never had any friends. Then I met this guy and after a couple of days he said, 'You know, there *are* other people like you in San Francisco. You should go to this bar, the Coffee Gallery.' So I got on the bus and I went."

It would take a few years before kids like Linda and Janis would make Haight-Ashbury the new bohemian mecca. In the meantime, North Beach provided an edgy destination for dropouts who made a point of confounding all kinds of socially enforced borders—between black and white, criminal and legitimate, and sometimes even gay and straight.

Janis and Chet's journey out West began badly. Their first night on the road they stopped in Fort Worth, where Chet's parents lived. When they left Austin, Janis had turned girly, clinging to Chet as if he were her boyfriend. But once they set foot in his parents' home, she metamorphosed back into a ballsy chick, stomping around the house and "swearing like a trooper." Janis's clothes—jeans, a half-open work shirt and no bra— didn't help matters. After dinner, there was a scene when Mrs. Helms squelched any ideas Chet and Janis had about spending the night there. She didn't care that they weren't lovers; that her son was friends with someone like Janis was distressing enough. Eventually Chet's brother drove them to the edge of town, where they hitched a ride with a trucker. Fifty hours and many rides later they arrived in San Francisco and crashed with David Freiberg, a fellow folkie who had played at UT a couple of years earlier as part of the Mendicant Folksingers for Peace.

Janis was clear about her purpose in North Beach: she had come to sing. Chet quickly hustled Janis a gig, persuading the owner of the hip hangout Coffee and Confusion to include Janis in her hootenanny. According to Chet, Janis was such a hit at the Grant Avenue coffeehouse that someone passed the hat—normally verboten there—and collected fifty dollars. From Coffee and Confusion Janis moved down the street to the Coffee Gallery. Janis was just one of many future rockers to play the Coffee Gallery as a folkie. Regulars included David Freiberg, who ended up with Quicksilver Messenger Service; Marty Balin, later of the Jefferson Airplane; David Crosby of the Byrds and then Crosby, Stills and Nash; Terry Garthwaite of Joy of Cooking; Nick Gravenites of the Electric Flag; and James Gurley of Big Brother. Chet also arranged some gigs at a couple of South Bay coffeehouses, where Janis met Jorma Kaukonen, who went on to play guitar with the Jefferson Airplane, and Jerry Garcia. Though Chet stopped helping with gigs shortly after the pair arrived in San Francisco, Janis quickly made her own way. She continued playing at North Beach coffeehouses and bars and performed several times with Roger Perkins, Larry Hanks, and Billy Roberts, the songwriter who penned "Hey Joe," later made famous by Jimi Hendrix. And that summer of 1963 she made her presence felt on the side stage at the Monterey Folk Festival.

Janis hadn't been in San Francisco more than a month when she met Linda Gottfried at the Coffee Gallery. It was Linda's first day in town and she had no place to stay until Janis offered to put her up. "So we met kind of magically," Linda says. Janis was living for free in the basement of a house on Sacramento Street. "These folksingers let her stay there for free because she was such a good singer," recalls Linda. "She'd come upstairs once a week and sing a few bars. That was all they needed." Janis and Linda "clicked right away." They'd both grown up feeling estranged from their families and their peers, and Linda says they even looked alike—a claim not substantiated by photos. "We recognized each other immediately. It was wonderful. We looked like twins. We loved each other. We'd both been very, very lonely. She came from the same kind of situation I did, not getting what you need to go into the world." Still, they didn't talk much about their pasts. "Our reality started when we got to North Beach," she insists.

Their reality was determinedly marginal. Janis and her friends lived on the very edges of mainstream America. After her death, Janis's father said she had lived "on the dole" during her years in North Beach, a disparaging term that reflected the shame he felt about his daughter's sponging off the state. Like many other young North Beach kids, Janis got by on unemployment checks, the occasional job, the few bucks she could pick up from singing, and the generosity of others. Of course, it was easier to be a slacker in those days: unemployment and homelessness were relatively rare; a resourceful person could avoid a regular job by eating free mission meals at the Church of Saints Peter and Paul in North Beach, making 4:00 A.M. runs to the produce district to salvage crates of damaged vegetables, and stopping by the Salami Factory for discarded ends. Merchants were more generous to bohemians when there were few of them. Diane Di Prima and her roommates used to keep fires going in their unheated New York tenement apartment by getting free wood from workers at nearby construction sites. "No one in those days had heard of beatniks or hippies, and so the guys who worked there were friendly and cheerful."

Shoplifting was another boho survival skill. Janis was busted in Berkeley for shoplifting during her second month in town. "We all stole steaks from Safeway when we didn't have any money," explains Chet Helms. "They fucked us over, so whatever we do is fair—that's the way we thought at the time." Janis had shoplifted in Austin, too, but mostly for the thrill of getting away with it; in San Francisco, stealing was a matter of necessity. She also panhandled at the corner of Grant and Greene. One acquaintance recalls Janis and a friend, a biracial girl named Shelley, singing for money with the Salvation Army band. When Janis was famous she joked that she even tried turning tricks but was too ugly to make it as a hooker. "We lived for the night," says Linda Gottfried. They weren't idle, however, she insists. Even when Janis was unemployed, "she *still* kept a schedule." She spent the days getting ready to go to North Beach at night to sing and studying music, especially the blues. "She had a routine," Linda remembers. "At twelve o'clock it was blues. And then she'd listen to the country radio station, which she loved. Basically, country was her roots. And then at three o'clock we'd watch *Dialing for Dollars*. That's for real." The afternoon TV show featured a movie and at its conclusion a viewer would be called and asked the amount of that day's jackpot. "She wouldn't go out of the house until *Dialing for Dollars* was over, so she

Janis, ca. 1957.
Sophomore year at TJ High
(Richard Hundgen)

TJ High's Slide Rule Club. Janis is in the front row on the far right; Tary Owens is in the back row, third from left. (Richard Hundgen)

The Waller Creek Boys, Austin, 1962. From left: Powell St. John, Lanny Wiggins, and Janis. "We'd hang out and get drunk," she said, "roll in the mud, drink beer, pick and sing, pick and sing." (*Cactus Yearbook*, Texas Student Publications)

Kenneth Threadgill, Austin's premier yodeler (Burton Wilson)

Dave Moriaty, Janis's high school friend, at the helm of the Rip Off Press, 1969. Virtually all of Austin's freak community relocated to San Francisco. (Bob Simmons)

Lamar Tech's Dave McQueen, 1971 (Steve Rahn)

Janis's University of Texas buddy Travis Rivers (Bob Simmons)

Linda Gottfried Waldron (Jae Whitaker)

Jae Whitaker, Janis's lover in 1963 (Jae Whitaker)

Janis's promotion
picture, 1963
(Jae Whitaker)

Janis at Austin's Eleventh Door, March 1966 (Bob Simmons)

"The Birth of a Scene"—
a handbill for the first Family
Dog dance at the
Longshoreman's Union,
October 16, 1965 (Drawing:
Alton Kelly)

Furthur, with Ken Kesey and the Merry Pranksters (Lisa Law)

Janis and Chet Helms outside the Pine Street apartment (Herb Greene)

could see if we'd won," according to Linda. "Then she would go across the street to the pool hall." More than anything, Janis was passionate about her music, says Linda. "She studied Leadbelly, Billie Holiday, Bessie Smith. On Sundays we'd go to various black churches and sit in the back and do gospel." The idea that Janis emerged from nowhere "is nuts," says Linda. "I mean, she *worked*."

During this period Janis also lived with Jae Whitaker, an African American woman and amateur musician who shared Janis's passion for music. She doesn't remember Janis keeping to a schedule, but she does recall her saying, "I'm gonna make it! I'm gonna make it!" She craved the spotlight, says Jae, who took Janis to a photographer's studio to have some publicity shots taken. The radio was always on in their apartment and they both sang along with it. When they'd go to the bars, they'd sing along with the jukebox, too. It was Janis who turned Jae on to Bob Dylan. "I remember we had a little grass and a little wine, and Janis said, 'I gotta tell you about somebody I just love. I gotta meet him one day.'" Janis put his record on the turntable and said, "Just listen to the words. He's just wonderful." Jae really liked his lyrics but "thought he was an old man. About sixty or seventy years old." Jae remembers Janis listening to everything from Hank Williams and Hank Snow to blues and pop songs. Bessie Smith was her idol, though. "She felt she was Bessie Smith reincarnated. She really did."

Within a few months, Janis's reputation began to spread, according to Toni Brown, who played in the Crabgrassers, a bluegrass band. She heard Janis singing "Black Mountain Blues" at Berkeley's Cabal and says, "She was incredibly strong. I'd heard about her because the word was out that there was this singer doing Bessie Smith. We all kind of knew we were listening to someone who was going to be very big." James Gurley, a future bandmate, remembers hearing Janis at the Coffee Gallery and thinking her voice was "incredible." Linda Gottfried says, "it got to the point that no other female singers wanted to sing when she showed up at hootenannies." Her voice was so powerful that whenever she sang she attracted a crowd. When she appeared at the 1963 Monterey Folk Festival she created something of a stir. Janis wasn't a featured performer, but she did sing at the informal hoots on the second stage. Jae contends that Janis won three hootenanny contests there and tickets to the shows on the major stage. "Everybody just loved her. She won every damn time she got up there and sang. They just went fucking wild. I started paying attention."

Others started paying attention, too. Every so often a talent scout from a record company would show up and express an interest in signing Janis, but nothing ever came of the offers. Of course, things didn't work out for most of the talented folksingers on the Bay Area coffeehouse circuit. San Francisco was a highly competitive market that at the time attracted little industry interest. But Janis had some special handicaps that undermined the promise of her first year in San Francisco. "She was hungry for some-body to back her up on guitar," says Edward Knoll, a beatnik friend, "but nobody wanted to play *behind* anybody." Though Janis began accompany-ing herself on the guitar, she was never a good guitarist. Most of Janis's problems, however, were self-inflicted. "I used to tell Janis, 'You're gonna make it in spite of yourself,'" says Linda Poole, another of Janis's North Beach friends. Poole set up a recording session for her with an L.A. pro-moter, but Janis didn't bother showing up. RCA Victor wanted to sign her, but she injured her leg trying to mount her Vespa motorbike when she was drunk, and the deal evaporated while she was recovering from the accident. Indeed, Janis's drinking was fast becoming a problem. Although Jae doesn't recall her putting away significantly more than anyone else, some say Janis drank heavily even then. One acquaintance says that when Janis first arrived in San Francisco she would hang out on street corners with friends boozing it up with the winos. She maintains that from the time Janis "hit the street with Chet, she juiced constantly." One night, she crashed the motorcycle that belonged to the man she was seeing at the time, a Detroit hipster named Malcolm Waldron. During a fight, she jumped on his motorcycle, roared off into the night, smashed his bike, and hurt her arm.

Another problem was Janis's "fuck off" attitude, which got her into trouble even in North Beach. When a powerful man in the local folk music scene came on to her she reportedly said, "Are you kidding, man? Get fucked by somebody else." As a result, she was banned from the Cof-fee Gallery. The bartender, an actor named Howard Hesseman, who was later on the TV series *WKRP*, would let Janis sing during his shift, but she had to beat it, even if she was midsong, whenever the man she had spurned walked through the door. Another night, right as she was poised to sign with another label, Janis walked out of the Anxious Asp, a North

Beach bar, and mouthed off to some bikers who were staring at her. According to Chet, "they beat the shit out of her." Janis was "pretty fucked up" by the beating, he says, and another opportunity was lost. Just about every time Janis was on the brink of getting ahead, she would sabotage herself. And then there were the drugs.

When Chet and Janis moved to San Francisco, they "walked right into a speed crowd," in Chet's words. Speed was the drug of choice in North Beach and other bohemian enclaves, and it was freely available. Long before Augustus Owsley Stanley III made his name turning out acid, he was running a methedrine lab. It's true that, at the time, speed was widely regarded as harmless, even by straight America. Diane Di Prima says she used speed for years. "My aunt used to bring home bottles of Dexedrine from the hospital where she worked. She thought it was so wonderful that we wanted to write more and study more. Nobody knew there was anything wrong with it. I remember one of my brothers had a bottle of a thousand and I said, 'Where'd you get it?' And he said, 'From Aunt Ella.' " Amphetamines were widely prescribed too, especially to women who were overweight or complained of feeling tired and depressed.

For the Beats, getting high was closely related to the artistic project. "The basic feeling was that all experience was good," says Di Prima. "Drugs could not help but broaden who you were as a human, but especially as an artist. Second of all, we were exploring the frontiers of consciousness, to be clichéd about it. And we were quite serious about that." Ginsberg wrote under the influence of laughing gas, marijuana, cocaine, heroin, speed, and psilocybin—and combinations of all these drugs. Burroughs was a junkie and Kerouac did vast quantities of speed, as did Carl Solomon, who wrote of "eating Benzedrine" in the late forties. Drugs and alcohol were considered essential to the creative process— part of living on the edge, which was what being an artist was about. "The amount of liquor consumed in the art world between 1950 and 1960 seemed like a flood," says the painter Helen Frankenthaler. Linda Gottfried recalls the days when she and Janis first started doing drugs as wonderful. "We thought we were growing by leaps and bounds. We worked night and day. We did more paintings, more poems, and more songs." Speed was the drug of the moment for artists and writers in the late fifties and early sixties, and Di Prima maintains "it made a particular kind of art, and a particular aesthetic, happen," the result of the perma- nently pumped-up, amped feeling. For Janis, too, getting high was part of living a creative life. After she was famous Janis would say, "A lot of artists have one way of art and another of life. They're the same for me."

Living down and out—which included getting juiced and doing speed—was not only generally part of the artistic life but, as Janis saw it, a necessary step to making herself into an authentic blues singer. To sing the blues you had to live the blues. "Somewhere deep inside she felt you had to experience everything you could to be a real singer," accord- ing to Sally Lee, a North Beach acquaintance whom Janis had first met back in 1961 on her hitchhike to San Francisco. "She felt she had to pay her dues to sing the blues. She felt in some sense that she had not suf- fered enough," says Chet Helms, who after her death blamed Albert Grossman—Janis's manager beginning in late 1967—for encouraging Janis to feel she had to be "down and out and junked out," for trying to mold her into a "white Billie Holiday."

But Janis felt obliged to be miserable well before Albert Grossman began to manage her; indeed, her meth and alcohol abuse long preceded Grossman's presence. "I really do feel Janis did a lot of things—even the drinking and the dope—to put herself on the lower rung," Jae Whitaker says. Janis wanted to make up for the fact that she hadn't grown up black or poor or even working class, according to Jae. "She wanted to feel this wretchedness and this pain so she could sing about it and write about it with feeling." Michael Pritchard, a guitarist who played music with Janis in this period, says, "I could play the blues technically but not emotionally or psychologically, because of everything the blues implies." That both- ered Janis, who would complain, "You're not playing the blues, man," but Pritchard would tell her, "One of the reasons I don't play the blues is that I don't want to get the blues." He had grown up in San Francisco with black people who'd abandoned the blues for that very reason—the suffer- ing involved.

Another obstacle to mainstream success during those years was Janis's assaultive singing style. Her voice expressed her marginality and authenticity, but the public wasn't ready for her rawness in 1964. Edward Knoll, who met Janis through her boyfriend, Malcolm Waldron, suggested to him that Janis start seeing a vocal coach. Knoll recalls Waldron saying, "No, no, she shouldn't do that. She ought to keep it raunchy." Ultimately, Janis would be vindicated, but in the midsixties, folkies still expected female singers to sound like Joan Baez or Judy Collins. Bay Area folk music mavens may have been impressed by Janis, but hers was not a style that yet had any mass appeal. On one of her trips through Texas, she stopped off in Houston with Frank Davis and Pepi Plowman and played the Jester, a local folk club. Not long into her act, Janis was kicked off the stage. Davis believes she engineered her own rejection. "I have a recording of her doing a song where she's yelling at the top of her lungs for ten minutes about dead black people. She was too damn strong for everybody."

Davis believes Janis was testing her audience in the same way that she tested her friends and lovers; she wanted to put the audience through "quite a trip," as Davis puts it. They'd have to take her as she was or not at all—onstage and offstage. Years later she told her manager, Julius Karpen, that she didn't just sing "pretty heavy," she lived that way, too. Guy Clark, a Texas singer-songwriter, thinks he heard Janis that night at the Jester. "She was playing the autoharp, singing John Jacob Niles ballads. 'Hangman, Hangman' was the one I remember particularly. I *liked* what she did. I thought it was far-out. I don't know if she was consciously doing it to make people hate her, but it was definitely unique." She sang in her Bessie Smith voice, and "she wasn't making any compromises. I thought she was wonderful." Back then, however, Clark was one of the few people willing to go on her trip.

Janis's approach to getting ahead was pretty haphazard. She drifted. After hanging around North Beach for almost a year, she headed off to New York for a brief visit, probably curious about the Greenwich Village scene. She stopped off in Port Arthur for Christmas and partied with her old buddies from Lamar and UT. Laura Joplin wonders how her sister felt coming back to Port Arthur, where her friends were leading settled, even married lives. Janis had always been different from the other girls, and her friendships were mostly with the men, but now her rootlessness and aimlessness set her apart from the guys as well.

By the summer of 1964, Janis had saved enough money from a keypunching job to purchase a secondhand yellow Morris Minor and she asked her friend Linda Poole to drive back East with her. Janis wanted to make it in

New York, according to Poole, but once she was there she slid deeper into drugs and alcohol. The two of them stayed with another friend, Ken Hill, a gay actor whom they had met in San Francisco. Andy Rice, a nurse's aide at Bellevue, hung out at Hill's Lower East Side apartment and says, "We basically partied twenty-four hours a day. We'd get a few hours of sleep here and there." Rice didn't drink much, but the others did. Hill was working as a bartender at the Old Reliable, where dropout kids were beginning to displace the Ukrainian, Polish, and Russian clientele. Janis and the others would stop by the O.R. before closing for a few rounds. Then they'd buy some booze, go back to Hill's apartment, and drink through the night. Hill lived right above another bar, which opened at 6:00 A.M., and the group would usually be its first customers. This was the schedule almost every day. Rice says she didn't much care for Janis. "She really intimidated me. She was a very strong woman, and I am too. But she was more sure of herself than I was. She came on like gangbusters." Janis *seemed* more confident, at any rate. To Rice she confided, though, that singing in public frightened her. "One of the strongest memories I have," says Rice, "is of her singing 'Walking the Dog' with the jukebox. This woman had it. I knew it then."

Before long Janis hooked up with Edward Knoll and his wife, Janice. The Knolls lived in a fourth-floor walk-up on Second Street between Avenues A and B. It was a typical Lower East Side tenement apartment, with the bathtub in the kitchen and huge cockroaches crawling everywhere. Janis hadn't known the Knolls, at least not Janice, for long when she stopped by their place with a stocky, short-haired butch lesbian named Adrianne. In her black motorcycle jacket, accessorized with a massive motorcycle chain draped around her chest, Adrianne was probably the more memorable of the two. As soon as Janis and Adrianne walked into the Knolls' apartment, they announced that they wanted to shoot speed. Shooting up wasn't like popping pills, which is apparently all Janis had done until this point. The Knolls did shoot speed, though not regularly and not a lot, and Janice Knoll felt no compunction about turning the two on. At the time, turning people on was like introducing them to an exciting new world, Janice says. If it was risky, well, that was part of its appeal. But the moment has haunted her ever since. "Man, I've lived with that guilt for over thirty years," she says.

Janis rarely performed while she was in New York, and no one can remember her having a job. Instead she hung out at the Old Reliable and supported herself by shooting pool, according to Mary Anne Kramer, a friend of the Knolls. "She'd go up to guys at the O.R. and say, 'Hey, don't any of you big strong guys want to play some pool with a little girl from Texas?' She'd sucker them because she was a really good player." Janis may have led her parents to believe she was making great strides in her career; Dorothy, in any event, sent her stage clothes—a black blouse embroidered in bright orange and covered with tiny mirrors and a luxurious white and red robe. Janis passed both items on to Janice Knoll, claiming they were "too flashy" for her. Only a few years later, Janis would laugh about how subdued those clothes seemed by comparison with her flamboyant current wardrobe. But in the early sixties, Janis and other folksingers were still in beatnik drag. On the Lower East Side, Janis never wore anything but black Levi's and a black V-neck sweater, with a very large gold watch on a gold chain hanging around her neck.

After four months in New York, Janis headed back to San Francisco, stopping off again in Port Arthur—unannounced, of course. Laura, fifteen years old at the time, recalls coming out of band practice to find Janis waving and yelling at her from her tiny yellow car. Janis showed a fleeting interest in her little sister, asking how she was and then quickly launching into a description of her own life. She gave her sister a battered old guitar, though, which Laura says "wowed" her, even though its neck was "warped and the strings were so far from the frets I had to use a capo just to play." The visit seems to have been unremarkable in any other way.

By September 1964, Janis was back in San Francisco and living in a hovel on Geary Street, an "infamous gay rooming house of transvestites," according to Linda Gottfried. Before long, though, Janis was back sharing a place with Linda, this time a basement apartment on Baker Street. That fall, Janis had a visitor—her father. Seth had flown out to San Francisco ostensibly on business but in truth to check up on his wayward daughter. During her two years away from Texas, Janis had visited a few times and written home occasionally, although only a postcard or two survives. Her letters were largely works of fiction. As Janice Knoll points out, she could hardly write that she was "strung out on speed and eating at the Salvation Army." Nor could she say that her plans to be a big-time folksinger had so far come to nothing. Nevertheless, Janis did write her father at least one letter that revealed her despair.

Years later, Seth talked about Janis's despondency during this period. He recounted that Janis felt nothing was good. "Is this all there's gonna be?" she wrote. Seth was sufficiently worried to pay his daughter a visit. Janis's despair prompted Seth to let Janis in on his grim view of life as a big swindle, as something to be endured. "Yes," he told his daughter, "that's all and you've got to find out how to live with it." Linda Gottfried remembers Seth telling them "the story of the Saturday Night Swindle, about how you hear over and over that if you work real hard you'll go out Saturday night and have a really good time. And everybody lives for that good time, but it never really happens." Linda thought Janis's father was "a wonderful guy and a real intellectual. I remember him saying if we were going to be dropouts the one thing we had to do was read *Time* magazine every week." Although Seth was terrified by Janis's pedal-to-the-metal driving style, Linda feels he wasn't especially judgmental about the way they lived. "He just wanted to make sure Janis knew how to get around in the real world. He understood her." By contrast, her mother still wished that Janis would straighten up and become a schoolteacher.

There is no other record of Janis's unhappiness at that time, but one source of despair might well have been her failure to make it as a singer. Although she had been in North Beach almost two years, Janis was more often accompanying a jukebox than singing onstage. Her appearances at the Coffee Gallery and the 1963 Monterey Folk Festival hadn't led to more recognition. Of course, when given a break, Janis had shown a remarkable knack for blowing it. "I had a couple of opportunities," she recalled later. "I just wasn't that serious about *anything*." Except getting high; Janis started shooting speed regularly. Maybe she thought it would help make her a better, more authentic blues singer, or perhaps she just wanted something that produced the same exhilaration she felt when she sang.

Whatever the reason, by the end of 1964 Janis was a speed freak. Chet Helms was so strung out that a friend intervened to break his addiction. All over San Francisco and New York young kids were spun out from shooting speed, their jaws locked in a perpetual clench, their talk rapid-fire, and their nights unrelieved by sleep. Many turned to heroin to help them come down. "When people fell into smack or extreme use of meth where they couldn't control it anymore, then they weren't exploring anything," says Diane Di Prima. "That was seen as a lost place to be." And by the midsixties there were plenty of lost people roaming North Beach and Greenwich Village.

Linda Gottfried remembers the moment she and Janis realized they were addicted. It was the fall of 1964 and they were on their way to the de Young Museum. According to Linda, they "just looked at each other and said, 'Let's go home and do some meth.'" Describing those days to a reporter, Janis said, "I wanted to smoke dope, take dope, lick dope, suck dope, fuck dope, anything I could lay my hands on I wanted to do it. Hey, man, what is it? I'll try it. How do you do it? Do you suck it? No? You swallow it? I'll swallow it." Michael Pritchard, with whom Janis sometimes played music, maintains that drugs weren't just "palliatives for pain"; they also created a sense of community. This was true especially when needles were involved. For kids who felt on the margins, shooting up not only dulled the pain, elevated their outsider status, and allowed them to feel enormously productive but seemed also to forge bonds between them.

Before long Janis was dealing as well as using. Sunshine remembers hearing someone pounding at her door one day. When she called down to see who it was, a woman shouted up, "It's Janis Joplin and I want to sell you some speed." John Jennings, who later played in the San Francisco rock band Wildflower, bought speed from Janis when she lived on Baker Street. It was just the right place for a speed freak, a windowless basement apartment accessible only through an alley. "There were no windows, so you'd have to keep the lights on. There was no night or day there." Jennings's most vivid memory is of Linda and Janis shooting up "just about anything they could get, but mostly speed. Then they had these little knickknacks that they'd sit around and polish. Or they'd paint pictures on little file cards. It was pretty strange." Jennings visited several times when Janis was dealing. "She was really happy to go out and score because she'd get a good piece of it for herself and she was pretty poor."

Altogether, Janis was in such sorry shape she even shot up watermelon juice one day. "She felt she was cracking up," says Janice Knoll, who was now living in San Francisco. She remembers that Janis tried committing herself to San Francisco General, but the hospital staff turned her away;

they suspected she was feigning craziness to scam the system. In 1965, during a meth drought, Janis started using heroin. Janis really liked heroin, Linda Gottfried says, because she was looking for "something that killed the pain."

At this point, Janis's dream of making it suffered two setbacks. George Hunter, who had moved to San Francisco from Los Angeles, had started a folk rock band, the Mainliners, later changing its name to the Charlatans. Hunter's initial success owed less to his musical ability than to his good looks and vision—he was among the first to understand that beatnik kids were ready to be lured out of the coffeehouses and onto the dance floors. When Hunter was putting the band together in 1965, Janis expressed an interest in joining. "I had no idea she was really a musician," he says, "because the whole scene we were a part of was connected to dope." Janis told him to check her out at the Coffee Gallery, but Hunter never bothered. "I don't know. I just couldn't see integrating her into the Charlatans. The interesting thing is that she had a record with some tunes by Johnny Dodds, a clarinetist, that I wound up borrowing from her. I should have been more perceptive—if she had those kind of records lying around then she knew something about music. Even though I was interested in having a female in the group, I still couldn't integrate her. At that point we might have ended up killing each other."

Indeed, Janis just rubbed him the wrong way. Because she was so amped, her loud cackle had become even more irritating. When Hunter would come home and see Janis's Morris Minor parked in his driveway, he'd mutter, "Oh, shit, *that* broad's here." And Janis didn't look the part. She wasn't a beautiful, willowy blond. In the Charlatans—a designer band of handsome boys outfitted in twenties-style threads and western cowboy gear—appearances mattered as much as, perhaps more than, musical skill. "Her looks, her manner, and everything" were a problem, says Hunter. "I still feel really stupid for having been so oblivious," he admits. "Ah, it's just unbelievable."

Then Janis was snubbed at an audition. One night when Richard Oxtot, a Dixieland jazz player, was playing the Blind Lemon folk club in Berkeley, Janis stopped by. Oxtot recalls a "tough-looking gal roaring up on a motorcycle." Janis asked if she could sing a few blues numbers and "knocked everyone out," according to Oxtot. He arranged a recording session, in part because he knew Turk Murphy, a major bandleader in the Bay Area jazz scene, was looking for a lady singer. Oxtot went into the studio with a pickup band and remembers Janis's being "sensational." He played the tape for Murphy, who also thought she sounded impressive and who agreed to let her audition for him at a club where he was gigging. Oxtot's wife dressed Janis for the occasion and the three went off together to the club. They sat at a table, ordered drinks, and waited for Murphy to call Janis up on stage. After a couple of breaks Murphy still hadn't called her. Finally, Oxtot went backstage to see what was going on. "I can't let her up here," Murphy said. "She's a beatnik!" Oxtot claims Janis looked "pretty good" that night, but apparently Murphy wasn't fooled.

Janis's dream of becoming a singer wasn't working out and neither was her love life. As in Austin, Janis's sexual relationships included both men and women. Not every beatnik girl was as sexually daring as Janis, though Diane Di Prima recalls that in New York "we went to bed with whatever we went to bed with—male, female, whatever." Sunshine says the boho women she knew tended to be looking for "what felt good" rather than what was socially sanctioned. Such flexibility was possible in the fifties and early sixties, when the Beat and gay worlds often overlapped, partly because both groups were underground, only barely visible to straight America, but also because a number of Beat writers wrote openly homo-erotic work. To Allen Ginsberg's friend Carl Solomon it seemed that "you needed apostles of heterosexuality in those days."

Janis had sex with lots of guys, too. "You didn't know what you might catch," George Hunter says, explaining why he turned her down. Mostly, Janis's affairs with men were very short-lived. For an intense two-week period she was involved with Michael Pritchard, who lived behind the Magic Theater for Madmen Only, San Francisco's ur–head shop. Music was the initial basis for their connection. When their affair began they didn't separate for six days. It was, according to Pritchard, "twenty-four hours a day, real intense." But Janis was so involved with music, he says, "that sex was just a kind of background thing."

Janis's most sustained relationship during her first two years in San Francisco was with another woman, however. She met Jae Whitaker in the spring of 1963 at Gino and Carlo's, a North Beach gay bar around the corner from the Coffee Gallery. For most of 1963 and 1964 Janis ran with a lesbian crowd, which is why Chet Helms and she drifted apart. Jae had seen Janis and Linda Gottfried hanging out at the North Beach bars, and it was Linda who first caught her eye. But Mark Evans, a bisexual man they all knew, told Jae to go after Janis instead. After all, Linda was heterosexual while Janis would swing both ways. "Jae was so cute," remembers Linda. "She had a real short Afro and looked a little like an androgynous guy. She was really sweet, and she loved Janis." Their relationship wasn't one-sided, though, at least not at first. Jae suspects Janis liked her partly because she was considered a catch in the lesbian community and knew old blues and R & B, but also because she was black. In truth, race was a factor for Jae, too. "We were both rebels," she says. "I mean, I was attracted to white girls."

Almost as soon as Janis moved in with Jae—a mere two months into their relationship—things started to go downhill. Whenever Janis was faced with a tender, considerate lover, she'd respond by radiating ambivalence. She would leave, hitchhiking for days at a time, and Jae was never sure whether Janis's traveling companions were just friends, as she claimed, or lovers. Jae was no homebody herself in this period but says, "I was too settled for Janis, even then. For her to go off to New York or wherever and expect that she could come back and be with me—I couldn't handle it." And then there was Janis's "nobody-wants-to-fuck-me" rap, which was something she used to say all the time. "What the hell you think I'm doing?" Jae would snap. "She'd say it in front of other people," Jae recalls, "letting them know she was still available." Jae suspects Janis did it because she thought of herself as ugly. "I didn't think she was ugly. I thought she was very attractive. But I told her, 'You just do some fucking ugly things.'"

Janis tested Jae as well, constantly asking whether Jae really loved her. But Janis was so obviously ambivalent that Jae held her feelings in check. More than anything else, Janis created distance between her and Jae by going on about how much she wanted the proverbial white picket fence. All the talk about the white picket fence, settling down with a man, and having kids gave Jae pause. "I knew I was transitional," she says, "yet she did move in with me. She didn't have to. I guess in some way I gave her that white picket fence." In early 1964 they broke up and Janis moved out. Jae saw her only infrequently after that. "Once she started going with men and shooting up, I just kinda stayed out of her life unless she called." When Janis got in touch it was usually to ask for money, and on three or four occasions Jae gave her twenty dollars.

"Janis was a walking contradiction," Jae says, looking back on their relationship. Janis would say she wasn't gay, but "you could almost take anything Janis said, turn it backwards, and that would be the truth, too," Jae observes. "I think she wanted kids, but I also think she really felt very good with a woman, yet she punished herself for that feeling. She didn't think it was right." When Janis picked her boyfriends, though, she chose guys that Jae thought would have given almost any woman second thoughts about heterosexuality. "I'd ask her, 'How are you going to get this white picket fence and a child and everything when you pick up the most chickenshit assholes on the street?' She'd say, 'Well, I will when I'm ready.' "

Jae's assessment of Janis's boyfriends received spectacular vindication with Michel Raymond (a pseudonym), whom Janis began to see in the fall of 1964, about nine months after she and Jae broke up. There is general agreement that Michel was profoundly screwed-up and possibly sociopathic. Janice Knoll was in Hawaii when she heard Janis was involved with Michel. Why would she be so stupid? Janice thought. And what was *he* up to? Michel was an electronics wizard who claimed to have an M.A. from McGill University and to have worked for the French army during the Algerian conflict. "Of course, this could have all been a lie," says Edward Knoll. Michel had been lying for years; after high school, he had appropriated a classmate's glamorous life as his own. He claimed to have grown up in a sophisticated, bicontinental family and told tales of a high-society aunt who hobnobbed with the likes of Dorothy Kilgallen, a regular on the TV show *What's My Line?* In fact, Michel had grown up in a troubled family in Niagara Falls, New York, and, according to a former lover, never even went to college.

Janis's new boyfriend was a brilliant, seductive imposter hooked on the excitement of high-risk living. He told one girlfriend he worked for the FBI, and she suspects he did. A year earlier, Edward Knoll had gotten involved with him in a crazy scheme to sell a communications system to revolutionary groups in the Middle East and North Africa. (Apparently, Michel's fantasies were all-inclusive: aiding the French one minute and helping out their adversaries, Algerian revolutionaries, the next.) They had tickets to Europe but got stuck in New York, where Michel was strung out on some very powerful and pure speed he had acquired illegally from a pharmaceutical company. With Michel acting like a madman, their dream of setting up a rebel broadcasting company fell apart. But Knoll doubts Michel ever planned to follow through. "He lived on the dream itself."

There's little doubt that Janis loved Michel, however. Edward Knoll remembers her patting Michel on the butt, the kind of affectionate gesture Janis never made, and he says, "There was real love in her eyes." Like everyone else who knew them both, though, Knoll doubts Michel loved Janis. "I don't know whether Michel liked anybody. I don't think he really disliked anybody, either." Perhaps it was his indifference that made him such an effective con artist. Sunshine knows of two women Michel got pregnant while he was seeing Janis. Someone else claims he lived with one woman who became pregnant and moved in another girlfriend, relegating the first girlfriend to the living room. To make matters worse, he was already married—one part of his past he shared with very few people. Apparently he'd been forced to marry a pregnant girlfriend back on the East Coast; he bailed out after only a few months but for some reason hadn't divorced her. Or so he said. As Janis told another of his exgirlfriends, "I think he kind of just is whatever anyone wants him to be."

Michel was a cad, but a very attractive cad. One ex-girlfriend says she suspects both she and Janis were drawn to him because he was that rare find—a smart, handsome, charismatic man who wasn't afraid of bright women. "When he was with you, he was right with you," she says. "And you could be yourself 100 percent with him. I know that's how Janis felt. He was very open-minded and accepting of who you were." Another of his former girlfriends ventures that Janis, like her, "saw his pain. We knew that pain and we thought he was like us, but he wasn't." One thing they did share, though, was an addiction to speed. Chet Helms saw Janis that spring and says she was totally strung out. "Janis would change her mind two hundred times before she got to the door. She was emaciated . . . almost catatonic, just not responding. . . . That's like terminal speed."

Linda Poole, who was working at a Safeway, brought Janis food and begged her to eat it because she was literally wasting away. The last time John Jennings tried buying speed from Janis, she said she was packing it in. "Ah, I'm not doing that anymore. I'm leaving town," she told him. "Her face was blue," he remembers, "like there was no circulation." Jennings wasn't sure whether her corpselike look was due to the drugs or just the cold, dank basement apartment. Michel was in even worse shape. Sometime that spring he became so delusional he customized his Land Rover with rifles that stuck out the air vents and told friends he was receiving messages from the moon. Janis seriously considered committing him but chickened out. He ended up in San Francisco General anyway, hospitalized with "speed paranoia" for some twelve days.

After Michel was released, he and Janis made plans to go straight, swear off speed, and get married. They decided Janis would return to Port Arthur to prepare for their wedding while he would fly to Seattle. Janis couldn't have found a more unreliable man to marry, a man who was, as Edward Knoll puts it, "a figment of his own imagination." She probably did not know he was already married, but she certainly knew about the other women. Still, Sunshine says Janis felt marriage would solve all her problems, and by now she was desperate to get away from the boho world before she totally bottomed out. Michel was sure to win her parents over, too: he could so easily transform himself to suit his environment. Janis knew her mother would approve of his impeccable manners, his blue serge suit, and black oxford shoes.

As for Michel, it's anyone's guess why he promised to marry Janis. "He'd say that to anyone," says Edward Knoll. "He probably intended to do it," an ex-girlfriend maintains—he had promised to marry her, too, a year before. In fact, he had even been the one to broach the idea. Perhaps Michel liked getting himself into jams with women. It wasn't helping revolutionaries in North Africa or scamming drugs from pharmaceutical companies, but there was certainly intrigue and high drama involved in playing boyfriend, even fiancé, to several different women at once. Concocting stories, juggling women—he thrived on it.

In May 1965, Janis's friends threw her a bus-fare party so she could return home. They all knew she needed to get out of the scene, whether the marriage took place or not. Michel felt he could neither help her nor handle her, according to Chet Helms. "The only thing he could think of to do was marshal everybody's efforts to send her back to her parents in Port Arthur." They raised the fare, but Sunshine says Janis didn't board the bus for Texas as planned. Instead, she followed Michel to Seattle. Once there, he completely freaked out, according to Sunshine, and had to be hospitalized for an extended period. Janis tried breaking him out of the hospital but gave up when he started hallucinating that spacemen were attacking them. Janis returned to Port Arthur alone, weighing all of eighty-eight pounds, shredded from speed, heroin, and life on the fringes. She had fled her hometown because she longed to sing and wanted something more than bowling alleys and drive-ins, and yet here she was back again in the Great Nowhere.

4

The Beautiful People

After the ravages of San Francisco, Janis resolved to go straight. Back in Port Arthur, she combed her unruly hair into a tidy bun, re-enrolled at Lamar, swore off drugs, booze, and singing, and set out to be the daughter her mother wanted. There were, however, a couple of hitches in her plan. For one, Dorothy already had the ideal daughter in Laura, who seemed to have been born straight. Although it galled Janis that respectability came so easily to Laura, she decided to take lessons from her. As it turned out; Janis was deficient in the basics: when Laura took her sister clothes shopping, Janis's cluelessness became apparent even before she tried anything on. As she started to undress in the fitting room, Laura had to run over to Woolworth's to buy her sister some underpants. Laura was six years younger than Janis, but she felt as if she were supervising her older sister. More mystifying was Janis's insistence on picking only long-sleeved dresses, even though east Texas was unbearably hot and sticky. Janis didn't mention the needle tracks on her arms that she needed to cover up.

That summer Janis concealed herself in every way. Like the turtle she compared herself to in "Turtle Blues," a song she wrote during that time, Janis curled up in her shell. At first, she even hid her talent, refusing to sing, for fear she would get messed up again. The only way Janis could imagine surviving Port Arthur, it seems, was by disguising herself. In time this would prove to be the other big hitch in her plan. There just wasn't any way Janis Joplin could camouflage herself enough to fit in, not in Port Arthur.

Janis had come back to Texas because that course seemed preferable to dying a speed freak in San Francisco. "She told me she'd been shooting methedrine," says Frances Vincent, Janis's Lamar classmate, "and one day she got a look at herself in the mirror and had what you might call an epiphany. It really scared her, enough to make her want to leave and come home." It's unlikely, however, that Janis would have returned had she not believed there was a good chance Michel was going to marry her. Fitting into Port Arthur required being married, and virtually all Janis's friends were. Actually, it was hard to be a single adult anywhere in America and not feel somehow like a "poison in the social system." For Janis, getting married was a necessary part of her camouflage. Jack Smith, her friend from junior high, recalls her going on and on about her fiancé. "He was supposed to be the be-all and end-all of everything." With Karleen Bennett she seemed less enthusiastic. If Michel loved her, Janis said, then their marriage must be right. Karleen tried pointing out that Janis might want to consider whether *she* loved *him*, but to no avail.

Meanwhile Michel certainly wasn't behaving like her fiancé. After Janis had left for Texas, he traveled with friends to Mexico, where he met Debbie Boutellier, a former San Francisco State student working for an airline. They took a shine to each other and he proposed following her back to New York, where she lived. First, though, she had to stop over in New Orleans. "Michel said he'd come with me to New Orleans," Debbie says, "because he wanted to go to Texas to break up with his girlfriend. So we flew back to New Orleans." After they checked into a hotel, she stayed behind while he went on to Port Arthur. No one in the Joplin family had a clue Michel had come to town to end his relationship with Janis, because he acted like the perfect suitor. Laura describes him as "terribly proper" and claims he "seemed devoted to Janis." He even asked Seth for her hand in marriage. When Seth announced to the family Michel's intentions and his own eager consent, Laura recalls that Janis "jumped up and down, hugging [Michel] and clutching his steady arm as if it were a tether to reality."

Michel had promised Janis he would stay several days, but he left abruptly, blaming his early departure on a recent death in his family. Of course, the truth was he couldn't linger in Port Arthur and leave his new girlfriend stranded in New Orleans. Michel later explained to Debbie that he'd had no choice but to continue the masquerade. Even today, she's not sure where the truth lies. "Maybe he didn't go there to break up with her." After all, she maintains, "he did love her." To Janis's family, Michel's impersonation of the ideal son-in-law was almost flawless. He wrote the Joplins a thank-you note and even sent Dorothy a silver-plated coffee service. Only one false note spoiled the charade. Michel requested the Joplins hold off before announcing Janis's engagement in the Port Arthur paper and said his parents would do the same. He claimed to need some time to take care of a few details. By this point, Janis must have known that the one big detail standing in the way of their marriage was that he was already married. Linda Gottfried, who had since married Janis's former boyfriend Malcolm Waldron, had met Michel's pregnant wife shortly after Janis left San Francisco and wasted no time in writing her about it. But even this bombshell failed to deter Janis from behaving as if her engagement were the most wonderful and conventional event. Exhibiting what her college friend Powell St. John calls a "real streak of ordinariness," she began readying her trousseau. She started making a Texas Star quilt and her mother sewed a wedding dress. Janis drove to Houston and shopped at Pier 1 for china, linens, and cutlery with her friend Patti McQueen. And then Janis did what she'd never before done—she waited.

In her year back in the Golden Triangle, Janis did many things she had never done before. She entered therapy, seeing Bernard Giarratano, a psychiatric social worker at a family services agency funded by the United Way. Frances Vincent had referred Janis to her own therapist there, whom Janis hadn't liked. It was "serendipity," says Giarratano, that Janis was then assigned to him. Janis exhibited none of her old bravado when she showed up at his office. "She said she wanted to be straight—those were her words," says Giarratano. "But she didn't say it as if it were a demand. She knew she wasn't happy. She knew she didn't fit, and she was down about it." What he most remembers about their conversations was Janis's intense concern about meeting the challenge of her family's conventionality. "And the models she always referred to were 'Mother, Father, and Laura.'" He was struck by how much Janis idealized her father as an intellectual and her sister for her propriety. "In our sessions Laura was Miss Straight, and, oh, if she could only have whatever the virtues were that Laura had." Giarratano knew nothing about Janis when she first came to see him, so he was astonished when she began to unfold. One day she sang for him. "Everybody came out of their offices, because she could *really* sing."

Giarratano recalls that Janis opened up to him easily. "I tend to be afraid to make judgments about people," he says. "My sense is that she felt safe with that." Safe enough, evidently, to confess her longings. "She wanted to work at going straight, which meant getting off the drugs, getting a college education, and doing God knows what after that. She didn't know." Janis pinned all her hopes on becoming respectable, imagining this would bring her the acceptance she craved; for Janis, "being straight and being accepted were one and the same thing," says Giarratano. He tried to get her to see there were other ways to gain approval, but sometimes it seemed to him that Janis wanted nothing so much as to "be like Port Arthur," which he deemed an utterly self-defeating goal.

Eventually, Janis realized she couldn't turn herself into a carbon copy of her sister. She talked with Giarratano about how she could remain sincere and true to herself "without provoking a lot of negative attitudes." Avoiding rejection while maintaining her authenticity was also an issue for her at Lamar, where other students found her weird. "Janis was really a bright woman," notes Giarratano. "And she would go to the classes and at the start she would want to participate or even foment some discussion, but she could see she was not accepted. I don't know if that had to do with her ideas or her gender." Janis's rejection at Lamar was disheartening given the efforts she was making to be like everyone else, but she persevered with her studies during the winter of 1965, earning Bs as she pursued a major in sociology. Frances Vincent claims Janis did become friends with one of her professors. "She thought he was a hoot, and she really enjoyed the hell out of that class." But he was very much the exception.

Although she felt miserable much of the time, during the first few months in Port Arthur, Janis refused to do what she loved best—perform. When Jim Langdon in Austin tried coaxing her back into singing, she declined, fearing anything that might undermine her bid for conformity. She also avoided hanging out too much with old friends whose drinking might lead her back to the bottle. She was still such a nervous wreck from the speed—ultrasensitive to movements and noises around her—that a physician prescribed a tranquilizer. Gradually, though, she started seeing some of her old gang. One evening Grant Lyons and his wife paid Janis a visit. "She had her hair pulled back in a bun, and she had on makeup for the first time I recall, and she was playing canasta with these very, very dull people that I myself would not have spent a moment with." It was obvious to Lyons that Janis was trying to become something she wasn't. She seemed very subdued, and when she smoked she couldn't keep her hands from shaking. Dave Moriaty, her high school friend, came across Janis at a party and remembers her as "very thin but enthusiastic about going straight. . . . She gave me all this propaganda about going to college and becoming a secretary, going straight and never again trying to be a beatnik." Janis had always been the life of the party, but now she was the proverbial wet blanket, chastising friends for cursing or drinking too much. Jack Smith refers to these few months as her "life as a nun." That November, at her mother's request, Janis even painted a nativity mural for her parents' front porch. Grousing about her good-girl drag, Jack Smith says, "I mean she got so straight, people didn't like being around her! She was downright *dull*."

While Janis was boring her old friends in Port Arthur, the place where nothing ever happened, San Francisco suddenly turned into the place where everything was happening. This was a totally new city by the Bay. As recently as May 1965, when Janis was last there, North Beach had seemed washed up: acoustic folk music had run its course and the Beat scene was completely played out. But soon after she left town, San Francisco's bohemian world began to transmogrify in ways Janis could never have anticipated. When she returned a year later the talk was of hippies, not beatniks, and Haight-Ashbury had supplanted North Beach as the epicenter of hipness. There were holdovers from the beatnik years—a little Zen Buddhism, marijuana, even the term *hippie* itself had been used by veteran beatniks to put down young wanna-bes, the junior hipsters. But there was also the new and the shocking—rock 'n' roll, Day-Glo colors, and LSD.

By the end of 1965, the new bohemia was electric with possibility. Peggy Caserta, the owner of the Haight's first hip boutique, remembers the moment when the extent of the changes finally hit her. It was early 1966 and she was minding her store by the corner of Haight and Ashbury. Outside, a photographer, Herb Greene, had just finished shooting pictures of the scruffy, shaggy Grateful Dead when her next-door neighbor, the barber, sensing his shop's impending obsolescence, said, "Peggy, *what* is going on here?" Within a year, the barbershop was gone, replaced by another of Peggy's stores. By 1966, convention—even history itself— seemed to have "come off the leash," and the unraveling felt inevitable, inexorable, sort of like an acid trip.

News of Haight-Ashbury spread quickly as boho kids on both coasts exchanged tales about the wild new scene. Bob Seidemann decided to move there in late 1965 when he ran into a fellow New York hipster who said, "Would you believe that people are taking LSD and dancing to rock and roll music in San Francisco?" The idea was as irresistible as it was implausible and the Haight began filling up with people like Seidemann who were eager to walk away from the straight world. All over America parents were receiving what Tom Wolfe dubbed the "Beautiful People letter." Such a letter would typically open with an apology for having disappeared, then go on: "I won't bore you with the whole thing, how it happened, but I really tried, because I knew you wanted me to, but it just didn't work out with [school, college, my job, me and Danny] and so I have come here and it really is a beautiful scene. I don't want you to worry about me. I have met some BEAUTIFUL PEOPLE."

It wasn't hard finding them, especially the guys with their Jesus Christ hair and beards. Beautiful people dressed to underscore their freakiness, appropriating the clothes of other times and cultures—Davy Crockett buckskin, military surplus, Buddhist robes, Edwardian suits, Errol Flynn pirate shirts, Native American headbands, capes, cowboy and Beatle boots, hats—bowlers, stovepipes, cowboy, Eskimo, anything—and beads, of course. Being beautiful was more than copping a look, though; it was an attitude, a stance, a vibration. Weirdness mattered, and so did a mellow vibe. Both tribal ("Everybody get together") and individualistic ("Do your own thing"), the hippie scene was philosophically thin: a little Eastern mysticism and the conviction that all things "natural"—with the important exceptions of electric rock 'n' roll and synthetic drugs like LSD ("Better Living through Chemistry," as one poster put it)—were better.

Many factors converged to create the Haight and the hippie counterculture, not the least of them drugs and rock 'n' roll, but the shift couldn't have happened on the scale it did had white America not been at that moment extraordinarily affluent. While white sixties rebels were rejecting what the playwright Arthur Miller called "a system pouring its junk over everybody ... maroon[ing] each individual on his little island of commodities," their revolt was subsidized and underwritten by America's unprecedented prosperity. In the Haight virtually everything, including the space, was surplus. Haight-Ashbury was itself an almost forgotten part of the city, a working-class, interracial area bohemians began moving into when the commercialization of North Beach caused rents to skyrocket. And in this sleepy neighborhood beatnik types didn't have to worry about police harassment, which had become routine in North Beach. San Francisco State College had been located on lower Haight Street until the early 1950s, and a few scattered student or teacher households remained, giving the neighborhood a mildly boho air even before the migration from North Beach began. Because rents were cheap and the area was one quick trolley ride to the new SF State, Haight-Ashbury began filling up with students, graduates, dropouts, and even some faculty. Two huge floors of a once-beautiful old Victorian house went for $175 a month, or you could rent a room in such a house, often for as little as $15 a month. Nor were the ballrooms and theaters that were home to the new rock dances in great demand either.

Beautiful people lived on leftovers, the discarded waste of a "postscarcity society." In 1966, an anarchist group called the Diggers began serving free food in Golden Gate Park. The Diggers, named after a group of seventeenth-century English radicals, were street-theater "guerrillas" determined to prod society out of its lethargy and passivity. "Everything was designed to jog consciousness," recalls Peter Coyote, one of several San Francisco Mime Troupe actors who formed the Diggers. The food the Diggers handed out was sometimes donated by bakeries, produce markets, and meat markets; other times it was "liberated." Although the Diggers were often praised as "anonymous good guys" or a "hip Salvation Army," some people considered them con artists who used the lingo of liberation to rationalize scamming anyone with even marginally greater resources. The Diggers also ran a free store, filled with used clothes and surplus from local companies like Levi Strauss. The Free Store was so awash in white button-down oxford shirts—nine-to-five wear that drop-outs no longer needed—that a Digger woman found an ingenious way of reclaiming them: tie dye. Before long, the new fashion was everywhere. Rejected Levi's designs would sometimes make their way into the Digger community, too. At one time almost all the Digger women were wearing supertight silver pants made from metallic cloth—designer rejects from Levi Strauss.

San Francisco's two army-navy surplus stores were another source for hip clothes, which included sturdy and dirt-cheap navy bell-bottoms, pea jackets, and army jackets. Truly enterprising hipsters like George Hunter spent hours at thrift stores, the Salvation Army, and Goodwill rummaging through secondhand clothing for cool Victorian and Edwardian styles. They also outfitted their apartments in an "old-timey" look, using unwanted, outdated furniture and appliances. Bob Seidemann remembers, "Everybody's house had the old-timey stove and the old-timey refrigerator even though the fuckin' refrigerator was lousy—the lightbulb didn't work and it didn't get the beer cold." Even the overhead projectors that light-show artists used during rock concerts were World War II vintage, available at military surplus stores. Many kids lived, as Janis had, on welfare. Richard Hundgen, a future roadie for San Francisco bands, claims that groups of hippies began calling themselves "families" because of their dealings with the San Francisco Welfare Department. All of a sudden lots of unrelated people were living under the same roof, and welfare workers began designating them families, he says, so they'd be eligible for food stamps. On the whole, these middle-class white kids worried not about whether they'd find jobs but rather about how they could best avoid them.

The kids crowding the Haight were partly driven to drop out by the "junk" but also by a vast sense of spiritual and emotional emptiness. Like Janis and Sunshine and other kids before them, they hungered for connection and an experience of intensity. Peter Coyote came to the Haight after "twenty years of marshmallow, plastic, and hopscotch," determined to "lay life." "I want to taste it, beat it, feel it, kill it, fuck it," he said, "and I want to have all those things done to me." Jim Haynie, who worked with Coyote in the San Francisco Mime Troupe, joined up because he was "tired of the gray life." After Janis became famous, the journalist Nat Hentoff once asked if she was concerned her voice could withstand the abuse she put it through when she sang. For her the question assumed generational significance. She believed you could "destroy your now by worrying about tomorrow. We look back at our parents and see how they gave up and compromised and wound up with very little. So the kids want a lot of something now rather than a little of hardly anything spread over seventy years."

And by May 1965, a UC Berkeley dropout, Augustus Owsley Stanley III, or just Owsley, was providing an instant cure for the lack of emotional, intellectual, and artistic stimulus that so many felt growing up in postwar America—lysergic acid diethylamide. LSD was legal but not widely available until Owsley, whose grandfather had been a U.S. senator from Kentucky, began manufacturing it with help from his girlfriend, a former chemistry graduate student from Berkeley. When Owsley's acid began making its presence felt in the Haight, people were eager to get psychedelicized and experience that "orgasm behind the eyeballs." Acid was the antidote to the "adventure shortage." Unlike most other drugs, it wasn't about feeling good. LSD trips were sometimes a "bummer"—originally a Hell's Angels' expression for a bad motorcycle trip—but mostly spiritually cathartic, even transcendent. Nor was LSD addictive, because, as one aficionado puts it, getting hooked on it would be "like being addicted to having the shit beat out of you." Psychedelics (originally called psychodelics) opened up the mind to that flood of stimuli that the brain under normal functioning reduces to a manageable trickle, as Aldous Huxley, an earlier advocate, had explained.

Jerry Garcia claimed that psychedelics allowed him to enter a reality he had "always thought existed but had never been able to find." For the most part, acid revelations were strictly of the moment, not easily translatable. Bob Seidemann remembers some "derelict" guy telling him during an acid trip: "The floor is neutral and the ceiling is positive." According to Seidemann, "That was a major revelation. My mind was blown, though I could never begin to reconstruct what truth was revealed to me then." Moreover, psychedelics affected the music people listened to and played. Folkies began to pick up electric guitars to make noise, to combat the adventure shortage, and to match in some way the monumental stimulus—the high-voltage charge—provided by psychedelics. The first time Phil Lesh of the Grateful Dead plugged in, he played for seven hours straight. When the music is amplified, Lesh explained, "you can hear it all. That's what the electronics do—they amplify the overtones to a degree never thought possible in an acoustic instrument." Acid and electricity just seemed to go together.

San Francisco's 1965 transformation from the home of folk to the home of acid rock happened just as dramatically. Acid hit, Bob Dylan went electric at the Newport Folk Festival, and British rockers kept pushing the limits with songs like the Rolling Stones' "(I Can't Get No) Satisfaction," the number-one single of 1965. Until the British Invasion there was little room in commercial music for anything that wasn't squeaky clean. Even the Shirelles' "Will You Still Love Me Tomorrow?" with its hint of premarital sex, was too suggestive for some. When the Kingmen's 1963 song "Louie, Louie" became a huge hit, the FBI launched an investigation into the meaning behind its slurred and garbled lyrics. While the Beatles proved the commercial viability of irreverence, the Rolling Stones proved there was a market for something darker and nastier. Ironically, the British Invasion conquered America with America's very own music—early rock 'n' roll, hard-driving R & B, and the blues—black music that had been unwelcome on American Top 40 radio. Hits like the Beatles' "Twist and Shout" and the Rolling Stones' "It's All Over Now" had already been recorded by black musicians in the States, but most white Americans were unaware of that. In a strange twist, mod young Brits had grown up worshiping America. "The most exciting thing about being alive was looking at Americans," recalls one British memoirist. "America was where we all wanted to be"—not drab Britain, where rationing lingered on and the economic recovery from World War II was taking decades. "The first books I ever bought were about America," the British musician Eric

Clapton recalls. "The first records were American. I was just devoted to the American way of life without ever having been there." Just a few short years later, Americans were gazing longingly at Britain as the epitome of everything cool, especially London's hip Carnaby Street.

Like everyone else, Bob Dylan was mesmerized by the modish Brits. By 1966 he was claiming folk had just been a "substitute" for rock during the late fifties and early sixties, an interim period when rock had devolved into teenybopper dreck. The English had changed all that, he said, by revitalizing rock music. Dylan had loved the Animals' 1964 rock version of "The House of the Rising Sun," a folk song he'd sung on his first album. When he toured England in 1965, he had hung out with the Animals and the Beatles and had fooled around in the studio with Britain's premier blues band, John Mayall's Bluesbreakers. Other American folk musicians, including the Cambridge purists, also admired the Beatles. Dylan's side-kick, the painter and guitarist Bobby Neuwirth, was "taken" by them; as far as he was concerned, they had moved "European harmonies into an Everly Brothers sack, shaking them up with a rock 'n' roll, rockabilly beat and throwing them back across the Atlantic." Geoff and Maria Muldaur of the Jim Kweskin Jug Band raved about the Beatles, too. Even in notoriously snooty Greenwich Village, folkies were enthusiastic, recalls John Sebastian, who would form the Lovin' Spoonful. And in California, folk music veterans like David Crosby, Gene Clark, and Roger (Jim) McGuinn were "Beatle struck" after seeing *A Hard Day's Night*. Crosby remembers "coming out of that movie so jazzed that I was swinging around stop sign poles at arm's length. I knew right then what my life was going to be. I wanted to do that. I loved the attitude and the fun of it; there was sex, there was joy, there was everything I wanted out of life." The three musicians formed the Byrds with Chris Hillman and Michael Clarke and quickly had a smash hit in the spring of 1965 with their folk rock cover of Dylan's "Mr. Tambourine Man." Neuwirth recalls hearing the Byrds' electric version as he sat with Dylan and Albert Grossman, Dylan's manager. "It was great because no one could figure out how anyone except Peter, Paul and Mary could ever cover any of Bob's songs." According to Roger McGuinn, Dylan first heard their version in Los Angeles, not New York, where the Byrds showed him their arrangement. "Wow, man, you can dance to it," Dylan said, astounded.

Much is made of Dylan's plugging in at the Newport Folk Festival in

1965, but as Eric von Schmidt and Jim Rooney, Cambridge folkies, point out, Dylan had already made his intentions known earlier that year on his fifth album, the half-acoustic, half-electric *Bringing It All Back Home*. So mercurial his friend Richard Fariña once dubbed him the "plastic man," Dylan was reinventing himself in the first of many reincarnations. The album cover shows Dylan "in the lap of outrageous luxury. Albert Grossman's wife, Sally, desirable, elegant, aloof, in flame-red, reclines behind Bob. . . . Dylan's attire is early English mod: French cuffs, button collar, no tie. . . . It was an optical celebration of opulence and disdain. A visual open letter to the Old Folk Guard: Kiss off." Dylan summoned the Paul Butterfield Blues Band, an interracial Chicago blues group, to back him at Newport because it was the only American band that came close to sounding like England's Bluesbreakers. Dylan's electric set, like the Butterfield Band's earlier set, antagonized the acoustic ideologues. Dylan's performance was especially jarring coming on the heels of a set by a traditional folksinger, Cousin Emmie, who sang the hopelessly hokey "Turkey in the Straw." Underrehearsed and ragged-sounding, Dylan's electric ensemble sped through three songs at ear-splitting volume. The musicologist Alan Lomax and Pete Seeger, both festival board members, were furious with Dylan and the sound mixers who refused to turn down the volume. A distraught Seeger yelled, "If I had an axe, I'd cut the cable right now!" Peter Yarrow of Peter, Paul and Mary supported Dylan's right to go electric but says it felt like a "capitulation to the enemy—as if all of a sudden you saw Martin Luther King, Jr., doing a cigarette ad." However, Dylan wasn't making music to please the old or young fogeys of folk; he was looking to beat the English at their own game. Paul Rothchild, a producer who would work with the Doors and Janis, recalls listening to a rough mix of "Like a Rolling Stone" with Dylan and Neuwirth. They'd already played it about twenty-five times when Rothchild showed up, and they were "grinning like a couple of cats who'd swallowed canaries." Rothchild soon understood why. "What I realized while I was sitting there was that one of US—one of the so-called Village folksingers—was making music that would compete with all of THEM—the Beatles and the Stones and the Dave Clark Five—without sacrificing any of the integrity of folk music or the power of rock 'n' roll."

Dylan could count among his greatest supporters the poets Allen

Ginsberg and Michael McClure. According to Ralph Gleason, the music critic for the *San Francisco Chronicle*, Ginsberg, Lawrence Ferlinghetti, Ken Kesey, and two Hell's Angels sat in the front row at Dylan's Berkeley concert in December 1965. The following week at Dylan's San Francisco show, McClure reportedly sat in Dylan's dressing room grilling him about "how you write a hit song and become a millionaire." To those who argued that Dylan had sold out, Ginsberg replied, "Dylan has sold out to God. That is to say, his command was to spread his beauty as wide as possible. It was an artistic challenge to see if great art can be done on a jukebox. And he proved that it can." Ferlinghetti, by contrast, was bitter about Dylan's success. In his view, Dylan was just some kid with an electric guitar and artistic pretensions, whereas he himself was a "major poet." But with Ginsberg weighing in on his side, Dylan seemed to have pulled off the impossible—reconciling the artistic with the commercial. For San Francisco folkies the ramifications were felt immediately. "When Dylan went electric," recalls Bill Belmont, then a San Francisco State student, "everybody went out and bought an electric guitar. Literally! That was the end of the beatnik movement and the beginning of electric rock 'n' roll as we know it." Terry Garthwaite of Joy of Cooking recalls returning to Berkeley in mid-1966 after a year abroad to find that Berkeley's acoustic folk club, the Jabberwalk, was now presenting Country Joe and the Fish, an electric jug band.

American prosperity, acid, the British Invasion, and Dylan's plugging in were the catalysts that sparked the hippie revolution, and San Francisco was uniquely poised to respond to the shift. Just south of the city in La Honda lived Ken Kesey, author of the much-acclaimed *One Flew over the Cuckoo's Nest*. Kesey had been psychedelicized in 1960 when he'd signed up as a $75-a-day guinea pig in an experiment at a local Veteran's Administration hospital. Kesey and his friends—the self-proclaimed Merry Pranksters—were acid proselytizers who began turning on San Franciscans in 1965. In contrast to the other major acid outlet, Timothy Leary's operation in Millbrook, New York, which appealed to an elite group of writers, artists, and jazz musicians, the Pranksters turned on anyone and everyone at their public happenings, or "Acid Tests." And while Timothy Leary devised a cautious protocol for tripping, which emphasized the creation of a controlled environment, the Pranksters would urge the people they dosed to "freak freely," their solution to the unpredictability of an acid trip. Unlike Millbrook, which was all cool and meditative—"one big piece of uptight constipation" to the Pranksters—Acid Tests featured rock music, weird electronic noodling, and spoken-word experiments. The Warlocks (soon to be the Grateful Dead) became the Pranksters' house band and would play loud rock 'n' roll on a sound system purchased by their biggest fan, acid king Owsley.

San Francisco quickly became the scene of wild parties, of which the Pranksters' were the most off-the-wall. According to Chet Helms, there was a "huge party circuit" in the midsixties because there were so few venues for live music. Many of the party goers were students at San Francisco State and the San Francisco Art Institute—people who later formed the core audience at the Fillmore and Avalon ballrooms. Many of the musicians who would form rock bands in San Francisco had hung out together at the same parties. Peter Albin of Big Brother says there was a "camaraderie there already between us." Bob Cohen, a transplanted New Yorker, was part of the party circuit and also lived at a notorious hippie house not far from Haight-Ashbury, 2111 Pine Street, a three-story Victorian with ten one- and two-bedroom apartments. There were several such houses on Pine Street, kind of extensions of the party scene; the house at 2111 was, by all accounts, the most outrageous. "In its heyday," Cohen recalls, "we had Ronny Davis and the people from the Mime Troupe, people from the American Conservatory Theater, artists. Janis Joplin lived there, and some of the Charlatans, some of Big Brother. We had everybody. It was amazing. And it was one giant party. I must have known over a thousand people."

The parties evolved not only from the music and acid scenes but also from political activism. The Free Speech Movement at UC Berkeley in 1964 had given rise to more protests as activists looked beyond the campus to end racial discrimination in San Francisco's restaurants, hotels, and auto dealerships and, of course, to rally against the escalating war in Vietnam. Political demonstrations were often followed by big bashes, and dissenters of all persuasions—the political and cultural radicals—would celebrate together, enjoying closer ties than were possible a few years down the line. One of the most visible left-wing San Francisco groups, the Du Bois Club—dominated by red-diaper babies, children of Communists, and fellow travelers—was famous for its postdemo parties. Terence Hallinan, a cofounder of the local Du Bois Club, was well known to the Haight's musicians and artists, Janis among them. Other members included Bill Resner, who with his brother, Hillel, would open the Haight's electric ballroom, the Straight Theater, and Luria Castell, who had been to Cuba, where she claimed to have met Che Guevara, and now resided at 2111 Pine Street.

San Francisco's artistic ferment was a multimedia happening, involving not only politicos, Pranksters, and musicians but artists, dancers, poets, and actors. Although it was the "San Francisco Sound" that grabbed journalists, the first rock 'n' roll dances featured poets, dancers, theater troupes, and light-show artists. One of Big Brother's first gigs was *The Blast*, a multimedia event that Dave Getz says was "way ahead of its time. There was a rock 'n' roll band on one side of the stage, a free jazz ensemble on the other side of the stage, with dancers in the middle, light projections, and this black operatic singer, Crystal Mazur. They projected comics on the screen and she sang the words. Sometimes both bands would be playing. It was totally spontaneous. It was so avant-garde no one's ever heard of it."

In fact, the Bay Area boasted a thriving avant-garde. The San Francisco poetry renaissance, spearheaded by Kenneth Rexroth in the late forties, had put the city on the literary map. Now the experimental Ann Halprin Dance Company created a stir with its nude dancing; the Tape Music Center was home to experimental electronic musicians like Pauline Oliveras, Ramon Sender, Morton Subotnik, Zack Stewart, and Steve Reich. This small but vital community of avant-garde artists also included Berkeley's Open Theater; an improvisational troupe, the Committee; and the American Conservatory Theater (ACT), from which Ronny Davis split to form the lefty San Francisco Mime Troupe, which performed hardhitting political satire, not pantomime. The painters Joan Brown, Wally Hedrick, and Jay DeFeo were part of the mix as well. The Pacifica radio station, KPFA, brought many artists and intellectuals together; KPFA regulars included Kenneth Rexroth on books, Pauline Kael on film, Alan Watts on philosophy, and Ralph Gleason on jazz. Despite all the activity, outsiders treated the Bay Area's art scene as if it were a mere echo of New York's—an idea that made local writers and artists bristle. When Tom

Wolfe asked Ken Kesey if an Acid Test was like "what Andy Warhol is doing in New York," Kesey's chilly reply was, "No offense. But New York is about two years behind."

Indeed, the light show, for instance, was a San Francisco innovation, invented by Seymour Locks, an art professor, in the early fifties. Unlike the light shows associated with Timothy Leary or Andy Warhol, in which static images were projected, Locks projected light through glass dishes filled with paint, which he would swirl and stir to trippy effect. He taught the technique to a student, Elias Romero, who in the early sixties became the "real Johnny Appleseed of light shows" in the Bay Area. Romero put on Sunday-night light shows at an old Mission District church that he and Ronny Davis rented. Romero was living in a funky house on Pine Street managed by Bill Ham, a painter. The two began collaborating and by the spring of 1965 Ham was presenting light shows in his Pine Street basement, sometimes to classical music and sometimes with a group of jazz musicians from an after-hours club around the corner. Alton Kelley, a future poster artist, recalls someone at 2111 Pine Street inviting him to Ham's place for a light show. "What the fuck's a light show?" he asked. He went along, wondering, "What's he gonna do, turn on little lightbulbs?" Instead "the windows were blacked out, the lights went off, and the music started. Then little dots started to move and swirl and change colors." The image was like a "moving abstract painting" projected against the wall and enhanced, of course, by plenty of weed.

Light shows, rock 'n' roll, psychedelics—by late 1965 the hallmarks of the hippie era were all in place. Today, however, few of those at the forefront of the "sixties" will admit to having been hippies. Dave Getz claims, "I never called myself a hippie, ever. I hated it." Bob Seidemann, the photographer, maintains, "We called ourselves freaks, never hippies." Carl Gottlieb, a writer, says, "hippies were the people who borrowed your truck and didn't return it." Even Janis's pal Sunshine, whose name alone seems incontrovertible proof she was a hippie, insists she was a beatnik instead. Hippies, she explains, were "people who just kind of showed up and didn't seem to have any sense. They didn't know how to take care of themselves. They didn't know how to wash their clothes, hold down a job, or make sure they were going to live through it." Robert Crumb, the cartoonist whose work appeared in almost every sixties underground paper, remembers being "swept up in the general optimism and sharing a lot of the same LSD-inspired visions and ideas." But he says he "never quite got with the hippie shtick. I wasn't beautiful enough. . . . I mean, in my soul . . . dark demons lurked in there. The hippies could tell. . . . They picked up on your vibrations." Even at the time, the Diggers denounced the whole hippie image as a "Love Hoax" and claimed the hip Haight merchants who perpetrated it were trying to mask "the overall grime of the Haight-Ashbury reality." Many longtime habitués of the neighborhood blamed the notion of hippies on the media. Janis's sometime lover Milan Melvin still snarls at the word. To him, hippies were the wanna-bes who flooded Haight-Ashbury when Scott McKenzie's insipid ode to the Emerald City, "San Francisco (Be Sure to Wear Some Flowers in Your Hair)" hit the charts just before July 1967's Monterey Pop Festival. That song, he argues, "was the real last nail in the coffin. The squares were on the march, kicking down little old ladies' picket fences to get flowers in their hair so they could arrive dressed to the code described in the papers."

The flower child wasn't invented out of whole cloth by the media, however. Reporters could always find young people who fit the profile easily enough. Chet Helms, now a full-fledged rock impresario, was among those willing to oblige reporters. His fellow Texan Bob Simmons recalls the press thinking Chet "looked 'just perfect.' Him in that Afghani leather jacket (that really smelled funny in wet weather), preaching love, enlightenment, renaissance, etc. Mostly everyone just said, 'Go, Chet, talk to the press, say what you want, just help keep the party going.' " Meanwhile, journalists intent on hyping the hippie codified and popularized a caricature that kids then came looking to become. Before long, the myth was set in stone: hippies and beatniks were polar opposites. Whereas the beatniks were all doom and gloom, the hippies were all dopey optimism.

It was never that simple, though. Before the media descended on the Haight, hippie and beatnik coexisted, one shading into the other. Both the underground and mainstream press used *hippie* and *beatnik* interchangeably until the spring of 1967. In fact, when *hippie* first appeared in the press in a September 1965 *San Francisco Examiner* article trumpeting Haight-Ashbury as "a sort of West Beach," the headline read, "A New Paradise for Beatniks." And when Janis returned to San Francisco in mid-1966, only a year after she'd left, she was still wearing jeans and a blue work shirt—regulation beatnik garb.

In a long essay on hippies in the *New York Times Magazine*, Hunter S. Thompson acknowledged the nuanced connection between the two groups. Hippies, he reported, "reject any kinship with the Beat Generation on the ground that 'those cats were negative, but our thing is positive.' They also reject politics, which is 'just another game.' They don't like money, either, or any kind of aggressiveness." Thompson did note, however, that if love was the "password" in the Haight, paranoia was the "style," and that the ex-beatniks in the love crowd saw hippies as "second-generation beatniks" rather than as a "whole new breed." Jerry Garcia later claimed greater affinity with the Beats: "The media portrait of the innocent hippie flower child was a joke. Hey, everybody knew what was happening. It wasn't *that* innocent. Our own background was sort of that deeply cynical beatnik space which evolved into something nicer with the advent of psychedelics." Bob Seidemann puts it more starkly: "Fuck the Love Generation! That was bullshit, man. That was a scam. It was always a dark, eraserhead world."

While Garcia and Seidemann saw the darkness, the media was slow to see the "apocalyptic edge" of "what looked like a huge party in perpetual progress" and certainly failed to connect the Haight's more self-destructive manifestations to the race riots and the assassinations, not to mention the Vietnam War. For young unmarried men not enrolled in school, which was most of the Haight's male population, the war wasn't abstract. The draft and the nightmare of serving (and possibly dying) in the jungles of Vietnam hung over their heads. And as the war escalated it got harder to avoid being drafted. Claiming you were gay or showing up at the induction center toothpick-thin, zonked out from drugs and lack of sleep—common strategies—didn't always work anymore.

Listening to the "hippie" music of the time, one hears almost as much dread and foreboding as flower-power goofiness. For every "Get Together" or "Wooden Ships" there's a song like the Buffalo Springfield's "For What It's Worth," with its memorable line "Paranoia strikes deep / Into your heart it will creep." Darby Slick's "Somebody to Love," which opens with the line "When the truth is found to be lies / And all the joy within you dies" doesn't sound much like a Love Generation tune. Nor does Country Joe and the Fish's antiwar anthem "Feel-Like-I'm-Fixing-to-Die Rag." When Grace Slick of the Jefferson Airplane sings "White

Rabbit" it's not bubbly acid enthusiasm you hear in her voice but something closer to menace.

The musicians themselves were not always emissaries of peace and love, either. Joshua White, a light-show artist, remembers the first time he encountered the new bands at Toronto's O'Keefe Center in late 1967. "For us this show *was* the San Francisco scene—the good vibes, the love—coming to Toronto. What came to Toronto, however, was an extremely unpleasant group of people known as the Jefferson Airplane and a very strange bunch of kind of hostile guys known as the Grateful Dead. And then there was the Headlights Light Show, which was two guys fighting with each other." It should have been obvious that, as Darby Slick puts it, there was a "darker side" to all this. When Janis died, her predilection for alcohol and hard drugs made it easy to claim she was anomalous, her death illustrative of the pitfalls of celebrity or her failure to embrace the psychedelic experiment. After all, Janis was a junkie and a boozer, not a *real* hippie. But then who was? Even America's favorite hippie, Jerry Garcia, turned out to have a heroin addiction.

Which is not to say that hippies were no different from beatniks. Even though Allen Ginsberg palled it up with the Pranksters and Neal Cassady actually drove their bus, not all the Beats were so enthralled. Kerouac walked out of a Prankster party Cassady had taken him to. Kerouac couldn't make sense of the scene, except as something un-American. Before he left, he rescued an American flag being used as a sofa cover. As he carefully folded the flag, he asked the Pranksters whether they were Communists. Diane Di Prima moved easily in both bohemian worlds and wouldn't have been rattled by the Prankster party. But she maintains "there were two different lineages. Those kids were raised softer than we were," not having "witnessed the blacklisting, the Rosenbergs, and the insanity of World War II. That's a different world." While the hippies were characterized as peace-loving and optimistic, Jack Kerouac perceived a strain of rebellion altogether more incendiary, more rejectionist than his own revolt of the fifties.

Yet more confident, too. Both Beats and hippies were nomadic, on vacation from work and the consumption it subsidized. The Beats, however, traveled unobtrusively, while the Pranksters, for example, advertised their weirdness as only those who feel untouchable can, crossing the country in a 1939 school bus painted in a rainbow of Day-Glo colors. The Pranksters represented, in the words of Tom Wolfe, "something wilder and weirder out on the road." If the Day-Glo paint didn't attract the cops, the words emblazoned on the bus—"Furthur" in front and "Caution: Weird Load" in back—did. Compared to the Beats, hippies seemed positively adolescent, or even younger. After all, it wasn't a car the Pranksters were driving but a school bus, the traditional site of childhood pranks. What better place for their public "put-ons" or "pranks"? The Beats had certainly never felt the sense of immunity or limitless possibility that characterized the midsixties, however fleetingly. Even a skeptic like Robert Crumb found it impossible to resist entirely the heady optimism of those days. And the Dead may have come out of a "cynical beatnik space," but they were drawn to the Beatles by the group's movies, which Garcia described as "very high and very up." That, he said, was "better than down and out."

Race and gender played themselves out differently, too. For Beats, blacks had signified hipness; the new bohemians, whether out of choice or necessity (by the midsixties, black power was beginning to eclipse fantasies of integration), insisted on their own hipness—Kesey claimed to have "outniggered" blacks, as he put it. Contrary to Tom Wolfe's claim, African Americans weren't completely irrelevant to the new bohemia, but neither did they occupy the central position they once had. Nor were relations between women and men quite the same. The Beat vision was explicitly masculine. Kerouac even claimed the "core" of the Beat Generation was "a swinging group of American men intent on joy." By contrast, Kesey and company were sexist for sure but coed. In fact, while the Beats were about escaping the family, hippies were about reconstituting it, in all its glorious inequality. "Hippies treat their women like squaws" was reportedly the blunt assessment of the mother of the Grateful Dead's comanager Danny Rifkin. In this way, the new bohemia was even less hospitable to ambitious, creative women than the older beatnik subculture, in which women could at least occasionally gain entry by acting like the guys.

These distinctions meant little to Janis in Port Arthur, but some of the transformations rocking San Francisco were already reaching Austin, where the folkies with whom Janis had played were also making the electric turn. Even before Bob Dylan played Austin in September 1965, Powell St. John, Bob Brown, and Wali Stopher—Janis's buddies from UT—had formed a rock band called the Conqueroo with Ed Guinn. Unwilling to cover Top 40 hits at frat parties, they began playing at the I.L. Club, a black East Side club whose clientele was less than totally enchanted by their "hippie folk music with rhythm and blues presumptions," as Guinn calls it. Lots of white UT beatnik students showed up, though, which meant the beer was flowing and the owner was happy. An interracial rock band playing to an interracial crowd at a black club in central Texas was a dicey proposition, but Guinn says "it basically worked." It continued to work through much of 1966 until a barroom brawl triggered by a white's use of the term *niggardly* put an end to their gig. Another Austin rock band, the 13th Floor Elevators, led by two psychedelic pioneers, Roky Erickson and Tommy Hall, had also begun to attract a "proto-hippie" crowd. Hall had come out of the UT folk scene, and the band included an electric jug in its mix. Widely hailed today as one of the premier psychedelic bands of the era (Peter Buck of REM rates the Elevators' debut record "far superior" to the Beatles' *Sgt. Pepper's Lonely Hearts Club Band*), the Elevators were known as Austin's leading rock band. ·

Janis stayed close to home throughout 1965. She certainly didn't make it to the I.L. Club or the New Orleans Club, where the Elevators played, and she was still listening to blues and folk music rather than the new rock sounds that were beginning to seduce other folkies. Keeping away from Austin and her old friends wasn't easy, especially because Janis was discovering that no matter how hard she struggled to be as dull and proper as her hometown she still wasn't accepted. Giarratano recalls her crying about the way people treated her. "But to them she was a weirdo, and they would have nothing to do with that." Bob Clark, a friend of Janis's from Lamar, agrees that despite her best efforts to be like everybody else she still didn't fit in. One night he took Janis to the ballet, and although she wore a very conventional dress and had curled her hair and packed it perfectly in a bun, "she *still* looked different." To Clark, it was obvious. "There was just no way that girl could be like the kind of people who run for Miss Texas." Jack Smith saw it similarly. "She was gonna will herself to be the kind of person who wanted that white picket fence," he explains, "and it didn't fly. It didn't fly at all." Janis herself would say of this period, "I was down there trying to kick [drugs], not getting fucked, trying to get through college, because my mother wanted me to."

Janis might have persevered had Michel acted like he was serious about marrying her. He was working as an engineer at IBM's Poughkeepsie office and living in New York City with Debbie, the young woman he'd met in Mexico. Janis suspected he was two-timing her, because Debbie frequently answered his phone. Predictably, Michel didn't come clean. "He told Janis I was his cousin," Debbie says, and for a while they all went along with his lie. Janis was so lonely and unhappy back in Port Arthur she wrote Michel every day, sometimes more often. Debbie remembers days when she'd find several letters from Janis in their mailbox and a package of her homemade pralines by their door. Over time, though, Michel's letters and phone calls to Janis dwindled. Then he reneged on his promised Christmas trip to Port Arthur, the visit in which he was supposed to give her an engagement ring. Janis continued to write and call him, but she was heartbroken. "She had been shot down much the same way in high school when she wasn't asked out on dates or for the prom," notes Sunshine. "Janis's self-esteem just went further down the tubes because of this." As painful as it was, Sunshine thinks his betrayal was liberating as well. If Janis seemed to have lost "an opportunity for a stable 'normal' life," Sunshine suspects she finally felt "it was okay to follow her heart. The loss freed her from living up to her parents' expectations and allowed her to be herself." Equally important were her therapist's efforts to help Janis see that conformity was not the solution to all her problems. By the New Year, Janis was coming out of her shell.

All along, the biggest stumbling block in Janis's attempted makeover was her longing to sing. "She talked about it," says Giarratano. "She knew she wanted to do that. She did not know how it would fit in with the straight world, certainly not with her mother and dad, even though she played the guitar at home and sang beautifully." But, he says, there's no doubt Janis was "burning" for a career. While Giarratano encouraged Janis to see if she could perform without becoming self-destructive, her parents offered no such encouragement. To Dorothy and Seth, singing was the road to ruin. Unfortunately for them, Janis's biggest fan was her old friend Jim Langdon, who was now writing a regular music column in the *Austin American-Statesman*. When Janis agreed to sing at Beaumont's Halfway House coffeehouse during Thanksgiving weekend, Langdon was in the audience. Beaumont was nowhere near Austin, but Langdon wrote a glowing review for his newspaper, calling Janis "the best white female blues singer in America." One of Dorothy's friends read the review and saw the handwriting on the wall. "Dorothy," she warned her, "you don't have a chance!" Dorothy scolded Langdon for the review. "*Stop encouraging her*. That's not doing her any good. That's doing her harm, writing things about her." Langdon later observed that Mrs. Joplin wanted Janis to go "back to school, to do this stenography. She did not want her to get back into singing, because of the drug associations."

Janis didn't resume performing in earnest until March 1966. Langdon was instrumental in getting her a gig at Austin's Eleventh Door, the town's first commercial folk venue. "She absolutely knocked out at least half of the audience," he says. "They were tremendously impressed, well, over-whelmed, really. And then there was a percentage of the audience that just absolutely didn't know what hit them because this wasn't what they expected. They were expecting a folksinger, a Joan Baez–type singer, and they were really uncomfortable with Janis's strength, with her forceful-ness." A week later she was back in Austin at the Methodist Student Center, playing a benefit for one of Tary Owens's discoveries, a penniless blind fiddler by the name of Teodar Jackson. Some of the old Ghetto gang showed up for her Austin gigs. Bob Brown of the Conqueroo caught Janis at the Jackson benefit and was shocked by how she had made herself over. "She appeared in a very adult and somber black dress—dress!—with her hair done up in a bun. And maybe even high heels! Everything was quite formal, the kind of performance you'd expect for an assembly of col-lege professors, entitled 'The Folk Song, Its History and Evolution in American Rural Culture.' We were proud of her and respectful but incredulous. It was an amazing transformation from the jeans-sweatshirt-bawling-cursing Janis we knew. In the time she'd been gone she had evi-dently decided to look professional." Powell St. John was also taken aback by Janis's new look. She wore "women's business suits, stockings and heels, and high necklines all the way up to her Adam's apple, and she had a serious demeanor onstage when she sang the blues." Powell thought she looked "very severe," but when she opened her mouth it was the Janis of old; she was "singing like Bessie Smith, absolutely authentic." In fact, he thought her look was "a nice contrast to the music she was singing. It worked great, sort of like the Blues Brothers in suits."

That spring, Janis began making the rounds of the Texas folk circuit, traveling from Austin's Eleventh Door to Sand Mountain in Houston and back to Beaumont's Halfway House. Her performances were so strong that word of her talent spread quickly. Frances Vincent was waitressing at the Halfway House and drove Janis to her Sand Mountain gig. "She was very anxious about it," recalls Vincent. There was a lot of buzz around Janis, and that night, Vincent recalls, "the place was packed. It was just incredible to see all these people there who were well thought of as folksingers. I thought, Wow, everybody is showing up just to hear this girl. And she blew them away, of course. They were astounded."

As elsewhere, though, some Houston folkies were more confounded than astounded. Don Sanders, a well-known Texas folk musician who saw Janis audition at Sand Mountain a few weeks earlier, says he "didn't know what the hell to make of it." Janis showed up in a pink iridescent minidress with bell sleeves and a scooped neck. Her hair wasn't coiffed but pinned back on one side. It was a weekday night and the place was nearly empty when she got up onstage and launched into Jelly Roll Morton's "Winin' Boy." "Now, in those days," explains Sanders, "girl folksingers were kind of ethereal and fine-featured." And though the music was not insignificant, the words, Sanders maintains, were still very important to most folkies. "So Janis got up there and wailed, 'I'm a winin' boy, don't you deny me my name.' Her face turned red and she kinda swung back and forth and whacked on her guitar and sang with all of her body. I was so shocked it didn't even make me critical. I had no reference point for it. I didn't think she had a chance in hell of communicating with the audience that came there." Today Sanders admits that what he found most shocking about her performance was the way it "so powerfully crossed the gender line." Female folksingers didn't sing "Winin' Boy" in a raucous voice that sounded like a male tenor's.

Yet what so impressed Jim Langdon about Janis's singing was her voice, or voices, because at this point Janis would sound husky one minute and use a clear "Jean Ritchie falsetto" the next. "She had a true chameleon's voice," says Langdon. "She could imitate anyone." Frances Vincent recalls

Janis singing in "both voices, but mainly in her bluesy, husky one. We had a conversation about it. I think in terms of marketing she was right. She was shrewd and savvy enough to know this was the way to go." Janis wasn't simply doing both voices, though. She was doing both the good girl and the bad girl suggested by each. Vincent, who remarried that spring, remembers Janis showing up at the wedding with her hair pulled back and wearing a "schoolmarmish blue dress that was so severe it looked like something out of the Depression." Janis had resumed her "wild life" by then, drinking and smoking weed, but Vincent emphasizes that she still "came properly dressed for a wedding at my aunt's house." Janis wouldn't keep playing both roles for much longer, though. When Karleen Bennett saw Janis that spring she tried talking Janis into getting married, but Janis said she wasn't interested. Instead, Janis tried to sell her high school friend on getting a tattoo.

Just as Janis was poised to shed her conservative suits, San Francisco's new bohemian scene emerged from underground and began exerting wider appeal. Acid and rock had come together to transform bohemia. Some say the fateful marriage took place at the Pranksters' Acid Tests, or at the Matrix, the first hippie nightclub, or at 1090 Page Street, where Chet Helms began holding jam sessions. Many more remember the first big rock 'n' roll dances. But a few would point to the Red Dog Saloon, a hip bar and restaurant in the Nevada desert hundreds of miles outside of San Francisco. In the spring of 1965, not long after Bill Ham began putting on his Pine Street light shows, Bob Cohen, who had assisted Ham, was approached by a guy dressed like a cowboy who pressed fifty dollars into his hand and invited him and Ham to bring their light show to Virginia City, Nevada. "I thought Virginia City was from the *Bonanza* show," says Cohen. "I didn't think it was real. So I went back to 2111 Pine Street and said to Ham, 'You'll never guess what happened. This crazy guy gave me fifty bucks to go to this place, Virginia City, Nevada, that doesn't exist. Does it?' " They pulled out a map, got into a Volkswagen bus, and drove to Nevada.

Virginia City was a former ghost town where a group of psychedelicized bohemians lived peacefully among the locals. The Red Dog Saloon was the brainstorm of Don Works, a member of the peyote-eating Native

American Church; Mark Unobski, a folk musician whose father was a rich cotton grower in Tennessee; and Chan Laughlin—the cowboy—former owner of Berkeley's premier folk club, the Cabal. Originally conceived as a folk nightclub, the Red Dog was supposed to give the town some much-needed entertainment by booking folk players traveling between coasts. "Mark was a true visionary," Cohen recalls. "He had this idea of restoring this bar to what it had been originally in the 1800s, with bartenders and waitresses in period costumes. They'd serve the best food and have live entertainment." Ham and Cohen, meanwhile, built an unusual light box, whose colors pulsed in time to the music. "I got the electronics going and Bill created the mobiles and things inside and it was art, it was beautiful." As it happened, Ham and Cohen weren't the only Pine Streeters involved in what some have called the first hippie saloon. While in North Beach, Laughlin had spotted two guys he thought were in the Byrds and hired them on the spot to come and play the saloon. In fact, he'd found two members of the Charlatans doing what they did best—posing as rockers. Although the Charlatans at this point were only "playing their tam-bourines in time" and had more publicity pictures than licks, they became the house band at the Red Dog. Lots of hip San Franciscans made the trek to Virginia City, including Darby Slick of the Great Society, who recalls that the band "managed to appear, at once, good-timey and sinis-ter." Milan Melvin, then a deejay in nearby Reno, spent time at the Dog that summer. At first most of the crowd were folkies, accustomed to sit-ting and listening to music. But "the Charlatans, God bless every one of them, forced folkies up out of their coffeehouse chairs and started them dancing."

For baby boomers raised on a steady diet of westerns, the Red Dog was a dream come true. Laughlin explained that the "Red Dog was to be mod-eled on the classic *Gunsmoke* movie-set saloon." For Bob Cohen, who spent the whole summer there with fellow Pine Streeters, the Red Dog scene was "vanishing America. It was the last place you could carry a gun. And we bought every gun in town. This was the Wild West, a big fantasy world where you could be whoever you wanted to be." Cohen was a trans-planted New Yorker, but he had a quick-draw outfit. Lots of people did. "That's where all the fringe and the leather came from, which became such a big part of that whole hippie image."

When the summer ended, the Pine Street group (now calling themselves the Family Dog) returned to San Francisco. Inspired by the Red Dog Saloon and convinced that the guys primary source of income—had grown too risky, they decided to put on rock 'n' roll dances instead. No one wanted to give up dancing, which is one sign that the sixties were truly on—having fun and showing it were a clear break with the cool coffeehouse culture. Psychedelics and the new rock marked an easing of the standards of cool. Luria Castell suggested the Family Dog hold its dances in the meeting hall of the International Longshoremen's and Warehousemen's Union. Jim Haynie of the Mime Troupe says the choice "was kind of poetic in a way because of what [red-baited] Harry Bridges and the West Coast Longshoremen's Union represented—lefty philosophy and the workingman, the working person. Justice, you know. We felt some poetry in being aligned with the most maligned people." The Family Dog named its first dance "A Tribute to Dr. Strange" after the Marvel Comics character, the "master of the mystic arts." Alton Kelley designed the poster, which was plastered all over town. Bill Ham did the lights and the Great Society, the Charlatans, and the Jefferson Airplane all played. General admission was $2.50, and $2.00 for students.

Somewhere between four hundred and twelve hundred people showed up at the Longshoremen's Hall the night of October 16, 1965. That weekend fourteen thousand protesters from across the western states gathered to march on the Oakland induction center in the Bay Area's first big antiwar demonstration. Turned back by the police on the first day and by the Hell's Angels on the second, some of them found their way to the Family Dog dance. Allen Ginsberg, who'd spoken at the march, was, like others, "astonished" by the "energy in the air and the number of strange people." Al Kelley remembers being "stunned by all the freaks who showed up. I didn't know there were that many freaks in town because we thought *we* were the cool guys." The shock of recognition hit everyone. John Cipollina, who in a few days would form the rock band Quicksilver Messenger Service, clambered onstage and was startled to see so many people with long hair who looked like him. As Chet Helms surveyed the crowd, he marveled, "They can't bust us all." Darby Slick maintains everyone was overwhelmed with the "certainty of the birth of a scene." Ralph Gleason raved about the dance in his *Chronicle* column, alerting more people to the emerging scene.

The Family Dog envisioned its dances transforming San Francisco into "the American Liverpool," but despite its role in launching the scene, its members weren't around long enough to preside over the transformation. While the group was still in business it offered its services to Bill Graham, the business manager of the Mime Troupe, which had just been busted for performing in the park without a permit after the Parks Commission had canceled its permit for alleged obscenity. Graham was organizing a benefit for the troupe, and Luria Castell and Al Kelley offered to help in exchange for a plug for the Family Dog on the poster. In the course of conversation, Castell and Kelley told him about the Family Dog's plans to hold dances in the old Fillmore Auditorium, which could be rented for just sixty dollars a night. A well-known R & B venue, the Fillmore was where Johnny Otis had discovered the great Etta James, but it had fallen on hard times. Graham was noncommital about the offer and promised to get back in touch. Before Castell and Kelley secured the Fillmore, Graham had signed a four-year lease on the theater. The Family Dog had never made big money off its dances, but Kelley claims Graham's actions "blew us right out of the water and out of business. We didn't know any other halls we could rent in San Francisco for that price." They held their last dance on February 4, 1966.

Born Wolfgang Grajonca, Graham was a frustrated actor from New York who had once waited tables in the Catskills. By day he worked as the office manager at a small San Francisco manufacturing company, but at night he caught plenty of plays, which is how he hooked up with Ronny Davis of the Mime Troupe. Graham's first benefit took place on November 6, 1965, and featured the poet Lawrence Ferlinghetti; an improvisation group, the Committee; the jazz saxophonist John Handy; the folksinger Sandy Bull; and two rock groups, the Jefferson Airplane and the Fugs from New York. Almost four thousand people showed up at the Mime Troupe's loft, which held only six hundred. Many people, including Dave Getz, were turned away at the door, but the troupe still took in more than four thousand dollars that night. The next benefit was held at the much larger Fillmore, in the heart of the black Fillmore district. The three benefits staged by Graham were the "towering cultural events leading to Haight-Ashbury," according to Peter Berg of the Mime Troupe, a real "cultural revolution." Robert Scheer, the editor of the radical magazine *Ramparts*, recalls driving up to the benefit on the back of

Graham's motor scooter and finding "this fucking line going around the building. It was *incredible*. People were all around. . . . We were saying things like, 'Wow! Wow!' Then Bill turned around on the motor scooter and said to me, '*This* is the business of the future.'" Graham and the Mime Troupe parted ways when he decided to continue promoting rock dances. Although the Mime Troupe was so chronically broke that its actors were "absolute art serfs," who survived, says Peter Coyote, by "stealing and swindling and doing what we had to," they voted against participating in the moneymaking dances.

Having discovered the business of the future, Graham wasn't about to share the booty. Definitely not with an acid head like Chet Helms, to whom Luria Castell had sold the name Family Dog before leaving San Francisco for Mexico. The Family Dog lost money on its last few dances, but Chet wanted to keep the rock 'n' roll going and joined forces with John Carpenter, then the manager of Grace Slick's group, the Great Society. To Jerry Garcia, who had noticed the "gleam" in Chet's eye at the second Longshoremen's dance, Chet was "always a businessman, a shrewd guy with an eye for a trend." But Chet was no match for Graham, with whom he and Carpenter formed a loose partnership in mid-February 1966. The Family Dog was without a venue so Graham allowed Chet and Carpenter to use the Fillmore every other weekend; in exchange they told him about the hot bands. From the beginning, relations were rocky as they fought over everything from percentages to dope smoking during concerts—Graham opposed it. Their partnership fell apart soon after the Family Dog brought the Paul Butterfield Blues Band to town for three shows that garnered over eighteen thousand dollars—an unprecedented sum. As they counted their take, Chet, Carpenter, and Graham talked enthusiastically about hiring the band again. But at six the next morning, Graham was on the phone to the band's manager, Albert Grossman, securing for himself all of Butterfield's San Francisco dates for two years, thereby blocking the Family Dog from hiring them. It was a story Graham delighted in telling. "Look, I get up early" was Graham's response when Chet confronted him. Less than a month later, on April 22, 1966, Chet opened the Avalon Ballroom, a smaller hall eight blocks from the Fillmore. The Avalon was in a building called the Puckett Academy of Dance, or the "Fuck It Academy of Dance," as it was soon known by the

Family Dog. In the thirties, the Avalon had been part of a chain of swing ballrooms, and with its red flocked wallpaper, mirrors, gilded booths, and columns, the Avalon retained some of its earlier elegance. Its sprung wooden dance floor, which moved in sync to the dancers, made it the trippiest ballroom by far.

Chet and Graham represented a new breed of rock promoters. Unlike rock promoters such as Dick Clark and Murray the K, whose teen cavalcade shows treated rock musicians like "pop plebes," they treated musicians like artists. Both men put on eclectic shows, mixing popular local bands with R & B, blues, or jazz acts little known to their young white audiences. Pete Townshend of the Who respected Graham for "taking the ticket money he earned from top bands like the Who and passing it on to people who weren't selling tickets at the time like Cannonball Adderly, with whom we played the Fillmore." Chet did the same thing, promoting the jazz musician Charles Lloyd and the bluesman John Lee Hooker, among others. But there the resemblance between the two ballroom promoters ended.

In contrast to Chet, Graham never claimed to be a nice guy. Having survived the Holocaust by walking across France with sixty-three other children at the age of ten, Graham felt that one had to either destroy or be destroyed. He was utterly ruthless toward his competitors, especially Chet, whose hippie softness he seemed to take as a personal affront. He tried forcing bands to sign exclusive contracts that effectively barred them from playing the Avalon or any other Bay Area club. Milan Melvin organized radio campaigns for both the Avalon and the Fillmore and recalls sitting in Graham's office on more than one occasion when Graham "looked at Chet's acts for the week, called the manager of one of the bands, and railed at him that if he ever let his band work for Chet again, he, Bill, would never use any of the guy's bands and would use all his power in the industry to put the manager and his musicians out of work." Although local bands usually resisted, out-of-town musicians sometimes capitulated.

Jerry Garcia said doing business with Chet was "like doing business with a hippie," whereas "with Bill, it was like the other end. . . . He was like a *Martian*." Graham's ballroom helped sustain the counterculture, but he was primarily in the business of rock dances to make a buck. To maximize his profits (admission was at first only $2.50), he routinely flouted Fire Department regulations, packing up to three times as many people as allowed into his second-story (956 legal capacity) auditorium. Philip Elwood, the *San Francisco Examiner* music critic, says, "I never understood what would have happened if there had been a fire there as the hall was upstairs and there was no access." One light-show artist claims his partner brought an ax with him when they worked the Fillmore because he was so afraid of getting trapped in a fire. Graham either avoided issuing tickets or sold them over again, so his real take was always a matter of speculation. Jim Haynie worked closely with him and maintains, "Bill's profits were enormous. We knew he was stuffing thousands of dollars away every week, and I thought he was sending it to Swiss bank accounts. I never knew for certain."

Still, unlike Chet, Graham held many benefits for political groups. Moreover, bands sometimes preferred dealing with him because he always paid them, whereas Chet was less reliable. "Money," recalled Jerry Garcia of his Avalon gigs, "was always a problem." Chet would try to get out of paying with excuses like "You know, I've got family. I can't pay right now." Most important, Graham was a fighter who wouldn't fold in the face of the authorities, who were eager to shut down his theater and much of the emerging scene. Graham liked nothing better than outwitting and outmaneuvering City Hall and the police. To Pete Townshend, Graham seemed like a "rock" in the middle of Haight-Ashbury; without him "all these airheads would fall to *bits*." Both loathed and loved, Graham, who had precious little patience with the subculture that made him rich, nonetheless held it together with his make-a-buck drive. Reflecting on Graham's 1991 death in a helicopter crash, one poster artist said, "It *would* take 100,000 volts to kill the motherfucker."

If Graham was the foundation stone of the electric ballrooms, Chet Helms, very long-haired and determinedly mellow, was their guru, motivated more by messianic zeal than the hunger for profit. Bob Simmons, who worked at the Avalon, says that for a time "Chet was kind of like the rooster who takes credit for the sunrise. He really thought he had invented the whole thing." In her 1967 essay on the Haight, Joan Didion skewered him. Chet, Didion noted, said things like "Just for the sake of clarity I'd like to categorize the aspects of primitive religion as I see it."

Or "There are only three significant pieces of data in the world today." Chet could be pompous, but in contrast to Graham he was generous and kind. He let friends in for free and gave complimentary passes to whole communes, the sorts of benevolent gestures that hurt business in his beautiful old ballroom. Equally damaging was his lack of organization, and his tendency to "work off the top of the stack." In the end, Chet was undone by his own grandiosity when he poured thousands and thousands of dollars into an unsuccessful ballroom in Denver, a move that doomed the Avalon.

Chet had begun moving into music promotion in the summer of 1965, six months before taking over the Family Dog dances. A marijuana legalization activist, Chet had supplemented his meager income by Dumpster diving for castoffs and selling the occasional nickel bag of marijuana. He started organizing jam sessions at 1090 Page Street, a boardinghouse owned by the uncle of Peter Albin, the future Big Brother bassist. Peter's brother, Rodney, managed the building in exchange for free rent and filled it up with the usual suspects—artists, beatniks, and freaks, mostly from SF State—that populated the Pine Street houses. "I thought it should have a flashing neon sign that read, 'DRUGS,' " recalls Sunshine, who lived there. There was a party her first night there and Jerry Garcia and the Warlocks, who knew the bluegrass-playing Albin brothers from San Carlos, dropped in, smoked dope, and partied.

The massive Victorian—soon known simply as 1090—was in a state of serious disrepair, but with its hardwood parquet floors and stunning redwood-and-oak spiral staircase it was still impressive. The building's real treasure was located, oddly enough, in the basement: a redwood-paneled ballroom off the kitchen. The ballroom was big, with imposing columns and large alcoves off to the side; it even had an outside entrance, making it the ideal party and performance space. Peter and his brother knew a lot of folk players in the area and several musicians began hanging out there and playing. John Jennings, who would shortly form the rock group Wildflower, says, "It was great. A beatnik wanna-be's dream." The place would soon be *the* hangout for aspiring rock musicians in the Haight. A scenester above all else, Chet Helms could see that something was happening there. It was his idea to organize informal jam sessions in the basement ballroom. The jams became so popular that he started charging seventy-five cents to discourage the crowds—a move that paradoxically only made the sessions more popular. At the height of the jams, as many as a hundred people would show up.

Out of these sessions a band began taking shape with Sam Andrew on guitar, Chuck Jones on drums, Peter Albin switching over from guitar to bass, and Paul Beck, a Bob Dylan soundalike, who came up with their first name, Blue Yard Hill. Initially Chet and Beck comanaged the group, which continued jamming at 1090, usually playing Rolling Stones tunes they didn't know had been recorded already by American blues artists. Before the year was out, Beck was gone and a second guitarist, James Gurley, was in. Chet took over managing the band full-time and was so central a figure in the early days he was included in the group's first publicity shot. It didn't take long for the band to come up with the name Big Brother and the Holding Company, the result of a stoned group rap about "1984, monopoly capitalism, holding corporations, and holding in the sense of possessing drugs." It was the coolest, most cutting-edge name of all the early San Francisco bands. Charles Perry, a hip journalist, remembers people wondering, "Oh wow, could you get busted for having a name like that?"

Like most other San Francisco bands, Big Brother began as a group of acoustic amateurs. Peter had the most experience, playing at folk clubs around San Mateo, a town twenty-five miles south of San Francisco where he'd attended junior college. He'd hung out at the Chateau in Menlo Park and the Boar's Head Coffeehouse run by his brother and George "The Beast" Howell, a beatnik whom Janis had known during her North Beach days. Peter had listened to rock 'n' roll when he was in his teens, but his real love was folk music. His parents had introduced him to the Weavers, Leadbelly, and Josh White by the time the Kingston Trio ignited the folk craze. Sam Andrew, the guitarist, was an air force brat who had lived all over the world, fronting his own rock 'n' roll band in Okinawa at age fourteen. He had attended SF State and played the coffeehouses around town, but it was "all very amateurish." After studying at the Sorbonne during 1963 and 1964, he moved to the Haight and was gearing up for graduate study in linguistics at UC Berkeley when he walked by 1090 and heard what turned out to be Peter playing his guitar. "I was coming out of a very academic, linear, abstract, scholarly Western European tradition," he says. A lot of what was happening in the Haight "was the opposite of that."

While the Haight was a learning experience for Sam, it seemed to be James Gurley's natural habitat. A transplanted Detroiter, "James," explains Sam, "was almost entirely nonverbal." He had spent four years at Detroit's Catholic Brothers of the Holy Cross studying to be a monk and then began hanging out at a local beatnik coffeehouse, the Cup of Socrates. There he met his future wife, Nancy, a straight-A student at nearby Wayne State University, who was working as a waitress. Soon the two were inseparable. At one point James had helped his father, a stunt car driver, who strapped his helmeted son onto the hood of his old Ford and drove him through a flaming plywood wall at local speedways. The "human battering ram" act was a hit with crowds, but the stunt knocked out James's front teeth and singed his hair so badly that he shaved it off. James and Nancy moved to San Francisco in 1962. With his bald head James became known in hip circles as "Weird Jim Gurley." The couple lived on Pine Street, where James would hole up in a closet for hours "with a stethoscope taped to the body of his guitar, finger-picking cascading notes into his own ears alone." James fit seamlessly into Big Brother, and he and Sam became a familiar sight in the Haight, "sort of walking down the street in a stoned aura of long-hairedness, playing acoustic guitars together." James's reputation as a Haight-Ashbury scenester was further enhanced when Bob Seidemann's photograph of him in cowboy drag holding an Indian feather appeared as a poster in Haight stores.

Seidemann had been a high school hipster who began hanging out in Greenwich Village cafés when he was a teenager. He had first encountered Nancy Gurley on an earlier stay in San Francisco and met James through her. He knew her as Nurse Nancy Nancy because, he claims, she worked as a receptionist for a "script doctor," a doctor who wrote prescriptions for sought-after drugs. Nancy would walk around town with a stuffed animal—a huge green toad—which she carried on her hip as if it were her child. To Seidemann, she was "a five-foot-four, large-breasted, not very pretty, supersexual, superdrugged-out, superhip female in her early twenties. We were friends who had sex."

Seidemann remembers dropping acid with her one evening. They were heading back to his place "to get it on" when they passed the Coffee Gallery and Nancy told him to wait—she had to talk to someone. Ten minutes later she came out with James Gurley and said, "I'm going with this guy." James and Nancy were among the coolest couples in the Haight, dropping some of the first acid to hit San Francisco and spending time in Mexico doing mushrooms with Indians—so much, in fact, that James never wanted to take psychedelics again. Nancy was unknown outside the community of hipsters, but she was an influential figure in the Haight.

Chet unveiled Big Brother in December 1965 at Berkeley's Open Theater, where the band played an almost entirely instrumental and improvised set while the experimental filmmaker Bruce Conner ran "a bunch of choppy bits" he'd edited from film he'd shot of the group jamming one night at 1090. Not long after, Chet booked them at the Matrix, the pizza-parlor-turned-nightclub located on lower Fillmore Street. Many bands got their start at the Matrix, although the place was so tiny that instruments weren't even miked there at first. Darby Slick recalls Chet "had been hyping the group to us all for some time," but hardly anyone had heard them play. Chet was "especially high" on James Gurley. The Matrix debut was by invitation only, and many local musicians showed up to catch the latest band. When Slick ran into Jerry Garcia outside and asked what he thought of James's playing, he answered, "He's cool," in a way that signaled "respect" but not "an abundance of personal enthusiasm." Slick remembers the band's aggressive playing and their treble-heavy sound. James Gurley used "finger picks and therefore played twice as fast as anybody else on the local scene." Peter handled almost all the vocals, which everyone agreed could use a lot of improvement. The biggest problem with the band was its drummer, who couldn't keep time, but eventually Dave Getz came onboard.

Dave Getz had moved to San Francisco to attend the Art Institute after graduating from Cooper Union in New York. Upon earning his MFA in 1964, he headed off to Europe on a Fulbright and came back to town just as the hippie scene was unfolding. Dave had always been interested in music, starting out as a rock 'n' roll addict but deciding in high school to be a jazz musician. Dave played drums in the Catskills, made second string in New York's extremely competitive All-High-School Jazz Band, and at nineteen toured Europe as part of a Dixieland band. Shortly thereafter, convinced he lacked the discipline to be a jazz musician, he put his creative energy into painting instead. He still listened to avant-garde jazz musicians like Ornette Coleman, though, and kept a drum set in his studio. In late 1965, he became interested in rock 'n' roll again and tried to form a band with Victor Moscoso—a future poster artist—and others at the Art Institute, where he was now teaching. "I was going through a parting of the ways with the old guard at the Art Institute," he says. Their style was "definitely this macho painter thing that involved drinking in bars and commitment above all else, never taking your nose off the grindstone." Increasingly certain that there was more creative momentum in rock music than in art, he also suspected he wouldn't be hired back at the Art Institute. After all, he was growing his hair and dropping acid.

Dave's relationship with Big Brother began when he spotted Peter Albin in a café directly below his painting studio. With his long hair, Peter was hard to miss. Although Dave had never met Peter, he walked up to him and remarked on the length of his hair. Peter explained he was in a rock 'n' roll band and told him about their gig at an upcoming antiwar rock concert. Dave had already been planning to go to the Peace Rock, which his friends at the institute were helping organize. The Great Society, Wildflower, Quicksilver Messenger Service, and Big Brother were among the bands scheduled to play the Fillmore on February 12, 1966. Big Brother's set was a revelation to Dave: "They knocked my socks off. I *had* to play with that band." They went through a couple of more drummers before approaching Dave in March about auditioning for them. "The first song we played was a Rolling Stones tune and we just didn't stop for about a half an hour. It was so intense nobody could stop." There was no question Dave would be their new drummer. "It was just like *I* was the drummer," he says. "Then we played the Matrix that night or the next."

Professionalism was frowned on among the new San Francisco bands. Professional meant slick, L.A., and selling out. Nevertheless, some bands were more professional than others. The Jefferson Airplane was by far the most polished, projecting "a vibe of success" from the beginning. After scoring two hits in 1967 with "Somebody to Love" and "White Rabbit," the Airplane became doggedly anticommercial, but at first it seemed better suited to L.A. than San Francisco. Darby Slick, whose own band, the Great Society, fell apart when his sister-in-law, Grace Slick, joined the Airplane, says the Airplane was "very show-biz" back then. "They smiled a lot, and projected a clean-cut image." Sometimes when Marty Balin was singing a ballad he'd even drop on one knee, crooner-style. By contrast,

Big Brother was "just *really* rough," says Sam Andrew. "It was kind of like art school students picking up guitars, conceptual art or something like that. The way I always saw Big Brother was untutored, but we had a concept." Dave Getz agrees. "We were absolutely a freak rock band. That's what we called what we did."

Among most San Francisco bands, spontaneity was a virtue and expertise suspect. "We were just going for it," Sam explains. "We had no musical knowledge. Actually, I was afraid to bring out what knowledge I had. It was very hard to show anyone anything then. Everyone wanted to arrive at whatever it was by experimentation. There was no linear approach in Big Brother, or way less than in other bands." Which is partly why an autodidact like James Gurley was, as Dave says, "the predominant force" during the early days of Big Brother. The band was driven by James's frenetic efforts to translate his idol John Coltrane's assaultive saxophone playing, his "sheets of sound," to the guitar. To Bob Seidemann, "James *was* the Big Brother sound. For a minute, James was Jimi Hendrix. For a minute he was *the* psychedelic guitar player in America. There was just nothing like it. He may have missed his string once in a while, or often, but it was all soul, all mood, all emotion, all pain, all suffering, all blues." Others felt musicians could have soul and hit the right notes, too. One night Charles Perry of *Rolling Stone* heard James take a forty-five-minute solo, a "logicless exploration of the highest and lowest register, sometimes getting hung up on one or two notes forever."

To the extent there was a "San Francisco sound" it consisted of extended jamming and soloing. Even if the bands had wanted to perform tight, concise songs, they lacked the chops to do it. Instead, they played long and sometimes tedious jams, like Big Brother's reworking of Grieg's middlebrow classic "In the Hall of the Mountain King" or Quicksilver Messenger Service's twenty-minute version of Bo Diddley's "Mona," all with plenty of feedback, which became yet another element in the stoned mix. James would often end the Grieg piece by picking up his amplifier, which would be screeching with feedback, and hurling it against the stage floor so it produced a thud that reverberated throughout the ballroom. If the musicians' inexperience made them more open to experimentation, so did performing high. As Darby Slick notes, being out of tune was one of the "prime characteristics of the San Francisco sound," caused not only by inexperience or the absence of the cheap electronic tuners used today but by all the grass that was smoked. Tuning a guitar while stoned, recalls Slick, is an exercise in frustration because "your ear seems, at once, too good, and then again not good enough. The string sounds too sharp, or maybe way too flat, all at the same time." It was quite possible "to chase a string's tuning up and down, up and down, for an hour or so." And then, there were five other strings, all of which had to be tuned correctly to the first string. "If the slight variation in pitch between one instrument and another in classical music is called warmth," Slick points out, "San Francisco music was extremely hot." So hot that record company talent scouts weren't in a hurry to sign these new acts. The music was just too primitive and weird.

Big Brother knew that to gain attention they'd have to find a singer. They tried auditioning all kinds of local singers, and then Chet mentioned Janis. Chet had lured Janis to San Francisco once before, that time with promises of coffeehouse fame. Both James Gurley and Peter Albin had heard her in the North Beach coffeehouses and claim they were intrigued by the idea. James says he remembered her incredible voice "right off." Chet, however, remembers some resistance from James and Peter, who feared Janis would "give too strange an aura to the band." He himself thought "she was strange and weird and off-the-wall and she raised the hair on the back of your neck." But so, he reasoned, did the band. After hitting a dead end with other vocalists, Chet set about bringing Janis to San Francisco for an audition.

What Janis said, in effect, was 'I'm going to go be what I am,' " recalls Giarratano. And above all else she was a singer. In the spring of 1966 Janis finally decided to move back to Austin to pursue her dream. She was worried about getting hooked on drugs again, but she had come to understand that Port Arthur spelled death as surely as drugs did, and Langdon's rave reviews and the gigs they generated gave her some hope that this time the outcome might be different. She and Giarratano talked about her move for two or three sessions before she left town. He could see that singing was Janis's only relief from despair, and he gave her "permission to develop and explore herself and to go sing," he says. Concerned that Janis not lose the self-awareness she had gained, he referred her to an agency in Austin where she could continue with therapy.

Janis left Port Arthur to resume her life as a folksinger, and yet almost as soon as she arrived in Austin she was thinking about joining a rock band, the 13th Floor Elevators. Tommy Hall of the Elevators, however, didn't think including her was a good idea, because the group wasn't a blues band. Besides, the 13th Floor Elevators already had Roky Erickson, a vocalist so fiery he "didn't simply sing a song," writes one critic, "he became them. . . . It was like he was screaming to get outside of his body." Janis was influenced by Erickson's approach, but the band's commitment to freaking freely probably put her off. It also put the authorities on their trail, and before the end of 1968 Erickson was busted for possession of marijuana. He pled insanity and spent nearly four years in the Hospital for the Criminally Insane, where he received shock therapy.

As Janis and the Elevators were eyeing each other, Travis Rivers arrived in Austin to find Janis and bring her to San Francisco for an audition with Big Brother. At least that's what Travis intended. After talking with her friends and discovering how well she was managing, though, he changed his mind. But when a friend told Janis that Travis was in town, she set about tracking him down. "No one knew where I was staying. To this day I don't know how she figured out where I was. At about six or seven in the morning I hear this pounding at the door. So I went to the door and asked who it was, and she said, 'It's Janis, honey, let me in.'"

Travis and Janis talked all day about the risks of returning to San Francisco. There were the drugs and the real question of whether she could sing rock 'n' roll. But the prospect of becoming a schoolteacher after graduation filled her heart with dread. Travis says he took her to an Austin bar where they shared a beer and listened to a rock band. After hearing several songs, Janis slapped him across the chest and said, "That's what I wanna do." Travis drove her back to the Golden Triangle so she could talk the move over with her parents. Travis remembered an awkward encounter he'd had with Seth Joplin several years before and opted to wait in the car while Janis went inside. "When she came back to the car, I asked, 'So what did they say?' and she said, 'They agreed it would be okay.' As it turns out, she didn't talk to them at all about going to California. It was a complete surprise to them."

After she became famous, Janis was fond of claiming that she had "been fucked into being in Big Brother" by Travis. "He just came, and *scooped* me up, and threw me onto the bed, whoo, baby! He just fucked the livin' shit out of me all night long! Fucked me all night, fucked me all morning. I was feeling *sooo* good." Travis says Janis told him she'd raved about his sexual prowess as a "favor" so he'd never want for girls. That is probably what she told Travis, but it's just as likely she invented the story to disguise her own considerable ambition and to advertise her unquench-able sexual lust. In any case, Janis barely hesitated before setting out with Travis. She did call Chet to confirm the offer and get his assurance he would pay her bus fare home should things not work out. When she con-fided in Chet her worries about drugs, he promised that everything was different now. The scene was "beautiful," he said.

Janis had not only failed to tell her parents about moving to San Francisco but had also lied about her purpose in Austin. Dorothy and Seth believed Janis had gone to visit the Langdons for a week and expected her home in time to begin the summer semester at Lamar. When she didn't return, Dorothy called Jim Langdon, who had the unen-viable task of explaining that Janis had left Texas, a step Langdon had counseled her against. He felt the move was premature, and he also wasn't thrilled to have her run out on gigs he had helped line up. None of this mattered to Dorothy, who blamed him for "making Janis think she could sing." She screamed at him, "Without your influence, my daughter would still be at home!"

On June 6, 1966, Janis sat down and wrote her parents a letter from San Francisco. Hers wasn't the typical "beautiful people" letter filled with wonder, awe, and vagueness. Janis's journey to the promised land had a purpose, after all. Janis explained to her parents that Chet Helms was now "Mr. Big" in San Francisco and that he specifically wanted her for this band. Chet, she claimed, had told her she'd become rich and famous singing rock 'n' roll in San Francisco. Careful to cover up her enthusiasm about being out of Texas, she stressed that she wasn't at all sure she wanted to be the "poor man's Cher" in San Francisco. She then assured her parents she'd be back for classes in the fall unless things worked out with the band. Throughout the letter Janis apologized for having once again disappointed them and emphasized she was determined to not blow it again. The letter is so relentlessly realistic and levelheaded it's easy to forget she's describing the stoned-out, freaky, flaky world of San Francisco rock 'n' roll in 1966. Janis's pragmatism, however, was only partly for her parents' benefit. Joining Big Brother wasn't just a lark for her. It was a career path. Although she made a point of sounding contrite, Janis couldn't completely conceal her excitement about being in the land of the beautiful people. The dances, she wrote, are "FANTASTIC."

5

Big Brotherized

Get rid of the chick," Bob Seidemann said to Dave Getz the night Janis made her debut with Big Brother at the Avalon Ballroom. "He was joking," recalls Dave, "and we both laughed because it was so obvious that she was good." The audience's reaction that night was mixed, though. Chet Helms felt Janis was a knockout, and many in the crowd agreed. Others, like James Gurley's friend Stanley Mouse, a poster artist, feared Big Brother would modulate its trippy, weird sound to accommodate her. But within Big Brother, the vote was unanimous: the band had found its singer. At her audition a few days earlier, Dave had felt disappointed Janis wasn't "the beautiful soul" he'd dreamed of, but he had no doubts about her singing. "From the moment I heard her I knew she was absolutely incredible. There was no question in my mind." Sam Andrew thought "she was really strong right away. Whether you liked her or not, you could tell that she was very extreme and unusual—a phenomenon." Peter

Albin agrees. "We knew we were going to use her from the first time she opened her mouth and started singing those great ballsy tones with her raspy voice." The most skeptical member of the band seems to have been James Gurley, whose guitar work defined Big Brother's early sound. "She was wearing torn Levi's, a sweatshirt, no makeup, and her hair was funky. She had a lot of acne and was a little overweight. If you'd said, 'This woman is going to be the goddess of music in two years' time,' I'd have said, 'Forget it, that ain't going to happen.' "

As for Janis, she spent the audition "in space city . . . scared to death." This was June 1966, but the only modern rock Janis had heard was on the radio or in that Austin bar with Travis Rivers. She had never been to a rock concert, much less tried singing rock 'n' roll with a band. "I sang blues—Bessie Smith kind of blues. . . . I didn't know how to sing the stuff, I'd never sung with electric music, I'd never sung with drums, I only sang with one guitar." Unlike some folkies, however, Janis wasn't ideologically opposed to plugging in. As Pepi Plowman points out, "Janis is a good example of someone who went from folk to rock without blinking." Janis's willingness to make the electric turn owed a lot to her experience at Threadgill's, where the old-timers disregarded the folkie distinction between acoustic and electric. According to Powell St. John, Threadgill and his regulars had no reservations about electric instruments. "They liked acoustic bluegrass fine, but they also liked George Jones and anybody making good music. It prompted us to look into commercialized country and western, and we found that, as in R & B, musicians using electric instrumentation could still make music that was absolutely pure." It's no accident that during Bob Dylan's 1965 tour Austin was one of the very few places where he wasn't booed during his electric set.

Switching to rock was a small step for Janis, but learning how to sing with that big electric blast behind her was a challenge. Big Brother's sound was also louder and faster than that of most other San Francisco bands, says Sam Andrew. "I can't exaggerate how fast we played then. *Prestissimo.* It was much faster than the punk rock that came later. The metronome setting was around Charlie Parker—300-plus quarter notes per minute." At first, Janis tried to keep up with this musical blur, an effort that made her sound like "a tape on fast forward," according to Sam. "It was as if she had caught hold of a passing freight train barreling through the night and was not sure if she could hold on." It was all she could do to hear herself over the band's cacophony. Often she ended up just screaming.

The band began rehearsing with Janis in a converted horse barn once used by the San Francisco Fire Department. Stanley Mouse and his fellow psychedelic-poster artist Alton Kelley rented the upstairs studio. One night the police showed up. "We heard a bang, bang, bang at the door," Kelley recalls. "I pulled open the door and the cops said, 'We have a report of a woman screaming.'" Kelley explained, "There was a band practicing and that was a girl *singing*." Janis and the band rehearsed a full week until they could perform a souped-up version of the gospel number "Down on Me" and "I Know You Rider"—tunes that Peter, Janis, and James knew from their folk past. The first night Janis appeared at the Avalon the band went onstage and played what Sam calls their "insane, free-jazz, speedy clash jam." Then Janis joined the guys for the songs they'd practiced. She looked out of place in her blue jeans and work shirt, and she knew it. "I didn't have any hip clothes. I had on what I was wearing to college." But her awkwardness vanished as she got into the music. "What a rush, man! A real, live, drug rush. . . . All I remember is the sensation—what a fuckin' gas, man. The music was boom, boom, boom and the people were all dancing, and the lights, and I was standing up there singing into the microphone and getting it on, and whew! I dug it. So I said, 'I think I'll stay, boys.'"

Word quickly spread that Big Brother had a new chick singer. Darby Slick of the Great Society saw the band play at the California Hall in late July. While he was impressed by Janis's strong, gutsy voice, he was equally struck by her ability to win over a crowd. "It was nearly impossible not to stare constantly at her," he says. "She pranced, she strutted, she shrieked, she whispered. The word of mouth was, a star is born." Janis's friend Sunshine, however, wasn't an immediate convert. "She didn't sound real good at first, and she was wearing a sweatshirt and jeans. You can't believe how bad she looked. I said to her, 'I need to tell you that lace, velvet, leather, and feathers look really great together.'" Bill Belmont, the future manager of Country Joe and the Fish, remembers people urging him to check out Big Brother. "Wow, you have to check out this girl," they'd say, "she's really incredible." He caught the band's act and thought them "uniquely terrible but a lot of fun. Gurley was doing a sort of rampant avant-garde Cageism, Sam Andrew was trying to play rock 'n' roll, and Peter and David were trying to be a rhythm section." Belmont wasn't wild about Janis, either. "She was out there screeching. Occasionally she'd get it together." Still, he thought the group was "entertaining in its wackiness."

In the first months, Janis spent a good deal of time each set just banging on a tambourine during the band's improvisational rock jams. Peter Albin still sang quite a few numbers, like "Oh, My Soul," "It's a Deal," and "Whisperman," that Dave Getz remembers as "kind of awful." For these, Janis would just do backup vocals or hit the tambourine. But she wouldn't stay on the sidelines for long. To make better use of their new singer, the band became less improvisational and more song-oriented. And Janis, for her part, learned to sing rock 'n' roll. As a folkie, Janis just "stood still and . . . sang simple," as she put it. But now she couldn't rely on the "big open notes" and "very simple phrasing" she had used when she was singing like Bessie Smith. "You can't sing like that in front of a rock band, all that rhythm and volume. You have to sing loud and move wild with all that in back of you." Dave recalls that in the beginning, "she had no restraint at all. She'd scream and holler and shout and oversing. At first it was kind of wonderful because she'd go out of tune and out of pitch and just didn't care."

Janis did care, however, because during her first year with the band she began to make herself over in every way. She saw a dermatologist who prescribed tetracycline for her acne, and she slowly tried to change her look. Afraid she'd seem ridiculous, Janis had never made much effort with her appearance. But now she was in the Haight, where hippie flamboyance rather than beatnik functionality reigned. Dressing up was the fashion, so Janis abandoned her usual uniform of men's shirts, sweatshirts, and jeans and began haunting thrift stores for eye-catching outfits. Janis's early efforts at stylishness were clumsy and reflected her habit of covering up rather than showing off her body. Besides T-shirts, beads, and Levi's, her wardrobe included a shapeless dress made from a madras bedspread and a poncho made from a lace tablecloth that looked like nothing so much as a giant doily. Over time Janis's fashion sense improved, with considerable help from Nancy Gurley, James's wife and one of the women responsible for creating the whole "hippie chick" look. Janis copped much of her style, including the zillions of bracelets and feather boas, directly from Nancy, who "set the standard of femininity with the Big Brother guys," according to Peggy Caserta. Although Janis would never wear a lot of makeup, when Big Brother worked on the British film *Petulia* in March 1967, Janis cornered a socialite-model on the set for some cosmetics tips.

Janis also transformed her voice to suit rock audiences. She began listening to soul music, in particular to Otis Redding, whom she worshiped. When Redding played the Fillmore that December she arranged for Bill Graham to let her into the auditorium hours before his performance so she could be right up front. Six months later, when Redding came to the Fillmore again, Janis and Sam Andrew planted themselves as close to the stage as they could get. Sam claims Janis "absorbed Redding's every syllable, movement, and chord change." She watched the way he made the song "visible" through his movements. "I started singing rhythmically," she said, "and now I'm learning from Otis Redding to push a song instead of just sliding over it." Although she had always rejected voice lessons, she even studied briefly with Judy Davis, the Bay Area's leading vocal coach.

In July 1966, one month after Janis returned to San Francisco, all the band members moved to Lagunitas, just over the Golden Gate Bridge in Marin County, where they shared a house. The Grateful Dead and Quicksilver Messenger Service were already living in Marin when Big Brother arrived. "It was the hippie version of getting a little money and going to the suburbs," Sam recalls. In Lagunitas there was no nightlife to compete with rehearsals. Big Brother practiced diligently and talked constantly about music and everything else. Sam remembers going on "for hours into the night, every night about 'God and the Universe,' a favorite phrase of hers, and about how to bring the essence of the blues into what we were playing without being purists—and yet without diluting the power of that beautiful music. We talked about what a different drumbeat would do here or a guitar chord there." Janis was always in the thick of these discussions. "If there was any telling what to do, it would be coming from Janis," says Sam. "But we were in it together; she was delighted with our discoveries and so were we."

When Janis joined Big Brother she joined a family, not just a band. Indeed, the band's communal style was one of the reasons she decided to stay in San Francisco. In the Bay Area's acid-rock explosion, bands frequently resembled large tribes that included close friends and lovers. Among the members of the Big Brother family was James and Nancy's baby boy, Hongo Ishi ("mushroom man" in Spanish and Yahi Indian); Sam's girlfriend, Rita; Peter's wife, Cindy, and their daughter, Lisa, all of whom lived together in Lagunitas. Then there were the friends, like Bob Seidemann, Stanley Mouse, and Richard Hundgen.

Whenever Big Brother played—which was just about every weekend— the family would be there. "We'd go to the Avalon and Nancy would bring Hongo and Cindy would bring Lisa and just put them on the couch in the back room to sleep," says Peter. "They'd go out and dance and come back to check in on them. There was always somebody in the room or at the door watching. The kids would sleep through most of it anyway." One night James remembers Jimi Hendrix babysitting Hongo backstage at Winterland, Bill Graham's other dance hall. "From the time he was a baby, Hongo's hair was white and in an Afro. Jimi Hendrix would see my son and just flip out. He loved that Afro. That night he stayed with Hongo the whole time."

Janis had promised herself to keep away from drugs, but then, she'd believed Chet when he'd assured her that in the Haight psychedelics had replaced hard drugs. Janis soon discovered that despite the ubiquity of acid, speed remained a popular drug, especially in her new band. "The Big Brother scene began with speed," says Richard Hundgen, a family member. "It was cheap and easy to get, and they'd learned to shoot up early." Not everyone in or around the band was shooting speed, but once Janis moved to Lagunitas she found little support for staying clean. In fact, one band member and his girlfriend were already dabbling in heroin. When the band wasn't rehearsing or playing gigs on the weekends, Janis often hung out at the Dead's house with a fellow boozer and blues maven, the keyboardist Ron "Pigpen" McKernan. Other times Hundgen recalls her shooting up with Nancy Gurley and Sam's girlfriend, "Speedfreak Rita," then staying up all night stringing antique glass and crystal beads, which they wore as necklaces or hung around their beds. Dave Getz claims Janis was "a maniac with needles. She loved to do other people up, loved the thrill of hitting somebody, shooting them up." Dave had never injected drugs before Lagunitas, but once he decided to try it, Nancy and

Janis fought over who would get to "do" him. He does not remember who won the battle, but he does recall staying up all night re-covering his drums.

Janis had found a family, but she was still the odd girl out. For one thing, not everyone found her charming. Bob Seidemann thought she was "an asshole who was really aggressive and abrasive and annoying." It was at this point that Seidemann took the famous picture that made Janis "the first hippie pinup girl," as she bragged. Posing her naked from the waist up, Seidemann draped a velvet cape over her shoulders and artfully arranged several strings of beads across her chest, leaving one nipple visible. Seidemann was ready to end the shoot when Janis said, "Oh, motherfucker! I want to take my fuckin' clothes off." She stripped, even though he told her to keep her clothes on. After rearranging the beads, Seidemann shot more pictures. Several days later Janis came into Mouse and Kelley's store, the Pacific Ocean Trading Company on Haight Street, where she saw Seidemann's contact sheets. "Do I look that good?" he claims she asked him. The collective answer of everyone in the store was no, according to Seidemann. Later on, Janis laid into Seidemann because she wasn't seeing any money from the sales of the poster. "You mother-fucker, you're taking all the money I'm making for you," she yelled at him. "She was a pain in the ass," he concludes.

Once again, Janis found herself the one single woman in a group of couples. There were James and Nancy, Sam and Rita, Peter and Cindy, and, within a matter of months, Dave and Nancy Parker, who'd been part of the Grateful Dead's family. Although Janis was still in touch with Michel, she no longer had any illusions about marrying him. In fact, later that summer she finally learned exactly what her fiancé had been doing during their "engagement." At Michel's suggestion, Debbie decided to look Janis up on a trip to San Francisco. The two women arranged to meet at the Avalon the night of a Big Brother gig. "I went backstage," Debbie recalls. "Janis had a bottle of Southern Comfort and we started to get into a girl-to-girl talk. We were starting to realize that things with Michel were a little bit different than we'd thought. We'd sort of known what was going on but hadn't copped to it exactly." The guys in the band kept interrupting, so Janis and Debbie locked themselves in the bathroom with the Southern Comfort and began comparing notes. "The more we found out, the more we laughed. He'd done things like sending us both a dozen roses with the same message on the same day. We were in hysterics. We knew Michel was a tricky kind of guy, but . . ." Janis didn't seem heartbroken, Debbie says. "What are you gonna do? You're either gonna cry, get angry, or laugh. And since we really liked each other, our first response was to laugh. It was as if we had a sisters-against-that-creature kind of bond." Whenever Janis mentioned Michel to Dave Getz, however, she would go on about how much he had screwed her over. "That motherfucker," she'd say.

Janis had a series of boyfriends, but her heterosexual relationships were so short-lived that none of her men entered the Big Brother family. Until the move to Marin County, Janis had been sharing an apartment with Travis Rivers, who had done Chet Helms—Big Brother's low-key manager—the favor of fetching her from Austin. Their relationship had started to sour as soon as they arrived in San Francisco, however, when Travis sheepishly confessed he had nowhere to stay in the city and couldn't put her up. Janis was annoyed until Chet advanced her a hundred dollars so they could rent a room in one of the hip Pine Street houses. They had been living there only a few weeks when she came home and found him with a group of people who were tying off. Dave Getz was with Janis and says the sight of people shooting up filled her with such terror and longing that she flipped out. Travis tried explaining that people were doing mescaline, a hallucinogen, not speed, as she imagined, but she didn't believe him. She told Dave she felt betrayed; they'd had a pact, she said: no needle drugs.

The next day, Travis asked Janis to marry him. Janis turned him down on the spot and Travis dropped the idea. His unwillingness to put up a fight may have signaled to Janis that he wasn't entirely serious, and it only made her angrier. "If you really loved me, you'd want to know why," Janis cried. She was "going to be big, really, really big." This would be the only time in her life, she said, when she'd be able to have any boy over the age of fourteen she wanted and she didn't intend to lose the opportunity. Janis's explanation was designed to provoke Travis, and when he again failed to react, she stormed out of the apartment, shouting, "After I've said something like that to you, you'd have to beat me up if you really loved me." Shortly thereafter Janis told Travis she'd be moving to Lagunitas with the band; several months would pass before the two of them would speak to each other again.

Very quickly, Janis realized that being a rock 'n' roll singer enhanced her sexual desirability. Big Brother was bringing her the acceptance she had never stopped craving, and sexual acceptance, which had always seemed so unlikely, so out of reach, was especially delicious. The stage became the arena for her sexuality, a place to advertise her sexual availability and desire. Janis's North Beach friend Edward Knoll remembers hearing her sing "Ball and Chain" and telling her, "That song is gonna get you a lot of lovers." He says, "She liked to hear that." Even the familiar story Janis told of Travis's fucking her into Big Brother revealed her feeling that singing and her own sexual desirability were inextricably linked. As she grew famous the connection between star power and erotic power would become hazardous, but for the moment she reveled in the attention.

Janis had been with the band only a few weeks when she and James Gurley began sleeping together. He claims to have been put off at first by her acne and her dumpiness but says the guys in the band weren't much to look at then, either. James thought they were both "a couple of desperadoes," and he was looking for an opportunity to expand his sexual horizons. Having grown up feeling "very uptight" about sex, he "had a lot of learning to do," he says. Years of Catholicism had left him feeling "shy, repressed, and screwed up," but the lanky, soulful guitarist was a sexually magnetic figure. "After shows, women would often ask me whether James would be in my room later," Peter Albin says. Lots of women were drawn to James, and Janis was no exception. Still, he wasn't the first band member she went after. Following one of the band's early gigs, in nearby Monterey, Peter recalls, "we danced and she was trying to come on to me. It was just goofy because my wife was back in the motel room. She was obviously putting out feelers: 'Who's easy here?' It was a bit of a power trip, too."

Once James and Janis became involved, he moved out of the apartment he shared with his wife, Nancy, and lived with Janis for two weeks. According to Janis, that arrangement ended the day Nancy came barging through the front door of Janis's apartment. "What an embarrassing situation," Janis told Jim Langdon later. "His old lady comes marching into my bedroom with the kid and the dog and confronts us." James has no memory of a bedroom confrontation; he does recall Nancy's showing up at a band rehearsal and asking him to come back. "It was sort of melodramatic," he admits. James continued to sleep with Janis for a while, but he did go back to Nancy. Soon all was forgiven. Dave Getz doubts Nancy was deeply concerned about James's dalliances. After all, she embodied "the hippie ethic of freedom, 'everybody do their own thing.'" Also, Janis "really liked Nancy," recalls Peter. And Nancy "loved Janis," says Dave. "In fact, she loved Janis as much as anybody." James thinks one reason the two women got along so well was that Janis was "very, very smart. And Nancy was one of the few people who was up to her caliber."

Janis's own sexual tastes were still "very broad," as Dave puts it. Shortly after joining the band, she and Dave went together to a North Beach bar, where Janis ran into her ex-girlfriend Jae Whitaker. Dave noticed some vibes passing between Janis and a striking woman playing pool. Still, he was shocked when Janis said, "Boy, am I turned on by her." Dave, who knew nothing of Janis's sexual proclivities at that point, exclaimed, "What did you say? *Her?*" Dave's background in the art world made him only a little more sophisticated than many people in the Haight, which was a relentlessly straight scene. Hippie boys may have looked like girls, but the counterculture was overwhelmingly heterosexual, despite straight America's association of long hair with effeminacy and homosexuality.

One person in the Haight who fell far short of the heterosexual standard was Peggy Caserta, the owner of the hip boutique Mnasidika. In the fall of 1966 she heard Big Brother at the Matrix and made Janis ecstatic when she told her how much she'd liked her singing. A month later Janis walked into Peggy's store, still looking pretty scruffy and funky in the same "dirty, faded, frayed jeans" she'd had on that night at the Matrix. Peggy noticed her eyeing a pair of $4.50 Levi's "as if they were made of the rarest silk." Janis was broke and offered fifty cents as a down payment. Peggy told her to take the jeans, because she'd so enjoyed her singing. Janis was amazed at Peggy's generosity and chutzpah and asked her worriedly, "Won't you get fired?" It never occurred to her that Peggy owned the store. Peggy not only owned it but was grossing several hundred dollars a day. It wasn't the first or last time Peggy would help struggling musicians. She lent the Dead hip clothes for their early promo shots and gave Peter Albin a snazzy pair of pants with silver stripes down the sides when she saw that the jeans he wore barely grazed his ankles.

After Peggy's kindness, Janis continued to drop by the store. She was physically affectionate, allowing her touch to linger on Peggy's arm, but Peggy thought little of it, assuming Janis was just one more straight hippie chick. Peggy was involved with a woman named Kim Chappell, and though they weren't "out" at the time, they didn't make much effort to disguise their relationship. People suspected they were lovers anyway, because Peggy was as conventionally feminine as Kim was stereotypically butch. "What is it with those two chicks?" Peter Albin once asked Janis. "Are they lesbians?" Janis told him she didn't know or care but thought they were "groovy ladies."

Altogether, Peggy was not your typical Haight-Ashbury habitué. She was an upwardly mobile entrepreneur who had grown up feeling perfectly well-adjusted, not freaky at all. Her hometown of Covington, Louisiana, was a mere three hundred miles from Port Arthur—a fact that always amused Janis. While they both grew up in the South, Peggy's childhood and adolescence were apparently as blissful as Janis's were miserable. Peggy had enjoyed a fabled kind of popularity; she'd even been a cheerleader. She might have ended up a suburban housewife, but she attended Mississippi's Perkinston Junior College, where she became good friends with the head cheerleader, who seduced her. Peggy casts herself as a reluctant participant in their affair, which she ended rather than confront the possibility she was gay. The two women remained friends, however, and after graduation they both got jobs as airline stewardesses and became reinvolved. Over the next few years, Peggy had affairs with both men and women. Indeed, Peggy's coming out unfolded gradually rather than in one defining moment. In 1964 she asked for a transfer to San Francisco and settled in the Haight, where she happened upon an apartment near Romeo's, a gay bar she frequented. When she arrived in town, Peggy was still wearing "super-straight little Peck-and-Peck-style dresses and pantsuits," but a boho girlfriend soon turned her on to pot and Owsley acid. Before long she decided to open a boutique for gay girls, calling it Mnasidika, an obscure literary reference (Mnasidika and her lover, Bilitis, were thought to be the first known lesbians in history) that a friend told her would be immediately recognizable to Bay Area lesbians. About the time Peggy figured out that it wasn't, she realized that the vaguely Eastern, cool-sounding name might appeal to the growing hippie market right under her nose.

Peggy had started seeing Kim Chappell, the daughter of a wealthy Carmel, California, orthodontist, shortly before meeting Janis. Kim had hung around the folk scene in Cambridge and Big Sur and knew folkies like John Cooke and Bobby Neuwirth. It was Joan Baez, however, who had brought the beautiful, androgynous Kim to Cambridge, in the guise of her personal assistant. In public, they acted like "buddies," so few people knew that they were lovers. Baez was never circumspect about her attractions to men, however, and after one flirtation too many her relationship with Kim had come to a very stormy end.

Janis learned of Kim's relationship with Joan Baez shortly after meeting Peggy, who got a kick out of telling people. But Peggy's star connection was only one reason Janis was so taken with her. Peggy also enjoyed the acceptance denied Janis, she was pretty at a time when lesbians were assumed to be ugly bull dykes, and she was self-sufficient, which, it seems, Janis admired more than anything else. "Janis idolized Peggy," Sunshine says, "because she owned a store in Haight-Ashbury and she had a gorgeous lover. And it was almost as if Kimmie was more important because she'd been Joan Baez's lover." The first time Janis mentioned Peggy to Sunshine, she'd said, "Well, Peggy's lover was involved with Joan Baez." Janis and Peggy were star-struck, but they were also seeking validation for their sexual nonconformity. In the search for role models, Joan Baez was irresistible.

In the spring of 1967, not long after Janis began hanging out at Mnasidika, she began seeing Joe McDonald of Country Joe and the Fish. Janis and Joe might as well have been from different planets, so it's hardly surprising their affair lasted only a month or two. Joe was a red-diaper baby who wore his lefty politics on his sleeve. Janis was left of center, but she wasn't much interested in the movement. Janis sought stardom while Joe scrupulously avoided it. Joe wanted to be able to walk down Telegraph Avenue, Berkeley's main drag, unhassled by fans, whereas Janis was thrilled when fans recognized her on the streets of the Haight. Joe shared songwriting credit with all the members of his band even when he was the sole songwriter, a move that mystified Janis. McDonald would go on to do important political work, especially among Vietnam veterans, but, in this period at least, he could be dismissive of those he considered unenlightened. Their relationship ended not in a political fight, however, but because Joe stood her up one night. Peggy took it upon herself to scold

McDonald, who was flummoxed because his plans with Janis had been so tentative. "I called Joe and fussed at him," Peggy says, "and he acted like he didn't know what I was talking about. 'I didn't stand her up!' he said. 'Well, she's here crying,' I told him. He went, 'Oh no.' " Thinking back on the incident, Peggy says, "Janis was *vulnerable*."

Janis had a series of other boyfriends, but none lasted more than a few weeks. Meanwhile, Janis and Peggy flirted with each other for many months before they ever made love. Peggy remembers their relationship heating up after the Monterey Pop Festival in June 1967. That summer when Big Brother finished some gigs in Los Angeles, Janis called Peggy from the airport to pick her up. "I can't," Peggy said, "I'm working." Janis complained, "You're always working. I want to get away." Proposing that she go alone to Peggy's Stinson Beach cabin, Janis stopped by the store for the keys. She hadn't been gone long when Peggy got a call from a neighbor near the cabin. "Man, you've got some friends!" he said. "That singer Janis Joplin is out here and no sooner did she pull up in the driveway than she yelled to me, 'Hi ya, fella, you got a local bar?' I told her about the Sand Dollar and I don't think she even went in your house. She went down to the Sand Dollar and got shit-faced, and then came back."

Janis kept after Peggy to join her, and Peggy finally relented. "We definitely had a little sexual something during that stay," Peggy says. "We undressed and played on the sundeck. I don't think we had wild, passionate sex, but we rubbed suntan lotion on each other and had an erotic day, kissed. And then I had to go back to work." Peggy can't remember where they first made love. "I know some people say, 'How could you possibly forget where you were the first time you made love to Janis Joplin? How could you forget that?' But God, we teased each other to death for months. We were like teenagers. We did everything but fuck. It was just like *Happy Days* in the fifties, where you parked and smooched until you were so hot you were about to explode." Looking back, Peggy believes that shyness kept them from going all the way. She was also in love with Kim and felt anxious about measuring up to Janis's expectations of her as an experienced lover, a largely self-imposed burden, she admits. "Maybe I thought I couldn't be as good as Janis thought I was going to be or as good as she thought a lesbian would be." She had no idea, however, that Janis had already slept with women. For whatever reason, Janis allowed Peggy to imagine she was "bringing out" a straight girl. Maybe she'd realized that straight Haight-Ashbury wasn't North Beach when it came to gay sex.

Janis was testing the limits of sexuality much as the rest of Haight-Ashbury was experimenting with new forms of partnerships and community—the large extended "families" and the turn away from monogamy, for example. Much about the Haight—the sex, the communes, and especially the rock 'n' roll—was makeshift. The bands, like the sexual liaisons and the big familial tribes, were often accidental, the result of chance meetings and shared moments of stoned-out bliss. Nevertheless, there was a method to the seeming randomness of Bay Area bands. As influenced as they were by the blues, Dylan, and the British Invasion, San Francisco bands were not trying to replicate a particular sound. For better or for worse, they were committed to eclecticism and experimentation, drawing on everything from free-form jazz and jug band music to Indian ragas. Sam Andrew recalls that in Big Brother, "what everybody wanted to do . . . was play real hard and fast for a long time and then whatever came out of that improvisation you'd work on."

Everyone was making it up as they went along, the musicians as well as their managers. Bands were often managed by friends or self-made impresarios and rarely had roadies or the money to pay for adequate transportation. When Big Brother played at the Vancouver Trips Festival in the summer of 1966, they had only enough money to fly to Seattle; Janis and the guys got off the plane, walked to the freeway, and hitchhiked to Vancouver with all their equipment in tow. "Janis carried a bunch of drums and I had a guitar and amplifiers," James Gurley recalls. Even after the success of Monterey Pop, "Janis would carry the bloody amps and the microphones," claims John Morris, one of Bill Graham's men. They were working a "frontier," he says.

The makeshift quality of the scene owed something, of course, to all the drugs. In those days, when being high was the great signifier of hipness, getting stoned was obligatory. Drugs helped alleviate stage fright as well. Although the musicians were part of a subculture that trumpeted the superiority of marijuana and psychedelics over booze ("the straight drug"), Darby Slick notes that many musicians continued to use alcohol "for its nerve-calming properties." Like Janis, Grace Slick carried around a little brown bag, only hers contained champagne rather than Janis's trademark Southern Comfort. Janis dubbed Big Brother an "alcydelic" band, and not just because of her own well-known penchant for alcohol. James Gurley claims everyone in the band "needed a couple of shots" of hard liquor before performing. "I had so much stage fright, in order to get onstage I had to get drunk." John Morris claims that when Big Brother debuted in New York at the Anderson Theater, he went out and bought the band "seven fifths and one pint of Southern Comfort," cleaning out the local liquor store. "Now there were, what, five people in that band? That's a lot of bloody whiskey in about a three-hour period."

The bands were high on something—anything—when they played, and so were the people who came to dance at the new ballrooms. Chet Helms's partner, Bob Cohen, who handled the sound at the Avalon, sometimes listens to old tapes of the shows he mixed. He loved the music at the time, but now he hears a lot of "out-of-key musicians and out-of-tune instruments," he admits. "But if you get stoned and turn the volume up, it sounds great," he adds. Ray Riepen, the owner of Boston's first electric ballroom, says, "I could've had two zithers down there as long as I had an overhead projector and a strobe light. They didn't care; they didn't know! It all sounds perfect if you've got five hundred mikes [micrograms of LSD] under your belt." According to Chet Helms, people didn't necessarily come to see the bands. "They came for the ambience, and the bands were a part of it. In the first year the band's name was of no great significance." More than just dances, the shows at the Avalon were a form of environmental theater, complete with light, sound, and music. In contrast to Bill Graham's Fillmore, where the audience was treated to a "high order of entertainment," according to Chet, the Avalon was about re-creation, nothing less than re-creating oneself through a "transformative and empowering experience."

Bob Simmons also worked at the Avalon. "The half-a-tab influence made a lot of things translate into way-out-of-hand peak experiences that I will never forget or say were not positive," he insists. "There really is such a thing as group ecstasy on a spiritual level and the cynicism of age and distance does not alter my memory of those moments. There were times when I was absolutely certain the floor of the Avalon was floating in a different dimension." But unlike Chet, he emphasizes the centrality of the music. "The audience was there for the music alone and their love of the bands, not for the cheesy 'multimedia' presentation and a place to have a trippy experience. The light shows were a wonderful idea, which sadly is what most of them remained, an idea that never went beyond squishing a few colors around on glass dishes on overhead projectors, interspersed with badly made experimental films." By the summer of 1968, no one would argue that the people flocking to the ballrooms were coming for the music. A year later, when the city's five hundred light-show artists went on strike for higher wages, Bill Graham simply canceled his light show, and his gate was unaffected; people continued to stand in line for blocks, waiting to get into his theater.

But even then, the audience had not yet deified the musicians. "The music was the thing, not the musicians," says Jim Haynie, who managed the Fillmore for Graham. "You knew the band and you dug the sound and you might even know some guys' names and stuff. But it wasn't like everybody was dying to meet them. You were going to hear the music." In fact, at this point, the audience could barely see the musicians. "There were no stage lights on the performers," according to Haynie. "We had one 750-watt ellipsoidal on the balcony that never moved and was one hundred feet away or something. It was *very* dim. All the light was from the light show spilling onto the stage." Most musicians preferred to be shrouded in darkness. "You didn't want spotlights," says Bill Belmont, the road manager of Country Joe and the Fish. "Some bands refused to allow spotlights. I think we specified in our rider for a long time that no spotlights be used."

San Francisco bands preferred light shows to bright lights because they were unwilling or unable to provide any visual stimulation. "The musicians barely did anything," according to Joshua White, a New York light-show artist. "They just played, and often with their backs to the audience. They would tune and tune and tune between songs. No one wanted to do a slick show. Anyone who did a really tight show in that very modest period of time—about two years—was considered slick and not authentic." Janis managed to be simultaneously dynamic and authentic, but she was anomalous. Indeed, for five years the Jefferson Airplane paid a light-show artist, Glenn McKay, 10 percent of their gross—a very substantial amount of money—because he "took the heat off" the band. "They made great music, but their stage presence often sucked," he says. "And when it didn't suck, Gracie was drunk and giving the kids a bunch of shit: 'I got here in a limousine, how'd you get here?' But mostly the band didn't relate to the audience. So they figured I was worth every dime of it because sometimes they'd get away with a stinky concert because I did a good light show." Bob Simmons claims the light shows served another purpose as well. "The light shows allowed the auditorium to remain dark so you couldn't see how dirty it was."

The backstage was invariably just as shabby as the rest of the hall. "You were lucky if they brought in Cokes for the band," says Lyndall Erb, one of Janis's friends. Even in 1968, when Bill Belmont began road-managing Country Joe and the Fish, he claims there was still no such thing as a dressing-room scene. "There were these funny, ugly rooms that had a terrible overstuffed couch that was falling apart and a garbage can with some Cokes and beer in it. You'd only stay in there if some groupie was harassing you and you didn't want to see her." The distance between audience and performer was minimal. In fact, pulling the musicians off the dance floor and getting them onstage could be tough. The scene was primitive and funky, with none of the big money and glitz that would soon come to characterize rock 'n' roll.

Which is not to say that the San Francisco rock world was an Edenic community of equals beyond the reach of commerce. The musicians might have mixed with the audience, but they were still set off by an undeniable aura of superior hipness. Nor were they indifferent to money. Paul Kantner of the Jefferson Airplane got into rock 'n' roll because, he says, "some of my friends were making five thousand a night as the Byrds." None of the bands—not even the Dead, whose scraggly, scowling keyboardist, Pigpen, was always scaring off record companies—was opposed to making money. The bands wanted high-paying gigs and lucrative recording contracts, but they didn't want to go the show-business route. Show business—its crassness, insincerity, and indifference to the artistic—was the enemy. San Francisco musicians weren't going to churn out two-and-a-half-minute bubblegum hits to please record companies and radio programmers; nor were they going to tone down their style so they could appear on *American Bandstand* or be featured in *Sixteen* magazine. They were auteurs, not crowd-pleasing entertainers. When Bill

Graham suggested that the Airplane go back onstage and give a bow after a spectacular three-hour performance, Paul Kantner snarled, "Fuck that. That's show business."

By the summer of 1966, all the leading San Francisco bands had record contracts, except Big Brother. The Airplane even had a record out. The only record company that had shown any interest in signing Big Brother, however, was Mainstream Records, based in New York. Bob Shad, the owner of the tiny label, had traveled to San Francisco to sign up some new bands—cheaply. During Big Brother's audition, he suggested to Chet Helms, still its manager, that they conspire to "lock this band down totally" with a lousy contract. Outraged, Chet declared the audition over before the band even had a chance to speak with Shad. Although Chet was acting in Big Brother's best interests, the band wasn't so sure. Worried that Chet had bungled the deal and convinced that he was too preoccupied with the Avalon to manage them effectively, the band fired him. Big Brother was just about to leave town for a four-week gig in Chicago when another offer came in. There was one problem: the offer was for Janis alone. Paul Rothchild, an artist and repertoire man for Elektra Records, had heard the band perform in Los Angeles, and now he approached Janis about joining a blues group that included Taj Mahal and Stefan Grossman. Rothchild promised that Elektra would rent a house for the group in L.A. and fund them until they were ready to record. Most important, he promised that the company would promote the hell out of the record. Janis was flattered and not only met with the group but seriously considered leaving Big Brother. After all, Elektra was an established folk label moving aggressively into rock and Rothchild was a hip guy who produced the much-admired Paul Butterfield Blues Band.

Janis wrote her parents an excited letter telling them about Rothchild's pitch and her ambivalent reaction. Rothchild had apparently warned her that rock 'n' roll might not last—an ironic prophecy, given his future role as the Doors' producer. Certainly, he said, rock music couldn't just continue growing "farther and farther out," a not-too-subtle dig at Big Brother, a band that was nothing if not far out. Janis was tempted by the prospect of singing the blues—her real love—with skilled musicians on a strong label. She wondered whether the guys in Big Brother really wanted to put in the hard work necessary to become a successful band. She worried, however, about letting her band mates down, and indeed they felt betrayed when she told them of Rothchild's offer. How could she ditch them just as Big Brother was beginning to come together?

Worse still, Janis kept raving, "He's gonna make me a star!" She was especially impressed by Rothchild's promise that if she signed on now she'd soon own a "Cadillac and a house in the Hollywood hills." The guys were all in shock, but it was Peter who finally locked horns with her. He couldn't believe that someone as avowedly alternative as Janis could be so easily seduced by the most vulgar aspects of the American Dream. He had assumed they'd all turned their backs on that bankrupt idea. "I felt I had to defend our whole lifestyle against this crass commercialism. I may have even used the word *family*." Being chastised as a sellout only provoked what Sam Andrew calls Janis's "schoolmarmish quality." It was like "Aunt Polly scolding Tom Sawyer." Peter put his foot down, though, and warned Janis that if she signed with Elektra she couldn't come to Chicago with Big Brother; they'd find another singer. "You're out!" he yelled. The whole time, Peter says, he was thinking to himself, "This woman with this pockmarked face and scraggly hair can't possibly make it on her own." In the end, Janis agreed to put off her decision until after Chicago, but the whole incident caused considerable strife within Big Brother.

Chicago was an unmitigated disaster. The band had no place to stay or even to crash. Motel clerks took one look at the scruffy group, with their long hair and equipment, and turned them away. "We were pretty damned scared," Dave remembers. "People were eyeing us like they were going to beat us up. White working-class people called us names on the streets. All the time, every day." Nick Gravenites, a North Beach folkie who had returned to his native Chicago, recognized some of the band members on the street. When he tried flagging them down, though, they were so nervous they almost turned on their heels and ran, thinking he wanted to beat them up. The musicians were finally saved from the streets by Peter's aunt and uncle, who agreed to put them up at their house in the suburbs and lend them a car to get to their gig and back.

Inside Mother Blues, an Old Town folk club gone rock, the crowds weren't much friendlier than the people on the streets. Audiences were mystified by Big Brother's look and sound, which was far too weird for Chicago in 1966. No one in the city looked even remotely like San

Francisco hippies. Janis had been excited about playing in the world's blues capital, but she clearly hadn't realized how strange Big Brother's blues would sound to those accustomed to hearing the genuine article. Chicago's own Butterfield Band, which at first played very straight-ahead electric blues, had also encountered resistance from blues purists like the musicologist Alan Lomax, whose idea of a bluesman was a "poor black farmhand," not some smart-ass white kids with amps. A few younger blues players stopped in to hear Big Brother. "Most of the hard-core blues people who came by would look and just shake their heads," recalls Dave. "To them it was like we were murdering the form." Even the Butterfield Band, which over time became more experimental, had little use for the San Francisco sound. Butterfield's Michael Bloomfield hated Big Brother, recalls Peter. "He always had a grudge that these white kids from San Francisco couldn't play their instruments yet were making more money than him." Similarly, white Chicago blues player Steve Miller griped that the Dead "could barely play 'In the Midnight Hour,' and they'd play it for forty-five minutes."

But Big Brother wasn't trying to produce faithful renditions of blues classics—quite the opposite. "We didn't want to imitate Erma Franklin, for example," contends Peter. "We Big Brotherized her song 'Piece of My Heart.' And we changed Big Mama Thornton's 'Ball and Chain' to a minor-key blues. We used the slash-and-burn method of arranging. The chainsaw method." Sam Andrew attributes the group's slash-and-burn style to their inexperience: "We didn't have a choice. Given our talents and capabilities that was the only thing we could do. Erma's 'Piece of My Heart' had a delicacy and a sense of mystery that was just beyond us." To purists, though, their music was a "full frontal assault" on the blues itself. Peter says, "We tried to do some of that blues stuff, like Howlin' Wolf's 'Moanin' Midnight.' Of course they were laughing at me because down the street was the real thing." Big Brother was "just too freaky," according to Nick Gravenites, who hung out with the Butterfield Band. "This chick had this hair hanging down and she was dressed in this *bedspread*! And the jewelry! Chicken bones! Voodoo shit! And this patchouli perfume, *reeking*! Her complexion was a wipe-out. She had this sore throat and was screeching like a wounded owl! I didn't really like the sound, but I was impressed. They were aliens and they were sticking it out!" Dave Getz remembers everyone in the band feeling "kind of intimidated" by the negative attention. At the same time, however, Dave felt a certain confidence. "We had our own thing and we also knew that the context out of which we developed was going to get to Chicago."

The band was committed to a month-long gig at Mother Blues, but after their first two weeks they were staring out at empty seats. Janis complained that the club owner was ripping them off, but he was in a pinch. He'd given the band a thousand dollars for the first two weeks; without any gate, however, he couldn't afford to continue paying them. Peter tried to enlist the musicians union to extract their payment but failed, and the band had no choice but to develop a stage show to attract customers. They hired a go-go dancer and named her Miss Proton, the Psychedelic Girl. She wore spray-painted and glittered leotards and a Saran Wrap hat. Janis later told an interviewer she cracked up trying to sing with "this half-naked chick dancing right there in front of me." Psychedelic go-go girls notwithstanding, Big Brother was flopping in Chicago.

The band was broke and stranded when Bob Shad approached them once again about signing with Mainstream. He told them Chet had wanted to take advantage of them by doing all the recording at the Avalon and then charging the band for use of the ballroom. Peter doubts this was true. "Shad told us stuff that would make us mad at Chet, that would get us to sign with him out of spite." The band had other reasons for signing, though. "The Airplane had made a record and the Dead had signed," recalls Dave. "It occurred to us," Peter adds, "that we could lock Janis in by signing this deal." As it turns out, Chet had been right to mistrust Shad. Sam later described him as "the master of rather sharp business practices," although, in truth, he was no worse than most owners of small independent record labels. Shad gave Big Brother the standard contract—a five-year exclusive deal with 5 percent royalties and song copyright held by the record company. It was a contract they would all regret soon enough.

Big Brother began recording its first album while still in Chicago, cutting four songs in one nine-hour session. They completed the record in Los Angeles later that fall. Sam recalls the recording process going smoothly; the band was still playing five or six sets a night at Mother Blues and had "ample opportunity to polish that rough Big Brother sound."

Shad, however, was more interested in recording radio-friendly product than in capturing the band's sound, its shrieking, extended guitar jams. He forced the band to shorten its songs, and his engineer, wary of distortion, refused to let the peak meters slip into the red during the recording. The engineer "was afraid of the needle going into the red," says Sam, "and that is where we wanted the needle to be all the time." The band was frustrated, fearing the record would be a tinny-sounding, toothless rendering of their distortion-heavy acid rock. Shad was no perfectionist either, limiting Big Brother to twelve takes a song. "If we didn't get it right, we'd choose one of the twelve takes, and that was it," Peter says. Everyone was pleased, though, with Janis's double-tracked vocals, especially Shad, who told her she was the most marketable part of the group. During the Chicago sessions, however, Janis most often sang backup; a month later, in L.A., she was featured on all six cuts.

Shad assured the band he would release their first single in a month or two. Janis was thrilled. In a letter home, she proudly announced that Big Brother would be making fifteen hundred dollars for an upcoming two-week gig in Canada. But what if the record was a hit? she worried. Then they'd be stars and the fifteen hundred dollars would seem downright measly. Janis needn't have worried: their first 45 release, "Blindman," received no airplay at all. The song had a generic folk rock sound, with vocal harmonizing very much like the Mamas and the Papas', but Peter's lead vocal left a lot to be desired. B-side songs rarely generated any chart action and Shad chose the unusual three-part harmony "All Is Loneliness," written by a blind New York street musician who called himself Moondog. Between May 1967 and February 1968, Mainstream would release four more singles by the band, but none of them registered so much as a blip on the national charts. Shad didn't release the album until after Monterey Pop made Janis famous. The band never made a dime from it, however, and the contract cost them dearly when they later signed with Columbia. Janis's ambivalence about staying in the band and the guys' eagerness to tie her down had long-term consequences for Big Brother. Had Rothchild not tempted Janis, the band might have held out for a better contract with a more established company. In retrospect, the Mainstream fiasco was the earliest sign of strains that would come to haunt Big Brother.

Shad didn't pay advances and had only given each band member a hundred dollars for the recording session. Too broke to fly home, the group (minus Peter, whose relatives paid for a plane ticket) crammed themselves and all their equipment into a borrowed car and headed for San Francisco, crossing parts of the country where long hair on men was nothing short of treasonous. San Francisco bands tended to stick pretty close to home; venturing beyond the Bay Area was a dangerous proposition. The band members were often the first long-haired freaky people locals had ever seen, and they risked harassment and even beatings when they hit the road. The offenses could be as trivial as wearing sandals without socks. Country Joe and the Fish were always being forced to wear socks with their sandals. The Fish's David Cohen was once thrown off a plane because he wasn't wearing socks.

On their way home, Janis and the guys were stopped by a highway patrolman who ordered them to drive into town, ostensibly because Sam's license had expired. As the police in town searched the car, they kept taunting Sam, James, and Dave. "Are you guys or girls?" they asked. Janis wasn't having any of it and simply yelled, "Fuck you, man." Dave recalls that "she was ready to get into a fight with them. The rest of us knew that if we answered back and took the bait . . . they would throw us into jail. Janis could be very dangerous in that way—she'd get into it with the wrong people and not have any sense of the danger or that she was always endangering the people around her." Dave shouted at Janis to shut up, and they got away with paying a fifty-dollar fine, leaving them barely enough money to get home.

Janis still had to break the news to Paul Rothchild of Elektra that she wouldn't be relocating to L.A. In the end, she told him she'd fallen in love with one of the guys in Big Brother and had decided to stay put. True, she was infatuated with James, but that wasn't really her motive. Janis was committed to the Mainstream record deal. Moreover, she had finally found a group—a family—that accepted her, and she loved the Haight scene, whereas L.A., despite its considerable allure, was an unknown. Big Brother had resolved, at least temporarily, the conflict between career and family that dogged Janis. In Big Brother, family and career were, in a way, one and the same. The band was now her "whole life," as she wrote her mother. "It did start to occur to me," says Peggy Caserta, "that Janis seemed to have a remarkable centeredness about things like getting to band practice on time." It could be a downpour, she says, but when it was time to rehearse, Janis would climb into her dilapidated Sunbeam convertible, with its torn top, and drive there. Dave thinks Janis realized at this point that she was the strongest part of Big Brother and that she would have faced a lot of competition in Rothchild's group. Taj Mahal and the other musicians were more accomplished than Janis; had she accepted Rothchild's offer she would most likely have been "relegated to a very conventional role," in Sam's view, "and not allowed to develop." In Big Brother, by contrast, she was able to step forward. "We didn't know enough to tell anybody what to do," Sam says. "In that way, she was really lucky to find us."

Even at this early stage, though, the Big Brother family was not a family of equals. During the band's first year together, Janis's growing power was held in check by the way the local press treated Big Brother as a group rather than as Janis Joplin's backup band. Journalists were used to covering the new British groups that way—the John-Paul-George-Ringo model. Moreover, the democratic ethos of Haight-Ashbury militated against any "star trips." When the band appeared on a local TV station, KQED, six weeks before Monterey Pop, Janis sang lead on only about a third of their songs, and she stood to the side rather than centerstage. Nonetheless, the balance of power within the band was shifting. Since the beginning of 1966, when the group came together, James had been the unacknowledged star, but Janis was displacing him and his guitar. Janis was also beginning to challenge Peter's position as group leader. Peter was accustomed to handling both the stage patter and day-to-day business matters, and he was entitled to an additional 20 percent of the group's earnings because he signed their union contracts. When Janis caught wind of this, she called a group meeting. She felt she was doing more for the band than anyone else, she said, and should therefore be the one signing the contracts. Stunned, Peter explained that he'd never taken an extra penny. In Big Brother, he lectured her, "we share everything." In time, Janis came to embrace the egalitarian ethic, forcing workers to change theater marquees when her name was singled out from Big Brother's, but it wasn't easy for her. Janis was hungry for the attention coming her way.

Sharing "everything" posed other kinds of problems for the band, nowhere more so than in their little Lagunitas house, where living together was getting to be a drag. There were the inevitable clashes over standards of cleanliness and tidiness and over late-night noise. "I always wanted to go to bed early," recalls Peter. "I'd say, 'My daughter's not even a year old, come on.' And they'd say, 'What do you mean you want to go to bed? It's only ten o'clock!'" James and Nancy had a German shepherd they seemed ideologically opposed to disciplining, with the result that the dog ran the show. "It would shit everywhere," says Peter. For Janis, living among couples was also an unpleasant reminder of her single status. When the lease ran out in January 1967, the band decided to move back to the Haight. Janis got a place near Mnasidika on Ashbury Street; a few months later she moved to Cole Street, also in the Haight.

Big Brother had been away only six months, but by the time they came back to Haight-Ashbury it was no longer an insider's secret. The streets now felt crowded, in large measure because the new bohemians made a lavish display of their strangeness. The Love Pageant, a celebration of psychedelic life, had taken place on October 6, 1966, the day LSD was made illegal in California. Then in January 1967, the Human Be-In confirmed San Francisco's position as the capital of weirdness. An effort to unite Berkeley radicals and Haight-Ashbury hippies, the Be-In drew anywhere from ten to twenty thousand people and countless reporters. Speakers included Allen Ginsberg, who chanted; Lenore Kandel, who read from her recently censored poems, *The Love Book;* Timothy Leary; and Jerry Rubin, a Berkeley politico at that point. Although the poster advertising the Be-In listed "All San Francisco Bands," Big Brother didn't play that day. The acid, though, was ubiquitous, because Owsley made sure it was. Linda Gravenites, who was living at the Dead's house, recalls Owsley's showing up there the morning of the Be-In with a "giant restaurant mayonnaise jar filled with teeny, tiny White Lightning pills. They were all gone by the end of the day." For reporters, one of the big stories was the peaceful commingling of Hell's Angels and hippies. They were amazed when the Angels offered to guard the power cable, which had earlier been cut.

For Linda Gravenites, January's Be-In marked a watershed, the moment when the Haight turned from a spontaneous expression of the counterculture to a hyped-up caricature. Most people mark that moment later, pointing to the Summer of Love in 1967, when thousands of lost kids descended on Haight-Ashbury. But the Be-In drew the press, which by focusing exclusively on sex, drugs, and rock 'n' roll, says Gravenites, pretty much determined what the nature of the Haight would be. "Up until then, people came because they were full to overflowing and were sharing their fullness," she adds. "After that, it was the empties who came, wanting to be filled." From the outset, though, it was evident that this paradise was going to leave some wicked scars. The Haight's "renegades, outlaws, misfits, and dropouts," as Bob Seidemann calls them, made for a volatile brew. "A cauldron," he says, "that's what this society was." More-over, the Haight was an interracial neighborhood and tension escalated as it filled up with middle-class young white kids renouncing the nice homes, good schools, and well-paying jobs that remained out of the reach of most blacks. Of course, drugs added to the destabilization. Hippies defended marijuana and psychedelics as mind-expanding "life" drugs, but mind-numbing "death" drugs, such as heroin, speed, and barbiturates, were around the Haight, too, and LSD was usually cut with speed. In fact, one reason good relations often obtained between Hell's Angels and hip-pies was that the bikers were an important drug connection, especially for speed.

Ken Kesey had inaugurated the relationship between the freaks and the Angels, perhaps in an effort to demonstrate the transformative power of acid or maybe just to out-hip everyone else. ("We're in the same busi-ness," Kesey told the Angels. "You break people's bones, I break people's heads.") In any case, relations grew a lot cozier between freaks and Angels in Haight-Ashbury, with the Dead and Big Brother leading the way. Janis insisted that the cover of Big Brother's 1968 album, *Cheap Thrills*, bear the Angels' emblem and the words "Approved by Hell's Angels Frisco." Janis went further than most when she hooked up with the Angels' infa-mous Freewheelin' Frank. Richard Hundgen of the Big Brother family claims the Angels were always dropping by Janis's place. "She could han-dle them. She played pool with them, challenging them to games, and they'd play for drinks and get totally fucked up." Of course Janis could handle them: compared to the types she'd met in Louisiana, the Angels probably seemed no big deal.

Some people in the Haight, like Jack Jackson, Janis's friend from

Austin, felt uncomfortable with the Angels' presence. "Janis and others thought that the Angels were part of the whole crowd, but they weren't," says Jackson. "They had a lot of hair, but they were the type of people we left Texas to get away from." The Angels might drop acid, moreover, but the counterculture's faith that LSD would transform them into cuddly teddy bears was, more often than not, misplaced. Jackson recalls "biker guys taking acid and smashing heads. It was like climbing in bed with Hitler." But at the time, people with concerns about the Angels were reluctant to voice them for fear of being branded uptight and uncool. The pressure to be cool always made it hard to know what to do with creeps, especially the Angels, who had the support of some of the leading lights of the Haight. One defense mounted on the Angels' behalf was that the real villain was large-scale, state-sponsored terror. The poet Michael McClure, for example, argued that President Lyndon Johnson was more evil than a bunch of guys on bikes who expressed the violence that most of us would rather deny. McClure and the Diggers Peter Coyote and Emmett Grogan hung out with the Angels and maintained that the bikers had to be judged individually, not as a group. Yet the Angels, whatever their individual talents, acted as a group. People were killed, women raped, girlfriends dumped, and goods stolen, all on orders of the club. "I can only believe it was the fascination the weak feel for the strong," suggests Bob Brown, another transplanted Austinite. "Maybe there was some sense that the Establishment had their cops, their thugs, and now we had ours." Except that the Angels behaved like thugs with just about everyone, hippies included. Bruce Barthol of Country Joe and the Fish remembers appearing at an outdoor event in Santa Clara where the Angels handled security. "Their method of clearing the stage was to push people off it. One guy took a bottle and smashed a girl's head with it." Defended as outlaws, the Angels were, in fact, quite conservative. Nowhere was this more pronounced than in their attitude toward women.

Sexism was pervasive in the Haight, a fact that helped the Angels' image as groovy guys. That period between 1960 and 1970, after the Pill was introduced and before feminism took off, afforded young men a window of opportunity. Carl Gottlieb, an actor and writer with the Committee, knows men who to this day are nostalgic for this time, when women were sexually available but not yet politically assertive as feminists. For women, the so-called sexual revolution was a mixed blessing. Women were having more sex (and with less guilt), but they were also more sexually vulnerable. Instead of undoing the deeply rooted sexual double standard, free love only masked it in countercultural pieties. Nor did hippie households pioneer an alternative to the traditional division of labor. Although many hippie guys managed to avoid nine-to-five jobs, few hippie females avoided housework. Baking, cooking, sewing, tending the children were a "women's thing." As Bob Seidemann points out, relations between men and women in the Haight were "old-timey," like the furniture. "The hippie ethos was a cartoon image of a woman making an apple pie and setting it on the windowsill while Dad, having toiled in the marijuana fields for the noble quest of selling pot, carefully folds it in plastic Baggies."

To Joan Didion, all the talk in the Haight about "the woman's trip"—her supposedly unique talent as housekeeper, mother, and all-purpose caretaker—seemed like nothing so much as Betty Friedan's "feminine mystique"; the sense of emancipation hippie women professed demonstrated people's ability "to be the unconscious instruments of values they would strenuously reject on a conscious level." In truth, most people in the Haight—women included—wouldn't have rejected sexism even had they been aware of its presence in their lives. When Travis Rivers, the manager of Haight-Ashbury's psychedelic newspaper the *Oracle*, proposed to his staff that the paper organize a roundtable discussion on women's issues with Margo St. James, a hip activist sex worker; the poet Lenore Kandel; and Janis, "there ensued a huge fight and virtually the entire staff quit." Travis was so angry he decided to stop publishing the paper, he says. "The vast majority of women in that scene were subordinate to men," Seidemann admits, but they seemed more than happy to be that way. "The women all wanted children real bad. Get pregnant, have the kid, and hit the welfare office." The women of the Haight were having sex with lots of different men and living in alternative families, but they were still expected—and many of them still wanted to be—pregnant and dependent. In this respect, the Haight was no less problematic than the straight world for a woman like Janis, who wasn't interested in "the woman's trip" and did not have an old man to call her own.

Years later the band reminisced fondly about the days before Monterey

Pop. To James Gurley, the best times were when Big Brother was a struggling band, lugging their equipment to gigs that paid them only $250. "That's when we were all together," he says. "We were united in our quest." But it is not at all clear that the band members ever shared a common quest. James, Sam, Dave, and Peter had been a freak rock band with dubious commercial potential when Janis joined them. They were not especially concerned with their market value at first, but it preoccupied Janis, whose letters home reveal a pragmatism and savvy at odds with her persona as a beatnik girl who just fell into singing. In these letters, Janis worries about what kind of music she should sing, but on strategic rather than aesthetic grounds. Would rock or blues prove more marketable? she wondered. She writes of wanting a gold lamé outfit that will look "real show biz," not like the street clothes she and everyone else wear onstage. Of course, much of what she wrote home was for her parents' sake. After all, when she finally told her parents she'd be staying in San Francisco rather than returning to Port Arthur, she made the preposterous claim that she missed her former life as a Lamar student living at home with them.

But Janis's talk of commercial viability wasn't mere pretense. Within the year she'd have that gold lamé getup. She wasn't just looking for an excuse to have a party; for her, music was about making it. This put her somewhat at odds with the guys in Big Brother, who didn't sneer at ambition but were more committed to collective endeavor, perhaps by necessity, than she was. With the possible exception of James Gurley, the other band members could have done something else with their lives, but Janis felt she had found the *one* thing she was good at, and she wasn't going to give it up. Commercial success seemed to offer vindication for past humiliations. She boasted to her parents about being a "celebrity" and an "important personage" in the Haight. Of course, being a celebrity in Haight-Ashbury was enormously gratifying, but it was nothing like the fame awaiting her. Everything would change in the wake of Monterey Pop.

6

Hope and Hype
in Monterey

Monterey is very groovy, man," yelled an obviously stoned Michael Bloomfield from the stage. "This is our generation, man. All you people, man, all together, man, it's groovy. Dig yourselves 'coz it's *really* groovy. . . . We love you all, man." Bloomfield's giddy Love Generation rhapsody echoed the feelings of the fifty-five to ninety thousand people who attended the Monterey International Pop Festival the weekend of June 16, 1967. The three-day outdoor festival felt like one big contact high. "Hippie heaven," declared *Newsweek*. More discerning was the music critic Robert Christgau, one of twelve hundred journalists covering the festival. "There are no hippies—they have disappeared in an avalanche of copy."

The hype notwithstanding, everyone remembers Monterey Pop as the cool, laid-back festival where musicians (even stars like Brian Jones of the Rolling Stones) mingled with the hoi polloi. "You could get food," recalled Grace Slick of the Airplane.

"You could go to the bathroom. People could see things. It wasn't too big. When it was over and you wanted to go home, you could just get in your car and *drive* there." Woodstock would grab all the headlines two years later, but Monterey was a landmark, the festival that signaled that what was happening on the streets of Haight-Ashbury was going national. America was turning. "Everywhere you looked beautiful people were in the majority," enthused the *Barb*, Berkeley's underground newspaper, in its report on Monterey. Otis Redding marveled at the scene. "Oh, these fucking hippies, man. They're smoking dope and shit like it's *legal* out here. See, *everybody's* high." For Redding and many others, the scene at Monterey looked like nothing short of a "cultural revolution."

The festival was the brainchild of Ben Shapiro, a booking agent "on the far fringes" of the counterculture. Inspired by San Francisco's Human Be-In, Shapiro and his partner, Alan Pariser, decided to organize a "music mart" showcasing the new, "serious" rock 'n' roll. They booked the Monterey County Fairgrounds, eighty miles south of San Francisco, and in a savvy move, they retained as their publicist Derek Taylor, the Beatles' former press agent. Shapiro and Pariser ended up joining forces with John Phillips of the Mamas and the Papas and their producer, Lou Adler, an L.A. music mogul. Phillips, an ex-folkie, convinced Shapiro the event should be an artist-run nonprofit festival like the famous Newport Folk Festival. Adler and Phillips had considerably more clout and chutzpah than Shapiro, and once onboard they took over the festival's planning and eventually bought him out. In no time, Adler managed to convince ABC-TV to film the event (for a hefty $400,000 fee) and lined up a number of leading L.A. groups—the Beach Boys, the Byrds, the Buffalo Springfield, and Phillips's own Mamas and Papas—even though musicians were only being paid expenses.

But Adler and Phillips had no clout among the musicians of the Haight, who considered them plastic hippies. Almost immediately, the two ran up against northern Californians' long-standing antipathy toward their southern neighbors. "L.A. hurts our eyes," sneered a member of Quicksilver Messenger Service. San Francisco's rock scene was parochial, chauvinistic, and automatically suspicious of anyone associated with Los Angeles, the hated capital of plastic. In the view of most Bay Area musicians, the festival organizers were just a bunch of "Hollywood sharpies" trying to "hijack and market the San Francisco sound" for their own profit. "We all resisted Monterey Pop because we felt it was kind of slicko L.A. hype," recalls Chet Helms. And once word hit the Haight of Adler's lucrative TV deal, musicians and their managers wondered why the bands weren't getting a piece of the action. This wasn't an easy sell for Derek Taylor, especially because the northern California groups were doing okay on their own. Before the end of 1966, they had garnered considerable press, with both *Newsweek* and *Time* weighing in with stories. And by the time of the festival, the Airplane's "Somebody to Love" was the number-three single in the nation. Chet Helms felt the festival organizers "were coattailing a bunch of L.A. acts on the success of what was happening in San Francisco." Although Adler and Phillips padded the bill with some of their musician friends, they also booked a number of acts—notably Otis Redding, the Who, and the Jimi Hendrix Experience—that weren't from any part of California.

San Franciscans had reason to worry, though. The organizers had already cashed in on the Haight scene with the dreadful Scott McKenzie tune "San Francisco (Be Sure to Wear Some Flowers in Your Hair)," penned by Phillips and released by Adler on Ode, his record label. Moreover, the Monterey brochure made clear that the festival was being plugged by association with the Haight. The audience was urged to "be happy, be free; wear flowers, bring bells." Or, as Christgau pointedly put it, "act like hippies, mingle with hippies, and hear hippie music." Then Derek Taylor tried drumming up support for the event by making vague promises about donating any profits to the Diggers, who he said would provide free food to the hungry hordes expected in Monterey. No one had contacted the Diggers, though, and Emmett Grogan and Peter Coyote denounced the organizers as "the scum of Hollywood." Monterey authorities were furious at the organizers, too, for encouraging mobs of hungry kids to descend on their town. To appease city officials, Adler and his cronies reversed themselves, promising that hippie organizations wouldn't see a penny of festival money—a flip-flop that confirmed San Franciscans' worst fears of them as unprincipled hustlers. In the end, though, San Francisco bands got over their loathing of L.A. and performed. Indeed, their music, their light shows, their groovy vibe—in short, the whole San Francisco scene—was what Monterey was all about.

Monterey is not remembered, however, for San Francisco's hippie bands like the Dead, the Airplane, or Big Brother. The stars of Monterey were Jimi Hendrix, the Who, Otis Redding, and Janis Joplin. Hendrix's otherworldly, acrobatic guitar playing (between his legs, behind his head, with his teeth) and the "vengeance" with which he "took back" and reworked the blues, as the Who's Pete Townshend put it, awed the audience. To Townshend, it felt almost as if Hendrix were telling white rockers, "You've taken this, Eric Clapton, and Mr. Townshend, you think you're a showman. This is how *we* do it . . . when we take back what you've borrowed, if not stolen." Few understood Hendrix's aggression the way Townshend did, but everyone responded nonetheless. Once relegated to the background in Little Richard's band, Hendrix dominated the stage at Monterey, playing with what the critic Nelson George called the "revenge of the R & B sideman." He even managed to "out-Visigoth" the stage-trashing Who, burning and smashing his guitar after humping both it and the amplifier.

With his charisma, dynamism, and intense, turbocharged vocals, Otis Redding succeeded in knocking out "the love crowd," as he called it. Redding had been wowing black audiences for years, but few besides Janis in Monterey's overwhelmingly white audience had ever seen him perform. Decked out in a snug blue suit, "Otis was king," the *Berkeley Barb* declared. One of the few African Americans to play the festival, Redding packed so much raw emotion into his singing that he went over with the crowd despite his tight, slick, soul revue act. By contrast, the nightclubbish routine of the twenty-year-old Laura Nyro (her first public performance) seemed weirdly affected and was so out of sync with Monterey's this-ain't-show-biz vibe that within the music industry "the phrase 'almost as bad as Laura Nyro' " became for a while "the definitive put-down for an inept performance."

And then there was Janis. Phillips and Adler hadn't expected much from Big Brother, whom they scheduled to appear on Saturday afternoon, distinctly non–prime time. Even the Dead, who were still pretty amateurish, had been given a coveted nighttime slot. Several other San Francisco bands were consigned to Saturday afternoon's program as well, which is why Chet Helms was appointed to emcee it. By the time of the festival, Big Brother had been playing together with Janis for exactly a year, but they were not yet one of the city's top draws. The Fillmore's Bill Graham hadn't started booking the band regularly; he didn't like Janis's singing and took offense when she told a tiny underground paper that his ballroom was for sailors and weekend hippies, while Chet's Avalon was the real thing. So the Monterey Festival was the band's first big unveiling and Janis was nervous. Peggy Caserta recalls a long-distance call from Janis, who yelled frantically into the receiver, "Peggy, I don't have a thing to wear!" She was barely exaggerating. Peggy suggested she wear her peace dress, a plain shift with peace symbols all over it that was popular in the Haight, but Janis appeared onstage that Saturday in jeans and a top. Janis was worried about more than her clothes, though. She was terrified of bombing, Peggy remembers. She told Janis to sing as if it were her only chance, which is precisely what she did.

Janis had appeared on a small side stage at the Monterey Folk Festival four years earlier, but Saturday she was center stage, facing her biggest crowd yet. "Janis was so nervous, it was crazy," recalls John Phillips. "But as soon as she hit the stage she just stomped her foot down and got real Texas." Janis ripped through the band's old standby, "Down on Me," and "Road Block," both fast-tempo numbers. Then she took her time with a haunting version of Willie Mae Thornton's "Ball and Chain," finally tearing down the house. By all accounts, the audience went berserk. "Where did she come from?" asked Lou Adler, stunned. Of the Bay Area performers, Janis was "the scene-stealer." The critics seemed to run out of superlatives; without a doubt, this was Janis's moment. Those who were hearing her for the first time were struck by the "terrible energy" she harnessed and "brutally compressed into the moment," as the rock critic Michael Lydon wrote, capturing the orgasmic quality of her performance. "In great shouts that send her strings of beads flying and knot her face into grimaces, the energy explodes and explodes again, sending out waves of electrical excitement." The jazz critic Nat Hentoff wrote similarly, claiming that, when Janis performed, "her voice and body hurled with larruping power" that left her "limp" and him feeling that he'd been "in contact with an overwhelming life force." Janis went so far out there when she sang that Greil Marcus, another critic, wondered how she ever managed to "get back." "Ball and Chain," in particular, always left Janis drained because, she explained, "it's about feeling things. . . . I can never sing it without really trying." Big Brother had totally overhauled the song. Now there was "this big hole in the song that's mine," Janis said, "and I've got to fill it with something."

And fill it she did, with all the pain and joy of her passion. "When I sing," she later told Michael Lydon, "I feel, oh, I feel, well, like when you're first in love. . . . I feel chills, weird feelings slipping all over my body, it's a supreme emotional and physical experience." You could see the "weird feelings" flashing across Janis's face, what Lydon called "the fierceness of joy breaking through anguish." More than Janis's irrepressible (and undeniably sexual) energy, more than her powerful voice, it was this quality of feeling that mesmerized audiences. In contrast to most other Monterey showstoppers, Janis "got a reaction based solely on her sweet tough self," said Robert Christgau. To Clive Davis of Columbia Records, Janis seemed "choked up at one point, laughing at another. . . . She seemed bursting with emotion; and it was so *pure.*" If Monterey's ultimate put-down was "plastic," then its highest compliment was "pure." Greil Marcus saw more contrivance than other critics did, but he considered it an asset: "By marshalling an array of blues and soul mannerisms, she contrives an act that in certain moments—and you can hear them coming—ceases to be any kind of act at all. The means of illusion produce the real." Janis always maintained there was no artifice in her singing. "It's real, it's not just a veneer, it's not just a performance," she said. Of course, she *was* giving a performance, but unlike the emotions many other singers summoned, Janis's seemed utterly unmediated, on the verge, even, of overtaking her.

Filmmaker D. A. Pennebaker was there with a crew that Saturday afternoon working on the TV documentary *Monterey Pop,* yet the only person caught on film as Janis sang was Cass Elliot of the Mamas and the Papas. Janis's killer performance was lost to posterity because Big Brother's new manager, Julius Karpen, had barred the producers from filming. Like several other Bay Area band managers, Karpen balked at signing a release form granting worldwide rights for use of the film "to the festival" without receiving some money in return. The band may have agreed with Karpen before their performance, but when Big Brother walked offstage they were sorry: the film was a rip-off, but they knew how hot they'd been; without doubt, they would have benefited in the long run. Backstage, Phillips accosted the band: he would let them perform again if they'd consent to being filmed. "Listen, you guys are blowin' it by not bein' in this movie," he counseled. But Karpen wouldn't budge. He was beginning to pose a problem for the band. A former Merry Prankster, Karpen was known as "Green Julius" because of his habit of conducting business while high. "He wouldn't do any business with anyone unless they got high with him on marijuana," Bob Seidemann claims. "So that put a real curb on his negotiating style." In fact, Big Brother only ended up with Karpen because Quicksilver's manager, Ron Polte, whom Peter Albin had asked to manage them, was too busy to take on another band and suggested his friend Karpen for the job. Unfortunately, Karpen knew next to nothing about the business, which may be why he approached every deal as a potential rip-off. Jim Haynie, who managed the Fillmore for Graham, heard that people were reluctant to do business with Karpen because of his paranoia. In any case, he was hurting the band.

Janis turned to the hippest, shrewdist manager of all, Albert Grossman, to advise the band. Albert was at Monterey to see two of the acts under his management—the Paul Butterfield Blues Band and Michael Bloomfield's new outfit, Electric Flag. He was also there to sign up promising new groups. Albert's major moneymaker, Bob Dylan, had been out of commission for almost a year since a motorcycle accident and showed no signs of returning to his hectic touring schedule. Albert was backstage with his wife, Sally, who remembers Janis as "totally frantic, screaming at Albert about what she needed." Janis and Albert "had a connection just like that," according to Sally Grossman, and he began to help her. He told Big Brother they'd be fools to hold out for film money, although he refused to let his own band, Electric Flag, take part in the documentary. Faced with a mutiny, Karpen relented and the organizers arranged a second slot for Big Brother on Sunday night. After her encounter with Grossman, Janis was heard saying, "Julius Karpen doesn't know it yet, but he has just lost Big Brother and the Holding Company."

When the band took the stage on Sunday night Janis was wearing a brand-new gold lamé pantsuit. "She pronounced it 'lame' to rhyme with 'fame' as in 'This outfit is really lame,'" recalls Sam Andrew. "We were mocking ourselves for grabbing at that brass ring, but we grabbed all the same." The band's second performance of "Ball and Chain" is captured in

Pennebaker's *Monterey Pop*, and it's hard to imagine their Saturday set had rocked any harder than this encore. The audience went wild once again. As Janis turned away from the crowd, she beamed, a little shyly, at all the adulation. With sweat dripping through the gold lamé, she was euphoric as she first trotted and then skipped offstage.

At Monterey Pop, it became clear that the real turn-on was Janis's raw, uncompromised presence. Janis wasn't conventionally pretty and didn't put on the usual kind of sexy show, but her performances would leave men, in particular, panting for her. Robert Christgau wasn't the only man to comment on her sexuality. The *L.A. Free Press* ran an article, "Big Brother's Boobs," in which the writer raved that Janis "makes it for me, like holy mojo lips caressing the dick of my soul." Richard Goldstein put it less crudely in the *Village Voice:* "To hear Janis sing 'Ball and Chain' just once is to have been laid, lovingly and well." Janis turned men on precisely because her emotional nakedness seemed almost obscene compared with the dolled-up, painted femininity of her time. And, of course, Janis was high-voltage, which many saw as a barometer of the ferocity she'd bring to any sexual encounter.

For Janis, Monterey was the ultimate vindication. The very thing that had gotten her into so much trouble back in Port Arthur—her inability to control her feelings, "to keep them down," as she said—now made her the darling of the counterculture. People everywhere were raving about the way she let all those powerful, unruly feelings take hold of her. She'd gotten that admiring reaction before, but usually in places like the funky Avalon. Several months after Monterey, Janis talked to Nat Hentoff about having grown up handicapped by her feelings. Her mother had always urged her to "be like everybody else," Janis said, but she just couldn't. "It nearly tore my life apart." Her openness to her feelings made her susceptible to "superhorrible downs," she went on. "I was always victim to myself. I'd do wrong things, run away, freak out, go crazy." Singing with Big Brother had changed that. "I've made feeling work for me, through music, instead of destroying me. It's superfortunate. Man, if it hadn't been for the music, I probably would have done myself in."

Jae Whitaker, Janis's ex-girlfriend, joined the band for dinner that Sunday night in Monterey and remembers Janis being extraordinarily happy. Janis described the festival as "one of the highest points in my life" and "the best time of all." The festival seemed to lend itself to all kinds of nostalgic reminiscences because the feeling of goodwill and "sanguine goofiness," as Christgau termed it, was so remarkable in the light of what followed. "Those were real flower children," said Janis of the audience. "They really were beautiful and gentle and completely open, man." Of the other musicians, her band mate Sam Andrew claims "there was truly an absence of any kind of competitiveness or stress." To Art Garfunkel, the magic of Monterey was that "it wasn't about money." Free of the ego tripping that would mar future rock extravaganzas, Monterey was nevertheless not quite the dawning of the Age of Aquarius: the festival of good vibes was also the site of fierce behind-the-scenes deal making. The machinations were intense as record companies practiced "check-book A&R," vying to sign new bands.

Nor were relations among the musicians always mellow. The Who and Jimi Hendrix fought over who would perform first. Hendrix, who had come back to the States from England to prove his guitar wizardry, struck fear in the hearts of all Monterey's wanna-be white-boy guitar heroes. Today, James Gurley admits that hearing Hendrix's astounding playing "made it real hard" for him. Sunshine was with James several nights after the festival, when Hendrix played the Fillmore, and couldn't help but notice the way "he sat there clenching and unclenching his fists." James was an inspired guitarist, but he never became an accomplished player. Instead he remained locked in his own style—a paralysis that had consequences for all Big Brother's musicians. Monterey Pop may have been a moment of reckoning for him, and Hendrix his excuse to stop growing.

Indeed, for all the guys in the band, the festival was a mixed moment, even as it was one of the high points of Janis's life. Within Big Brother the power shifted decisively as the national press and the music industry discovered Janis Joplin. Nobody cared about Big Brother, which simply became known as "the band with the incredible chick singer." From Monterey onward, Janis more or less obliterated the band. After all the work they'd put into Big Brotherizing "Ball and Chain," all anyone could talk about was Janis's singing. Christgau raved about her stage presence and her voice, calling it "two-thirds Willie Mae Thornton and one-third Kitty Wells," but wrote nothing about the band. Even Janis's left nipple got more attention than the four men in Big Brother.

No one was more taken with Janis than Albert Grossman and Clive Davis. Albert was willing to advise Janis on the film but didn't press the issue of representing the band. Clive Davis, the newly appointed president of Columbia Records, however, was so entranced he wanted to sign Big Brother on the spot. Upon returning to New York, Davis was reportedly "berserk with ecstasy. He loved Monterey Pop and he loved Janis." Although Janis was his favorite performer to emerge from Monterey, Davis also went after the Steve Miller Band and Quicksilver, only to find himself outmaneuvered by Capitol Records. RCA had paid $25,000 for the Airplane the previous year, but in the wake of the Airplane's success nobody came that cheap anymore. Capitol shelled out $40,000 each for the Steve Miller Band and Quicksilver, and Davis paid $50,000 for Electric Flag.

Monterey Pop marked "the creative turning point" for Clive Davis; it tipped him off, he said, to the social and musical revolutions of the sixties and led him to stake his company's future on rock music. It was a smart move, since Columbia Records was immensely powerful but financially troubled. His decision wasn't, however, just a cynical business move. Most record executives sneered at rock 'n' roll as music that "smells but sells." This attitude led to some remarkably stupid decisions, most notably Capitol Records' initial refusal to release the Beatles' first singles, produced by EMI, Capitol's English parent label. Columbia Records, which prided itself on tasteful music, was especially stodgy. Transforming "the label of Robert Goulet into the label of Janis Joplin," as Fredric Dannen put it, was a bold move, particularly because Mitch Miller, Columbia's leading A & R man, openly and publicly loathed rock 'n' roll. Davis made many enemies in the makeover, both in-house and outside the company, as he snatched up musicians who would go on to become the most critically acclaimed artists and biggest hit makers in the new field. Within a three-year period Davis signed Janis and Big Brother, Santana, Chicago, Laura Nyro, and Blood, Sweat, and Tears. Davis's legend (and his ego) grew accordingly. Joe Smith, his rival at Warner Brothers, had a convention audience in stitches when he introduced Davis by saying, "Let me read the official biography. Clive was born in a manger in Bethlehem."

When Davis decided to sign Big Brother, Karpen and the band's new attorney, Bob Gordon, tried unsuccessfully to finagle their way out of the

The Charlatans. "Everybody's house had the old-timey stove and the old-timey look…" (Bob Seidemann)

The Grateful Dead at the old barbershop on Haight Street, next door to Peggy Caserta's boutique (Herb Greene)

Country Joe and the Fish at the San Francisco unemployment office, 1967. Joe McDonald is on the far right (Bob Seidemann)

Big Brother and the Holding Company. Clockwise: James Gurley (top right corner), Dave Getz, Janis, Peter Albin, Sam Andrew. "The first time she opened her mouth and started singing those great ballsy tones, we knew we were going to use her," said Peter Albin (Lisa Law)

Janis, 1967, the first hippie pinup girl (Bob Seidemann)

Pat "Sunshine" Nichols
(Jim Smircich)

Peggy Caserta in the
Haight (Herb Greene)

Peggy at Stinson Beach
(Peggy Caserta)

James Gurley with feather,
a popular hip poster in the
Haight (Bob Seidemann)

Nancy Gurley and Hongo Ishi
(Lisa Law)

Milan Melvin
(Steve Rahn)

Big Brother and the Holding Company in Woodacre Park, 1967 (Lisa Law)

Janis, 1967 (Lisa Law)

contract with Bob Shad of Mainstream Records, claiming he had only recorded a demo tape of the band. Shad was nobody's fool. The contract was iron-clad; only money, and a lot of it, would release the band from Shad's clutches. Throughout the negotiations Big Brother was hamstrung by Karpen, who wasn't up to such high-stakes maneuvering. Soon after the festival, Bill Graham asked Big Brother to open for the Airplane and the Dead at the Hollywood Bowl in late 1967. Against the band's wishes, Karpen nixed the deal because he felt Big Brother should be the head-liners. Graham gave the band members pause when he phoned them individually, saying Karpen was hurting their careers and they should dump him. Karpen only added to their uneasiness when he refused to open up the books. Matters came to a head when he declared, "I'll leave you the books and I'll leave too." He did go but left no books behind, just mounds of random receipts. Before he quit, says Dave Getz, he managed to lose the band's earnings in a bad investment.

"It's so weird when you think of it now—the people who managed these rock bands," Dave recalls. "Chet was a guy who dealt grass who got into the business of putting on dances; Bill Graham was a real business-man, a force as a person and well-equipped to manage bands. But most of these guys were hippies who had a little more business skill than the peo-ple they were managing." And Big Brother went through many managers. "We were just so vulnerable and inexperienced," Dave explains. After the band fired Chet, "Peter met this guy one day and he was like a nobody and next thing he was our manager for two weeks. Then we went to Ron Polte, the manager of Quicksilver, and he said, 'Well, I have a friend and his name is Julius.' Well, Julius was kind of slimy and unpredictable. He was also very secretive. He wasn't forthright about anything. Everything was wrong with the guy, except he had a good heart." Other bands fared no better. Danny Rifkin and Rock Scully, who handled the Dead, were "another example of hippie managers who were great guys, funny guys, in the scene, really swingin' with everything that was happening, but totally incapable of running a business," Dave recalls. "And then there was Albert Grossman, a multimillionaire with his suite of offices and the clout of managing Bob Dylan. Anything associated with Dylan had to be God-like." Janis and the band "were just so jazzed at the thought of Albert managing us, lowly *us*."

When Big Brother approached Albert Grossman about taking over from Karpen in 1967, he was the most powerful and respected manager in the business. In fact, Albert has been credited with inventing the concept of the power manager. Outside of San Francisco most rock managers were just flesh peddlers; the last thing they cared about was the music. Albert, by contrast, was a music lover who prided himself on his impeccable taste. He enjoyed making money but refused to represent acts he considered lame. When he began working with Dylan in 1962, he was only thirty-two, but, overweight and prematurely gray, he already looked old. After hanging out with Dylan for a couple of years, he went "native," exchanging his tortoiseshell glasses, five-button suits, and crew cut for au courant wire-rim glasses, blue jeans, and longish hair, which he sometimes tied back in a short ponytail. To many, Janis included, he resembled an updated version of Ben Franklin. In fact, though, Albert was the first rock manager as hip as his clients. He hung out with Janis, Bob Dylan and Bobby Neuwirth, Emmett Grogan and Peter Coyote, and anyone else he considered cool. Coyote remembers his having "the best grass and hash and acid and introducing you to gorgeous women." Long before Woodstock, New York, became the epitome of hip, Albert owned a beautiful home there. Dylan and the Band were just a few of the many rockers who followed his lead and moved there, a migration that gave the town such luster that it was chosen as the site for 1969's big outdoor rock festival. "If it hadn't been for Albert," as Robbie Robertson of the Band later pointed out, "we'd probably be known as the Poughkeepsie Generation."

Nicknamed "The Bear," Albert could be a teddy bear, but in business negotiations he was a grizzly, a "son of a bitch," according to his client John Simon, a record producer. He loved the exercise of power, which in his case often involved saying no—when he wasn't being deliberately enigmatic, that is. Robert Shelton, a music critic for the *New York Times*, felt that Albert "seemed to enjoy saying no just as some lawyers enjoy threatening action." Albert had another nickname as well. Nick Gravenites and Michael Bloomfield of Electric Flag called him "The Cloud." "You could see it," Gravenites explained, "huge, gray, and august—but when you went up to touch it, it wasn't there."

If Albert was enigmatic and evasive, his power felt very concrete to anyone on the other side of his desk. The most innocuous conversation could still leave one feeling diminished. "It was the most intimidating experience in the world to come up into this guy's office," recalls one of his associates, Mike Friedman. "It was like a cave. There was a mahogany desk and a Tiffany lamp with like a twenty-watt bulb. Files piled so high on the desk you couldn't see Albert behind them and a visitor's chair so low that when a guest sat in it he couldn't see Albert anyhow. I used to call it 'the sucker chair.' People were looking around, barely able to concentrate on what they were doing." And barely able to hear. "He had a loud air conditioner going behind his desk," says Elliot Mazer, a record producer, "and he spoke quietly with his hand in front of his mouth so that you couldn't really hear what he was saying." It wasn't just the surroundings that made an encounter with Albert so discomfiting. He wasn't especially comfortable with himself. Somehow, though, he had learned to use his uneasiness to his advantage. "He could wait anyone out," says one record executive. "He could just take command of a room and make everybody come to him." Nick Gravenites recalls, "He'd enter into some kind of a business discussion and say five words. And the person would talk, and Albert would say nothing. He'd pick at his tooth with his little finger. Then there'd be silence, and the other person would start talking again, revising the deal."

Although Albert claimed to have earned a degree in economics from the University of Chicago, he had in fact attended un-tony Roosevelt College. Upon graduating, he had gotten a job with the Chicago public housing authority on the city's predominantly black South Side. Albert didn't like his job or the system, which didn't seem to him to serve poor blacks especially well. He began hanging out at a folk club and in 1957 opened his own club, the Gate of Horn, and started managing artists. Although he handled several musicians, he built his reputation representing Odetta. After producing the first Newport Folk Festival in 1959, he moved to New York, where he became a fixture in the folk music scene, holding court in funky Greenwich Village coffeehouses. He had a habit, says Robert Shelton, of smoking "a king-size cigarette the way an oil sheik would hold a hookah, making a circle of his thumb and forefinger, slightly crooking his little finger, and blowing smoke out slowly through his hand."

There were only two managers on the East Coast specializing in folk music when Albert started out—Manny Greenhill, who represented Joan

Baez, and Harold Levanthal, who managed Pete Seeger, the Weavers, and Judy Collins. Their orientation was left-wing politics, not show business. Albert was left-leaning, too: the filmmaker Mike Gray says Albert once handed him a brown paper bag filled with five thousand dollars in cash, which allowed him to finish his documentary on the Black Panther Party. Albert also let Emmett Grogan and Peter Coyote use his New York office to drum up support for a number of causes, including the student strikes in France in 1968. In contrast to Greenhill and Levanthal, however, Albert didn't see any reason why politics should get in the way of making money. And there was money to be made in folk music. Robert Shelton was friendly with Albert but still pegged him for "a Cheshire cat in untouched acres of field mice." Unlike the other folk music managers, Albert grasped "the show business principle," according to Bobby Neuwirth, that "you should get as much money as you can." Albert bragged about his hefty 25 percent commission and, when asked why his cut was so steep, said, "Because every time you talk to me you're 10 percent smarter than before. So I just add that 10 percent on to what all the dummies charge for nothing."

Albert wasn't just smart, he had vision as well, and he respected his clients. "Albert was the first guy to insist his artists be treated like artists," claims Jim Rooney, who managed Cambridge's famed Club 47. And in many ways, his insistence transformed the music business. Albert made sure Peter, Paul and Mary retained creative control of both the recording and the packaging of their music, an unprecedented demand in 1962. Consequently, Peter, Paul and Mary "would take as long as they wanted to record their album," says a high-powered Warner Brothers executive. "Deliver it when it was finished and mastered to their satisfaction. Ignoring entirely any schedules we had for its manufacture. And they would deliver artwork for the front and back. This was unheard of. Unheard of!" Fred Goodman, who has written authoritatively on the music industry in those years, believes that Albert's "greatest achievement was creating a commercial environment in which his clients could make a lot of money but preserve their artistic integrity." The marriage of art and commerce that revolutionized popular music in the sixties was embodied by Bob Dylan, but to a great extent Albert Grossman engineered the union.

And made a lot of money out of it—too much, some thought. Mary

Travers of Peter, Paul and Mary admired Albert until she discovered he was making more money than anyone in the group. A large share of his income came through the music publishing companies he established for some of his artists, such as Bob Dylan. Publishing royalties generate large sums of money, which few artists had ever seen before Albert changed the rules of the game. But Albert benefited, too, awarding himself 50 percent of publishers' royalties. Dylan came to feel Albert had taken advantage of him and eventually he broke away. The criticisms weren't restricted just to Albert's wealth, however. Grossman didn't suffer fools gladly, and though he could be quite kind, he wasn't concerned that he be seen as nice. Mary Travers has said that she loved Albert dearly even though he wasn't a very nice man. At first, Odetta saw Albert as a "marvelous, wonderful, delightful, humane person." She did notice, though, that he wouldn't laugh at other people's jokes. "He had to feel superior," she says, a view seconded by George Wein, a promoter who called Albert "a strong one-way street." Others faulted him for his temper and his meanness. "Albert could be very cruel and nasty in a flash," according to Elliot Mazer. And Levon Helm of the Band accused him of using divide-and-conquer tactics to "isolate the star" of the group, Robbie Robertson, and "fuck the other guys."

Albert has many defenders, though. Peter Yarrow of Peter, Paul and Mary claims Albert only went after phonies, and his band mate Paul Stookey agrees. Albert was "brutally honest," Stookey contends, and he had "an early-warning bullshit-detecting device that show[ed] personal annoyance very openly." His widow, Sally Grossman, admits, "You definitely did not want to incur Albert's wrath," but she believes his anger was a virtue. "He got rid of it right away. He used to tell me I didn't get angry and it wasn't healthy." The worst thing, she says, "was when he was disappointed in you. That was devastating because he was so great and he'd do so much for you, for everybody." She attributes much of the negative reaction he provoked to the insecurities of others. "He was such a charismatic, strong person and so smart that it was very easy for people to feel insecure if they were insecure." Even those who found his personal style off-putting acknowledge his uniqueness in the world of music management. Myra Friedman, the publicist in Grossman's office, believes "no manager had the class and taste and love for the music itself that Albert had. He was a breed that no longer exists." Peter Yarrow concurs: "There would never have been a Peter, Paul and Mary, there would never have been a Bob Dylan who could have survived and made it without Albert Grossman."

Of course, those who most disliked Albert Grossman were the many people to whom he said no—record-label executives, concert promoters, and the press. Robert Shelton ran into trouble when he mentioned his interest in writing Dylan's biography. Albert promptly threatened litigation. But mostly he just said no, forcing people to pay top dollar—or more. In the end, Albert Grossman reduced many powerful men to supplicants and that's why they hired him. "We used him as the ultimate weapon," the record producer Elliot Mazer concludes. "It made the labels crazy because Albert had the power."

He ran Clive Davis," Elliot Mazer says of Albert's relationship with Columbia's president. One way or another, Albert persuaded Davis to shell out $200,000 to release Janis and Big Brother from their Mainstream contract. Columbia charged Big Brother $100,000 as an advance against future royalties, and the company, in Davis's words, "had to swallow the rest." Mainstream also got a 2 percent override on the next two Big Brother albums. In the end Big Brother was $150,000 in debt—$100,000 of its first album royalties, plus $50,000 for recording costs, which were also charged against royalties. But the contract was quite a gamble for Davis and Columbia as well—to the tune of $250,000. Albert's clout is written all over the deal: not only did Davis agree to the exorbitant terms, but Albert's client John Simon was hired to produce Big Brother's next album, which had to succeed for Columbia.

Before Big Brother signed with Albert, he flew out to see them in San Francisco. When the band asked what he would do for them, Albert turned the tables. What did *they* want from a manager? he said. They were nonplussed—no one had ever posed such a question. If they wanted to be rich and famous, Albert reportedly told them, he could make that happen. If they wanted to keep a low profile, touring only occasionally and making just enough money to get by, which his client Richie Havens preferred, he could see to that as well. The choice was theirs. "We want to make good money," they answered. "We were so naive," says Dave Getz, that when Albert asked how much they had in mind, he replied, "We want *at least* $75,000 a year." Dave had arrived at that figure by taking the money they'd earned that year and multiplying it by three. The sum seemed vast, but Dave suspects Albert knew it was well below what they would earn. After all, since Monterey they had been making $2,500 a night. This kind of conversation was Albert's métier, and he just shrugged and said, "Make it a hundred thousand." He even suggested putting it in writing. "If I can't make you that, I'm in the wrong business." After the band's succession of flaky managers, Albert seemed rock-solid. "He exuded such an air of sophistication and confidence and knowingness," Dave recalls, and seemed "so low-key," with none of the flashy, fast-talking hype that characterized most East Coast managers. There were a couple of disquieting moments, though. "Don't ever trust me," Albert said at one point, and when they asked him what he meant, he smiled. The band couldn't tell whether his comment was a joke or a warning.

Albert was crystal-clear, however, when it came to heroin. "One thing," he said. "No schmeeze." He would have nothing to do with smack. "I've seen terrible things with it and if anybody here is messing with it at all, there's no point in going any further." Albert never revealed the havoc it had wreaked in his personal life, but his first wife had been a junkie. The band members nodded earnestly and assured Albert they'd never touch it, even though James, Sam, and Janis had already done heroin on more than one occasion. They were only using infrequently at this stage, usually when someone backstage would offer it; none of them were making enough money to buy smack regularly.

Albert had an immediate effect on Big Brother's fortunes. Even after Monterey Pop, the band was still playing gigs up and down the California coast. Within two months of signing with Albert, they had joined Columbia's classy roster and were on their first East Coast tour. Their lives would now be spent on the road in pursuit of rock 'n' roll stardom, but with a road manager and a roadie to ease the burden of touring. Janis herself could now afford the caretakers she'd never had—Albert to manage her career and a new roommate, Linda Gravenites, to help handle her increasingly chaotic life.

A clothes designer, Linda was house-sitting for the Grateful Dead when she met Janis and agreed to make her an outfit. Linda's house-sitting gig ended abruptly, and she crashed at Janis's place, an arrangement that became permanent one night when Janis looked helplessly at the sinkful of dirty dishes and sighed, "Oh, I need a mother." Linda, broke at the time and calm by nature, thought to herself, "I could do that." In no time she moved in and "did everything Janis didn't want to do," even before "she knew she wanted it done." They both palled around with Sunshine and Suzy Perry, Stanley Mouse's girlfriend. All four of them were the same sign, and they were known as the "Capricorn ladies" around the Haight, where people mostly got out of their way, according to Linda. "We'd walk down Haight Street raucously laughing and carrying our Rainier Ale in paper bags," she says. She could take care of Janis, she felt, as long as Janis's place wasn't a "junkie house." And it wasn't at first, but with fame and fortune right around the corner and a life of pain to forget, it wasn't long before Janis began turning to that other caretaker, both more reliable and less demanding.

Monterey Pop brought other gifts, too. Janis became a lot more attractive to men in the wake of the festival. Sunshine recalls hanging out together leaning against the parking meters on Haight Street and drinking Ripple. "People would just swarm around her. It blew her away." Sunshine imagined Janis thinking she had to be beautiful if all these people were drawn to her. Men, in particular, started coming around. Janis had long made a conversational staple out of her inability to "get fucked," but the claim began to seem ludicrous. "Lots of people were fucking her," claims Bob Seidemann. "And because she was a singer, she got the cute guys," says Stanley Mouse. If her sudden popularity was gratifying, it was unsettling, too. "Before she was famous, people didn't think Janis was attractive," observes Peggy Caserta. "She could barely get laid, and now she had all these admirers." Janis was well aware that the sudden attention was pretty shallow. "Don't think she didn't know," says Peggy. George Hunter remembers coming on to her one night after a show. "Janis gave me a bunch of shit, saying, 'How come you never wanted to come over to my place before?' I gave her some line about always liking her." Janis didn't buy it, but she had a brief affair with him anyway.

George Hunter wasn't the only guy who started appearing backstage after shows. There were a lot of one-night stands in the fall of 1967, some with other rock stars. Supposedly, Janis had sex with Jimi Hendrix backstage in a dressing room. (Linda Gravenites, however, claims Jimi was with her, not Janis, that night. "I'd been celibate for three years and then there was Jimi. I'm a believer in extremes, and it was too good a joke to pass up.") What doesn't seem in dispute is that Janis went to bed once that fall with the self-proclaimed "lizard king," Jim Morrison of the Doors. Linda recalls that the Doors were in town and invited Janis out to dinner. Morrison arrived with his girlfriend, Pamela Courson, in tow, while Janis showed up with Sam, Dave—the band's roadie—and Linda. After dinner they all moved on to Janis's Lyon Street apartment, where Linda claims "Janis and Jim sort of dragged each other into the bedroom. Morrison's girlfriend left in tears, with Sam in hot pursuit." It wasn't a good match, though, and on a subsequent occasion, in a much-recounted story, Janis knocked Morrison over the head with a whiskey bottle after they had gotten into an argument in which he had grabbed her by her hair. "She hated Jim Morrison," says a West Coast booking agent who worked with both bands. "We could have all made so much money had she allowed a Doors/Joplin package to go on. But she refused. He didn't like her that much, either. They were two of a kind and they hated what they saw in each other."

This was when Janis started hanging out with Freewheelin' Frank of the Angels. He wasn't as violent as some of the other Angels, but he was a serious speed freak. "A piece of work," says Linda Bacon, one of the many Austin refugees who lived in the Bay Area. She remembers a harrowing car ride one night with Janis, Frank, and a frenetic guy behind the wheel. "He was driving like a complete maniac and Janis and I were saying, 'Listen, we want to get out.' We drove down the peninsula quite a way and he ran a couple of red lights and sideswiped a couple of cars. This took several hours and I only found out in the middle of the trip that the driver was Neal Cassady. Everybody but me was drunk and crazed."

Bob Seidemann also ended up in bed with Janis around this time, though he didn't much like her. "The first time we had sex it was sort of like alligator wrestling. She was insatiable, literally." But Stanley Mouse, another lover, speaks better of her. He loved the way she would "light up" when he came backstage to hobnob with the bands between sets. She was passionate the night they slept together, but her carrying-on seemed excessive and he wondered if she was able to stop and actually enjoy herself. By all accounts, there was sometimes a theatrical quality to Janis's lovemaking, and she was more than dimly aware of this. In 1970, she told a reporter, "I used to ask guys I was balling, 'Do I ball like I sing? . . . Is it really me or am I putting on a show?'" For several months, Sunshine lived with Janis and Linda Gravenites in a small two-bedroom apartment with very thin walls, and whenever Janis was particularly noisy and the sex especially quick, she felt certain Janis was indeed performing. "I'd lie in bed and just crack up," Sunshine says. Janis didn't fake it most of the time, she emphasizes—a point confirmed by George Hunter, who says, "Janis *really* knew her way around a mattress." Janis's sexual passion wasn't contrived with Milan Melvin, either.

An ad salesman and deejay for the underground rock station KMPX, Milan Melvin was one of Janis's more enduring yet intermittent partners of this period. His roommate, Carl Gottlieb, says that having Janis as a "frequent sleepover was pretty intense. I knew she was extremely sexual. I knew it from being on the other side of a small apartment." Usually Janis was afraid to drop acid, but she felt close enough to Milan to trip with him several times. One night they dropped acid "on the roof of KMPX during a red lunar eclipse, which she described as God's bloodshot eye staring down on us through the wrong end of a telescope," Milan recalls. Another time they turned on in a hot spring in the northern Nevada desert during a beautiful snowstorm. Milan recalls laughing a lot on both occasions. "No sign of sadness at all. We were loving it and each other and it was pure joy. When she was happy, there was no one more effusive," he says. "Perhaps it was these moments of unbridled ecstasy that made many of her other moods seem almost sad."

Milan claims he was serious about Janis, so serious he took her home to meet his parents. "I remember the look on their faces as we jangled through the door, my mother probably thinking about the grandchildren this union would produce, my father wondering how he would explain this to the guys at work. Then Janis and I reverted to the dutiful, polite children we'd been raised to be, all the while desperately wishing an end to the visit so we could get back to our real lives and some serious misbehavior. We laughed about it on the way back to San Francisco." Milan was aware of the contradictions in Janis. "One side of her was pure tomboy, a tough, scrappy bitch unwilling to take crap off anybody; the other side was china-doll fragile, a person living in fear of further hurt."

He soon discovered how easily she could be wounded. One night when she was performing at the Fillmore, he forgot to pick her up on his Harley-Davidson to take her there. He had dropped mescaline and when he finally showed up at the ballroom she was hurt and angry. "I don't ever remember hurting her deliberately. I just goofed, but, wow. . . . It was like I drove a stake in her heart. It was a minor fuckup but she took it as though I'd left her for somebody else." Soon enough, however, he began seeing another woman, Mimi Fariña, Joan Baez's sister, and the relationship led to marriage. Linda Gottfried Waldron recalls Janis being devastated by Milan's marriage to Fariña. To make matters worse, Linda Gravenites was hard at work sewing Fariña's wedding dress in their apartment. And then, in January 1968, right around her twenty-fifth birthday, Janis had an abortion; the father was most likely a musician in the proto-metal band Blue Cheer. Later Janis confided to Linda Gravenites that she regretted having the abortion, although at the time there was hardly room for a baby, a fact underscored by her insistence on performing just days after the procedure.

Big Brother was scheduled to appear at a club in Los Angeles, according to their booking agent, Todd Schiffman. The band arrived to find the club had been taken over by the mob, and the owners had sabotaged the P.A. system in retaliation. Schiffman found Janis in her dressing room "in terrible, agonizing pain." She told him she'd had an abortion two days earlier and asked him to help her to the telephone so she could call a hospital. Schiffman literally "picked her up off the floor and almost carried her down the hall," as she could barely walk. Meanwhile, thousands of people were waiting to see her. Schiffman suggested that she use the broken P.A. system as an excuse to cancel the show, and she eagerly agreed. In the meantime, however, the promoters had let kids inside the club and gotten the sound system working. Schiffman told Janis, "You can't go on, so just walk out onstage and explain there are problems, and they should come back tomorrow." But once Janis was up onstage—with Schiffman's help— she said, "There's a lot of bullshit going down here tonight. There are guys backstage walking around with guns and all. But, you know, you're here and I'm here and we're going to do it." The band came out, according to

Schiffman, who says, "I couldn't believe it. She put on an hour show and you wouldn't have known she was sick. I couldn't believe my eyes. That tells us what kind of dedication and craziness she had." Or the depth of her insecurities, says Linda Gravenites. Janis was a dynamic performer, she argues, because she was "so insecure. She needed the return that she got."

Janis herself felt transformed by the stage and the audience's adulation, which is why she needed so desperately to perform. "I'm on an audience trip. . . . I need them and they need me," she once told a reporter. Up onstage, she believed she was pretty, even beautiful. "You know, it's funny," she said in an interview in the last months of her life. "Like most girls, I'm always really self-conscious about do I look fat, if my legs are short, if I'm weird shaped, but when I go onstage, man, it never occurs to me. I think I look beautiful." The difference was visible to others, too. "When Janis was performing she was probably the most sexual woman I've ever seen in my life," says John Morris, who produced many of her concerts for Bill Graham. "Any night she was performing I think she could look out at the audience and say, 'You, or you, or you. Meet me backstage.' " Some nights she did just that. During a particularly inspired performance of "Ball and Chain" at the Fillmore, Glenn McKay, who ran the light show, recalls that he was so moved by her rendition that he jumped up on a table when it stopped and screamed, "Janis, I wanna fuck you so bad." Janis saw him waving his arms and grinned. "We're on," she said, and they were. James Gurley recalls hearing Moby Grape at the Avalon. "This girl came out to sing with them. And I thought, 'God, who is that? Man, what a beautiful girl!' And then she started singing and I went, 'What, that's Janis!' I didn't even recognize her. She just looked so beautiful onstage . . . it was like an aura came over her."

The rush Janis felt onstage was a temporary fix, of course, and up close her insecurities and vast neediness continued to drive some people away. Seidemann was put off by her neediness the time they had sex: "Whoa, it's too big for me, I can't fill that hole. I'd be shoveling all day. I think that's what it was about. That was her tragedy—she couldn't fill that hole." Milan, by contrast, believes he and Janis gave each other all they craved sexually, although he admits he was not willing "to Velcro" himself to "her side while she dealt with the backstage madness or the personal problems created by making up and breaking up with her bands or put on a business hat to go toe-to-toe with Grossman." For Milan, however, the problem was not just Janis's needs but the pressures of celebrity. From now on, as her fame grew, being with Janis would mean taking on an enormous burden.

The support Janis still sought certainly wasn't going to come from her family, no matter how much she wanted her parents' approval. In August 1967, at the height of the Summer of Love, Janis's family came to visit San Francisco. Her parents wanted to check up on their daughter, still harboring some hope she might return to Port Arthur and Lamar Tech. Janis should have known they'd be shaken by the Haight-Ashbury scene, but she was determined to show them what a big deal she had become. She even arranged for Big Brother to play a few songs at the Avalon, although the band wasn't on that weekend's bill. But just before their arrival she panicked and asked her old boyfriend Travis Rivers to come to her apartment for moral support. "I assured her that everything looked lovely, that it looked real homey." Nevertheless, Janis's family was, in Linda Gravenites's words, "very uptight." Predictably enough, there was a cultural collision from the moment Janis ushered her family into the apartment and they found themselves face to face with a wall of Bob Seidemann's provocative "hippie chick" posters. The Joplins were silent, and Janis felt her parents' disapproval. "It hardly shows, Mother," Janis said reproachfully. She might have thought the pose bared her breast discreetly, but her mother, of all people, would never agree. Janis might as well have given Dorothy the finger.

Still, the visit continued. Janis took her family on a tour of the Haight, her stomping grounds, which looked pretty seedy, nobody's idea of utopia. Their day ended with a visit to the Avalon, where her family didn't linger. The family looked and felt hopelessly out of place among all the spaced-out long-haired freaks—all except Janis's brother, Michael, who, following in his sister's footsteps, tried desperately to bum a joint off anyone. As they were leaving the Avalon, Janis kept saying, "Isn't it wonderful?" To everyone but her brother her pride must have seemed mystifying at best and horrifying at worst. "Oh, can't you see?" she begged them. As they walked away, Janis seemed perplexed. "I think Janis realized then that we didn't, and couldn't, and probably weren't going to see," Laura

Joplin wrote. The family went through the motions of warmth, exchanging hugs and kisses as they parted.

A year after Janis's return to San Francisco, her parents finally realized they would never get their daughter back. The Joplins "could have no effect," Laura wrote; Janis's scene was "so different," and at this point she was "so internally successful." Laura underestimated the power of her parents' opinion, but it is true that Janis had abandoned all efforts to live her life to satisfy them. She got far too much gratification out there onstage. A year later, James Gurley met the Joplins backstage during a Houston gig, and it seemed to him that they "were just appalled at everything they were seeing." Janis's family never would understand her life.

Monterey Pop lasted a mere three days, but the festival's reverberations were still being felt many years later. In their wildest dreams, Lou Adler and John Phillips could never have imagined all that would happen in the wake of their event. The whole rock juggernaut—not just Woodstock and Altamont—had its origins in the festival. Within months Jann Wenner launched *Rolling Stone* magazine, featuring, ironically, a cover story lambasting the festival's promoters for lining their own pockets. Record companies now courted rock musicians and made *Rolling Stone* required reading for their executives. Rock 'n' roll was no longer the bastard child of the entertainment industry but its shiny new jewel. An especially "happy accident" for the music industry, Monterey Pop spawned "the next billion-dollar business," in the words of Robert Christgau. In 1962, record sales totaled $500 million; by 1996 they grossed over $20 billion, largely on the basis of rock 'n' roll.

Until this transformation, rock musicians, however popular, had earned far less money than what they made for others. In the new order, they gained control over their creative output and made money for themselves and not just for the businessmen. On tour, rock acts had long been consigned to the world of lousy flat rates, while "class" acts like Danny Thomas and Harry Belafonte received some 60 percent of the gross, always a more lucrative arrangement. Todd Schiffman was one of the first booking agents to buck the system whereby rock was "subsidizing the

Thomases and Belafontes." He began demanding 60 percent for his acts, not the standard $5,000 flat fee that most bands—even the Rolling Stones—received. No longer the "asshole" of the entertainment industry, rock musicians like Janis and Big Brother were now in a position to negotiate with managers, booking agents, and promoters.

Warner Brothers Records had a preview of this changed world three months before Monterey Pop when two of its executives appeared at a Grateful Dead concert to present the band with copies of the band's freshly pressed first album. Joe Smith—the company's vice president—and his boss, Stan Corwyn, couldn't have looked more out of place with their short hair and official Warner Brothers blazers. Smith stepped up to the mike. "I just want to say what an honor it is for Warner Brothers Records to be able to introduce the Grateful Dead and its music to the world," he said. As Smith and Corwyn stood onstage, quintessential company men, the Dead just rolled their eyes. Finally, Jerry Garcia took the mike back and offered his droll response: "I just want to say what an honor it is for the Grateful Dead to introduce Warner Brothers Records to the world." To help negotiate the shores of the new music world, Warner Brothers hired Andy Wickham, a music lover and freak, to assist with the transition. Columbia also brought in its own "house hippie," Jim Fouratt, who had worked closely with Abbie Hoffman in the Yippies. Columbia even began to promote its acts with the much-ridiculed "But the Man Can't Bust Our Music" ad campaign. Most veterans of the San Francisco scene thought it simply a crass attempt to cash in on the youth revolt, but the FBI reportedly worried about the money record companies were pouring into the coffers of radical underground newspapers with such "hip" ads. For a while it seemed as if Lenin's maxim that capitalists would sell the rope with which to hang themselves might come true.

The line between hooking up and cashing in was precariously thin. Clive Davis, a Harvard-educated lawyer, claimed his Monterey weekend not only marked the "creative turning point" in his life but had changed him "as a person." Walter Yetnikoff, who had worked for Davis at Columbia, didn't buy his former boss's breathless enthusiasm. " 'I went to the Monterey Pop Festival, and I was instilled with Love, and Joy, and the Flowers were in the Air,' " he said, mocking Davis. " 'Then I came to Los Angeles, and a Cop stopped me. Can you believe what they did to the

Love? Then I signed this, and I signed that. . . .' What is this bull-shit?" Yetnikoff asked. The festival may have loosened Davis up, but, as Yetnikoff points out, it in no way interfered with his interest in making money. The whole Haight-Ashbury shtick was easily recuperated by the music industry. Christgau would write a year after Monterey, "Art and social commentary were absorbed, almost painlessly, by the world's schlockiest business." Citing as evidence a trade journal's review of a new single as " 'a highly commercial rock allegory of perishing society,' " he would grouse that, "apparently, society itself would perish before the record industry." The humorist Cynthia Heimel recalls the time in June 1967 that she and her hippie friends spied a press kit for Moby Grape, one of the new San Francisco bands. "It looked psychedelic, yet it was done by ad people. I believe the word 'hype' was coined that very day."

But the commercial takeover of rock 'n' roll wasn't the straightforward assault that myth has made of it. According to the familiar story, sixties rock set out to change the world and found itself transformed instead. Journalists began sounding the alarm as soon as the music became com-mercially viable, but the account—a remarkably durable boomer myth—exaggerates the bands' hostility to the commercial music industry and minimizes the significance of the cultural revolt wrought by Janis and her peers. San Francisco bands promoted sex, drugs, and rock 'n' roll and saw themselves as an alternative to AM teenybopper fare, but they were never averse to making money, much less at war with capitalism. In 1967 Bob Weir of the Dead, the least commercial of all the bands, told a reporter, "If the industry is gonna want us, they're gonna take us the way we are. Then, if the money comes in, it'll be a stone gas."

It *was* a gas for the Airplane and Big Brother and, years later, for the Dead, which through perseverance, and thanks to sixties nostalgia, would profit far more than any of the other San Francisco bands. And once the money began coming in, they all did what successful entertainers have always done—they bought fancy cars and expensive homes. San Francisco's nouveau riche rockers also spent lots of their flashy money on expensive marijuana and hashish and on harder drugs as well. The Bay Area music scene quickly "turned into who can buy the most cocaine," Nick Gravenites said. As the bands became more successful, they also became quite insular. Opinion varies on the cordiality of relations between the bands, but Ed Denson, who managed Country Joe and the Fish, claims that "a lot of the bands hated each other. They wouldn't let each other on the same bills, formed little cliques." According to Bill Thompson, the Airplane's manager, the bands didn't work cooperatively and form their own label because "everyone had their own fiefdoms." Even Bill Graham felt it was a "tragedy . . . that the musicians never really did anything communally." Bill Belmont of the Fish adds, "The bands were created by the audiences, but did they ever do anything for the audience? Did they ever pump anything back in?" Perhaps the radical activist Abbie Hoffman, who was thrown off the stage at Woodstock by Pete Townshend of the Who, said it best when he called rock musicians "the high priests of our culture" but added, "unfortunately, most of them are assholes."

By contrast, Janis avoided ostentation, buying a used Porsche and, in the last year of her life, a less-than-palatial Marin County home that she filled with secondhand furniture. She loved making money, though, and might well be said to have been among the first rock 'n' roll stars to find a corporate sponsor—of sorts. While the Airplane became flacks for Levi Strauss, then under fire for exploitative labor practices, Janis decided the Southern Comfort folks owed her for all the free publicity she was giving their product. She directed Albert Grossman's office to flood the company with newspaper clippings mentioning her fondness for Southern Comfort, and the company ended up giving her a check for twenty-five hundred dollars, which she put toward the purchase of a lynx coat. Once she got the coat, Janis plugged herself, not the product. "Oh man, that was the best hustle I ever pulled—can you imagine getting paid for passing out for two years?"

Although the bands may have allowed themselves to be "swallowed by the voracious maw of corporate America," in Heimel's words, they transformed the country's cultural landscape in the process. The Airplane's Bill Thompson recalls the band's gig at Grinnell College's homecoming dance. There they were in Iowa: "The girls were in ruffled dresses all the way down to the ankles with corsages, and their *families* were there. We started the light show and we had three sets to do that night. The first set, it was like we were from Mars." The parents ducked out early, and by the second set "people started dancing a little bit. . . . The third set, people went *nuts*. Off came the corsages. Shoes were coming off. Guys were ripping off their ties. They went *nuts*. It was one of the greatest feelings I ever had. It was like the turning of America in a way. We went out and played everywhere and did that. We were the first band to do that out of San Francisco."

Janis saw herself quite consciously as a cultural provocateur. "Kids from the Midwest, their whole fucking thing is to sit in row Q47 and be still. . . . It's never occurred to them that they could *not* go in the army. You know, it's a thing I do. . . . If you can get them once, man, get them standing up when they should be sitting down, sweaty when they should be decorous, smile when they should be applauding politely . . . I think you sort of switch on their brain, man, so that makes them say: 'Wait a minute, maybe I can do anything.' Whoooooo! It's life. That's what rock 'n' roll is for, turn that switch on, and man, it can be all." Claiming that she and her performance were one and the same, Janis nevertheless understood her power as an iconic figure. "People aren't supposed to be like me, sing like me, make out like me, drink like me, live like me," she later told reporters, "but now they're paying me $50,000 a year for me to be like me. That's what I hope I mean to those kids out there. After they see me, when their mothers are feeding them all that cashmere sweater and girdle ———— [expletive deleted by the *New York Times*], maybe they'll have a second thought—that they can be themselves and win." If the bands didn't manage, or even set out to, overthrow corporate America, they did encourage American youth to trample on all the old certainties.

When bohemia finally went mass—largely through the success of the bands—Haight-Ashbury paid a heavy price. Rock music had made San Francisco the epicenter of hipness, but it was an honor veterans of the Haight would have gladly palmed off on any other city during 1967's disastrous Summer of Love. That spring, the crowds in the Haight had grown so thick—and progressively thicker every weekend—that people realized the neighborhood was on the cusp of a much larger influx. The Diggers predicted a hundred thousand newcomers would descend on the district that summer, and along with the Straight Theater, the Oracle, the Family Dog, they formed the Council for the Summer of Love to organize celebratory events and serve as a liaison to the straight world. The coming invasion of kids had prompted entrepreneurs to convert anything and everything into Love Cafés and Love Burger stands. In a one-month period, fifteen storefronts either changed hands or changed their names to capitalize on the hippie craze. In April, the Gray Line Bus Company began its Hippie Hop Tour, advertising it as "the only foreign tour within the continental limits of the United States." Pete Townshend visited the Haight around the time of Monterey and was surprised and saddened by how thoroughly commercialized the area had become. Bob Seidemann shot a Summer of Love photo essay in which he recorded young people making their journey through Haight Street. "You don't see any hippies. You see people looking for hippies," he observed. As the newcomers progressed up Haight Street they'd stop in boutiques so they could "get their act together." They'd buy an earring, then a groovy T-shirt, followed by a hip pair of bell-bottoms.

Increasingly, the crowds at the Fillmore and the Avalon neither knew nor cared about the origins of the scene. They cared only about the music. The Red Dog Saloon, 1090 Page Street, and Ken Kesey's Acid Tests were largely forgotten. Less than two years after the original 1965 benefits, the Fillmore held another dance for the San Francisco Mime Troupe. "Some of the musicians remembered us from the old days," said its founder, Ronny Davis, "but the new rock fans . . . knew the bands but not the Mime Troupe." He tried talking to them, but "it was like speaking into a cotton candy machine." By the Summer of Love, the scene had changed, growing, as Ken Kesey observed, "tighter and stranger."

Seventy-five thousand kids spent their summer vacation in the Haight, and by the end of the Summer of Love, "Haight Street was lined with people with problems," Don McNeil reported in the *Village Voice*. "Behind the scenes, there were only more problems." The streets of the Haight were "griseous and filthy, psychedelic weirdburger stands springing up in mutant profusion," wrote Ed Sanders in his book about Charles Manson. It was "like a valley of thousands of plump white rabbits surrounded by wounded coyotes." A community that had relied on long hair and weed as the badges of authenticity and cool found itself vulnerable to the faux-hippie con artists flooding into the neighborhood and other hip enclaves across America. "There was a six-month period," recalled the folksinger Arlo Guthrie, "when you could look down the street and you could tell who was your friend and who wasn't. . . . You knew who had a roach on him . . . but soon after you had guys who looked exactly like you sellin' you *oregano*." Oregano was the least of it: bad drugs, stickups, rape, and venereal disease were now increasingly common in Haight-Ashbury and other "love ghettoes." Racial tension escalated as thousands of middle-class white kids came to divest themselves of the very material goodies that were beyond the reach of the vast majority of African Americans. Bob Seidemann says, "Blacks began showing up on Haight Street and they weren't looking like Jimi Hendrix. They were looking like bad guys." And, of course, there were the cops, who in October 1967 busted the Grateful Dead's house on 710 Ashbury Street.

Before long the old Haight habitués either fled or stayed indoors. "Uh oh, the street people have become the house people," Raechel Donahue, a KMPX deejay, recalls her husband, Tom, saying. The Dead began moving away soon after the bust. Janis and Linda Gravenites stuck it out longer than many, but by the beginning of 1968 they too moved. "I didn't realize I'd been looking a block ahead for bad trips until I moved and didn't have to anymore," says Linda. The community lay in shambles as the bands pulled up stakes and escaped, usually to Marin County, that "outpost of Nirvana." After the triumph of Monterey, the Haight's swift decline came as something of a shock. "Ain't nothing like it ever gonna happen again," Janis said of Monterey Pop in late fall 1967. "For a while there were kids who believed they could make it better by being better. And they were better and it didn't make a bit of difference." Though she confessed to some bitterness, Janis wasn't going to lose any sleep over her disenchantment. After all, she'd never been much of an optimist or a true believer. "I've always believed people are screwups and are gonna lie," she once said. By the fall of 1967 Janis was betting on Janis. To many, the Summer of Love stood as a cautionary tale about the perils of publicity and hype. On the brink of superstardom, Janis need only have looked around the ravaged Haight to see what a bitter harvest hype could reap.

7

Bye, Bye Baby

How do you want us to promote you?" Big Brother sat in Albert Grossman's New York office, dazed and disoriented, like all first-time visitors, and the question just hung in the air. But it wasn't Albert who asked the question or Myra Friedman, the new publicist, but Albert's assistant. An "awful silence" followed as the band members looked at one another nervously. "We didn't know what they were talking about," Dave Getz admits, but Albert's assistant just barreled ahead, oblivious to the discomfort now blanketing the room. "I mean, what kind of image do you want?" the assistant asked, looking straight at Janis. Myra claims to have been as puzzled by the question as the band. What could you do with a "bunch of beaded musicians born out of the San Francisco hippie milieu"? she wondered. She couldn't imagine "what athletics of transformation" her colleague was contemplating.

The question of promotion was quickly dropped, but Dave

Getz contends the future was clear at that February 1968 meeting. "What they were trying to get at was, 'We're going to promote Janis instead of the band.'" As evidence, he points to the press kits that followed, in which the band was virtually invisible, and to the change in billing that occurred later that year: "Janis Joplin with Big Brother and the Holding Company." Myra Friedman vigorously denies that Albert's office hatched such a plan. Perhaps, but Myra, who had just joined Albert's staff, knew very little about her cryptic boss's plans. "He was never exactly Mr. Communication," Myra allows.

Albert brought Big Brother to New York to kick off their first East Coast tour and to sign their Columbia Records contract. Until February 1968 the band had stayed pretty close to home, playing mostly in the new rock ballrooms and clubs on the West Coast. Now they were in New York, the capital of America's culture industry. From this point on, the city would be their home base whenever they played east of the Mississippi. During the rest of that year, the band spent as much time in New York as in San Francisco—and the ill effects began to show quickly. Many believe that the city alone was almost entirely the cause of Big Brother's fate: the band was caught in nothing less than a cultural collision between the East and West Coasts. *Rolling Stone,* then located in San Francisco, played up the East-West divide. According to one apocryphal story it ran, when the band signed at CBS's famed New York skyscraper, James Gurley tested Clive Davis's claim that Columbia Records wasn't as stuffy as everyone thought by jumping on his desk, stripping naked, and yelling, "Can you dig it?" The story of 1968 is more complicated than a simple East-meets-West face-off (after all, many East Coast critics and fans embraced the San Francisco bands), but in the late sixties New York and San Francisco were still worlds apart.

At the time, San Franciscans strained to be mellow while New Yorkers seemed to take a perverse pleasure in their harsh city and in the toughness required to live there. "My first trip to San Francisco," says the New York record producer Elliot Mazer, "I remember looking around and saying, 'Why are all these people smiling?'" New York, by contrast, was not a city of smiling faces, especially if you looked like a hippie. "New York in that era was terrible," Bruce Barthol of Country Joe and the Fish remembers. "It was hostile, cruel, and the most provincial place I'd ever been. You were hassled really badly there for long hair by people on the streets of Manhattan." Barthol looked tame by comparison with Sam Andrew and James Gurley, whose hair was even longer than Janis's mane. And then there was Janis herself, whose look hadn't yet traveled across the country to New York. "Janis was a freak, even on the Lower East Side," insists Mazer, and she got a lot of static for it. "She was the first woman to walk into a restaurant wearing a feather boa, sit at a table, and say, 'Fuck you,' to a rude waiter." Janis, of course, was no stranger to rudeness, especially when she ventured out of San Francisco. Actor Howard Hesseman once took Janis to a Los Angeles deli where the waiter refused to serve her unless she put on a hair net. "She gave him an earful and we split."

What made New York so daunting for Janis and the band was its vibe—what Janis called the "ambition, pressure, and pushiness" that drove the city. Coming out of laid-back, low-pressure San Francisco, Big Brother hadn't had the requisite schooling in hard knocks. They discovered that New York's musicians weren't so forgiving of bands playing out of tune and out of time, the "hot" sound of San Francisco. After just a few weeks, Janis told a reporter that New York "seemed to have made us all crazy." It was "dividing the unity of the band."

Still, there was Albert's office to provide the stability of a road manager and a publicist, luxuries most rock bands went without. "Nobody had road managers," recalls John Cooke, who filled that function for Big Brother. "We thought Albert invented road managing," he laughs. Cooke hooked up with the band in December 1967, just before they came East. He met them in their rehearsal space and immediately ran up against Janis's prickliness. "Before I sat down, somebody said, 'What's your sign?' I said, 'Libra.' James said something like, 'That's cool,' but Janis sort of shrugged and said, 'Oh, I never cared much about Libras one way or the other.' It wasn't totally negative, it was just standoffish. But it left the door open."

The son of the British journalist Alistair Cooke, John was no stranger to the folk music scene. As a student at Harvard he had been part of a Cambridge bluegrass group, the Charles River Valley Boys. One of the many folkies who turned to rock, he counted among his friends Bob Dylan's friend and road manager, Bobby Neuwirth. From hanging out with Dylan's entourage during his 1964 New England tour, Cooke says, he "kind of had a sense of what a road manager does." Nevertheless, Neuwirth gave him some advice. "What I should not be from the first moment," Cooke was told, "was their buddy, because you have to tell them what to do."

Neuwirth's advice may have been on the money, but it immediately caused problems for Cooke. The members of Big Brother were accustomed to roadies who hung out with them and shared their laid-back ethos, and so they quickly bristled at Cooke's aloofness and drillmaster style. "Within a month," he recalls, "I got a call from Albert, who said, 'John, what's going on?' " The band had complained about him. "Basically I knew what they were talking about. I wasn't growing my hair as long as theirs and I didn't hang out with them." Cooke called a band meeting and lectured them. "Listen, if you want someone to be your hang-out partner and carry your guitar and go get cigarettes for you and a pint of whatever you drink, we can get somebody to do that for fifty dollars a week and he'll be a gofer. But if you want me to do my job, let's try this a little longer." At that point, somebody, maybe Dave Getz, said, "What *is* your job?" They didn't know what Cooke was doing and they were worried their earnings were being swallowed up by their new overhead. After all, the band members' weekly draw amounted to only two hundred dollars, a mere fifty dollars more than Cooke's salary. "They were sure they'd never see a dollar," Cooke says. "San Francisco was so paranoid about Albert Grossman, the East Coast manager."

The band came to understand Cooke's importance as their touring increased and life became more complicated. Cooke made sure the band and their equipment arrived at gigs on time, found doctors when they were needed, and had no qualms about going toe-to-toe with sleazy promoters, or even cops for that matter. By all accounts, Cooke was the best in the business. His was a demanding job, and his haughty air served the band well on any number of occasions. His devotion to precision and efficiency, not to mention his way of barking orders, however, earned him the reputation of "road Nazi." Janis grew very fond of him, but his persnickety manner once led her to ask Myra Friedman, "Man, can you imagine scrambling an egg for John Cooke?"

Cooke wasn't a San Francisco hippie, but he was closer to Janis's world than Myra, the band's able publicist, who really was an outsider. She wasn't straitlaced, but she was rather straight—not an asset among rock's emerging hipoisie. Being female, moreover, put her at a disadvantage in Albert's office. "Bobby Neuwirth went to Europe and everywhere. And both Bobby and Emmett Grogan went around with charge accounts and charged it all to the Grossman office. But I couldn't do those things, because I was female," Myra contends. "Albert respected me, but it didn't manifest itself in my paycheck or the freedom to charge airline tickets."

Despite their differences, Janis and Myra became friends. Myra was attracted to Janis's "magnetism" and "the painful urgency in her eyes." She wasn't fooled by Janis's tough-girl act, which she considered "just about the phoniest front" she'd ever seen. Around her, Janis was some-times "frighteningly fragile," a quality, Myra says, that "had a stabilizing effect on my own temperament, which could not exactly be called sub-dued." Janis "was noisy even when she was totally *quiet*," Myra maintains, and her powerful exertions of feeling may have made Myra feel well-adjusted by comparison. Next to Janis's gargantuan insecurities, Myra's own initial uncertainty about working in the "Vatican" of the rock world might have seemed more manageable.

For her part, Janis welcomed a Myra in her life, someone who would set limits and act as a surrogate mother. Myra went along and played superego to her charge's raging id when Janis was in New York or called long-distance about the latest calamity in her love life or career. Unlike many other people in Janis's life, Myra generally told her when she felt Janis had gone too far, which evidently was a good deal of the time. Throughout her 1973 biography of Janis, Myra "groans," "grunts," "hisses," "yells," and "snaps" at her, like an exasperated mother stuck with a delinquent teenage daughter. But if Myra sometimes responded to Janis with maternal disapproval, she cared for her, a fact Janis apparently grasped.

Big Brother made its New York debut on February 17, 1968, at the Anderson, an old Yiddish theater on the Lower East Side. The Anderson had literally gone from staging such Yiddish staples as *The Bride Got Far-blundjet* (*The Bride Got Confused*) to Country Joe and the Fish. John Morris and Joshua White, two Carnegie Tech theater grads, were among those putting on rock concerts there in the hope of luring Bill Graham back to his hometown. Graham was reluctant to expand into "big time" New York—he didn't want to "fall on his ass," as one friend put it. Morris and White were convinced they could woo Graham there with Janis, whom New York rock fans had heard about but never witnessed in the flesh. "Ever since Monterey Pop," White recalls, "we'd been hearing these rumors about this woman from Texas who could sing Grace Slick off the stage."

John Morris spent most of that February afternoon with Janis, who was "scared shitless" about the night's performance. "I ain't so sure we're ready for New York," she confided to him. Backstage with the band and Albert's staff, Janis worried about absolutely everything, including her age. "Do I look old?" she kept asking. B. B. King opened for Big Brother, which only made the band feel more anxious. Dave Getz and Janis wandered out to the orchestra pit to listen. They were both in awe of King's musicianship and felt they had no business being the headliners that night. Self-deprecatingly, Janis said, "We're just a sloppy group of street freaks." Then, according to Myra, "smiling childishly, she snuggled up to Albert."

"B. B. King slayed 'em," Morris says. "It was the first time he'd ever played to a white audience downtown. He did seven or eight encores. He had to keep doing them. And Janis was terrified to follow him. She didn't want to go on. I remember putting my arm around her before she went on and saying, 'Just go kick their asses.' She charged out, literally went from halfway upstage toward them." Janis always made a habit of running onstage. "I go whooooosh," she said, "so that by the time I get to the microphone my blood's going bump-abump-abump-abump." That night, Big Brother started with the fast-tempo tune "Catch Me Daddy," and as Janis sang the first notes, "the roar from the audience was so strong it knocked her back, it physically drove her back upstage," Morris says. "She had 'em. I'd never seen a performance like that in my life. Before that curtain went up she was a scared little girl, she wasn't 'Janis Joplin.'" But then, "she tore the place apart," Morris remembers. "I think I've done about four hundred concerts in my life, and probably seen eight hundred, and that would have to rank with the top two or three of all of them." Like the rest of the audience, Myra Friedman was stunned. "Never before had I heard a sound like that!" The band did four encores, the last of which was the smoldering "Ball and Chain." Bill Graham was backstage surveying the packed house, and Joshua White saw "the click in his eyes. I saw him realize this is do-able." When Graham opened the Fillmore East across the street less than a month later, Big Brother was the headlining act.

"Everyone was exhausted after the show," recalls Morris. "Janis was wrung out but overjoyed." Neil Louison, a writer for *Crawdaddy*, a rock magazine that had helped put on the show, claimed Janis was "like a big kid squealing with happiness; she spotted Albert, ran over, hugged him, and screamed, 'Oh Albert, I'm so happy, I want to fuck you!' " Eventually, Albert would devise an effective way to deflect Janis's generosity, according to Myra. "If I turn out to be a lousy lay, I may not be able to keep you as a client," he'd say smilingly. The band was scheduled to rehearse after the show in preparation for the Columbia album recording. But Sam Andrew snuck off with Linda Eastman, then a pretty, well-connected rock 'n' roll photographer, and the others decided to party, leaving Janis feeling deserted and pissed off. She walked from the theater down the street to a dive on Second Avenue, possibly one of the bars she'd haunted during her stay in New York in 1964. Louison spotted her there and thought it strange, "her sitting at a bar alone with seven Ukrainians." Janis complained about her band mates to Louison, the man who would write so scornfully about her after her death. It wasn't the first time the guys had partied after a show while Janis consoled herself with a bottle in some dive, but this time she was angry at the guys, who she felt were "fucking up." And they resented her for getting all the attention. The fissure in the group was growing.

Tensions had been simmering back in San Francisco, but when the band first arrived in New York it was still technically a group of equals, Big Brother and the Holding Company. By the time they opened Graham's Fillmore East in March 1968, the band appeared on the marquee as "Janis/Big Brother." Janis asked Joshua White, who was hired to do the light shows, to change the marquee. "She didn't want to stick out," recalls Morris, the manager of the Fillmore East. "She was a band member. Now, she stuck out by a hundred miles, but she kept saying, 'I'm not the star.' I heard that sentence quite a few times." "That was sort of like bullshit," says Joshua White. "We knew better. But there was a lot of that kind of crap in those days." The idea of hierarchy was such a taboo in Big Brother that when the band discovered the roadies staying in their Chelsea Hotel suite, the guys just let the mixup stand. Janis, however, wasn't happy about losing her more commodious digs. "What is this crap?" she snapped. When one of the roadies, her friend Dave Richards, shot back, "Right, Janis. We're just workers, and you're the star," she just said, "Aw, fuck you, man," and left. The roadies kept their suite that night, but the band's false egalitarianism wouldn't survive New York.

The hype swirling around Janis after the Anderson Theater gig gave the band's fragile unity a lethal knock. "The incredible commotion over her," Myra recalls, "was simply overwhelming." Myra was completely unprepared for the press's immediate and headlong infatuation with Janis. Robert Shelton of the *New York Times* had never heard Janis live and rushed up to Myra after the concert, yelling, "She's fantastic!" He asked for her picture and was stunned when Myra admitted she had none. "Whadda you *mean*, you don't have one!" Myra ripped a poster of the band off the wall and handed it to him. "I don't *want* this! I need a picture of *her*!" When he asked who played what, Myra couldn't provide those details either, prompting Shelton to ask, "Don't you *want* me to write this review?" Shelton's flat-out rave appeared as the lead story of his paper's Arts and Culture section. The Grossman office had no picture of Janis so the *Times* cropped the group shot to eliminate everyone else. Although Shelton noted that Big Brother was worthy of its star, he gushed about the lead singer, who, he claimed, was "as remarkable a new pop-music talent as has surfaced in years." After comparing her to Aretha and Erma Franklin, he wrote, "comparisons wane, for there are few voices of such power, flexibility and virtuosity in pop music anywhere. Occasionally Miss Joplin appeared to be hitting two harmonizing notes at once." Altogether, the New York critics were enthralled by Janis and if they had doubts about the band, they didn't voice them.

Indeed, the band's press party several days later was a mob scene. When Myra asked Dave Getz how the band was holding up, he said, laughing, "Ahhh! Gettin' drunk. This is ridiculous! I feel like we're putting people on." Janis was surrounded by worshipful people intent on catching her every word. She thrived on the attention, but her mood changed abruptly when, swinging around too quickly, she brushed the face of a woman next to her with her hair. "Who do you think you are!" the woman snarled at Janis. Myra was shocked to see how utterly defenseless Janis became. Her face suddenly turned "tight, masked in splotchy pink," and she looked on the brink of tears. All the adulation couldn't wipe out this one stupid slight, which seemed to send Janis right back to Thomas Jefferson High School. When Myra tried to make her feel better, Janis looked wistful and said, "Well, let's face it, I've got ratty hair." Within a few minutes, though, Janis was her old self, "yammering away breathlessly about her spontaneity as if nothing had happened." Later, when Myra asked how she was feeling, Janis frowned. "I don't know what this is all about. I'm no star!" she protested. Yet the very next moment "her eyes were darting expectantly around the room" until she saw a photographer and struck a pose. Janis may have found the adulation discomfiting, but she still ate it up.

The truth is that Janis took to publicity quickly and well. She was "very intent" on publicity, more so than the rest of the band. In fact, when Myra met with them all to gather biographical information for their press packet, she ran into some resistance. Rather than talk about his past, Sam Andrew got into a long and tedious reverie about acid. "Listen," Janis finally broke in, "she's just trying to get inside of our heads, man. Cooperate." Janis understood the importance of Myra's role right away. "She was going to tell me anything I asked and then some," Myra says, although she insists that the whole media circus around Janis "sprang from the ground quite on its own momentum." It was not, she maintains, in any way orchestrated by the Grossman office. "Had I *wanted* to 'hype' her—it was not my style—I would never have had the chance," she rightly observes, noting how sudden the Janis tsunami was. The speed of adulation defied the normal rules of star making; after all, the band didn't even have a hit record. All they had was the Mainstream LP, an album Janis found so embarrassing she had thanked Ralph Gleason of the *San Francisco Chronicle* for panning it.

In the end, the press went into overdrive not because of Janis's willingness to cooperate or because of any Myra- or Albert-hatched master plan but because reporters saw who Janis was: a uniquely powerful singer and personality whose success signaled a seismic shift in the culture. She was not just a white girl singing the blues but a white girl laying claim to raunchy rock 'n' roll, previously the turf of bad boys. There were other women who rocked full tilt, but they were black—Etta James and

Tina Turner, in particular—and racism robbed them of the fame they deserved. And then there was the question of Janis's looks. As the record producer John Simon points out, "Singers usually had to have that starlet look, and Janis was pretty average-looking." But in 1968 this worked for Janis, as did her boast that she'd always been an outsider, "on the other side of society," as she told *Vogue* magazine. The media fell in love with Janis because she seemed to embody the rebelliousness, spontaneity, honesty, and authenticity of her generation. If she preferred alcohol to acid, that was okay. Janis was the real thing. Journalists declared her "a social phenomenon," a phrase Janis quickly satirized into "social phe-nomonemone," pronounced fe-nom-o-nem-o-nee.

Not that Janis's manipulation of the press didn't help. "She was absolutely captivating," says Myra, a "wizard with words," and she also "said all these things that were outrageous." Janis did the unthinkable: she talked about sex. "At that time to say that performance was like orgasm was the most outrageous thing that anybody ever heard," Myra points out. Janis understood her cultural capital was her ability to shock and began playing it up almost immediately. Once she discovered something went over well with reporters, notes Myra, she'd embellish and refine it, creating the perfect sound bite. At first she likened performing to "falling in love twenty times" or to "having a baby," but within months she'd shock and delight journalists with the racier analogy. "It's like an orgasm," she announced. She also concocted the story of her parents kicking her out of the house when she was fourteen. Back in Port Arthur, "little resentments stewed" because of the story, but Janis was expressing a truth she felt about her relationship to her family, and it made great copy.

Despite all Janis's talk about spontaneity, Myra maintains that Janis, "in some ways, was about as spontaneous as the Manhattan Project." In the spring of 1968 she thought up the Southern Comfort publicity stunt. She insisted Myra call the company's corporate headquarters and "point out all the PR she was giving them and—hint, hint—shouldn't they recognize that in some way?" The call resulted in the famous lynx coat. Another time, she ordered Myra to publicize her fight with the Doors' Jim Morrison. Myra remembers Janis calling her with news of their altercation. When Myra responded disapprovingly, Janis grew irritable. "Maybe you don't like the story," she replied, "but his people think it's somethin' and they want pictures." In the end, Myra preferred discretion and she won. But a year later Janis didn't even bother with Myra, instead ordering her friend Richard Hundgen to call Jann Wenner about her one-night stand with the New York Jets' studly star quarterback Joe Namath. "Tell him Janis fucked Namath and I want it in the next *Rolling Stone*." When the story appeared in the very next issue, Janis cut it out and framed it.

After Big Brother's New York debut, it became harder to deny the obvious, despite Janis's having the Fillmore East's marquee changed. In the recording studio, "Janis was the focus of it all," John Simon maintains. "Things couldn't start till she got there. She was the leader of that band, no doubt. It may have been a democracy in intention, but it certainly was not in practice." The interview requests from *Vogue*, *Glamour*, *Time*, the *New York Times*, *Eye*, the *Village Voice*, and everywhere else started piling up. "The press began focusing on Janis at Monterey Pop," says John Cooke, "and the guys were getting periodically pissed: 'Hey, it's all Janis this and Janis that.'" John Morris remembers the guys growing unhappy about their increasing invisibility. "Of course they resented it, they're men. They wanted to be as talented as she was. They weren't." At this stage, Janis's mesmerizing performances weren't the only thing setting her apart from the guys. Her offstage behavior was getting her lots of ink. The men, by contrast, were less interesting to the press. "Who cared what a bunch of guys thought?" says Myra. "They couldn't get this through their heads." Myra tried to deal with the media's indifference by telling publications, "Listen, if you talk to the guys, I'll set up an interview with Janis later." It was all very demoralizing.

Worse was to come when Big Brother began recording their first Columbia album, *Cheap Thrills*, and had to confront the withering contempt of its producer, John Simon. The son of the founder of the Norwalk Symphony, he'd been an all-star jazz player at Princeton and had early distinguished himself at Columbia Records as someone whose perfect pitch couldn't tolerate musicians playing out of tune. "A wonderful producer," insists the album's engineer, Fred Catero. "He was one of those people who really knew what they wanted and what they were doing." No one ever questioned Simon's competence, but pairing him with Big Brother was a questionable move. "What? This guy can't produce this band," was

John Cooke's first thought. "He doesn't have a clue what this music is about." At twenty-eight, Simon was only three years older than Janis, but he had little use for most rock music. In the wake of the British Invasion, Simon says, "most of the bands we signed were without discernible evidence of any talent. They had great hair and looked right in their clothes, but they had no talent." For Simon, talent was largely reducible to instrumental skill. Once he determined that Big Brother's artistic ambitions outstripped their musicianship he apparently made little effort to disguise his disdain. Simon himself admits that his social skills in those days were underdeveloped.

By all accounts, Simon thought Big Brother was a disaster from the beginning. In December 1967 he'd flown to San Francisco for a preproduction recording of the band at Golden State Recorders and he wasn't encouraged. Simon missed the band's Anderson Theater show in New York but asked Catero and Elliot Mazer to check it out. "Janis appeared to be much better than the band," Mazer thought, but he still felt "you could really do something good with them as a unit." In fact, he left the theater that night thinking the recording would be a snap. Mazer delivered "the incredibly unpopular view" that Big Brother had given a great performance. "Our job is to capture that," he told Simon, who just rolled his eyes.

In all probability, Albert Grossman thought Simon's exacting ear would counter the sloppiness that often characterized Big Brother. Dave Getz recalls, "Albert just told us, 'John Simon will be your producer. You need him and he's going to get two-sevenths of your royalties.'" Simon had worked well with one of Albert's other clients, the Band, on *Music from Big Pink*, their first album. But he loved the Band's music, which was a pretty good indication that he wouldn't take to Big Brother. After all, *Big Pink* was a deliberate rebuttal of psychedelic music, "with its flaming guitars and endless solos and elongated jams," as the Band's drummer, Levon Helm, put it. Dave recalls Simon's playing the band a prerelease tape of *Big Pink*, and announcing, "*This* is what I like." Simon claims he wasn't trying to disparage Big Brother's music, but that's the way the band felt.

Simon took his first serious stab at recording them at Detroit's Grande Ballroom on March 1, 1968. He, Mazer, and Catero had all come along that weekend. If the strength of San Francisco's sound was "live," as Janis herself said, then it made sense to play up the group's stage qualities—its garage-band energy and grittiness. "The idea was that Janis would sing on-stage and the audience reaction would build the tension," Catero recalls. "The band would get into it and it would happen." Recording live required a remote crew to set up the control board, which was a "monstrously heavy thing." It was stationed right off the stage and Big Brother's "roar of sound"—the band always cranked their amps up high—made recording a nightmare. "I'd just look at the meters," Catero says, "and hope for the best. Well, we'll mix it when we get back, I thought." They recorded for two days and Catero remembers Janis "singing like you never heard." The audience, however, was just stunned. "They'd never heard a woman sound like that," Catero says. "Everytime she'd finish a song, people were just, like, Huh? There was no reaction. It was so funny." Mazer agrees the audience was lackluster but claims that the Detroit performances weren't the band's best shows. More important, Detroit's own beloved MC5 had opened the gig and killed the crowd for Big Brother.

The band had their live audience, but there was no response, no tension, no buzz. Nobody took this harder than Janis, who desperately wanted the Columbia album to be a hit, especially after the disappointing Mainstream record. Janis was not in great spirits that weekend. "I was in the control booth," recalls Catero, "and she'd just finished one set. We started playing back the tape and I guess she came down to hear a little of it. The door hit her hand, spilled her drink, and she just went, 'Aw, fuck,' and walked away. She didn't even hear the tape."

Catero remembers going to a bar with Janis, Mazer, and Simon after the last set. Janis said, "I want five." So, according to Catero, the waiter very politely brought her one drink. "Where's the others?" she asked. And he replied, "Well, I'm bringing you the first one." But Janis wanted to chug them in a row. "She was really depressed," Catero says. "At one moment I was sorta thinking, 'Gee, what a hard woman, what a hard life.' And she looked at me and said, 'I look old, don't I?' "

Back in New York, Simon, Mazer, Catero, and Albert Grossman listened to the Grande tapes and decided they were unusable. "Except for Janis, they were terrible," says Catero. Simon decided not to continue recording the band live but to bring them into a studio. Sessions began in Columbia's Studio B and they were grueling for everyone. "After a few takes it was becoming very evident that the band was not together,"

Catero remembers. "They didn't seem to know their parts. They were out of tune. They forgot when to come in, when to do this, when to do that. But Janis was a killer. She made my hair stand up. She sang her ass off." After three or four takes, Janis was drained. "She was sweating," Catero says, "while the guys were very mellow, taking tokes off joints like, 'Hey, man, what's the big deal?' Simon would say, 'No, it's not right.' And Janis was like, 'Am I going to have to do this again?' Finally Simon said, 'Look, let's call it a day.'" Nothing much was accomplished during these early takes, according to Catero.

Within days, the studio was transformed into a stage, because the band felt their playing suffered from the closed environment. "Everything's fairly isolated," Peter Albin points out. "You have headphones on. The vocalist is in a soundproof vocal chamber. The drummer is baffled like crazy. You can't see the drummer most of the time. It's a very nontogether way of recording." So a stage was improvised with risers, the curtains were lowered, and a spotlight was added to create the necessary atmosphere. The band even chose to set up a P.A. system in the studio rather than have Janis hear the music through headphones, the usual way of recording. "It was the first time anybody tried to simulate the feeling of a stage in the studio," claims Mazer. "And it's why the record has that great ambience." Once again, Janis sang her guts out. "She walked in with her little bottle of Southern Comfort and kicked ass," recalls Catero. "But nothing changed. The bass player was out of tune, the guitarist forgot to come in—you know, all this kind of stuff." Simon kept telling the band to get it together. After many tries, they were just on the verge of getting a usable take when Janis entered the control booth. "She knew it was wrong and was livid," Catero says. "Simon told her they had to do one more take, but she said, 'I ain't going to sing with those motherfuckers,' and walks off and slams the door. And Simon was just left sitting. I remember him saying, 'All right, we'll have to deal with this somehow.'"

The sessions left Simon—usually a "cool, unemotional man," according to Mazer—gnashing his teeth. At one point, he tried to stop a take but the P.A. was so loud the band couldn't hear him and kept on playing. "There's Sam Andrew hunched over his guitar with his hair falling in front of his face," Mazer remembers. "Fred Catero walked out of the control booth and parted his hair and waved at him to stop playing. It was kind of symbolic. There was no communication between the band and John."

Simon insisted that the band do their numbers over and over again. "Here's this dude from Princeton with perfect pitch telling this band they're playing their guitars out of tune, and telling her that she's singing out of tune, and making them do a million takes," says Mazer. D. A. Pennebaker filmed one of the early recording sessions (included in the documentary *Janis: The Way She Was*), and the footage shows Janis's obvious impatience with both Simon and her band mates. Simon brings them all into the control booth to listen to a take of "Summertime." As he plays the track, Janis holds court, growing so boisterous that she drowns out the music. Exasperated, Simon stops the tape and asks them to cut it out, to no avail. Janis was not usually disruptive in the studio, though. "While no one in the band was a slacker," Mazer says, "Janis was twenty times more serious than the guys. She was always the first one there and the last to leave. She wanted to know what was going on. She wanted to have some control over it. While someone else was doing a guitar part, she'd be in the control room doing beads, asking questions, listening." But not that day. Tired of listening to one botched take after another, she sabotages Simon's Music 101 session. At another point, as the band discusses how to proceed, Janis defies Simon's efforts to make the guys play right and slights the guys themselves by insisting, "What you hear is what's up front and that's the vocal. Unless the instrumental really makes a mistake you aren't gonna hear it." If she was trying to get the boys off the hook, she also seemed to be saying that they didn't much matter, that their part was negligible next to her wondrous voice.

In the end, no amount of spotlights and curtains could change the fact that Simon was the band's producer and his expectations clashed with theirs. "John was fighting to get great takes to make popular records," explains Mazer. "And the band wanted to be in a situation where they felt they were doing art. Instead they were worried about making mistakes." Simon's censoriousness only made matters worse, but what could he do? Mazer asks. Ignore all the clunkers? "John has more skill than anyone I've ever known," he says. "When you have perfect pitch, you can't stand to hear stuff that's out of tune and out of time, and they played out of tune and out of time." Janis seemed to internalize Simon's critique of the band, telling a reporter, "We're passionate; that's all we are. And what we're trying to get on record is what we're good at—insisting, getting people out of their chairs." The band was trying to record music of the moment for a producer who believed records should be forever. The New York sessions lasted almost two weeks but netted only three songs. In April, Simon and the band returned to the studio—this time in L.A.—and spent at least a month recording the LP.

"John acted like he was being tortured," recalls Dave Getz. "He acted like he hated our music, like he was only there because he was doing us a favor or because Albert made him do it." Today Simon says Big Brother's musicianship "was not at the very bottom of the competence scale but certainly in the lower half." When he spoke with Myra Friedman in the early seventies, Simon was harsher: the band had no business being in a studio, because "they couldn't make music." To be more precise, Big Brother played "tribal" rather than "studied" music. "What they *should* have had," he told her, "was an Alan Lomax field recording from San Francisco." The only reason the band ended up in Columbia's Studio B, he argued, is that, "for some probably sociological reason, Clive Davis forced them to make a record." Big Brother was a "great *performance* band," he conceded, that "made a lot of people happy," but it was the drugs that caused this collective delight, he believed, and his judgment included Janis. "That's how Janis Joplin could happen in the first place. Everyone's mind was fried."

In all probability, Big Brother would have run into problems in the studio whoever their producer was. "Beatle records were what companies thought were records," Elliot Mazer explains. Virtually all the labels expected polished, catchy tunes that clocked in at two and a half minutes. "But one just wasn't going to get a Beatles record with Big Brother and the Holding Company," says Mazer. Nor with most of the other San Francisco bands, for that matter, which is why the studio was often a frustrating and fraught experience for musicians and producers alike. The Grateful Dead was "branded as an undesirable group in almost every recording studio in Los Angeles," according to a top executive at their label. All the San Francisco bands specialized in "endless jams" that lost a great deal when they were translated to vinyl. "Most people didn't really have the chops to record," admits Bill Champlin of the Sons of Champlin, a veteran of the scene. In fact, John Simon attributes the development of multitrack tape recording to "the fact that rock groups couldn't really cut it in the studio. Until then, things were recorded on three-track, or on four-track for something special. But usually it was three tracks with the vocal in the middle and the band in split stereo because all the musicians could cut it. They'd walk into the studio and play whatever they had to play. The Band was like that."

Simon didn't much care for Janis personally, either. She was smart enough, but he found her loud, not especially funny, and not at all sexy. "She could be very gracious," Simon admits. One day she walked in on Simon playing the piano with the Electric Flag in an adjoining recording studio. "You're good. How come you're not playing piano for us?" she asked. Simon was "very flattered and touched" when she proposed he play on "Turtle Blues." Janis was okay when she was mellow, he maintains, but most of the time he found her "so overbearing she was scary." "There were some people who were very negative about Janis physically," says Myra Friedman. "They just didn't like the way she looked, and John did not like the way she looked. He didn't find her attractive at all. He thought she was a comical figure." Sensing his dislike and feeling rejected, Janis became harder, as if to "amplify her coarseness." And of course, Janis was stung by his lack of regard for her singing. "She was really pissed off at John," Mazer says. "She wanted people to accept her and think she was great and wonderful. She had a huge inferiority complex." But to Simon, Janis was "much more important as a sociological phenomenon than as a musical phenomenon. At the time, it seemed that she was the champion of the less-than-glamorous young girl." In his view, Janis's popularity was rooted in her "liberation of all the plain-looking, over-weight, loud young women."

In addition, Simon was put off by "her lack of spontaneity" as a singer. "She was really quite studied," he says. "She went into the studio with an idea in her head to make a song using elements of Tina Turner, Big Mama Thornton, Etta James and incorporating them into her style very con-sciously. It was *her*, but it was not utterly spontaneous. Quite the oppo-site." Talking to Myra Friedman, Simon said, "She was planning out every single moan and shriek as she went. . . . We'd do a take. She'd say, 'I like that.' The next take she'd do it the same." Janis's way of singing a song did change over time, Mazer maintains, but in the studio "Janis would sing a song basically the same way every damn time. The guys working on the 1993 boxed set at Columbia would call me up and say, 'It's amazing! Seventeen takes and she sounds the same on every one!'" To Mazer, though, this was a virtue. "She was really smart, about the smartest artist I ever worked with. She had a vanity about her singing and she sang the words, the meaning, and orchestrated a way of doing it that was very moving. It was this incredibly powerful combination of intellect and spontaneous feeling. There's a magic to it that few people can get." Whatever the roots of Janis's studied approach—her vanity, her insecurity, her intelligence, or a background in folk rather than in improvisational jazz—it was certainly effective, even if curiously at odds with her self-presentation as a blues singer who just "feels things."

Simon's exacting standards may have frustrated the band, but he did make them sound better. Big Brother's version of the Gershwin standard "Summertime" included a diminished chord that was unique and "exquisitely beautiful," in Simon's words. Sam Andrew had appropriated the Prelude in C minor near the beginning of Bach's "The Well-Tempered Clavier" and played it at half tempo as the song's opening. Simon noticed, however, that the band "seemed to think you could simulate Bach when each musician played a stream of steady eighth notes. They hadn't paid much attention to the fact that the eighth notes always had to create harmony between them. As a result, the 'Bach' they made was much more dissonant than I suspect even they had hoped"—a view Sam doesn't dispute. On "Summertime" and other songs, Simon certainly left his mark. He also overcame the band's musical limitations by overdubbing some of the instruments. "The whole album," explains Mazer, "is chock full of little bits and pieces and splices." The *Cheap Thrills* version of "Ball and Chain," for example, was recorded live at Winterland (Bill Graham's second San Francisco ballroom) except for one part. "John Simon could hear a mistake in an eight-minute song," notes Mazer, "and know that it was measure 134. He could call up another take of the same song, find measure 134, and know if it was the right tempo and whether the splice would work. He's a mathematician. He's brilliant."

Simon's real stroke of genius, however, was to create the sound of a live album. "John was good," Dave Getz admits. "He came up with a real concept for the album that worked. It created a picture for people who hadn't been to the San Francisco ballrooms." From the very first line— Bill Graham introducing "Four gentlemen and one great, great broad, Big Brother and the Holding Company!"—the album sounds live, even though all but one track ("Ball and Chain") was recorded in the studio. Simon says he "set up fake audience loops and everything," because he reasoned listeners would be more forgiving of the band's flaws if they thought the group was playing live. "If the listeners assumed these were live tracks, then bad or out-of-tune playing would be sort of more permitted than if it had been called a studio album." The acoustic track "Turtle Blues" even includes background noise from Barney's Beanery, an L.A. rock 'n' roll joint Janis frequented; James and Janis went there with a tape recorder and James kept the tape running as Janis provoked an argument with someone.

Most of the live effects were captured in the studio, though. In "Turtle Blues" Dave Getz and Bob Neuwirth break wine glasses, creating the crash that punctuates Peter Albin's guitar solo. The audience on *Cheap Thrills* was not the crowd at the Fillmore or the Avalon but secretaries, engineers, and various hangers-on in the studio. "We gave them tambourines and whistles and stuff," recalls Fred Catero, "and said, 'Can you stand out here, and whenever you feel like reacting just whoop and holler, shake your tambourines, and blow your whistles?' " For a band that so valued spontaneity and authenticity, it is something of an irony that the album's live sound was largely contrived.

According to some accounts, Simon actually quit in frustration before finishing the album. Simon denies the accusation, and in fact he did deliver a mix to Columbia, a mix that Dave Getz, for one, loved. Simon's version included "Harry"—a "Frank Zappa–like song," Dave wrote—and the band's version of "Happy Birthday," but Columbia rejected them as too raw. By that point, June 1968, the album had dragged on for over three months and Simon was already committed to producing the Band's second album. As a consequence, delivering a new mix and "mopping up" were left to Mazer, who found himself having to fend off pressure from Clive Davis to hurry and finish. Mazer was still "trying to figure out how to put the second side together" when Davis notified Janis that *Cheap Thrills* had been certified gold. "It was really infuriating," recalls Mazer, who wanted the time to complete a good record. As it turned out, the rules changed and a record had to be sold before it could be certified. Mazer believes *Cheap Thrills* would have been even stronger had Columbia not been breathing down his neck to finish. Although Janis and James are credited with the final mix, Dave says the whole band was involved in the album's marathon thirty-six-hour mixing session. Sam recalls emerging from the studio feeling convinced that the band really "had something."

When *Cheap Thrills* finally came out, Simon's name was nowhere on it, oddly enough. He knew all along the record would be big, Simon says, but months before the final mix was completed, he had decided against taking producer's credit, a "highly unusual" move, in Fred Catero's words. Almost everyone associated with the band assumes Simon refused credit because he disliked the album, but he claims otherwise. "I was working on the movie *You Are What You Eat* with Howard Alk," he explains, "and Alk said, 'Credit corrupts. Once you put your name on something you automatically start wondering what people will think of you, based on this piece of art. And that nullifies the purity of the art.'" He and Alk went on to make a pact to leave their names off their work. It just so happened that Simon's next project was *Cheap Thrills*. "A few months later," he says, "I decided it was a philosophically interesting concept but a stupid thing to do in the real world. And I've put my name on every album I've done since."

"He told me that dopey story, too," says Dave Getz, "and it's such bullshit." Myra Friedman also doubts Simon's account. "Well, I don't think that's the truth," she says. "He didn't want his name on the album because he didn't like the way it sounded." Elliot Mazer is one who confirms Simon's story of his pact with Alk, but the *Rolling Stone* review of *Cheap Thrills* noted that Simon wasn't listed as the producer and quoted him as saying the album "was as good as the band and that's about it." Little wonder that people thought he was distancing himself from the record. For Big Brother the kicker was that Simon refused to associate his name with their record but nonetheless earned tens of thousands of dollars from it.

Cheap Thrills was released in late August 1968 and sold a million copies in its first month, despite mixed reviews. With all the success, though, the process of recording the album undermined Janis's confidence in the band. When Paul Rothchild was pursuing Janis in 1966, she'd admitted to her parents that she had doubts about her band mates' seriousness, their willingness to "work hard enough to be good enough to make it."

But her misgivings faded as she grew acclimated to the Bay Area rock scene, where virtuosity had so little to do with making it. No one in San Francisco cared that Big Brother sounded like a garage band. "The band had a sound and was cool live," recalls Bruce Barthol of the Fish. "They were a little notorious for being out of tune, although that was Gurley to a great extent." In late 1967 when Janis returned to Port Arthur for the holidays, her friends Frances Vincent and Jim Langdon advised her to ditch the band. "Both Jim and I said, 'Jan, you've got to get rid of Big Brother,' " recalls Vincent. "They're lousy musicians." Janis didn't defend them as musicians; instead she said, 'Oh no, I slept with all of them. They're like my family. I've balled 'em all.' " Janis hadn't slept with them all, but she certainly did feel they were her family.

After several weeks in the studio, though, Janis began wondering if she'd be better served by another band. She wanted a solid foundation behind her, not the erratic if inspired Big Brother, with their lurching sound. The endless takes wore her out, and the band racked up expensive studio costs more accomplished musicians would have avoided. Myra noticed the first signs of friction between Janis and the band at an early-April 1968 gig at a Greenwich Village club, but the tension had begun earlier, almost as soon as the recording started. Janis avoided complaining about the band to the press, however, preferring to tell reporters that Big Brother was "passionate and sloppy." After several weeks in New York she admitted to Nat Hentoff that the city had taken its toll on the band, but she insisted they were "learning to control success, put it in perspective, and not lose the essence of what we're doing—the music." Inevitably, the band could hardly stay focused on the music when everybody treated Janis like the star and Big Brother like her backup band. This was not the deal the guys had struck two years earlier. While she was unhappy with their musicianship, they began to accuse her of thinking she was "hot shit." Janis started complaining to friends that the guys were trying to make her feel guilty for being more talented than they were.

Her increasing disillusionment with the band has often been attributed to Big Brother's treatment in the rock 'n' roll press. "The reviews were relentless," according to Clive Davis, "saying again and again that she was far superior to the musicians backing her." Nick Gravenites of the Electric Flag believes that after "reading review after review" that praised her while calling Big Brother "dog shit," she "got real crazy, and she felt she'd have to drop the band and get a band together who were really good as musicians." Dave Getz blames the press, too. "Once we left warm and cozy San Francisco, the critics attacked Big Brother because we were very limited musically. Ultimately, that's what split up the band." In truth, Big Brother garnered few negative reviews before the summer of 1968, though Janis was clearly the one who excited critics and fans. New York critics like Robert Christgau, Ellen Willis, Robert Shelton, and Richard Goldstein devoted little ink to the band, but neither were they negative.

In the fall of 1967, however, the band did get an unequivocally negative review, in the *L.A. Free Press*, Los Angeles's underground paper, which praised Janis but argued she was "too full of soul for Holding Company partners." And throughout 1968, Big Brother was trashed by the Bay Area's very own *Rolling Stone*. Jann Wenner's new paper was still a funky-looking rag, but it had quickly managed to acquire enormous influence. You didn't want to get a bad notice in *Rolling Stone*. Early that year the paper reviewed the band's Boston gig, calling the group "messy and a general musical disgrace." Condemnation of this sort was actually rare outside the pages of *Rolling Stone*, but it affected the band. "We started looking at ourselves that way," says Dave.

Janis was rattled by another source of criticism: other musicians and their increasingly pointed comments about Big Brother. New York players, most of whom were studio musicians who could read music, often took a dim view of the San Francisco bands, whose appeal they couldn't quite fathom. Big Brother's East Coast booking agent, Lee Housekeeper, overheard "lots of disparaging comments about the band's musicianship" among New York players. "But," he adds, "there was great respect for Janis and her abilities as a singer. The old blues cats who'd worked with Aretha and others would say, 'Oh man, what a voice! All you need to do is get some good musicianship behind her.'" Janis had to have known what people were saying, but attacks by other musicians did not make their way into the press until Michael Bloomfield, the guitar wunderkind, blasted Big Brother in the pages of *Rolling Stone* in April 1968. "Big Brother is just a wretched, lame group of cats who she carries for no reason at all," he said, an opinion seconded by Wenner.

Clive Davis and Albert Grossman had never been great fans of the band, either. Davis doubted "that Big Brother could grow any further."

And Albert had always been enamored more of Janis than of the guys. He'd even suggested a personnel change early on, after seeing one of the band's gigs in Huntington Beach in September 1967—the show that garnered the negative review in the *L.A. Free Press*. James had been so drunk and stoned on downers he could barely stand up, much less hit anything resembling the right notes. Albert was appalled and after the show called a band meeting to which James was not invited. He was completely open, advising Big Brother to give James "some time away from the band." Offer him a lump sum of ten thousand dollars and hire another guitarist, he suggested. Predictably, the band rallied to James's defense. Replacing James, whose screaming psychedelic guitar had so defined the band's sound, was unthinkable.

Albert didn't push his view, but once Michael Bloomfield and John Simon, clients whose opinions he respected, began publicly knocking Big Brother, he may have decided his star's career (as well as his own impeccable taste) was on the line. In August 1968, Big Brother turned in a sizzling performance at the Newport Folk Festival. The audience loved the set and demanded two encores. But afterward, Albert took the band aside and told them the rhythm section was a problem. "It's just not working," Peter remembers him saying. Dave found it hard not to take Albert's criticism to heart. "I thought he knew everything," reflects Dave. "I bought into it. A lot of us bought into it because he exuded such an air of sophistication and confidence and knowingness." But Albert's view was shared by a cocky young Boston rock critic, Jon Landau, whose savage review of Big Brother's Newport performance was published in *Rolling Stone*. Landau ripped into the band, declaring that Bloomfield had been "charitable" in describing the group as lame. "Gurley and Andrew don't know a decent rock or blues chorus between them. . . . And the rhythm section never happens." Not that Landau exempted Janis from his blistering attack. "Her melodrama, overstatement, and coarseness are not virtues. They are signs of a lack of sophistication and a lack of security with her material." True, Landau pilloried all the stars who played Newport, preferring B. B. King and Janis's old Austin friend the "modest but moving" Kenneth Threadgill and his Hootenanny Hoots.

Landau had never taken to Big Brother (or to psychedelic music—he'd panned Jimi Hendrix's *Are You Experienced?*), but even the admiring critic Vince Aletti had some harsh words after a Fillmore East appearance in early August. The "band in back of Janis is usually just that: in back of her. Sounding OK, but generally unexceptional," he wrote. "You get the feeling that without her, they would still be in San Francisco." Of Janis he wrote, "some things about her singing . . . are beginning to become set into a style—mainly the harsh, raspy quality of her voice." He lamented her refusal to use "the more natural range of clear and sweet sounds she is capable of," a range he believed would "heighten the impact of her whiskey voice." Several weeks later when she played the Singer Bowl with Jimi Hendrix, Aletti faulted both of them for recycling old performances, but he wrote that "at least Joplin will cut short any period of stagnation when she leaves Big Brother."

Understandably, Janis came to believe the band was hampering her. She didn't want to worry about whether or not the band would be "on" that night. She was tired of the rushed rhythms and out-of-tune playing. One night during the band's disappointing Grande Ballroom show, the microphone picked up Janis reprimanding James Gurley, saying "you gonna play the wrong chord all night?" Mazer left the aside on the 1972 record *Joplin in Concert;* the wrong chord, he observes, "was typical of what she had to put up with. Being a real perfectionist, she had to work hard to get what she wanted out of the band." Sam remembers their June performance at the Fillmore as a "turning point" in Janis's relationship with the group. After a less-than-stellar show—two band members were sick—Janis complained that she was "busting her ass" to get the songs right while the guys weren't really trying. Later she'd say it always made her "goony" when a musician behind her screwed up. And in Big Brother screwing up happened all too often. "We didn't know our scales that well, and we played a lot of wrong notes, a lot of clunkers," admits Peter. Janis also wanted to move into soul music. Like many white rock 'n' rollers, Janis was infatuated with the tight horn-based soul bands that backed Aretha Franklin and Otis Redding. The prospect of working with sea-soned professional musicians frightened her, but she felt her musical growth demanded the move.

The concerts were also feeling formulaic to her. "What drove me crazy," she said, "was that I couldn't dredge up any sincerity in the music anymore." Certainly it was hard to sound sincere as the band embarked on their second year of playing "Down on Me," "Ball and Chain," and

"Combination of the Two"—the same songs night after night, week after week, month after month, and now year after year. Janis felt the band had grown lazy. Rather than come up with new material or approaches, she claimed, the others "thought, 'why work, man, they like it.' " The performances were all just so much "shucking," she told one reporter. "I don't mind selling pleasure if people want to pay for it, but who wants to get paid ten grand for acting like you're having a good time? That's shameful, and I saw it before the band saw it." Peter thinks Janis was the one "shucking," but he agrees the band was growing stale. "She was able to digest new stuff and we were lagging behind," he says. Even at the time, Peter admitted that "Janis was the best musician; she could experiment onstage." The rest of the band, however, "needed time and rest to do new things. So for us it got to the point where all we wanted to do was play our tunes and split." In the wake of *Cheap Thrills*, Big Brother "became a very good, monster act with one killer set," according to Dave. He concedes that Janis was growing at a faster pace, though. She had always been restless, wanting to be more creative, and the band's inertia drove her nuts. "I wasn't doing anything but standing still and being a success."

Her decision to quit, however, wasn't reached breezily or lightly. Janis agonized over it for months. Walking away from the guys tore her apart. "She said it was like getting a divorce," Linda Gravenites remembers. "It was a very sad thing, man," Janis told a reporter later. "I love those guys more than anybody else in the whole world, they know that. But if I had any serious idea of myself as a musician, I had to leave." Big Brother had been her family, her anchor, and had allowed her to reconcile, however imperfectly, her conflicting impulses toward conventionality and self-expression. In a way, she was choosing between career and family, and unlike most other women of that era, Janis chose her career, perhaps because her success had already soured relations with the band.

As early as June, Janis confided to Sam Andrew that she was thinking of leaving the group, but he kept the secret to himself. Finally, in September, she took him aside and said, "I want to play with horns, do something different. I want to sell out. Just show me where I can sign. I want to be rich, and I want you to come along with me." Janis never broached adding a horn section to Big Brother, either because she knew she'd face resistance or because she was just weary of Big Brother's freak rock, the band's smear of sound. As it happens, Sam says he would have agreed to add horns and he thinks Peter and Dave would have as well. "But James would have been unalterably opposed and then Peter would have gone over to his side. James didn't want to change anything ever." Peter maintains he would have opposed hiring horn players but was amenable to adding horns to certain songs. The whole point is moot because Janis had essentially decided to make the break. "She could have just been tired of looking at our faces, along with all these other reasons," Sam speculates. "Maybe she just thought, 'I really *am* great! I thought I was great before, but now I know I'm great because the whole world thinks so. What's lying out there waiting for me?' Maybe it was just intellectual curiosity." Linda Gravenites simply attributes Janis's discontent to all the hype she read about herself. "When Janis started believing what she read about herself, it was pretty awful," she contends.

Sam suspects money was also a crucial factor, and as her confidant within the band he's in a position to know. "What's often overlooked in this is that maybe she just saw a chance to have all the money to herself. She probably thought she was earning it all anyway, and in some ways she was. I *know* that played a part." After several weeks in New York, Janis knew unequivocally that she was the star attraction—with all the pleasures and burdens that followed from her key role. "I don't think it's possible to be on a San Francisco free thing with me and the band totally, because I'm in front," she told a reporter. "I'm in the spotlight, and if something goes wrong I'm the one who has to carry it."

In mid-September, less than a month after the release of *Cheap Thrills*, the Grossman organization wrote a press release announcing that Janis was quitting Big Brother. The band now had a hit record, but it was unable to generate any new material, according to the release, and Janis had been "pretending" onstage. Before the press was informed, though, Janis called a band meeting and presented her departure as a fait accompli. "She just basically said, 'I'm outta here,'" Peter recalls. No one was really surprised, but Peter still launched into a rant about what a back stabber she was. The guys felt burned by her partly because they'd yet to see any real money from the band. Albert had upped their weekly draw, but it was still only three hundred dollars. Everyone knew Janis was on her way to making big bucks.

Later that day, Dave met with the remaining group members to plan "a whole new life for the band." Dave felt Big Brother could still make a lot of money even without their star attraction. Several hours after the meeting, though, Sam ran into Dave in the Chelsea Hotel and said he'd be leaving with Janis. Dave was furious. "Thanks for telling me, Sam. Why are we sitting around making plans about what to do? That's the end, if you're going to go. That makes it impossible." Janis had vacillated about bringing Sam along; they had collaborated on some tunes and did sing together, but it was probably the terror of striking out alone that prompted the invitation to join her in a new band.

"I didn't know if Big Brother was going to be a viable unit," Sam says. "There were a lot of drugs, and it was kind of the end of an era. But my biggest regret is Janis leaving and my leaving with her. I wish we wouldn't have done it. It was insane to quit when she had a number-one record. I think she should have given it another year. But even if she left, I wish I would have stayed in. That was the biggest mistake I made, easy." Sam's defection was certainly a blow, but James Gurley thinks the band's greatest error was not finding another female singer to do their signature tunes. After Janis left he vowed, "No more chicks! I don't want to work with no more chicks!"—a miscalculation, he now believes, because "Janis took all the band's arrangements and claimed them as her own. We could have gone out just as logically and rightfully and done 'Ball and Chain' and 'Piece of My Heart.' " The band later teamed up with Kathi McDonald, a Bay Area vocalist who could have "gone toe-to-toe with Janis," James claims. Still, the guys were, in his words, "all burned out on the whole thing and wanted something more low-key."

Peggy Caserta echoes the feelings of many hip San Franciscans when she observes that "Albert was the kiss of death for the band." Nick Gravenites, who, as part of the Electric Flag, was also managed by Albert, agrees. Gravenites saw him in action on a number of occasions and says, "Albert would say, 'You love these guys but I'm more interested in you. I will get you a deal for two million dollars, but only if *you* get it. I won't put it into the guys' pockets.' " Indeed, Janis bragged to her parents that Albert had told her she could expect to make a cool half a million dollars in the coming year. According to Elliot Mazer, Clive Davis played a role, too. "I think Clive was pushing Janis to do slick stuff. We all loved Memphis soul music. Those who heard Janis sing thought she sounded better doing that than she sounded doing rock 'n' roll. I went along with it because there was this general decision encouraged by Clive Davis to convert Janis into an Aretha Franklin or a Barbra Streisand. He was looking to Las Vegas. I think Clive had his eye on a ball that was different from Janis's ball. He had these big goals for her. I don't think he was very sensitive to her or her needs. And I was very angry with him for years because of that." Davis, on the other hand, claims Janis called to ask his opinion about leaving the group. "I could tell from the way she spoke that she'd already made up her mind," he says.

Janis was nobody's pawn but her decision was undoubtedly influenced by rock's premier manager and the president of the world's largest record company. Most of all, their view of the band coincided with her own longing for the approval stardom had begun to bring her. She could hardly choose staying with the band if that hurt her popularity. As Linda Gravenites says, "Janis began to feel Big Brother was holding her back from giant success, which she wanted."

Grossman's office described the split as "amicable," but relations between Janis and the band deteriorated rapidly. "Even being in the same room with her was a total stone drag," said Peter. Big Brother still had some gigs to play out that fall after the announcement of Janis's departure, and there were several public flare-ups. In Minneapolis, Janis and Peter nearly came to blows during the show. After one especially exhausting song, Janis panted into the microphone. Peter felt she was trying to impress upon the audience that she was giving them her all. "Now we're doing our Lassie imitation," he joked. The audience cracked up, but Janis looked straight at him and snarled, "Fuck you" right into the mike. Never one to back down, Peter raised his fist to her. "You start talking like a man, I'll treat you like one," he shouted. "Maybe it was chauvinistic," he conceded later, "but when someone says 'Fuck you' to me onstage—be it a guy or a girl—I get pissed off." Backstage, Janis was in a rage, yelling at the band's road manager, John Cooke. "Man, he called me a dog. Onstage in front of everybody. I don't have to take that shit." After the show she laid into Peter. "No one likes to be called a dog," she shouted. "Panting into the mike had become one of her devices," Sam explains. "People who perform have all these little tricks. She was kind of overdoing it, like, 'I've really worked hard and I've given all of myself.'" When Peter made his Lassie remark, he "punctured that illusion abruptly," Sam says. "She wanted to be honest and direct and that's what she was preaching, and here Peter had exposed her. She just freaked. She was beside herself." Janis felt exposed, all right, but not just as a performer using tricks. She felt mocked as an ugly woman, a "dog," and as Sam suggests, the combination must have been horrifying, especially in front of thousands of people.

Although Janis and Peter had fought before, she had always been buddies with Dave, calling him the "solidest guy" in the band. But at their final New York concert, at Hunter College, Janis, screwed up from speed, Seconal, Southern Comfort, and lack of sleep, clashed even with Dave, who was tripping on acid. During his drum solo the band left the stage, as always, but Janis soon returned with his tiger-skin drum, triggering applause. As she placed it next to him, he kicked it away. "Fuck you!" she shouted as she jumped back. They resumed their fight backstage. "I was just trying to be nice to you, man," Janis yelled. "I was just bringing this drum out to you. That was a really nice thing for me to do and you, you fucker, you embarrassed me in front of three thousand people." Dave countered, "You were just trying to upstage me and get your ass onstage again. You put it where I couldn't even play it!"

As Big Brother fought their way through their final tour, *Cheap Thrills* was burning up the charts. The album held the top position for eight weeks, and "Piece of My Heart" reached number twelve on the singles chart. The band had originally wanted to call the record "Sex, Dope, and Cheap Thrills," but accepted the shortened, sanitized version when Columbia balked. With the Hell's Angels' stamp of approval on the cover, the claim that "all live material" had been recorded at the Fillmore, and R. Crumb's cartoon images, the record felt like a real slice of Haight-Ashbury. Originally, Columbia's art director, Bob Cato, had planned a different cover—a photo of the group in bed in a hippie crash pad. When the band arrived at the shoot they discovered a bedroom done up in pink frills—like no hippie pad they'd ever been in. "Let's trash it, boys," Janis declared. And they did. The shot of them, in bed and naked (with the exception of Peter), the bed covers pulled up only to their waists, was junked in favor of Crumb's caricatures.

Cheap Thrills was certified gold within days of its release, but the critics were divided on its merits. Robert Christgau gave it high marks and argued that it proved Big Brother was "always underrated and ever-improving." Bill Fibben, a writer for Atlanta's underground paper, called it "one of the greats." Janis sounded, he wrote, "kinda like a lady James

Brown—one of the great female singers of our time." Fibben thought the album was recorded live and compared it favorably with the band's previous release; the two records stood as proof, he argued, that Big Brother sounded best live. Annie Fisher of the *Village Voice* approved, too. The album, she wrote, "does sound just like [Janis], the group's improvement is noticeable, the live quality is all there, it conjures an instant mental picture of her in action." Although she called Janis "very special indeed," Fisher also wrote, "I hope Janis finds her voice before she destroys it, because it strikes me that we've never heard it." Ignoring Janis's own "Turtle Blues," she faulted her for singing "marvelous re-creations of someone else's message" and urged her to sing "blues that are original and have to do with Janis Joplin here and now."

Predictably, *Rolling Stone* panned the album, calling it "a fair approximation of the San Francisco scene in all its loud, exciting, sloppy glory." Detroit's *Fifth Estate* grumbled, "Janis Joplin has a good voice but can't sing. James Gurley is a very poor guitarist and as a whole the group slides along on an infallible cushion of mediocrity." Worst of all was the *New York Times*, which savaged the band. "Every cut on the album rings false," declared Bill Kloman. As for Janis, he found "enough indications of an interesting vocal quality to suggest that if she knew what she was doing she might be able to sell a song." All the same, he observed, "there are chicks like her in bars all over the Southwest, who sing along with the jukeboxes and dance with soldiers for beer. Like Tiny Tim, Janis is an authentic slice of mid-century Americana but, for the present, a major talent she is not." If Janis was a star, he ventured, it had a lot to do with "the hippie myth that there's a knock-out artist hidden in each of our breasts, if only we'd let it out and start singing or writing poems, or whatever." Janis's success proved you didn't have to take voice lessons, he wrote, before delivering the final blow: "Get yourself a press agent instead." Indeed, the negative reviews often shared an exasperation with the hype surrounding Janis. *Rolling Stone* huffed that after "all the hoopla" the album was a "real disappointment." The *Fifth Estate* argued that the album's success showed "if you put up a big enough front, and Janis has, you can get away with anything." Trashing *Cheap Thrills* became a way to strike a blow against hype and what Joni Mitchell would dub the "star-maker machinery" of the rock business. Ironically, though, as soon as Janis quit

Big Brother, some critics—including Ralph Gleason, the dean of San Francisco rock criticism—started to wax nostalgic about the band. The *New Yorker's* Ellen Willis even wrote that Big Brother "was a good foil for Janis; better musicians might have tried to compete." In his 1972 review of *Joplin in Concert*, Lester Bangs ignored everything but the Big Brother cuts. Decades later, most critics feel Big Brother was Janis's best band, although "passionate and sloppy" plays better today in the wake of punk and grunge than it did thirty years ago. Writing about the boxed set of Janis's recordings, released in 1993, Christgau argued that the rawest music was the most compelling, especially her "rough anything-goes with Big Brother." At the time, Elliot Mazer went along with the critical dismissal of Big Brother; now he feels differently. "They were a very original-sounding bunch of musicians. They created a lot of energy, made a nice noise, an original noise, had some unusual arrangements and ideas, were certainly unique, and passed one test: you hear thirty seconds of Big Brother and you know who it is. How many bands can you say that about?"

Mazer is not the only one to reverse his opinion: almost twenty years after the release of *Cheap Thrills*, a panel of critics assembled by *Rolling Stone* voted it one of the fifty best records of the previous two decades. *Cheap Thrills* captures the band's unexpected darkness as well as its wild exuberance and it remains one of the most powerful recordings of sixties rock 'n' roll. The guys in Big Brother now like to stress their music's kinship to punk, but *Cheap Thrills* is unmistakably a product of the sixties—listen to the whispering of "hiiiigh, hiiiigh, hiiiigh" on "Sweet Mary."

Janis's reworkings of "Piece of My Heart," "Ball and Chain," and "Summertime" also bore the indisputable stamp of her time as she filled them with all the sadness, rage, and incomprehension she felt about life. Her renditions didn't please blues purists, but then, that wasn't her aim. She could do faithful versions of Bessie Smith and Jean Ritchie, but in *Cheap Thrills* and onstage she was hardly just recreating someone's else's message. She took the songs apart and made them hers. She transformed Willie Mae Thornton's ballad from a jilted lover's lament to a brooding meditation and protest against the unfairness of life itself. "Tell me why everything goes wrong," she pleads, exhorting both her lover and the audience to explain it to her. "Maybe you could help me, come on, help me," she shouts. These lines don't appear in the original, nor do Janis's closing cries, where she wails that it just can't be that love—and life—is like a ball and chain. Her singing is sometimes overwrought and screechy, but consider the context—the cute, coy singers who dominated Top 40 radio, from Diana Ross, to Lesley Gore, to the Dixiecups. Janis could sound sweet, but she was damned if she would. Big Brother's compressed metal crush and Janis's raw, assaultive vocals are what gave *Cheap Thrills* what Lester Bangs called its "errant energy." For all their annoying sloppiness, Big Brother was the one band that generally matched Janis's intensity and abandon.

Fittingly, Big Brother ended things where they all began: the band's final gig, in December 1968, was a benefit for Chet Helms's Family Dog. Chet and his partners had been forced out of the Avalon by the San Francisco Board of Permit Appeals on a noise complaint. Big Brother and Chet's Avalon ballroom dances had set out on their path together, and now both were unraveling. After the benefit, the Family Dog tried to make a go of it on the outskirts of town but soon went under. And as Dave had predicted, Sam's departure nixed Big Brother's future plans. James was already contemplating a leave from the band to deal with his heroin addiction. Peter and Dave tried to put together a group, but nothing came of their efforts. Finally, almost a year after the breakup, they accepted an offer from Country Joe McDonald to join the Fish, which had also fallen apart. Big Brother went on to re-form with some new players, including Nick Gravenites, who handled vocals. Janis remained friendly with her former band mates and even joined them onstage twice in the summer of 1970, but they were no longer family. "There are dysfunctional families, you know," says Peter Albin, reflecting on the split. "We had our problems. Sometimes people in the family don't work out and they have to leave. Did Janis have to leave? I don't know."

When Janis struck out on her own, she lost much of her community as well as her family. San Francisco fans reacted to the split as if it signaled the end of the dream, the end of the sixties. "Janis, please don't leave Big Brother," read the spray-painted graffiti on a billboard right off Haight Street. The band's infighting and unraveling "seemed a failure of the whole hip spirit," one rock critic, Michael Lydon, wrote. And in a world where women were just chicks and old ladies, Janis was seen by some as an uppity, back-stabbing bitch. Following her success, she was considered an obnoxious diva whenever she got huffy with a stagehand, even though the same behavior was perfectly acceptable in male rock stars.

Janis's fame had revealed the limits of the "San Francisco free thing," but her real sin was in being a ballsy broad, a chick with acne who took up too much space in the boys' club of late-sixties rock 'n' roll. The rock culture of those years was so profoundly masculine that the first time *Rolling Stone* paid any attention to women, it was in an issue devoted to groupies. As Robert Christgau once noted, "rock and roll was a shitty place for women." And San Francisco was no more enlightened than the rest of the country. Women musicians there encountered "very primitive attitudes," says Tracy Nelson, the female singer of Mother Earth. Nor did success insulate Janis from sexism; in fact, the more famous she became, the more difficult life grew. When Bob Simmons asked one of the guys in the band if Big Brother would play a benefit for the Avalon, he was told to call Janis: "That's the man you gotta talk to." Janis wasn't exaggerating when she said about those difficult months, "They sure laid a lot of shit on me."

The nastiness directed toward Janis had a lot to do with the media blitz. No other San Francisco musician approached Janis's celebrity in this period. *Newsweek* even put her on the cover of its May 29, 1969, issue for a feature article on blues music. In his *Rolling Stone* review of *Joplin in Concert*, Lester Bangs declared that, "having our noses rubbed in hype for months on end, it was only natural that we should resent her to some degree." She was everywhere: "Janis The Spirit Of the Blues, Janis The Spirit of Bessie Smith, Janis on the cover of *Newsweek* magazine and represented inside as what We ('we'?) were all about," Bangs went on. "Janis Suffering, Drinking, Going Through Changes and Searching For The Right Band and The Right Man, her every swig and sigh duly recorded." Some rock fans "wished that damn yammering bitch would just go away," he recalled, seemingly having shared that view. By the end of 1968, Janis, the quintessential countercultural icon of authenticity and spontaneity, was being packaged, as was the sixties spirit she represented. The backlash was inevitable; Janis had become just too big for everybody.

Increasingly, Janis relied on her public persona, even when she was alone with friends. Myra Friedman told her soon after she left Big Brother that it was time for a change, that she should play less to the press's expectations of her as a red-hot mama. "That stuff made me famous!" Janis snapped. "Everybody loves it." Everybody but her friends, who were distressed at how easily Janis could slip into "doing" the tough-assed blues belter. The rest of the world expected her to be outrageous and sassy rather than intelligent, so she rarely revealed how smart she was. Yet many people remember her sharp intellect; one doctor who treated her even thought she was "bordering on brilliant." Hiding her intelligence had begun in Texas, where women were not encouraged to be intellectually superior, according to Janis's Austin friend Fredda Slote. Within the counterculture, being smart, while not precisely a liability, was regarded somewhat suspiciously, as a way of setting oneself apart from "the people." There's no doubt, however, that fame made Janis more reluctant to show off her intelligence. Because she so frequently acted like a boozy broad, "the public didn't know how smart she was," insists Elliot Mazer. "You can hear both people speaking on *Joplin in Concert*, and I did that deliberately."

Linda Gravenites felt Janis was "losing huge chunks of herself" as she played to her image. "Because of the hype, after a while everyone meeting her expected her to be her persona—the tough little chick from Texas. And that was only a smidgen of who she was. But that's the part they sought out and talked to and the part that answered them. And the rest of her fell by the wayside. It was sad to see this whole person becoming a caricature." Linda had always enjoyed talking with Janis because she was well-read and had wide-ranging interests, but now she became difficult to engage on any topic but herself and how she appeared. And more and more, she seemed oblivious to everyone's feelings but her own. Shortly after leaving Big Brother, Janis asked Dave to teach her new drummer how to play a passage in "Summertime." She seemed to have no idea, Dave remembers, that this was an insensitive request. To Bobby Neuwirth, who, as Bob Dylan's sidekick, perhaps knows nothing so well as celebrity, it's very simple: "If you practice long enough being a big, brassy blues mama, you become one. You start to expect it of yourself just as others expect it of you." Of course, Janis had been perfecting the part for years. The character she'd eventually name Pearl, the fast-talking sock-it-to-me broad, had been keeping people at bay with her bravado as far back as Port Arthur. But once she became famous, claims Peter Coyote of the Diggers, there was such "pizzazz and amplification of the media, and it had everybody so freaked, that they couldn't get next to her."

But, of course, Janis's armor was the flimsiest of shields. Janis herself said that "Turtle Blues," for example, was "about me trying to act tough, and nobody noticed I wasn't." In truth, lots of people preferred the front, the larger-than-life Janis, to the "unsettled mix of defiance and hesitancy, vulnerability and strength"—as Michael Lydon called it—barely below the surface. Certainly, the "ballsy, funky" Janis was the "easiest Janis" for reporters to write about, as David Dalton points out in his book about her. "There was nothing enigmatic or ambivalent about it. Janis barreling into town, trading raunchy stories with the boys, setting up drinks. It was so put together."

Janis could still be disarmingly revealing, though, even on occasion to strangers. Dalton once witnessed her open up to a starstruck hippie reporter from Louisville, Kentucky, telling him how insecure she felt about her looks. After he left, Janis worried whether she had been nice enough to the nervous writer. Dalton tried reassuring her, pointing out the obvious: people were nervous around her because she was a star. "I can't relate to that, I can't relate to that," Janis protested. "If they know anything about *anything*, they know I'm not a star. They know I'm a middle-aged chick with a drinking problem, man, and a loud voice, and other things, too . . . but what am I supposed to do? Turn around and say, 'I'm a person'?" In fact, she had done just that by confessing she was as self-conscious about her looks as the next girl. The conversation ended with Janis insisting, "I'll never be a star like Jimi Hendrix or Bob Dylan. I figured out why—cause I tell the truth. If they want to know who I am, they ask me and I'll tell them." Janis didn't always tell the truth, but her moments of self-disclosure could be as disconcerting as the pizzazz.

One thing is sure: fame did nothing to diminish Janis's fragility, whatever other aspects of her character were less in evidence. Two years after the fact, she was still complaining about that "bitch" at the New York press party who'd insulted her. Indeed, fame seemed to magnify rather than ease her defensiveness. According to Dalton, Janis would assume that "the couple laughing at the next table were laughing at" her or that a roadie's offhand comment was meant to hurt her. Slote recalls telling Janis she thought it was "a hoot" that Janis was famous. "And she said, 'Well, no, Fredda, I think I'm a very *good* singer.' And I said, 'Janis, honey, you're an excellent singer, but you were always an excellent singer. It's just a hoot they finally discovered you. You're a wonderful singer and you deserve everything you get and you work real hard for it.' She was reassured then, but it was like, poor baby." Todd Schiffman, the band's booking agent in the early days, remembers how hurt Janis was by the comic Don Adams when she appeared on *Hollywood Palace*. Schiffman says Adams "thought he was being funny" when he cracked the old generic hippie joke "You know, it's hard to tell which ones are the guys and which ones are the girls." But Schiffman found Janis in the dressing room afterward "crying, crying her heart out. It really, really hurt her."

Indeed, Janis's expectations seemed to set her up for crushing disappointment, imagining, as she did, that fame would bring her parental approval and force her hometown to its knees in guilty admission of how wrong it had been about her. In the summer of 1968, at the very height of the hype, when journalists from *Time* and *Life* were falling over themselves to interview her, Janis asked her mother hopefully if the *Port Arthur News* had run anything. "If so, please send," she wrote. What Janis wanted from fame was more than just vindication. She wanted it to banish the feeling of emptiness and desolation hounding her. She wanted it to make her lovable and acceptable.

The neediness seemed to make Janis far too trusting, even naive, about the people seeking out her company—at first, at least. Some of those hanging around Janis in 1968 were "perfectly nice people," in Fredda Slote's words, but "some of them were manipulating her, using her to use her credit card. I kinda didn't want to say anything to her about it because I didn't want to burst her bubble, but I felt I had to just point out that she really ought to be very careful who she gave the card number to, just because later on she might have to justify it. And she said, 'Oh yeah, sure.' But I don't know if she ever did. . . . She would see only the good in people, even the people who were dangerous to her. She wouldn't realize at all what she was opening herself up to." To Fredda, it was Janis's insecurity that left her so open to being used. "If people would love her for what she had, she would accept it, even if they weren't loving her for who she was." In time, Janis's tolerance for being used would give way to the understandable suspicion that people were taking advantage of her.

Early on, Myra Friedman realized she couldn't "toughen" Janis so she decided to protect her instead. This would prove an equally daunting task because people assumed Janis could take it as well as she dished it out, and not just because of her bravado. All but her closest friends believed that anyone as successful and savvy as Janis, even a blues singer acting out her misery, surely understood her own inner fabulousness. Even some friends had a hard time reading her, according to her Austin friend Pepi Plowman, who with Tary Owens visited her backstage in 1969. "As we were leaving," Pepi says, "Janis was looking back at me with those eyes like, 'Help me, help me,' and I said, 'Tary, I'm really worried about Janis.' And he said, 'Oh, don't worry about Janis. She always thinks of Number One.' " Of course, Janis isn't the only star for whom the assumption of a healthy self-regard was unwarranted, but in her case it was spectacularly wrong. She remained so convinced of her ugliness that a man's indifference could devastate her and so haunted by the fear "she couldn't sing at all" that any criticism "tended to atomize her," according to Myra. Janis had always been prickly, but now her interior reality—the wounded adolescent girl—kept running up against her outsized reputation as a tough-talking broad and America's biggest hippie star. "Janis threw up her tough tomboy side to the outside world," recalls her boyfriend Milan Melvin, "but internally she was screaming, 'Dear God, send me someone to help me figure this shit out!' "

Lillian Roxon, a journalist, ran into Janis on the streets of Manhattan while *Cheap Thrills* was the country's top LP. "She looked too lonely and lost for a girl with her first number one album," Roxon said, but lonely and lost were how Janis felt that fall. Leaving the band was a tremendous loss that must have had painful echoes of her alienation from her own family. Was there really no place for her? Would she always stick out? Was she doomed to feel alone and adrift in the world except when she was onstage? In fact, being onstage had become one of her primary sources of solace. When Janis and Big Brother played Houston during their final tour, Patti Skaff and her husband, Dave McQueen, joined the Joplin family backstage. They arrived just in time to see Janis dressing down a stagehand who'd closed the curtain before she'd left the stage. "Why don't

you take her home?" Patti asked Seth Joplin. "She needs to go home."
Seth shook his head and wearily said, "It's just too late." After Janis had
verbally demolished the stagehand, she turned to her family and friends.
Patti remembers that they "kissed and hugged, and Janis said, 'You be the
mother and I'll be the star.' She wanted to be a star. It fed her. She said
she was only alive when she was onstage."

But being onstage meant being on the road, and Janis had a love-hate
relationship with all that the road involved. During much of 1968 and
1969, the road was Janis's home. By 1969 she made enough singing one
night a week to "pay for everything," but still she asked Albert to increase
her bookings. "I told them I wanted to play more. The most fun I have is
when I'm playing. I live for that one hour onstage," she told the L.A. critic
Robert Hilburn. Nevertheless, she also complained about the dreary
seamlessness of it all. "You don't see anything but the inside of airports,
Holiday Inns, and men's gymnasiums. I'm alone all the time, in god-
damned airplanes when it's too early and I'm hung over from the night
before." Or, as someone in Albert's office described Janis's situation, she
was "a chick laying in a fucking hotel room with nobody and nothing."

The road was especially tough for a single woman. When the singer
Maria Muldaur struck out on her own after the disintegration of both the
Jim Kweskin Jug Band and her marriage, she discovered just how "ludicrous" it was. "People are drooling over you in the audience, but where is
the one guy who will come in afterwards who isn't just a teenager with his
tongue hanging out? Just a nice dude in the town who'll take you for a cup
of coffee." After the band's mediocre show in June 1968 at San Francisco's
Fillmore, Janis and Bill Graham went for a bite to eat. After stopping at
a burger joint they drove out to the Marin headlands, across from the
Golden Gate Bridge. "She was a little loaded," Graham recalls. "Her life
was not going well." She began describing the frustrations of the road.
"I'm in the Holiday Inn in Toronto. After the gig, all the guys go upstairs
and freshen up. Then they come down and score chicks." Graham
remembers a pause before Janis said, "What does a woman do?"

8

Little Girl Blue

On December 21, 1968, just three weeks after her last show with Big Brother, Janis and her new soul band made their debut in Memphis, Tennessee. The band had not been named and the players—Sam Andrew, Brad Campbell, Terry Clements, Bill King, Roy Markowitz, and Marcus Doubleday—had been hurriedly assembled, yet the opportunity to perform at the second annual Stax-Volt Yuletide Thing seemed too good to pass up; it was the ideal place to unveil Janis Joplin's new group. Though Stax Records, the sponsor, had lost its star, Otis Redding, and most of his backup band, the Bar-Kays, in an airplane crash a year before, the label was still "Soulsville, USA." Stax was it, the real thing. To smug San Franciscans who thought their music scene was the hippest of all, Janis declared that Memphis was "where it's at!" Like Jimi Hendrix, Janis didn't have many black fans, but, banking on her crossover appeal, Stax nevertheless invited her to play their big year-end bash. Janis was the only non-Stax artist to appear and she received major billing, ahead of the Staple Singers, Booker T and the MG's, Albert King, and everyone else except Johnnie Taylor, whose megahit "Who's Making Love" earned him the coveted closing spot.

Even with the tightest band, Janis would have been up against very stiff competition. But Janis didn't have a tight band; she barely had a band at all. Her friends Nick Gravenites and Michael Bloomfield, who had left the Electric Flag, a horn-based soul band similar to the one she wanted behind her, and Elliot Mazer, the record producer, had helped pick the musicians, but the group hadn't begun rehearsing until a week before the Memphis show. It was all very unnerving—Gravenites and Bloomfield, who went to Memphis to lend his support, wouldn't be available forever, and this was supposed to be Janis's group. She'd never fronted a band of professional musicians. How could she tell them what to do when she didn't even have the vocabulary to describe what she wanted to hear? "It was her constant fear that she'd look bad behind a bunch of good musicians," explains Mazer. "None of us thought the band was ready," he says of the Stax show, "but they had the gig and they wanted to go." Moreover, Albert had advised Janis against letting too much time elapse before hitting the road with her new group.

As she and the musicians stood backstage watching the other acts, they began to comprehend the enormity of their mistake. Memphis, it turned out, was a lot more like Las Vegas than San Francisco, where everyone but Bill Graham collaborated in the fiction that what they were doing wasn't show business. Bay Area audiences wanted realness, not slick displays of showmanship. Janis's group realized the extent of the chasm separating them from the other acts when the re-formed Bar-Kays came out wearing "zebra-striped flannel jumpsuits." Janis was dressed up, too, wearing a cherry-red jersey pantsuit with matching red feathers at the cuffs. But she and her band didn't know the dances. And there were the Bar-Kays doing the sideways pony, followed by the boogaloo, and much, much more. Stanley Booth of *Rolling Stone* looked on as Michael Bloomfield's eyes got very large and members of the new band shook their heads in disbelief. Booth observed, "It was the first sign of the cultural gap that was to increase as the evening progressed."

Janis was the next-to-last performer. In San Francisco's electric ballrooms everyone assumed bands would take forever setting up their equipment and getting in tune. Not so in Memphis, where the salt-and-pepper audience turned cold as Janis's band spent ten minutes putting their act together. Janis decided to save "Piece of My Heart" and "Ball and Chain" for the encore and opened with "Raise Your Hand" by Eddie ("Knock on Wood") Floyd, who had performed right before her, and "To Love Somebody" by the Bee Gees. The only people in the stands at the coliseum who'd heard of Janis Joplin, however, were white teenagers there to hear her big hits. Both opening songs fell flat, and by the third unfamiliar tune the crowd was so unmoved it was obvious there'd be no encore call. "At least they didn't throw things," she muttered backstage after it was over. Worst of all was the fact that *Rolling Stone* was covering the event. For Janis, the magazine was rapidly assuming "the significance of the military-industrial complex," as David Dalton puts it. She knew her defeat would be painstakingly chronicled in its pages, and true to form, the paper proclaimed, "Janis Joplin died in Memphis." The problem, Stanley Booth conceded, wasn't Janis's singing but the band, which he found both ragged and soulless. Janis was stunned—all the agony she'd gone through quitting Big Brother, only to get the same review yet again. To Dave Getz, Janis's Memphis misadventure confirmed Albert's fallibility and arrogance: "He thought he knew everything." To Sam Andrew, the show "was sheer insanity. Janis wanted to emulate Aretha and Otis, but before we even had the repertoire down, we were going to play in front of one of the most demanding audiences in the country, our heroes from Stax. . . . It was intimidating, playing the blues for black people. . . . How dare we get up there and play their music? Naturally we were kind of nervous. We just blew it."

Of course, Janis had received negative reviews before, but she had rarely faced an indifferent audience. Memphis was her first defeat since she'd reinvented herself as a rock singer back in the summer of 1966, and of all places, Janis hated bombing at Soulsville. She had always feared that one day people would wake up and realize she was an imposter, a talentless girl whose powerful voice fooled people into thinking she could sing. As she lay awake at Memphis's Lorraine Motel less than a month before her twenty-sixth birthday, Janis worried that she was all washed up.

Her failure at Memphis, however, wasn't the result just of the band's raggedy performance or even of the soul–acid rock schism. The Stax-Volt show signaled a decline of the interracialism that had marked popular music during the midsixties and the opening of a divide that would only widen in the years to come as black and white music diverged. In the waning days of the decade, white artists like Janis, who had "traded off the black," and black artists like Jimi Hendrix, who had "traded off the white," as Lou Reed put it, would find it harder to cross the racial borders of popular music. Hendrix found himself confronted by Black Panthers demanding he be blacker, while Janis was scolded by white critics for trying to sing "black" music. Martin Luther King's assassination at the same Lorraine Motel only months earlier had ended all sorts of possibilities, including the cultural hybridity Janis Joplin and Jimi Hendrix represented. The appeal of a white girl singing the blues like no white girl had ever before would quickly become Janis's ball and chain. R. Crumb had unknowingly captured this shift in his *Cheap Thrills* cartoon of Janis as a sweaty prisoner struggling across a barren landscape with a heavy black ball (marked "Big Mama Thornton") chained to her ankle. As the year came to an end, however, racial typecasting was only one of the burdens Janis was dragging along.

A "big warm blanket" is how the musician David Crosby describes the feeling of shooting smack. In the summer of 1968, Janis had begun wrapping herself in that big warm blanket more and more frequently. "I just want some fucking peace, man," she growled at Linda Gravenites, who couldn't understand why her friend was doing heroin. She'd tried it once and hated the way it "makes everything get foggy and gray and go away. I didn't want that nothingness." But what felt like nothingness to Linda felt to Janis like euphoria, offering at least some relief from the anxiety and depression hounding her as Big Brother was coming apart.

Some accounts claim Janis didn't start using regularly until 1969, but her old friend Sunshine puts the date much earlier—the summer of 1967. Janis apparently began dabbling in heroin after the two met up by chance in the Panhandle section of Golden Gate Park. Janis told Sunshine she needed "somethin' new" and asked what she'd been doing. On her way to score some dope and feeling the aches and pains of withdrawal, Sunshine wasn't in the mood to talk with anyone. "But she and I rapped a little," Sunshine recalls, "and she asked me about it." Janis told her she had tried smack back in her North Beach days, but it had only made her sick. Sunshine assured her heroin was a groovy high, as long as you didn't get strung out. "Janis was so adamant when she came back from Texas that she wasn't going to use anything except booze," Sunshine says, "and she promptly had speed thrown in her face by Nancy Gurley and Speedfreak Rita. And then there was me." She felt a little guilty that she was the one to turn Janis back on to heroin, although others dispute Janis's claim that she hadn't liked the drug in North Beach. Sunshine believes Janis was drawn to heroin in part because "she had gone through her relationship with Joe McDonald, and despite being the poster chick of the scene she was having a hard time finding 'one good man.' " Even though Janis had a new lover, a rocker in the band Blue Cheer, she told Sunshine that their three-week affair was nearing its end. In any case, once Janis started using smack, she needed no encouragement to get high. Sunshine recalls that all they "had to do was look at each other and we got a twinkle in our eye and that was it."

In 1967, James Gurley insists, "none of us were strung out." Linda Gravenites agrees, characterizing Janis as a casual user, what's called a "chipper." Janis and James started out together as dabblers, shooting up only when someone backstage would offer to get them high. It was, he explains, a way to come down and chill out after their "adrenaline-raising" shows. But neither Janis nor James remained chippers for very long. In March 1968, during the effort to record Big Brother live in Detroit, Elliot Mazer saw a nickel bag of heroin fall out of a band member's pocket. He quickly called Albert, who "had a high level of concern about smack," Mazer says. Albert canceled the band's weekend gig and ordered the members to Woodstock to confront the issue of their heroin use. Despite his attempt at an intervention, Big Brother's use accelerated during the *Cheap Thrills* recording sessions. They had more money, and smack was always available. Peter and Dave stayed away from it, but Sam began using, too. After a concert in Cincinnati, Dave remembers a fan taking the group to a party where some of them shot up. "It didn't seem insane to us at all, then," says Dave.

At the time, Janis had lots of reasons for shooting heroin, including the nightmare of leaving Big Brother. As the aggrieved party in the breakup, Big Brother received a good deal more support than Janis, who really suffered. "She cried, threw a fit, and shot dope, cried, threw another fit, shot some more dope, and then left the band," recalls Peggy Caserta. She was also away from San Francisco for most of that year, becoming intimate with what she called the "abject boredom" of life on the road. Linda Gottfried Waldron remembers the time in 1968 that Janis visited her in Santa Cruz. She had come to kick her habit. "I put black curtains up on the windows and came in about three hours later. She was shooting up. I said, 'Janis!' and she looked up at me and sang, 'You can't eat yogurt and sing the blues.'"

Richard Hundgen, a roommate of James and Nancy Gurley's, remembers Michael Bloomfield saying "the only way white musicians could fully emulate black soul is by using heroin." Sam Andrew can't recall anyone in the band actually talking about heroin as a "shortcut to soul" but says the assumption "was always lurking there." Janis herself once told Linda Gravenites "it was the blues-singer mystique, like Billie Holiday, to get real messed up." "Chemical soul," sighs the singer Tracy Nelson. "They knew all the old jazz and blues greats did drugs. I can't tell you how many times I heard Ray Charles's name invoked in that context. . . . They just didn't get it. Those people weren't soulful because they did heroin. They did heroin because they were in pain. It was such an artificial, bullshit way of trying to get down and it killed a lot of people." Nelson believes "white people doing black music carry a lot of guilt and it might have been a punishment thing as well. But mostly," she says, "it was, How can I be like them? I'll do everything those people do and maybe that'll work."

By 1969, many more white musicians were trying to "be like them"— enough, in fact, to warrant a *Newsweek* lead story in May of that year declaring the "Rebirth of the Blues"—with Janis emblazoned on the magazine's cover. Young white blues enthusiasts like Janis, Michael Bloomfield, Paul Butterfield, the Rolling Stones, and Eric Clapton had sparked intense renewed interest in the older blues greats, some of whom had stopped performing until the revival led to their rediscovery.

Young whites had started turning up at blues shows as far back as the early sixties. For the most part, black musicians appear to have been bemused by their new audience. The kids worshiped them, and the attention was gratifying and flattering, if a little disorienting. By 1967, veteran blues musicians were no longer appearing only in small clubs and taverns within the black community; they were moving into electric ballrooms, where freaky-looking young white kids who often knew nothing about the blues danced to their music. In fact, that strange white audience became essential to the musicians' survival. Young African Americans had largely abandoned the blues, gravitating instead toward the soul music of Motown, Atlantic, and Stax Records. "Blues has something to do with that bastard part of life most black people want to forget," reflected Big Bill Hill, a Chicago deejay and former blues singer, in 1969. "They don't want to be reminded of sad memories." Muddy Waters claimed to be glad whites were doing blues because without them the music would have died. And B. B. King once told Bill Belmont of Fantasy Records that the Rolling Stones had made his career when they took him out on tour with them. "I will always be indebted to those guys for thinking of me," King said.

For many of the old-timers, though, whites' appropriation of the blues—no matter how loving—had to have been a bittersweet experience, especially once the blues revival was in full swing. All too often, they found themselves opening for Big Brother, the Jefferson Airplane, or some other headlining act that earned top dollar. White audiences respected the blues masters, but the musicians with whom they identified were Eric Clapton, Michael Bloomfield, and Janis Joplin. It rankled that young kids who'd learned their licks from older black players could parlay their music into a level of fame and fortune the originals could never have. Cream's "Strange Brew" remains a staple of classic rock radio, but few people know that Eric Clapton's playing was "a note-for-note cop" from Albert King's "Oh, Pretty Woman." Remarkably, black players expressed little overt hostility toward young whites. Not all black musicians, however, were willing to pass on their wisdom. Sam Andrew once asked Muddy Waters's guitarist about a chord he used to close a tune, but the musician refused to answer. Sam didn't blame him, nor did Peter Albin when Howlin' Wolf snubbed him. "I liked the way he played harmonica," says Peter. "So I came up to him at the Fillmore. No one was around and I said, 'Mr. Wolf, how do you play the harmonica like that?' He growled, 'That's for me to know and you to learn,' and walked away."

Much as black musicians were revered and emulated by their new fol-lowers, they remained in some crucial ways invisible. There was the time Bo Diddley played a three-week gig at Chet Helms's Avalon Ballroom. "Bo had been so used to playing in tiny clubs for shady promoters that the idea that people really wanted him there took a bit of getting used to," Chet recalls. "To white audiences that had been cutting their teeth on his 'Mona,' which had been a staple of Quicksilver's act, Bo was a legend." Sometime into Bo's stay, Chet's partner organized a big dinner in his honor. The menu consisted of fried chicken, okra, and, yes, even water-melon. Bo, who'd been born in Mississippi but raised in the North, took one look at the spread and barked, "I don't eat shit like this. Get me some food I can eat." To young white freaks, African Americans were all soul-fulness, sensuality, and spontaneity—the qualities so glaringly absent in middle-class white America. Nick Gravenites's reminiscence of his early days hanging out in Chicago blues joints rivals Norman Mailer's "The White Negro" in its romantic evocation of black life in the inner city, "that carefree blues lifestyle, the whores and pimps, the dope fiends and the dealers, the wine, women, and song, the way late night life, the hot music, the petty thieves and con men." White players who were trying "to tran-scend a whole lot of whiteness," as Michael Bloomfield once put it, were usually well-intentioned, but they sometimes held caricatured views of black people.

Like her friends, Janis, too, invested blacks with greater soulfulness. In fact, she had even less experience with African Americans than Gravenites, Butterfield, or Bloomfield, all of whom grew up in the North and hung out with black musicians in Chicago. Nevertheless, her years with hard-living and hard-drinking Cajuns and working-class whites in Texas had taught her that blacks did not have a monopoly on living on the edge. "I keep trying to tell people that whites have soul too," Janis told Nat Hentoff in early 1968. "There's no patent on soul." She thought she had an idea how "this whole myth of black soul" came about. "Because white people don't allow themselves to feel things. Housewives in Nebraska have pain and joy; they've got soul if they'd give in to it." When Hentoff told her she was the first white female blues singer he'd heard "since Teddy Grace, who sang the blues out of black influences but had developed her own sound and phrasing," Janis was delighted. "God, I'm so glad you think that," she said.

Most black performers echoed Hentoff's respect for Janis's singing. "Janis Joplin sings the blues as hard as any black person," declared B. B. King, who shared many bills with her. Little Richard once had the difficult task of following Janis onstage. "She had been sucking on that Southern Comfort bottle. When she took off her shoes I thought, Oh Lord. And when she started leaping up and down I thought, Look at this woman. And you know, she could scream, too. I thought, Oh, my God. She stopped the whole thing. Got three standing ovations. She was dangerous, that girl." Big Mama Thornton applauded Janis's version of "Ball and Chain," saying, "That girl feels like I do." In fact, John Morris of the Fillmore East says he "never met a black musician who didn't love her. The greatest thing was Janis and Mavis Staples on the same stage at the Fillmore East. To get the two of them to sing together was so obvious and was only difficult because each was so in awe of the other. They were both afraid of being embarrassed."

If black musicians were fond of Janis it was in part because she always credited performers who had influenced her. Odetta was the first singer Janis tried to imitate. "Every time Janis and I were in the same area," she says, "Janis made a point to thank me profusely." Janis even picked up half the cost of providing Bessie Smith's grave with a proper headstone. Fiery Etta James was initially angry about all the attention Janis received, but she, too, was won over by her. "She gave me respect, and I began feeling proud to be her role model. When I heard her sing, I recognized my influence, but I also heard the electricity and rage in her own voice. She had balls. I loved her attitude."

While black musicians embraced Janis, she nonetheless encountered plenty of resistance when she tried fronting a soul band. Had Janis pursued straight-ahead rock, her new group might have succeeded. Mickey Hart of the Grateful Dead had approached Janis about joining him, Jerry Garcia, and the Airplane's Jack Casady in a supergroup, but she'd turned him down. She wanted to sing soul, and her timing couldn't have been worse. King's assassination destroyed the dream of interracialism as black power and its critique of integration gained greater support and credibility within the black community—a shift that reverberated culturally as well as politically. "Everything changed at Stax," maintains June Dunn, the wife of Donald "Duck" Dunn, the white bassist with Booker T. White and the MG's. For the first time, writes Peter Guralnick, an "undercurrent of racial division" threatened the "surface harmony of the Stax family." Blacks began questioning the racial hierarchy whereby "blacks made the music, blacks made the audience, but the ownership was white," as Homer Banks, a Stax songwriter, put it. Whites, who were accustomed to feeling as though they existed in a racial twilight zone where race was irrelevant, learned otherwise. "All of a sudden people are noticing that we're white," recalled one Stax musician, Wayne Jackson. By the early seventies, many of the whites involved in southern soul music—most notably, Jerry Wexler, Rick Hall, and Phil Walden—left the field rather than be attacked for making money off black people.

The ascendance of black power chipped away at racial inequality in the record business and elsewhere, but it fortified what Eldridge Cleaver called the racial Maginot Line. If black power promoted black pride, it also encouraged essentialist notions of "blackness" and the blacker the better, an imperative that some African Americans experienced as a racial straitjacket. Jimi Hendrix, for one, didn't want to play sock-it-to-me soul music like Otis Redding and Wilson Pickett. "We did Dylan's 'Like a Rolling Stone' and 'Wild Thing,'" he said in 1967, "but we're not going in for any of this 'Midnight Hour' kick—no gotta, gotta, gotta because we don't have ta, have ta, have ta." But by 1968, Hendrix was under increasing pressure to play "black" music. The corollary, of course, was that only black musicians could play black music. Of white blues bands Muddy Waters said in 1969, "They can *play* most anything. But they didn't go to the Baptist church like I went. They didn't get that soul down deep in the heart like I have. And they can't deliver the message. They're playing the white folks' blues. I'm playing the real blues . . . the same thing the old master liked to hear when you're working for him." His comment underscores the tangled relationship between black and white in the history of the blues. While much recent writing emphasizes the syncretic nature of American popular music, that view hardly held sway in the late sixties, when blues and soul music were hailed as the embodiment of authentic blackness.

Rock critics—twenty-something college-educated white men, for the most part—too often upheld these racially based categories, becoming the arbiters of ethnic authenticity in much the same way that Alan Lomax had. The ironic result was that black musicians who didn't sing or play with the raw power associated with the grittiest of soul music circa

1967, while often quite popular with black and white audiences alike, were raked over the coals by white critics for being sell-outs, that is, too white. *Rolling Stone* lambasted Motown acts as "Tom travesties" who were "locked into a plastic nightclub style of performing." Years later, Mary Wilson of the Supremes, responding to what she called "the misguided notion that a black who was singing and didn't sound like Aretha Franklin or Otis Redding must have been corrupted in some way," pointed out that the Supremes' musical roots weren't in the church but rather "in American music—everything from rock to show tunes." White critics' impatience with black musicians whose work they deemed too slick and sophisticated—ergo, too white—prefigured the critical dismissal of disco in the seventies. One British critic would ask, "What happened to the days when black music was black and not this mush of vacuous Muzak and pretentious drivel?"

If the Supremes were going to take a licking, critics weren't going to let Janis or other white artists get away with fronting a soul band. By mid-1968, the equation of soulfulness and blackness was so unassailable that even *Time* magazine claimed soul music "has the authenticity of collard greens boiling on the stove, the sassy style of the boogaloo in a hip discotheque, the solidarity signified by 'Soul Brother' scrawled on a ghetto storefront." In one of the earliest attacks, Ralph Gleason accused Michael Bloomfield of trying to act black. Even before Janis had formed her second band, critics began taking her to task for not being the real thing, for being a purveyor of ersatz soul music. Jon Landau of *Rolling Stone* accused her of oversinging to disguise her lack of soulfulness. Erma Franklin's version of "Piece of My Heart," he argued, "has soul. Janis Joplin's has balls." Worse, the *New York Times*'s critic, Bill Kloman, attacked *Cheap Thrills* as a "stereophonic minstrel show" that came off as "a kind of plastic soul that lacks the humor and relative integrity of the Amos 'n' Andy shows."

By late 1968, Janis's fame and fortune had begun to undermine her credibility as a blues singer, too; she was no longer seen as just some funky hippie chick. Richard Goldstein was one of the few critics who balked at the trend, lambasting white blues mavens who embraced only certifiably down-home musicians: "How much more authentic Albert King seems, with his open-collar shirt, sipping orange juice between riffs, than Jim Morrison, who is all leather and lanolin. How much easier it is to adore Ma Rainey, who is black and rural real, than Janis Joplin, who is white and nearly rich." And indeed, Steve Katz of the Blues Project and Blood, Sweat, and Tears, said of Janis, "when you're making $10,000 a night, you're just not funky anymore—you can't come on hard luck and trouble. She's selling something she no longer is. How can you be a blues superstar? It's such a contradiction in terms." Of course, it was a contradiction many black blues musicians would have gladly embraced.

Janis dealt with all the criticism by arguing that blues music was universal and by bending over backwards to credit and promote black singers. When an overzealous fan wrote in an underground paper, "This is where Janis shows Aretha what it's all about," Janis assured *Rolling Stone* (which had sneered at the claim), "I understand I'm not Aretha Franklin." Moreover, she differentiated her blues from traditional blues. Hers were the "Kozmic Blues," spelled with a "K" because, she explained to David Dalton, life was "too down and lonely a trip to be taken seriously; it has to be a Crumb cartoon. . . . It's like a joke on itself." She went on to distinguish between traditional blues and her blues. "I don't know if this is grossly insensitive of me, and it may well be, but the black man's blues is based on the 'have-not'—I got the blues because I don't have this, I got the blues because I don't have my baby, I got the blues because I don't have the quarter for a bottle of wine, I got the blues because they won't let me in the bar. Well, you know," she said, "I'm a middle-class white chick from a family that would love to send me to college and I didn't wanna. I had a job, I didn't dig it. I had a car, I didn't dig it." For a white woman like her, Janis seemed to be saying, the blues weren't about material deprivation or, in the end, even about lost lovers but about existential loneliness and despair—"waking up in the middle of the night blues," as Sam Andrew puts it. "One day, I realized in a flash, sitting in a bar, that it wasn't an uphill incline, you know, that one day everything was going to be all right," she said. "It was your whole life." Janis's protest—"No, it just can't be"—would turn up in more than one of her songs.

Janis's second band was reason enough for her to sing the blues. For months people had urged her to dump Big Brother. That's what she'd done and it had gotten her nowhere. Nobody, Albert included, had seriously considered the possibility that the second band might fall flat on its face. Nobody thought about the country's shifting racial politics and no one had prepared Janis for the burdens of being a band leader. She was expected to take charge and make the group work—all by herself. Tina Turner at least had Ike, even if his free-floating anger tyrannized her, and Aretha Franklin had a husband who, though far from a model mate, dealt with shady promoters and refractory band members. Initially, Janis's friend Michael Bloomfield, whose *Super Session* with Al Kooper and Stephen Stills was one of 1968's biggest albums, agreed to help her— perhaps with encouragement from Albert Grossman, who managed him, too. Bloomfield had an encyclopedic knowledge of the blues, but he also had certain ideas about Janis's band that clashed with hers. Janis had hoped to hire him as her musical director but, according to Nick Gravenites, "Michael was so headstrong . . . and it just conflicted too much with Janis's ego, even though she wanted him to work on her music." So Janis was without anyone to lean on when her trumpeter, Marcus Doubleday, left the group and her organist, Bill King, was drafted several weeks after the Memphis show. "She's doing the hardest thing you can do—carrying a whole band on her shoulders," Nick Gravenites said.

After the Memphis debacle, Albert decided to avoid further embarrassment by scheduling Janis's next date (billed as a "sound test") for the obscure town of Rindge, New Hampshire. That was followed by a "preview" concert in Boston, a prelude to the band's debut at New York's Fillmore East on February 11 and 12, 1969. Janis's return a year after she'd first conquered New York was one of the rock events of the year; the shows were sold out almost as soon as tickets went on sale. *60 Minutes* was on hand to televise a segment on the Fillmore East, which it dubbed "Carnegie Hall for Kids." Reviewing the concert, Ellen Willis would write that a friend of hers had a curious nightmare the night before the gig: in the dream "the concert was a flop, Janis kept walking down the aisles futilely begging the audience to respond." Willis, too, had worried before the concert: "Will Success Spoil Janis? . . . Did Big Brother perhaps give her more than we realized?" She admitted, "I felt as if I were going to watch my best friend put herself on the line." The concert wasn't a flop, although the audience reaction was more subdued than it had been a year before. But, then, Janis was singing new material for the most part.

Although she performed "Piece of My Heart," "Ball and Chain," and "Summertime," she also sang two new songs by Nick Gravenites, covered the Chantels' "Maybe," Eddie Floyd's "Raise Your Hand," and the Bee Gees' "To Love Somebody." After the concert, she ventured that, once she got "the new tunes on a record, then the kids won't mind." The *New York Times* compared the new band favorably to Big Brother and once again gave Janis a flat-out rave. Willis, writing in the *New Yorker*, attributed any deficiencies to growing pains. Janis had decided to "stop killing herself," Willis felt, and to experiment with "a cooler, subtler delivery that would contain her energy without diluting it." She did notice, though, that Janis seemed to lack authority with her new group. No one felt the band had yet gelled, but *Rolling Stone* was especially harsh, claiming "the band made all local stops while Janis was an express. The singing and playing simply failed to mesh, Joplin constantly projecting and the group continually receding."

If Janis acquitted herself onstage, her postconcert phone interview with Paul Nelson of *Rolling Stone* was a disaster, plastered in the magazine's pages for all to see. "Janis Joplin: The Judy Garland of Rock?" blared the headline, alluding to the torch singer's well-documented insecurities. Throughout their conversation, Janis kept seeking reassurance from Nelson, who found the whole experience disconcerting. "It is difficult to imagine," he wrote, "a Bob Dylan or a John Lennon peppering an interview with constant nervous interjections of 'Hey, I've never sung so great. Don't you think I'm singing better? Well, Jesus fucking Christ, I'm really better, believe me.'" Nelson didn't agree. She had the potential to be great, he said, but he argued that she "doesn't so much sing a song as . . . strangle it to death." No doubt sensing his skepticism, Janis complained the band wasn't pushing hard enough and that she might try remedying the problem by adding "a great big ugly spade cat" on baritone sax. The interview was uncannily like the nightmare Willis recounted as Janis came close to begging Nelson to agree that what he'd seen was a new, improved Janis Joplin. "One gets the alarming feeling that Joplin's whole world is precariously balanced on what happens to her musically," Nelson wrote perceptively, "that the necessary degree of honest cynicism needed to survive an all-media assault may be buried too far under an immensely likeable but tremendously underconfident naivete." Of course, Janis's world did hinge entirely on what happened to her musically. As she explained to Nelson, "I've been really scared because this is *important* to me." Usually Janis acted like one of the guys, but that night she couldn't hide her insecurities and she acted like a girl—not a smart move. Nelson himself admitted to preferring the image over the real-life star with all her insecurities.

Some two weeks later, Janis's San Francisco shows were treated in the local press as an unmitigated disaster. Ralph Gleason called the band a "drag," a "pale version of the Memphis-Detroit bands from the rhythm and blues shows." He thought Janis was in "good voice" but noted that she seemed "bent on becoming Aretha Franklin." Gleason closed his review by suggesting Janis "scrap" her new band and "go right back to being a member of Big Brother . . . (if they'll have her)." The audiences were lukewarm, too. The opening-night crowd at Winterland didn't even call her back for an encore. Janis was devastated by the rejection. She was especially furious with Gleason, whose suggestion she return to Big Brother she called "she's-gettin'-too-big-for-her-britches shit."

Thankfully, the band spent most of April 1969 in Europe, where the crowds went wild for her. European audiences didn't care about Janis's split with Big Brother, nor were they bothered by a white girl singing the blues or soul music—far from it. "There were no prejudices over there," claims the new group's road manager, John Cooke, who had stayed with Janis after Big Brother. "The band was good because they felt there was nothing to overcome." Moreover, the band was finally beginning to come together, Cooke says. At last, *Rolling Stone* gave Janis some good press. Covering her triumphant Albert Hall concert in London, Jonathan Cott and David Dalton proclaimed, "Janis came and London came with her." The band reportedly played well, never "drowning her out," as they had in New York. "The people in Albert Hall got up and danced," recalls Cooke. "You can't imagine how much that delighted her." The British press was beside itself. "Soul," proclaimed the magazine *Disc*, "is what Janis is all about." *Melody Maker* enthused, "Janis broke through the wall of British reserve, loosening the audience, shaking them up, opening them out and turning them on."

For American GIs stationed in Germany, the question that spring, one ex-serviceman recalled, was, "Hey man, you going to the Joplin thing in

Frankfurt?" Over two thousand people, most of them GIs, crowded into Lieder Hall to see her. Some soldiers traveled two hundred miles for the concert and they all dressed in whatever "hip thing they could find, borrow, beg, steal. It looked like a masquerade ball for short hairs." But Janis didn't care if the audience seemed straight. "In the States," she joked, "the only way to tell the good people is by their damn long hair. Over here it seems to be the opposite." The audience "screamed, they loved her," according to the former soldier. Janis called people up onstage "to feel and touch and love her. They filled the stage, leaving only a horse-shoe area for her to perform in."

Europe couldn't last forever, though, and the band left for the States on April 24 for a gig in Springfield, Massachusetts, the very next day. Clive Davis was reportedly anxious that Janis begin recording her first solo record, *I Got Dem Ol' Kozmic Blues Again Mama!* Proving once again he was not omniscient, Albert chose Gabriel Mekler to produce the album. Mekler was best known for his work with Steppenwolf, which had scored Top 10 hits with the biker-rock songs "Born to Be Wild" and "Magic Carpet Ride." John Cooke immediately had doubts about Mekler's suitability for Janis. "Once again I thought, Why on earth?" Before Janis set foot in the studio there were problems. Mekler didn't like Janis's band and wanted to hire his own musicians. Although he didn't prevail, he succeeded in replacing the trumpeter, Terry Hensley, with Luis Gasca and—halfway into the recording—the drummer, Lonnie Castille, with Maury Baker. Still, when recording began on June 16, he was far from satisfied and he let it show, which didn't endear him to Janis or the band.

Even before Mekler's intervention, the band's personnel was constantly shifting, one reason the group never quite gelled. Only one musician—Terry Clements, the alto saxophonist—had been with the group from its beginning in December 1968. The bassist, Brad Campbell of the Paupers, a Canadian group Albert managed, joined the band after the Fillmore East gig, replacing a temporary bassist, Keith Cherry. Both the organist, Richard Kermode, who took over from Bill King, and the baritone saxophonist, Cornelius "Snooky" Flowers—"the ugly spade cat" whom Janis had spoken of—were with the group almost from the start. But the band went through three drummers—Roy Markowitz, Lonnie Castille, and Maury Baker—and four trumpet players—Marcus Doubleday, Terry

Hensley, Luis Gasca, and Dave Woodward. John Till came onboard as guitarist in July 1969. "Everyone felt as if tomorrow could be the last day," Sam Andrew says. Appropriately, the band remained nameless until after it was disbanded in December 1969, at which point it came to be known as the Kozmic Blues Band, after the album. During its existence Janis sometimes called it Squeeze or the Band from Beyond and joked with the press about naming her group Janis Joplin and the Joplinaires (after Elvis's Jordanaires), Janis Joplin's Pleasure Principle, Janis Joplin's Sordid Flavors, and even Janis and the Jack-Offs.

Some of the band members resented being treated like mere employees, but Sam claims he "kind of liked that idea. I kind of got caught up in the romance of it all. We were really idolizing a lot of Stax-Volt players and Aretha and B. B. King, and they all had big bands," he says, referring to musicians who remained anonymous. "And I could do that. I've been in bands where everyone's reading from the sheet." Maury Baker claims Janis was "very friendly with all the guys. She was the biggest-loving person I'd ever known." A number of the players, however, "would talk shit about her," claims their roadie, Vince Mitchell. There was never a family feeling in the group. Sam didn't feel as connected to the others, because they were professional musicians who simply "weren't as interesting to be with" as Peter, Dave, and James. Heroin also had something to do with the band's chronically slipshod sound, as Janis and Sam were hardly the only users. One of the horn players missed the first day of rehearsals because he'd gotten hung up trying to score. "When he did arrive," Sam says, "his works were jammed in the bell of his horn and he couldn't extricate them." Too many of the musicians were "buying balloons" of heroin rather than concentrating on the music, Sam maintains, one more reason the band just never got it together.

The mediocre concert reviews, the revolving personnel, and Gabriel Mekler's habit of ignoring the players' suggestions shot the band's morale to hell. "We were musicians and we knew how to play," claims Snooky Flowers, still testy after all these years. "We weren't just a bunch of hippies running around playing three chords. Luis Gasca had left the Count Basie Band to play with Janis Joplin. And I had played with all the known R & B bands that came through the Bay Area." Flowers believes Janis was uncomfortable with the group because she realized the "band was better than she was, musically beyond her." Sam doesn't entirely disagree with Flowers, but "Snooky could upstage anyone," he says. "He upstaged Janis and he did it a lot. She probably finally just lost patience with it." To Sam, Janis's problems with this collection of experienced musicians "highlights that she was lucky to find Big Brother in the first place."

The recording sessions lasted only ten days, but they were chaotic, according to the bassist, Brad Campbell. "Everybody was putting down everybody else. It was a mess, a total mess." Mekler was a hands-off producer, the opposite of John Simon, who produced *Cheap Thrills;* and Sye Mitchell, the new album's engineer, remembers "saying more and doing more" than Mekler. Janis was very involved in the making of the record, too. In fact, Clive Davis installed Mitchell after Janis became so abusive with the first engineer, Jerry Hochman, that he quit. Mitchell had witnessed Janis's reaming of Hochman—complete with many choice four-letter words—and wasn't anxious to relieve him. He told Davis he'd quit if Janis became belligerent with him, and he warned Janis, "If I hear any of that from your mouth, I'll walk out the door." Janis agreed and behaved, says Mitchell, like a "pussycat, always polite, courteous, and hardworking."

Janis was dynamic, but too often the band lagged behind her as it had four months earlier at the Fillmore East. To make matters worse, Snooky Flowers says, "We never got a chance to finish the album. We had to go on the road. We were supposed to come back to the studio and finish the record, but we never did." Under other circumstances, the bad notes would have been remedied before the album hit the stores, but there was a bigger problem plaguing the album. As Janis's father would later point out, "the brass in her second group didn't suit her. Her voice was an orchestra in itself." Janis found herself competing with the horn players, whose playing rarely approached the subtle work heard on most Stax records. As a consequence, *Kozmic Blues* finds Janis at her screechiest.

Still, the record has some sublime moments. "Maybe," Janis's radically reworked version of the 1957 girl-group hit, and the bluesy "One Good Man," cowritten by Janis and Sam and powered by Michael Bloomfield's scorching guitar, both really soar, in part because of the uncluttered arrangements. The album's showstopper, though, is Janis's version of "Little Girl Blue" from the Rodgers and Hart Broadway show *Jumbo.*

Like Nina Simone, who recorded a haunting cover in 1958, Janis dispensed with the song's opening verse, where the middle-aged heroine sings of how the circus dazzled her as a youngster. But in contrast to Simone and every other vocalist who's tackled the song, Janis sings from a position of empathy and identification. Instead of the line "What can you do? Old girl you're through," Janis sings, "I know you feel that you're through." And Janis's kozmic version makes no wistful mention of a tender blue boy coming to little girl blue's rescue. "Go on, sit right back down," she sings in the final verse, as if she's exhorting herself to rely on her own strengths and keep going—"Count your fingers," as the song puts it. Janis added and discarded so many lines that the woman administering the Rodgers and Hart estate refused Myra Friedman's request to publish the song's lyrics in her biography of Janis. "She just hated Janis's version," Myra says laughingly.

Although *Kozmic Blues* went gold, it generated a mixed critical response and no Top 10 singles. The band's lone African American, Snooky Flowers, insists the rock press trashed the album because the group was playing R & B—black music. "Big Brother represented the sixties, and they thought Janis was in her purest form in that band. We had horns and sounded more like a polished R & B band, and they weren't accustomed to that." In truth, the band had two strikes against it: first, it was predominantly white at a time when soul music was supposed to be played by blacks; second, it confirmed the prevailing stereotype of white musicians sounding uptight and stiff, too "white." Most reviewers of the album faulted its cumbersome arrangements and the band's sluggish playing. *Rolling Stone* ran two reviews: one was lukewarm while the other raved about Janis's singing but indicted the group for sounding "lumpier than a beer hall accordion band."

At concerts, the audience's reception was sometimes cool, too. Janis had always derived enormous pleasure from performing, yet with her new band either lagging behind her or overpowering her she was connecting only sporadically with the audience. "They didn't get me off," she told David Dalton. "You know, I have to have the *umph*. I've got to *feel* it, because if it's not getting through to me, the audience sure as hell aren't going to feel it either." Performing, one of Janis's many drugs, was failing her. She worried all the time about her singing now that critics were no longer quite so keen. "Janis would go, 'You know, some day they're gonna find out the truth,' " Peggy Caserta recalls. "I said, 'Being?' And she hesitated for a long time and we kept looking at each other. 'Being that I can't really sing,' she said. 'Oh Jesus, is that what you're worrying about today?' I asked, because each day would be a new problem. I think she knew after a while she had developed something she'd captivated the audiences with, but she didn't really believe she was good."

Janis was afraid of competitors, too, and by 1969 there were many more women on the scene. Tracy Nelson was making waves with Mother Earth, and Berkeley's Joy of Cooking was fronted by two women, its keyboardist, Toni Brown, and its guitarist, Terry Garthwaite, whose gutsy vocals were often compared to Janis's. When Joy of Cooking opened for Janis, Brown recalls her standing "in the back while Terry was singing. She was watching Terry very intently because Terry had a lot of the same kind of presence, and Janis was the queen." When Clive Davis introduced Janis to Laura Nyro backstage, Janis completely snubbed her. Nyro wasn't well known, but Janis surely remembered her from Monterey Pop. "Laura wanted to tell her how much she loved the performance," recalls Davis, "but Janis barely nodded a greeting as she drank straight from a Southern Comfort bottle and talked to a new boy she was eyeing." Once Nyro's career took off, Janis snapped at Davis, "I can see I'm not the Number One female in your eyes anymore. . . . You're turned on to Laura now." And when Joni Mitchell's star started to rise, Janis "was not exactly friendly" to her either, reports Mitchell.

Transient band members, new competition, flat concerts, and mixed reviews—Janis was besieged by anxiety throughout 1969, and heroin offered the tantalizing possibility of "life without anxiety," as Steven Tyler of Aerosmith, an ex-junkie, puts it. It worked so well for Janis that she began stretching out her weekends to accommodate her habit. Peggy recalls their beginning Thursday and ending Monday night, until soon shooting up became a daily event. Eventually, it didn't matter if the band was on and the energy was good—Janis still needed a fix after the show. When close friends expressed concern about her heroin use, Janis boasted she came from "good pioneer stock." After an actor she knew died of an overdose, she told Linda Gravenites, "Well, some people die and some people are survivors. I'm a survivor." But by the time she left for Europe in April, Janis was well on her way to being strung out. As her addiction grew, the dope stopped producing "its best effect, the dreamy, warm, safe return to your mother's womb" that her onetime boyfriend Milan Melvin describes. Like all other addicts, she craved the drug more as she came to use it more, shooting up just to ward off the inevitable muscle aches, brain ache, paranoia, and extreme irritability.

Janis used heroin throughout the three-week European tour, even though the concerts couldn't have gone better. Bob Seidemann, who was living in London at the time, remembers walking down King's Road with her. "She had a little blood on her satin psychedelic pants. It was do-up blood from the night before and she hadn't changed her pants. She didn't give a shit." Not giving a shit pretty much describes a junkie's life. Michael Bloomfield started shooting up in 1964, though he didn't become a hard-core user until 1968. "A junkie's life," he said, "is totally, chronically fucked. . . . Shooting junk made everything else unimportant." Or, as the legendary junkie William Burroughs put it, "Junk is not a kick. It is a way of life." And so it was with Janis, who later admitted she'd looked "gray" and "defeated" that April. Linda Gravenites accompanied her on the European tour but decided to stay in London and work on a commissioned vest for George Harrison rather than return to San Francisco and watch helplessly as Janis withdrew further into heroin.

Close friends and even some people in her inner professional circle knew Janis was using heroin. Most people, however, were fooled by her very public and prodigious boozing. When Janis appeared wasted, most people assumed it was from alcohol. With "her talismanic bottle of Southern Comfort," as *Newsweek* called it, Janis managed to "float in and out of Holiday Inns and backstage at hundreds of concerts without arousing the slightest suspicion" she was a junkie, according to Myra Friedman. Yet, in Myra's view Janis generally did little to hide her habit, especially around people whose concern she was eager to elicit. Curiously, others claim Janis was closeted about her habit and suggest this was typical of people—even rockers—who were using. "There was no heroin chic back then," insists Carl Gottlieb, who roomed with Milan Melvin. "No one was shooting up and nodding out in public back then," he says. Milan qualifies

Gottlieb's claim, pointing out that among the users he knew, heroin enjoyed considerable cachet. He agrees, though, that the drug was stigmatized in the larger culture and says that he and his friends were anxious to hide their habits from non-users. John Cooke, for example, was deliberately kept in the dark because he worked for Albert and was considered fairly square. Sye Mitchell saw no evidence of drugs during the *Kozmic Blues* sessions and Maury Baker, the drummer who played with Janis from June through December 1969, was completely ignorant of her addiction. So was Myra, who only learned of Janis's habit when a reporter from *Playboy* told her about it in June 1969. In fact, Peggy Caserta claims that Janis was usually very careful to cover her tracks, as it were. "You know," recalls Peggy, "she was an interesting junkie. I'd end up with a hundred syringes in my nightstand. But she would always fix and then clean it all up, wrap it up, and put it away. Most junkies start out like that but somewhere along the line, at least with me, the wrapping up and putting away goes by the wayside. But she was tidy till the day she OD'd. She'd be sloppy about other things. She'd pass out with a candle burning by a curtain, but she would have put the works away."

Disguising one addiction by broadcasting another was a diversionary tactic Janis applied to other areas of her life, not just heroin and booze. She concealed her feelings for women, for example, by endlessly drawing attention to her insatiable heterosexual appetite. "Look at that fine piece of ass," she'd say more times than anyone can remember, or "Isn't he cute?" or "God, I'd love to fuck him." With Janis this sort of talk was constant and unrelenting, at least when people were watching. "The private side of her sexuality didn't affect what she did in public," Elliot Mazer insists. But Janis's relentless, even frenzied pursuit of cute guys was, in fact, related to what she did with women behind closed doors. She always advertised her heterosexual conquests, making sure, for instance, that *Rolling Stone* reported her one-night stand with Joe Namath. And days later at her December 1969 Madison Square Garden concert, Janis moaned into the microphone, "Joe, where are you, Joe?" This isn't to say that Janis didn't like booze and men, because she did, but she also had other, less acceptable desires. Drug abuse and homosexuality are often mentioned in the same breath, as though they are equivalent evidence of an underlying pathology. Janis's habit and her "queerness" are linked here only because in both cases she mounted rather elaborate masquerades to disguise behavior that must have felt somehow shameful to her.

If Janis didn't boast about sleeping with women, she didn't deny the fact either. For the most part, though, people didn't ask. Sam Andrew played with Janis for three years and says they just didn't talk about "sexual preferences." To those who did broach the subject, Janis tended to emphasize the lopsidedly heterosexual nature of her sexual scorecard, the preponderance of her heterosexual home runs. Her friend Richard Hundgen recalls her reaction when a Bay Area underground paper claimed her as a lesbian and a role model to all independent women. Hundgen showed her the article backstage in San Diego. She was between sets, drunk, and "mad as hell. She was shaking the paper and said, 'You fly up there tomorrow and tell this bitch that Janis has slept with thousands of men and a few hundred women.' That was her way of proving she was straight," Hundgen laughs.

Of course, the Janis of myth was totally at ease with her expansive sexuality. Janis worked hard to keep up her rebellious reputation and some friends prefer not to tamper with Janis's iconic status as the sixties most-liberated chick. Old Austin friends, in particular, claim she was utterly comfortable being bisexual, as do some of her close "family" from San Francisco. As to whether she wanted people not to know, "I don't think she gave a shit," claims Milan Melvin. "We laughed about it." Linda Gravenites agrees. Asked if Janis found it difficult dealing with her feelings for women, Linda smiles. "Oh! She dealt with them all right. Like with Peggy. 'Oh God, Peggy has the most gorgeous tits in the world,'" Linda mimics Janis. Dave Getz remembers Janis commenting to him on the young women that hung around backstage at Big Brother concerts. "She always seemed to have a take—similar to a guy's—about these various chippies." Dave maintains that, while Janis took pains "to portray herself as blatantly heterosexual," she seemed to have no problem, at least around him, "objectifying women from a point of view that was not typical of most women at that time." Myra Friedman, however, contends Janis was no carefree sybarite. "She was terrified that people would think there was something going on between her and myself," Myra points out. Janis suggested they not hang out together so much at Max's Kansas City. "People might think . . . I mean, they might wonder . . . I mean, I don't have an old man and they might . . . well, I guess it's silly," Janis said to her.

Tellingly, few people remember Janis exhibiting sexual interest in women. Peter Albin was surprised, years later, to hear old stories of Janis coming on to women at parties. "A couple of women told me they'd been accosted by her. Janis gave one the eye and said, 'There's a free room down the hall.' I'd never heard those stories until recently, though." And John Cooke insists he never saw Janis show the slightest sexual interest in women. Undoubtedly, context is everything, and Janis apparently felt more comfortable around Dave, Linda, and Milan than around the sometimes supercilious Cooke, or Peter, the one member of Big Brother with whom she neither hung out nor made out, or even Myra, a single heterosexual woman who Janis might have assumed to be skittish about lesbianism. After all, Janis was nothing if not attuned to others' disapproval.

Peggy believes that Janis's reticence may well have stemmed from shyness; she wasn't sure how to approach the women—invariably straight—who were part of the rock scene. Once Janis called Peggy from the road and said, "I did what you do," explaining that she'd asked a woman up to her room. When pressed about what had happened, Janis admitted, "Well, it didn't quite work the way it does with you." Peggy suspects that Janis, realizing the girl was clueless about her intentions, suffered a loss of nerve, apparently suggesting dinner, if that.

In any event, Janis grew up in the fifties; she could hardly have emerged unscathed by the sexual shame that haunted most people whose desires were deemed queer. And being an outrageous hippie chick was still a far cry from being gay or bisexual, even in the sixties. The Summer of Love may have helped spur the great migration of gay men to San Francisco in the late sixties and early seventies, yet gays expecting to find a liberated zone of sexuality quickly discovered they'd have to create it themselves. Janis had little contact with this gay subculture, but Peter Albin believes that during 1968 more people in the inner circle did learn of her bisexuality. Peggy claims that Janis went public just once, at Woodstock in 1969, where she apparently grabbed one of Peggy's breasts in front of a gaggle of reporters.

Janis's fondness for heroin and women came together in the person of Peggy Caserta. Most accounts of Janis's life have relegated Peggy to the sidelines, but she was one of Janis's best friends, and their on-again, off-again affair was probably the closest Janis came to having a long-term relationship. Those who are eager to heterosexualize Janis would rather write Peggy out of her life, especially in the light of Peggy's embarrassingly overheated memoir, published in 1973. *Going Down with Janis* opens with the unforgettable line, "I was stark naked, stoned out of my mind on heroin, and the girl lying between my legs giving me head was Janis Joplin." Peggy denies responsibility for the book's more salacious language, including the opening line, which, she claims, was the work of Dan Knapp, the writer to whom she told her tale. "I've had to live under the shadow of that book's first fucking line for over thirty years," she snaps. Despite her annoyance, the book, which infuriated Janis's friends, actually figures in the coming-out stories of many thirty- and forty-something lesbians and bisexuals, even though it is in no way a heroic coming-out story on the order of Rita Mae Brown's *Rubyfruit Jungle*, published the same year. In fact, Peggy never entirely fit anyone's notions of a lesbian. "I know Janis was affected by the fact that at that time I was such—I hate to say it—but I was so much more feminine than I am now," Peggy admits. "I know that was intriguing to her. I could get a date, I could get a boyfriend. I could get laid. And I didn't want to." That Peggy did sleep with men and appeared more bisexual than lesbian probably made her especially attractive to Janis, who seemed to feel that lesbianism involved settling for second-best. There was nothing second-best about Peggy. The only drawback was that during their three-ways, guys invariably preferred Peggy.

"I know I'm not the kind of lover you're used to," Janis would tell Peggy. Indeed, when Janis first went to bed with Peggy she seemed completely ignorant about lesbian lovemaking. "If Janis had any previous experience with a woman, she definitely deserves to be recognized as an actress, because she was just too blown out by it," Peggy says. Still, Peggy describes their sex as "electrifying" and says that what Janis lacked in technique, she more than made up for in flamboyance and passion. "She'd get so silly," Peggy recalls. "We'd fix and fuck the night away." Heroin entered the picture very early on. Peggy had dropped acid and smoked dope, but she'd never done heroin. "It started like this," she says, explaining that one day after a violent fight with her lover, Kimmie, she went over to Janis's place. Janis began sexily stroking Peggy's arm, and said, "I could take away all your pain, and you could take away all my fear." Peggy was persuaded and Janis shot them both up. "She was right. We fucked all night and I didn't even think about Kimmie." Shooting up became part of their sexual routine, as compelling as the sex itself. It was part of the foreplay. On occasion, they'd get no further than foreplay because Janis would be so loaded from booze and smack she'd pass out, leaving Peggy feeling as if she were making love to a corpse. What's the point? she'd think, and stop in midcourse.

Peggy says she took on the project of building Janis's confidence. "I tried to get her to understand that she was not a loser. She was not ugly to me. She had her moments when she was unkempt and she'd been shooting dope and drinking and she'd get funky and everything, but I've seen her when I just wanted to eat her up." One night early on, Peggy told Janis she was beautiful. "You could see the pain in her face. 'Why would you say that?' she asked. I caught a look on her face . . . she saw I really meant it and was blown away. 'No one's ever told me that before,' she said. Then she held on to me like we'd just jumped off the *Titanic*. I think the guys for the most part felt that she was easy," Peggy goes on. "It wasn't a conquest at all. Too bad, guys. I had so much fun with her and I know that'll never happen again in my lifetime. Not so much the sex part, just the magic of those times, and we were young. I had more youth, more money, less sense."

Janis and Peggy were lovers on and off for at least two and a half years. Janis had Peggy helicoptered into Woodstock and she was so well known at the Landmark, the seedy rock 'n' roll motel where Janis often stayed in Los Angeles, that the staff routinely gave her the key to Janis's room. Peggy claims Janis never ditched her for a man but did kick a couple of guys out to accommodate her. One night Janis was flirting with a guy at Barney's Beanery as Peggy looked on. "He thought he had her and made his pass," she recalls. "She just said, 'I've got my date for the night,' took me by the arm, and sauntered out of the place."

The evidence is that Janis was taken with Peggy. A successful businesswoman, she was an anomaly both inside and outside the counterculture: she could pay her own way. Peggy's money came to count for a number of reasons. As Janis began using more and more dope, Peggy was the only friend who could afford a habit as big as hers and Janis hated subsidizing her friends' addictions. Her fame and the smack had also begun to disconnect her from other friends. With Peggy, at least, Janis wasn't worried that her money was the attraction. And the two women had been friends long before Janis was famous. "I started digging Janis on a street level before I'd seen her perform," Peggy contends. Theirs was, nonetheless, a limited relationship, or as Linda Gravenites puts it, "they were friends who fucked." Indeed, throughout their affair Peggy and Kimmie remained partners, while Janis pursued one-night stands with her characteristic stamina. Moreover, Janis still clung to her dream of finding an "old man" with whom to settle down. She never reconciled her desire for women with her fantasy of heterosexual marriage, even as she spoke to Peggy of living together. "Sometimes she would say, 'Why don't you move in with me?' And I would go, 'And be what? Your flunky? I like my beach house.'" Once, after Peggy told her she was still in love with Kimmie, Janis asked, "Didn't last night matter?" At the same time, Janis continued to talk of the straight life. "It was always, 'I'm going to marry and have two kids and a house with a white picket fence,'" Peggy says. "She was almost corny about it. She really didn't have a hit on who she was at all. I remember being in the supermarket and she'd try to buy the cheapest cheese and the cheapest jam and the cheapest crackers. And I'd say, 'Why are you doing that? You don't have to look at labels and prices anymore. Just zero in on the one you want.' And she literally looked at me and said, 'Really, I guess that's true.'"

Milan Melvin believes Janis's sexuality was genuinely liberated and beyond definition. In 1969 he walked into what looked like a lesbian orgy. "This is my life now," Janis said provocatively as Milan peered behind her door. Milan insists Janis's meaning that night was far from clear, though. "She was flirting in a way, being titillating. I think she was playing with me by indicating she was a lesbian. I don't even know if we went home later that night and got in the sack or not. . . . Did she mean she was a lesbian? I don't think so. It was just heightened sexuality." Peggy, Kimmie, Janis, and he were all sexually adventurous, Milan explains. "Janis wasn't a committed lesbian and she wasn't a committed heterosexual, she was just a supersexual woman, and that went every which way. I mean, there are some things I can't tell you that we did. That's what was fun about Peggy, Kimmie, and Janis for me. Because they were game to play and there were no taboos. Janis's attitude was, 'What's the big deal about defining yourself as this or that? Just be it.'" The very indeterminacy of Janis's sexuality—that she was beyond straight or gay—now seems the epitome of sexual liberation. But Janis's very real fixation on one good man and her relentless heterosexual boasting suggest that the conventional and the experimental coexisted rather unsteadily in her.

Janis's sexual confusion aside, both she and Peggy had every reason for not taking their relationship more seriously. "We're talking 1967 or 1968, not only was it not an 'out' time, it wasn't an 'out' society," claims Peggy. "It was a very heterosexual group of kids in the Haight. And look what we'd be getting involved in: two girls together in the sixties and one of them real high-profile." It wasn't just the pervasive homophobia of the period, though, that bothered Peggy. "She's an international star, she's going to be on tour. I really didn't want to go along and be invisible. I was into my house, I was still having some kind of a relationship with Kimmie, and I saw myself as a dyke, or a lesbian." And as far as she was concerned, Janis certainly didn't talk like a lesbian—not the way she'd go on about finding a guy who would fix everything, anyway.

Peggy claims she was also afraid of falling for Janis. "Every time I'd think, God, I really dig her, I'd feel bad, like, Ahh fuck, do I want to embark on something here where I let my heart go? I'd seen Kimmie when Joan Baez would come on the radio, and it'd be like a sledge-hammer hit her in the chest. And I thought, How am I going escape this woman's voice? I just didn't want to take a chance on feeling a dagger in my heart so deep that I might never be able to pull it out." In the end, Peggy never quite knew what Janis had in mind. "Some people say I've exaggerated this relationship. Others say I've actually underestimated it. People would tell me, 'She's crazy about you,'" she remembers. "The moments we had together, laughing and playing in bed, going out and being girls, buying clothes and going to the movies, eating chocolate fudge sundaes for breakfast and going back and debauching—it was so fun, so close." And always, there was the dope.

By the time Janis returned from her European tour in late April, she was supporting a hard-core addiction. "That girl had a needle in her arm," says

Peggy. "We both did. I had one in my arm every four to eight hours for years. And so did she." Between the summer of 1968, when she started using more heavily, and late 1969, Janis reportedly overdosed six times, once seriously. One reason people overdose is the variation in quality. "You *never* have a consistent supply," Milan points out. "No one brings in one huge shipment and keeps it in a warehouse and sells the same grade all the time. It's such a sleazy world, and the stuff gets stepped on [cut with other substances] in so many different ways. But Janis never took precautions. Some of us did; we tasted it first. But she went for the rush." Vince Mitchell, with whom Janis was briefly involved, once asked her why she didn't snort heroin rather than shoot up. "Why jack off when you can fuck?" she barked in reply.

Her most serious OD occurred in March 1969, after San Francisco's rock press panned her second band. Linda was in their Noe Street apartment when she heard a faint *oooh* sound from Janis's bedroom. Suspecting something was awry, she burst into the room, where Janis lay crumpled on the floor, all purple because she'd stopped breathing. Luckily, Sunshine, who was also living there at the time, knew what to do. She and Linda dragged Janis to the bathtub and put her in a cold bath, where gradually she began to revive. Linda made Janis walk for hours up and down the hills of their neighborhood to keep her from falling back into unconsciousness. "I was so furious with her," Linda said. "I mean, you don't do that to friends."

However, Janis did far worse to her junkie friends. With friends whose habits she was subsidizing, Janis would sometimes withhold dope, then make them beg for it. When they did, she'd act disgusted that they'd stooped so low. She put others at risk, too. One night, anticipating a hot three-way with Milan and Peggy, Janis cooked up a pile of heroin. Alarmed by the amount she was preparing, Milan said, "I've been clean for a while, so really back up. I just want a little hit here." Milan remembers her being very insistent. "Listen, I don't want this to be too much," he said. "I'd never let anyone either mix for me or inject me before. But she was really coming on: 'Look, I can do it for you, look, we'll have such fun.' . . . I hit the deck and it's the last thing I remembered till morning. I woke up frozen in the same position. That's the dumbest thing I ever did in my life. I think about that all the time. How could I have ever let anybody do that to me, even her?" After Milan passed out, Peggy worried she'd end up like him and cautioned Janis against giving her too much. Soon she was in a heap on the floor, too. "I was pissed," Milan recalls. "The next morning I told her, 'You almost killed me. There was no reason to do that.' She never apologized but reacted by saying, 'You're too light-weight. We could have had such fun.' Well, we could have died, too." A year later, in 1970, Sunshine OD'd while Janis was with her. Janis shoved her into a shower stall, turned on the water, and left the motel room.

"We all started recognizing the shadow that heroin cast," Peggy says. "The prince of darkness, it's called, and the scene did start becoming darker. We'd go into our hotel room and light a candle instead of turning on the light, fix, pass out, wake up, and debauch. We'd eat and smoke and Janis would drink and we'd fix again. It was debauching. When we looked up and realized we were really hooked, the party ended abruptly. Then we all knew that each and every day was gonna cost us a couple hundred dol-lars. When the addiction got really severe, Janis and I wouldn't buy a bag. We'd buy $1,200 or $5,000 worth of heroin. We weren't out for $50 or $100 bags. We'd buy $1,000 at a pop so we could stay inside for a couple of days before we'd need it again. George, our L.A. connection, would charge us $1,200 for an ounce, and Janis and I could shoot it up in two to three days." If they ran out of dope before they could reach George they'd call up somebody and say, "I'll give you an extra five hundred fuckin' dol-lars to get me an ounce of heroin here tonight," Peggy explains. "So you pay $1,700 instead of $1,200. If you can't get it, and you're getting sick, you'll pay to get it." Janis had a higher tolerance for the pain of withdrawal than Peggy. "She could go longer than I could without bitching. I'd start really writhing and getting nervous. I'd say, 'Well, have you called George yet?' I'd crank out to the hysteria mode that we weren't going to get fixed for the night before she would."

It had started as a way of getting down, getting soul, annihilating pain, and living on what Janis called "the outer limits of probability." But shoot-ing smack had become a very down-and-dirty scene. Bob Seidemann remembers walking into the party that followed Janis's Albert Hall gig in London to find Sam Andrew in a bathtub full of cold water with a groupie sitting astride him. He'd never seen such "interesting therapy . . . adminis-tered to an OD patient before." He heard that Janis was so hard up for a fix one time that she drew water into her syringe from a toilet. "Everyone took the risk and every time you took the needle to your arm death could happen, and we all knew that," Seidemann says. "Nobody was stupid. People OD'd and never came back." Nancy Gurley was one of them. "She didn't plan on dying that afternoon," Seidemann adds. "It was a mistake. They were just having fun."

Nancy and James Gurley had been going through hard times even before Big Brother fell apart. Nancy, who was pregnant again, had cut back on heroin, but James, who had been strung out on smack for some time, was still struggling to get clean. After living apart for a while, Nancy and their son, Hongo, had moved back in with James and his roommate, Richard Hundgen. The weekend of July 4, 1969, the Gurleys decided on the spur of the moment to take a camping trip with Hongo. James apparently saw the trip as an opportunity to get clean, but he took along a $100 bag of heroin. After an afternoon of drinking as they rafted down the Russian River, the couple camped and shot up. James was so wasted he missed his own vein entirely. Nancy wasn't so lucky. The heroin was powerful, her tolerance low, and James scored a perfect hit on her. As Nancy started to read a story to their three-year-old, she suddenly fell forward. James rushed her to the nearest hospital, but before they got there Nancy's face had already turned black. Had James hit his vein rather than his muscle, he too would have died. Instead he was charged with murder. With the help of Michael Stepanian, a lawyer who, with Brian Rohan, had founded the Haight-Ashbury Legal Organization, James ended up with only two years' probation.

James quit heroin immediately, but his life was in shambles. "I was totally shell-shocked," he says. "I couldn't tie my shoes. I didn't know if it would be the right thing or the wrong thing." Janis and Sam were devastated when they heard the news. Janis adored Nancy, from whom she'd appropriated much of her style, and dedicated the *Kozmic Blues* album to "Nancy G." The first thing she and Sam did upon hearing of Nancy's OD, however, was to go out and buy dope. In recounting the event to friends, Janis emphasized not only her distress about Nancy's death but her hard-core junkie reaction. "It was almost like braggadocio," says Dave Getz, "the way she talked about immediately going out and copping dope."

Within weeks of Nancy's death, though, Janis invited Sam to her room and fired him. Myra suspects Albert had a hand in his dismissal; Sam was, after all, Janis's junkie pal in the band, and Albert hoped that without him around she'd be less likely to put the needle in her arm. Of course, it made no difference. Shooting heroin kept the pain—and all Janis's other feelings, too—at bay. It deadened her, which is why she never shot up right before going onstage. "She had a thing about fixing before a performance," Sunshine says. "She knew what she was going to get from an audience." After all, Janis was on an "audience trip," as she herself put it. As soon as the gig was over, though, Janis would do up. It was a routine that Ed Rothschild, a doctor whom she later consulted about her addiction, thought curious and telling. She had "gotten all that satisfaction in theory from what she did and from the audience response," he reasoned, puzzled that it was at this moment that she should choose "to turn herself off and insulate herself from what should have been a beautiful world."

But walking offstage meant confronting her life. Like most other performers, Janis loved the stage in large part because it offered her a reprieve, however brief, from the real world. Janis might have received four standing ovations, but she'd still go back to her dressing room and fall into depression and insecurity, recalls Powell St. John. She was hardly unique in this respect. "The saddest part of performing," Nina Simone once said, was "that it didn't mean anything once you were offstage." For Janis, using heroin became a way of prolonging the onstage high by fending off the inevitable postperformance depression.

And then there was the scene backstage, which was hardly the beautiful world Rothschild imagined. Backstage was crawling with people who wanted something—an interview, an autograph, a picture, a fuck. Or confirmation of their coolness. Lou Reed met Janis in 1969 when she was in New York hanging out at Max's Kansas City. "Who can you talk to when you're famous and alone and all the people idolize you and want . . . to . . . get high with you and show you that they too are HIP," he wrote, reflecting on Janis two years later. Shooting up also helped distance her from what Milan Melvin calls all "the grabbing and the grasping" that started as soon as she ended a gig. "Janis hated the backstage scene," he recalls. "It felt out of control to her and she felt out of control." With her clothes sweaty and smelly and her hair disheveled and stringy, "Janis looked her worst at the moment that people expected her to look her most radiant," recalls Sunshine. Negotiating the backstage scene was especially difficult because Janis went so far out to the edge when she performed. "She threw herself so completely into it," Odetta observes, "that she almost disappeared and became this musical thing. That amazed me. She was so naked. And before she even got her skin back on, she was surrounded by people who needed this and that and everything."

In the end, the postconcert down and the backstage ugliness played minor roles in Janis's addiction. She looked for highs—performing, having sex, shooting up, and being a star—but they were all evanescent. No high could compete with her lows, with her conviction that she was worthless. That was the bottomless pit of neediness that caused her friends and lovers to complain; that was what made her so greedy, to use Linda Gravenites's word. Dope and booze and sex and fame could not fill up her yawning need or distract her from it. That's why she did all those encores, why she craved adulation, giving her audience yet another little piece of her heart.

One night at the Fillmore East, a critic caught a glimpse of Janis in the wings just after she'd finished her encore. As the audience called for another song, Janis "stood back there, pulling herself together for one more time, and her evident exhaustion was raw and frightening. I'd like to forget that look, but I won't for a long time." As Toni Brown of Joy of Cooking observes, "For Janis it was never enough to have all this applause and to have all these strokes. She needed it all the time. There was this big hole, and it was, 'Something come in here and calm me down, take care of me.' What did this woman do when she didn't have this scene around her?" Brown wondered. "Onstage I make love to twenty-five thousand people," Janis once said, "then I go home alone." She was rich, she was famous, and she was little girl blue.

9

Trading Her Tomorrows

In August 1969, strung out and unhappy with her band, Janis played Woodstock. Most musicians managed to avoid the mud and the hassle, but not Janis. "I can't fix in the tent," she complained to Peggy, who'd been helicoptered into the festival along with the musicians at Janis's request. "There's too many people coming and going. There's no privacy. Come on," she said to Peggy, "let's go find a place to fix." Peggy remembers wading through a sea of people to make it to the one place they'd be assured of privacy—the portapotties. "We got there and there's a huge line so Janis throws an 'I'm a star' fit and the crowds back off and let us in. There's shit piled up so high you couldn't sit down, and I'm gagging from the stench. 'Oh, Peggy, stop it,' Janis yelled." Janis Joplin and her girlfriend shooting up in a filthy portable toilet doesn't exactly jibe with the legend of Woodstock. But, then, the myth of Woodstock, nurtured by boomer chauvinism and nostalgia, can't easily accommodate the many bummers of that August weekend, much less all that followed in its wake.

Woodstock wasn't the first big outdoor music festival, but it was the one that came to stand as a defining event of the decade. At a time when America was riven by assassinations, urban riots, and talk of "bringing the war home," Woodstock, which was on the brink of disaster all weekend, defied all the dire predictions by proceeding peacefully. "The only . . . real surprise was that there was no riot," wrote the *New Yorker's* rock critic, Ellen Willis. Food and water may have been scarce and the ankle-deep mud and bad drugs ubiquitous, but the gathering of a half-million people never turned violent. Even the *New York Times*, which asked in an editorial headlined "A Nightmare in the Catskills," "What kind of culture can produce so colossal a mess?" admitted that the "great bulk of freakish-looking intruders behaved astonishingly well," showing "that there is real good under their fantastic exteriors." For one brief weekend—or until the press discovered Charles Manson several months later—the counter-culture stood vindicated as hippies became the country's model citizens.

Even before the festival was over, it had achieved mythic stature, which was then reinforced by Michael Wadleigh's 1970 documentary film, *Woodstock*. "I can always tell who was really there," claims Barry Melton of Country Joe and the Fish. "When they tell me it was great, I know they saw the movie and they weren't at the gig." True, the festival didn't end in catastrophe, but for many the experience still wasn't exactly pleasant. "Instead of the widespread notion of joy and an outpouring of goodness, the people I met told tragic stories of lack of consideration, non-existent sanitation, . . . fear and pain," wrote David Clurman, a former assistant attorney general for the state of New York, the unlucky official in charge of handling all festival-related complaints. "Woodstock was horrible," says Pete Townshend of the Who. Some people may have "managed to go through it completely unscathed and have a really good time," he concedes. The Who, however, had an all-too-typical festival experience when they arrived backstage ready to perform and were told the production assistant who'd ferried them there had gotten it all wrong. They were on in fifteen *hours*, not fifteen minutes. Backstage there were all kinds of squabbles as musicians demanded to be paid and sometimes ended up with only half of what they'd been promised.

At least the performers had been flown into the site by helicopter, while everyone else was stuck in the world's worst traffic jam. And once in the area, the musicians were installed at the Holiday Inn or the Howard

Johnson's, where they stayed dry and dined on steaks and champagne. The audience, on the other hand, was mired in the mud, listening to music made fuzzy by a sound system gone awry from all the rain. These stark differences spoke to the distance traveled in the two short years since Monterey Pop, where the line separating performers from audience was still permeable. Bill Graham was appalled by the festival's lack of organization. "They expected the audience to accept whatever short-comings they had. Oops, I'm sorry. Oops, sorry. Sorry, sorry, sorry." And the audience did accept every last apology, prompting Ellen Willis to ask if it was really "beautiful, transcendent acceptance" that kept Woodstock mellow or "plain old passivity."

In the era's lore, Woodstock has become synonymous with the "good sixties," with the beautiful people of the counterculture, while Altamont, the Rolling Stones' free concert just four months later, has come to stand for the decade's dark underside and the end of all that was hopeful and optimistic in the hippie revolution. Grace Slick of the Airplane, who performed at both events, sums up the difference succinctly: "Woodstock was a bunch of *stupid* slobs in the mud and Altamont was a bunch of *angry* slobs in the mud." A hastily thrown-together open-air concert at a speed-way on the outskirts of San Francisco, Altamont so reeked of bad vibes that Emmett Grogan of the Diggers dubbed it the "First Annual Charlie Manson Death Festival" days before the concert took place. The Hell's Angels, who'd been hired to handle security, ran amok, beating people up at will. As the Stones performed "Under My Thumb," the Angels targeted a black fan and stabbed and stomped him to death when he pulled a gun. Altamont, which occurred fittingly in the last month of the decade, came to symbolize the final gasp of the sixties. In its aftermath, the radical activist Todd Gitlin asked "whether the youth culture will leave anything behind but a market." But while Altamont was undoubtedly among the most disillusioning events of the decade, it was Woodstock that put an end to the era that had begun with the Family Dog dances and the Mime Troupe benefits.

The lesson of Woodstock for managers and musicians alike was that one big gig was preferable to several smaller gigs; ironically, the festival sounded the death knell for electric ballrooms, cultural spaces that had made Woodstock possible. "Before Woodstock the Jefferson Airplane still played four shows at the Fillmore East and earned $12,000," recalls Joshua White, a light-show artist. "Only really big acts—the Stones and the Doors—played Madison Square Garden. After Woodstock many more played the Garden. I knew—everybody on that stage at Woodstock knew—the future wasn't in rock theaters. The future was in arenas—big spectacle shows—and the musicians were going to start doing grander acts." Six months after the festival, White left his light-show company to start a video-projection business. "One of the reasons I got hired was that the bands playing these arenas felt a little guilty. And so they would make up to their audience for playing one show in a 20,000-seat arena by paying me $14,000 to project them up on a giant twenty-by-thirty-foot screen. I was there to help ease the blow of that big arena." Before 1969 was over, Janis joined the growing number of rockers playing the Garden. The new rock music was already a commodity before Woodstock, but the festival accelerated the process of commercialism by suggesting to corporate executives a way to reap untold profits off rock and the generation gap.

Woodstock was something of a defeat for Janis, as well. She had spent the two weeks before the festival in St. Thomas, at the home of John Morris, whom she knew from his days managing the Fillmore East. Morris, the festival's production coordinator, saw Janis when she arrived at the site and asked how her vacation had been. "Just like everywhere else," she said. "I fucked a lot of strangers." Morris was troubled. "I'll never forget that sadness," he says. "My first thought was, Uh-oh, we're in trouble. I knew her well enough to know we weren't going to get a great performance."

Indeed, Janis sang as if she were struggling to overcome the band's sluggishness and her own weariness. She had the misfortune of being sandwiched between the Grateful Dead and Sly and the Family Stone. Sly Stone and his band looked like a bunch of hippies, but they were tight in a way that Kozmic Blues never managed to be, even after eight months of gigging. In addition, the festival was running ten hours behind schedule, upsetting Janis's usual timetable for boozing and doping. Many people report that she was four sheets to the wind, at least from all the drinking she'd been doing. John Morris claims Janis had a bottle in each hand and was "totally ripped." Still, together with the band, Janis performed a sizzling "Try (Just a Little Bit Harder)," and until fatigue got the better of her, she sang a transcendent version of Nick Gravenites's "Work Me, Lord." The band's rendition of "Ball and Chain," however, with its loud and clumsy horns, was execrable, overblown like the arena rock that would follow in Woodstock's wake. Henry Diltz, one of the cameramen, described Janis as "tortured and crying in the microphone. . . . She really screamed in agony in those songs. She really meant it. You could see that in the way she contorted her face and her body and everything." At one point, her voice broke badly and you could see she wanted to kick herself, curse herself, just get offstage. "I can't relate to a quarter of a million people," she grumbled to Myra as she finally dragged herself off the stage. For Janis, too, Woodstock was a long way from Monterey Pop. Once backstage, she said something that would have been unthinkable just a year earlier. When Myra asked if she'd talk to a reporter from *Life* magazine, Janis, the inveterate publicity hound, barked, "I'm not fucking talking to anybody." Then she turned to Peggy and said, "I wanna go back to the motel room."

Everything upset Janis that weekend—her band, her singing, the vastness of the event, and the fact that neither the audiences nor her fame were working for her anymore. (Though, like many others, Janis learned to love Woodstock after the fact; during a visit back home in Port Arthur, she raved about its cultural significance.) Sometime later, an old Austin acquaintance asked Janis if she enjoyed what she was doing. "I wrote the part," she snapped. She did write the part, but she had never anticipated the loneliness that awaited her. For a while, fame brought her relief from the pain of feeling unloved and unlovable, but the exhilaration of celebrity couldn't dislodge "the underlying bleakness," as Myra called it. "Always her eyes would drift off just at certain moments to linger in some haunted, solitary space." By the fall of 1969, Janis was beginning to grasp what Susan Cheever, writing about her famous father, calls "the real secret" of success, namely, "It doesn't make any difference." "Success gets in your way," Janis said to *Newsweek*. "There's so much unspoken crap in the air that you're really alone." For her, success was bound up with outrageousness, was contingent on being a loud, freaky alcoholic chick, and so hobbled her even more. When Janis played at the University of Texas that October, her old friends Pepi Plowman and Tary Owens asked how it felt to have hit the big time. "Oh, this is no kind of life," she said. "I witnessed people coming into her room and basically kissing her ass," says Pepi. "It was so false. I mean, my shit detector was going boing, boing, boing. It must have been really bad to think that no one loved you, but then to have people trying to make you think they do . . . You're never really sure." Another old Texas pal, Dave Moriaty, ran into her in Berkeley. "Well, you've really done it," he said. "The whole damn Cinderella story." Janis stopped him. "I don't know, man. . . . I never get to talk to people I want to, I'm not meeting any more good people. It's just brought a different kind of alienation." Tellingly, Moriaty noticed that right after she'd complained to him, Janis "yodelled some more to draw a bigger crowd."

Her relentless unhappiness made her craving for all kinds of highs, including the rush from performing, that much more intense. It was no longer so easy, however, working the audience into a frenzy. After all, the shock value of seeing a white woman move and sing like Janis did was wearing off. And even though she was playing before sold-out crowds, the tour, which had begun that February, grew unbearable. "It just got worse and worse," she later told David Dalton. "We weren't getting along, and the music wasn't together," but she couldn't cancel the tour. Janis had always measured her success as a performer by whether she succeeded in getting a crowd out of its seats. To Myra, it seemed the "audiences had to be swarming the aisles, pressing toward the stage, whistling, yelling, shrieking, dancing, or it wasn't a Joplin concert; it wasn't the testimony of love." She would try everything short of igniting a riot to rouse the fans. "If Janis couldn't get them really riled up," Maury Baker, one of the band's drummers, recalls, "then it seemed she believed the show was a failure. There were no calm concerts."

Dancing in the aisles and on the seats became an issue in 1969, now that the new rock stars were playing in city-owned arenas and auditoriums with real police or nervous rent-a-cops, not in the hip electric ballrooms with their own security. A clash was inevitable given the cops' commitment to order and, in Janis's case, her commitment to defiance. After all, teaching kids not to accept their fate passively was part of her mission. "It was like Janis against the cops every time," recalls one of her musicians. Things came to a head in mid-November in Tampa, Florida, when jittery cops began moving fans out of the aisles and away from the stage. "Listen, Mister," Janis said politely, "I've been to more of these things than you have and no one's ever hurt nothin'. . . . Leave them alone." But as Janis launched into her signature ballad "Summertime," a policeman with a bullhorn interrupted her again. "Don't fuck with those people," Janis shouted. Asked to tell the kids to sit down, she snarled, "I'm not telling them shit," and resumed singing. After the song, she told the crowd, "Now listen . . . if we don't hurt nothing they can't say shit." It was no use, though, as thousands of kids were now standing and dancing on the upholstered seats, much to the consternation of the hall managers, who cut the power and turned on the lights. As she left the stage, Janis walked over to the cop with the bullhorn, called him a son of a bitch, and threatened to kick his face in. At midnight she was arrested in her dressing room and charged with two counts of vulgar and indecent language. Later Janis told reporters, "I say anything I want onstage. I don't mind getting arrested because I've turned on a lot of kids."

There were no showdowns with the cops at her sold-out Madison Square Garden concert on December 19, but once again Janis was provocative. This was the final stop of her tour, and during the Otis Redding tune "I Can't Turn You Loose," Janis paused. "It would be illegal for me to say, 'Why don't you get up and dance' because it would be illegal for you to do it. So don't think I'm suggesting anything like that, but I don't know what the fuck you're doing sitting down—this is rock and roll! Ain't nothing complicated about that." According to the *Village Voice*, people then "started pouring into the aisles and up to the front of the stage." Before Janis had finished the song the entire audience was on its feet and the main floor at the Garden started to shake so much some worried it might collapse. There was no trouble at the Garden, but her efforts to rouse her fans did not go unnoticed by promoters and hall managers in other parts of the country. The city of Houston actually banned Janis—"for her attitude in general."

That fall when Janis wasn't working the crowds into a lather, she was doped up, her eyes glassy and dull, the old spark gone. From the end of October until the third week of December she was often in New York, where Myra saw her fairly frequently. "She might as well have been slumped, nodding out in a public doorway, for the resemblance to her former self that remained," Myra noted. At the Rolling Stones' Thanksgiving concert at Madison Square Garden, "Janis was pretty down and she got really fucked up," Myra says. "She must have done up, and she was behaving really crazy and Tina Turner came over to me and said, 'Is there anything I can do?' Because it was just terrible. There was always this amusement about Janis's drinking onstage, but to see somebody in such a state is something entirely different." Ike and Tina Turner were opening for the Stones that night. During their set Janis made her way onstage and broke into their act. Generously, Tina embraced her and the two sang a duet.

At the same time, Janis knew she was screwing up and made some effort to get herself together. After her own gig at Madison Square Garden, she decided to disband her backup band, this time without any hand wringing. In November, she had bought a house in Larkspur, just outside San Francisco in Marin County. Earlier that fall she had called Linda Gravenites, who was still in London, and begged her to come back and move in with her. She followed the call with a letter in which she admitted dope wasn't the answer to her kozmic blues. Janis was ready to try the "other way," she assured Linda. She might even take up yoga, learn to play the piano, and start taking long walks in the woods. Janis claimed she'd seen the light, but she still didn't give up the needle.

Though drugs were de rigueur among rockers, Janis's heroin use was so out of control people finally began calling her on it. Once Linda was back in the States she and Myra confronted her. Janis responded angrily, but back at her hotel room with Linda she broke down and cried. The next day she called Myra with the news that she'd made an appointment to see Ed Rothschild, an endocrinologist whom Albert had recommended. Despite Albert's efforts to get Janis to see a doctor, he has been criticized for failing to act aggressively enough. Myra, echoing the feelings of others, thinks Albert "failed to take real command of the drug situation and Janis's personal behavior" and cites as evidence his reluctance to talk with her about her heroin problem. Sally Grossman, however, insists that her husband "never would have discussed this with Myra. Never. Because he didn't discuss it with me. He didn't discuss it with anybody. It was between him and Janis. I suspect Albert knew what was going on. And there's no way he'd discuss it, especially with the publicist. With all the artists he represented, privacy and confidentiality were major concerns." Nor was Albert the sort of manager to take control of an artist's life, says

Peter Yarrow of Peter, Paul and Mary. "He was not a sycophantic, hyper-protective stage mother," says Yarrow. "He urged his clients to be responsible for themselves. And Albert always said an artist had a right to destroy himself."

In any case, Janis's contrition was short-lived. Rothschild, who had treated a number of addicts before Janis, doesn't believe she was ready to quit using when she came to see him. Once again, Janis boasted about her ability to handle heroin. "I can do this," Rothschild remembered her saying. "It's the best thing in the world. I don't know why everybody's getting so upset about it." They talked about her drinking, too, and Janis claimed she'd been treated for alcoholism at seventeen. When test results showed her liver was functioning normally, she bragged, "Well, that just shows I'm really a strong, healthy person because the way I've been drinking you'd think my liver would be shot!" Rothschild tried to warn her of the cumulative damage caused by drink and dope. He was concerned about her diet as well, which in typical junkie fashion was heavy on sweets—the reason her weight fluctuated radically, from 115 pounds to 155. In the end, he gave her a ten-day prescription for Dolophine, methadone in pill form, to help her kick.

Janis claimed to feel better while she was taking Dolophine, but the day after her prescription ran out, which was also the night of her Madison Square Garden concert, Myra thought she seemed "edgy." When she finally showed up at Clive Davis's lavish postconcert party in her honor, Janis's face had "a green-white glow," suggesting to Myra she'd probably fixed after the show. John Cooke, her recently departed road manager, thought to himself, "Gee, am I glad I left the tour when I did. I didn't want to watch this happen to her." The next day, Janis returned to the Bay Area. She settled into her new Larkspur house, where she planned to take a well-deserved vacation from performing. Once she was back in California, her stance on quitting dope turned into "Not yet." According to Sunshine, Janis had kicked but had five bags she'd been given and wanted to shoot up with her because, she said, "I'm going to be clean from now on."

If anything, Janis's habit worsened during January. She resolved to get off drugs by getting out of town and had the idea of going to Carnival in Rio. She contacted Rothschild to get more Dolophine for the trip, then called her parents, who, Laura says, tried to "act supportive" when Janis told them she intended to take a vacation from "the bizness." When Seth ran into Karleen Bennett, her high school friend, and told her of Janis's plans, however, he didn't disguise his feelings. "I don't know why she's going to all the trouble to get to Brazil. All she's going to do is get drunk, and she can do that as easily at home." Peggy Caserta claims she declined an invitation to come along because, she says, "Janis was going to kick, and I wasn't ready. I was enjoying my addiction. Any junkie can tell you that if you can take it right to the doorstep of when you start to feel sick you feel so much better when you've fixed. So I was having fun with the habit and I didn't want to kick." Before boarding the helicopter to the airport, Janis gave Peggy her remaining dope, worth over two thousand dollars.

Linda in tow, Janis arrived in Rio in early February, popping Dolophine and drinking booze. She quickly hooked up with another American in town for Carnival, David Niehaus, a handsome blond who'd grown up in an affluent part of Cincinnati. After college he'd joined the Peace Corps, worked in rural Turkey, and returned home to attend law school briefly before hitting the road again. Niehaus was drawn to Janis even though he didn't know who she was. He endeared himself to her when he said, "You know, you look like that rock star, Janis Joplin." But Janis couldn't stand being out of the spotlight. Unable to keep her private life private, she held a press conference in Brazil and announced she was "going off into the jungle with a big bear of a man." She told Myra she'd totally forgotten about her career and suggested Myra phone *Rolling Stone* with that news flash.

After five weeks in Brazil, Janis had kicked the dope and was on her way back to San Francisco. Niehaus decided to follow her but was detained at the Rio airport because he'd overstayed his visa. After screaming, "You're a cunt and this is a cunt country!" at Brazilian officials, Janis boarded the plane, stopping over in L.A. just long enough to score dope. By the time Niehaus appeared at Larkspur two days later, Janis was back on the needle and tied up with Peggy. "Janis and I were pretty thick by the time she dragged that fucker home from Rio de Janeiro," recalls Peggy. As far as she was concerned, Niehaus was just some guy Janis had picked up. "When you stop using, you get pretty horny," she says. "To me, he was just like this dork. And what I resented about it was that all of the sudden it was like he was the love of her life and they might get married." Both Linda and Myra, however, had the impression that the relationship was genuine and substantial. Niehaus was put off by Janis's doping and her whirlwind scene. "Every time we went out of the house she had five hundred people screaming around her car. . . . It just wasn't fun," he said. The real drag, though, was coming back to Larkspur after a two-day trip to find Janis in a heroin haze, in bed with Peggy.

When Niehaus announced he'd be leaving, Janis countered by trying to talk him into becoming her road manager. He briefly considered the proposition, but what he really wanted to be was a teacher, with Janis at his side. "He's determined to turn me into a schoolteacher's wife," Janis groaned to Linda. When he couldn't persuade her to give up her life, Niehaus chose to continue traveling around the world, prompting Janis's send-up of hippie guys "out on the road looking for their i-d-e-n-t-i-t-y" in at least one concert version of "Cry Baby." Janis ad-libbed, "Don't you know you got a good woman at home?" and then cackled, "That oughta be identity enough for any man." Yet Janis had tried to bend his life to *her* will—after all, she had wanted to turn Niehaus into her road manager.

Once he was gone, Janis went racing all over Marin County and San Francisco looking for something new to distract her from herself. It was all "motion, motion, motion," as one friend put it. Janis finally had a home, which many say she regarded as an important accomplishment, but she was rarely there. She made the Trident, a hip Sausalito bar, her regular hangout. "Occasionally we'd get a call saying that Janis would be at the Trident," recalls Bob Brown of the Conqueroo, who had moved to the area from Austin. "We'd go down there and she'd sort of hold court with this circle of cronies around her." To Linda, a lot of the cronies were sycophants and she couldn't bear them. Nor did she like the way Janis was changing. "When I returned from England, things that had once thrilled her, like being ushered to a table at a crowded restaurant, she now expected as a matter of course. I remember one night at the Trident there were no tables and she got abusive. It was a shocker."

Linda was also exasperated by Janis's continued heroin use. There was no escaping the stuff, even in the Larkspur house, which had a separate wing for Linda. When she would venture into the kitchen, for instance, she'd risk running into Peggy and Janis doped up and staggering out of the bedroom in search of sweets. There was the time Janis, Peggy, and Michael Bloomfield shot up together. Linda opened the door to her bathroom and found Peggy and Janis trying to revive Bloomfield, who'd OD'd. "This is disgusting," Linda sneered, according to Peggy. By the end of March, Janis and Linda were barely speaking, and one day in early April, Janis brusquely announced that her roommate would have to either change her attitude about dope or move out. It was, Linda emphasizes, the only time Janis was ever mean to her, but she'd had enough and decided to clear out the next day. Janis was devastated, yet with little sense that she'd let Linda down by reneging on her promise to try the "other way." Instead, she felt abandoned by Linda. "You think I'm going to be a junkie for the rest of my life, do you?" Janis yelled. Linda didn't miss a beat. "Yes," she shouted back, convinced Janis needed to understand the repercussions of continued use. Janis knew that Albert would never dump her, despite his promise to drop any client using heroin. "He makes too much money off of me," she said. So Linda resolved to stay out of her life lest Janis trivialize her concern, too. Before Linda left, Janis turned remorseful, claiming she hadn't meant what she'd said. "Yes, you did," Linda said, standing her ground. "But you're my security blanket," Janis pleaded. She'd blown it with her best friend, the woman who had functioned as her surrogate mother for two and a half years. "Linda was her ground wire," observes Peggy. The day she left, Janis was on the phone to Myra sobbing uncontrollably about Linda's betrayal. Linda made it easier for Janis to feel victimized because she'd also taken five hundred dollars—money that Janis had put in Linda's account for house expenses—which she used to get settled elsewhere. Janis's great fear was that her friends only hung around because she was a star with lots of money. Linda had never before taken any for herself and felt it was owed her, but Janis was hurt nonetheless.

Like all the rest of the inner circle, Linda had come to resent Janis's insatiable neediness. "She was an extremely sensitive soul," Linda says, "but only for herself." The more famous she became, the more solipsistic she grew; the larger world receded, becoming a mere backdrop to every precious detail of her life. And who had the patience to listen to her velvet-lined woes? Here she was, an internationally famous rock star whose gross annual earnings were a staggering $750,000, yet she was perennially dissatisfied, whining about not having a boyfriend or not having the right band. "This hole in her gut, this clutching kind of need," as Dave Getz calls it, simply wore her friends down.

Even Peggy felt exasperated with Janis on occasion. When Janis played the Hollywood Bowl in September 1969, she gave Peggy and Sam Andrew tickets and a limo ride to the show. Sam, already out of the band, was incensed that the new guitarist was copying his old licks. He got up and left before the concert was over, Peggy trailing after him. They had Janis's driver take them back to their motel, assuming, Peggy says, that he would return to the Bowl for Janis. Instead the chauffeur went home, leaving Janis stranded at the concert. Furious with Peggy and Sam, Janis walked back to the motel, her way of compounding her grievance. "What's the fucking idea, going off and leaving me?" Janis yelled as she stormed into the motel room. "You suck, Sam. You really suck. And you . . . when it comes to him you're like some fucking . . . *jellyfish.*" Sometimes Peggy cackles at the thought of Janis left high and dry at the Bowl, other times she pleads innocent, and yet other times she exhibits sheer impatience. After all, what star in her right mind would walk home when she could have called a cab? Then again, what sort of friends except angry and resentful ones would walk out in the middle of her set and hijack her limo? Myra got in a dig one day, too. She remembers sitting around with Albert and Janis, who was "moping" about what would happen when she was no longer number one. Would Albert give her a job? Janis asked. "Sure, you can have the clipping service," Myra piped up, referring to the lowliest job in the office. "She looked like I had punched her in the stomach, and Albert glared at me. I couldn't resist it, because she was just being absurd and childish. It was the only mean thing I ever did to Janis."

When Linda left, Janis arranged for Lyndall Erb to move in and take care of the house. A clothes designer, Lyndall had grown up in San Francisco but had spent the last couple of years in New York, where she'd hung out in a rock 'n' roll crowd that included Country Joe and the Fish and Janis, for whom she'd designed some outfits. When Lyndall returned to the Bay Area, she resumed her friendship with Janis, sometimes sleeping over at her Noe Street apartment and taking care of her dog when Janis was out of town. Eventually, Janis invited Lyndall to move in and take over Linda's role. At Albert's suggestion, Janis then put her on the payroll. Albert was rumored to have hired Lyndall to keep an eye on his client, but she denies this. In any case, within a month of Lyndall's moving in, Janis, determined to prove Linda wrong, swore off heroin. She started seeing a shrink to get more Dolophine and eventually took the hardest step of all: telling her severely addicted friends, including Sunshine and Peggy, she didn't want to see them until they were clean. Every so often that summer Janis called Sunshine, asked if she'd quit doping, and hung up when Sunshine said she hadn't. Quitting dope and walking away from her friends took incredible strength. Too much, it turns out. Janis could no more stay totally clean throughout the summer than she could become a teetotaler. She started chipping, though few people knew it because she was no longer strung out and the worst of the junkies around her were gone. For weeks at a time Janis may have managed to stay clean, but Linda Gottfried Waldron contends Janis was using in July when she came to Hawaii. Sam Andrew saw little of her that summer, but claims that whenever he stopped by her home she'd bring out the works and the dope. (Lyndall confirms that Janis's abstinence was short lived but questions both Linda's and Sam's accounts. The guys in Big Brother rarely saw Janis at that time—they were still too angry; Linda never actually saw Janis in Hawaii, while Lyndall was with her constantly and never saw evidence of heroin.) Travis Rivers contends that Albert arranged for Janis to visit a spa, where she kicked again, perhaps that July.

With Linda out of her life, Janis became more vulnerable to the parasites that always hang around stars, and she came to depend even more heavily on employees and wanna-be jet-setters. Bob Brown remembers "the huge entourage of people who just sucked off her" and attributes the preponderance of creeps around Janis to "the hippie creed that everybody should be accepted. So when creeps descended on you nobody knew how to get rid of them." Odetta also recalls the "spotlight seekers and star fuckers" who populated Janis's scene. "Janis had a fabulous innate intelligence, but she was emotionally bereft and she tended to look to others for emotional support," says Carl Gottlieb, an actor and writer who is a friend of Milan Melvin's. "When those others were wise, or kind, or good she was in good hands. But when they were driven by their own egos and had their own agendas or were just not very smart, she unfortunately put the same faith in what they told her." In the last year of Janis's life, Gottlieb thinks, "the harmful influences outweighed the beneficial ones."

Many of her old buddies from Austin were now living in the Bay Area, but Janis saw them only on rare occasions, often when she was holding forth at the Trident. She kept in regular touch with Julie Paul and had plans to see Pepi Plowman and Fredda Slote later that fall. Janis seemed ambivalent, however, about renewing contact with people who'd known her in a less glorious incarnation. "It was like, 'Hey, I'm on top of the world now. I'm not a warthog that nobody wants to climb in bed with. Everybody wants to climb in bed with me now,'" says Jack Jackson, who worked at the Avalon. "So it was kind of embarrassing and awkward." Powell St. John was one Austinite Janis loved to see, but he kept away, not wanting to "wade through all those weirdos to get to her."

In time, Janis's Larkspur home became a magnet for freeloaders, which began corroding her trust in everyone. According to her roommate, Lyndall, Janis disliked the parasitical quality of the scene, yet she felt she needed these people around her. "Janis was real good to her friends. She'd throw big parties, she'd give them drugs. She'd do just about anything for them, partly because she was real insecure." Displays of generosity would be followed by periods of gloomy worry. She fretted—not unreasonably—that the guys coming around wanted to sleep with her only because she had drugs on hand. Myra heard many of Janis's rants about hangers-on but believes she was so invested in feeling victimized by others that she repeatedly created situations in which her worst nightmare—being used—would be realized. According to Kris Kristofferson, the singer and songwriter, who met Janis that spring, she'd bring people into her house "and then bitch because she was giving them bed and board." Bad as it was, being exploited seemed preferable to being alone.

"Around her success there was a terrible loneliness that was unbelievable," recalls Odetta. She suspects the people who were working with Janis might have been "selfishly keeping others away so that their space wasn't threatened." "I've seen this phenomenon in operation several times over," says Carl Gottlieb. "When you become rich and famous in show business there comes a point where the only people you talk to are the people whom you pay. And it's very rare, almost impossible, to find people who depend on you for their livelihood to tell you something you really don't want to hear, tell you something that's going to make you hassled, tell you something that's going to make you dislike them. So they hold back, either by design, which is fairly sinister, or out of self-preservation. And that happened to Janis." Indeed, Janis even told Myra that the only people who loved her were on her payroll. "It's true!" she cried. "Nobody really loves me, nobody!" She made "horrible whimpering sounds" before correcting herself. "The only people who love me," she said, "are the junkies I used to know!" Janis had scaled the heights of rock 'n' roll superstardom, yet she still felt unlovable.

Around this time, spring 1970, Janis adopted the nickname "Pearl" for the ballsy, hard-talking, barfly image she so often took on. Playing the tough girl had always been Janis's protective strategy against feeling vulnerable, and now she played the role with a vengeance. Laura Joplin claims the Pearl character grew out of conversations with Bobby Neuwirth (who, for reasons no one can fathom, was still on Albert's payroll and part of Janis's entourage). He and Janis talked about the need to have a "separate stage persona" apart from one's "most intimate self." The invention of Pearl seems to have been an effort to preserve "the real Janis," separate from her legendary image. Only the nickname was new, however; Janis had been crafting the character since her Port Arthur days. Still, Pearl was way over the top, an often grotesque self-caricature. Her closest friends cringed when she trotted out Pearl with feathers in her hair, not to mention all those boas. To Dave Getz, "Pearl was a simplification and ludicrous exaggeration of one aspect of her personality." Moreover, the loud, cheap broad act almost swamped the "intimate self" Janis had wanted to protect; there was a new hardness about her now, solidified by her eternal loneliness, the suspicion that everyone was out to use her, and not least, her twenty-four-hour boozing.

Alcohol had always been a staple in Janis's repertoire, but once she cut back on heroin she began drinking all the time. "From the moment I met Janis until the day she died, she was an alcoholic," maintains Linda Gottfried Waldron. Perhaps the first song Janis ever wrote, in 1962, was "What Good Can Drinkin' Do," about the futility of using booze to chase away the blues. Now she switched from Southern Comfort to a new favorite. When Myra asked if she was feeling better off the needle, Janis said, "If you call drinking a quart of tequila a day being better, then I'm better!" In May, Bobby Neuwirth and Kris Kristofferson showed up at her house and they all embarked on a three-week drinking binge they dubbed The Great Tequila Boogie. The long days of boozing culminated in a party where people got tattooed by a tattoo artist named Lyle Tuttle.

More drunk than sober, more Pearl than Janis, she was locked into a hard-bitten character that exacerbated her inability to feel loved and almost invited abuse. If Janis was going to act like a tough, cheap broad, there were plenty of people willing to play along with the fantasy. Pepi Plowman recalls seeing her that spring at a concert in Marin where the band New Riders of the Purple Sage was playing. "Janis got up onstage and shouted, 'I wanna sing some country.' She was completely drunk, and one of the guys onstage came up behind her and said, 'I'll give you country this way,' and pushed her from behind as if he were screwing her." And then there were the Hell's Angels. Janis had hung out with Freewheelin' Frank and other Angels, but in the wake of Altamont she and many other hip San Franciscans had come to reconsider the wisdom of embracing the Angels. She'd had a run-in with the bikers in the fall of 1969 when they'd crashed a party of hers and stolen a stack of her prerelease copies of *Kozmic Blues*. So when the Angels told her they wanted her to perform at a mid-May party of theirs, she agreed reluctantly. At the bash, one Angel accosted her and demanded a swig of her booze. Nobody pushed Janis around, not even a biker, and she turned him down. Gripping her bottle, she yelled, "Fuck you." A brawl ensued until the Beat poet Lenore Kandel's boyfriend, Sweet William, rescued Janis from the pile of people on the floor.

Even as Janis became more and more outrageous, she sensed the trap Pearl represented for her; she felt tyrannized by the caricature she'd created. She wanted to cut back on the boozing and find somebody special, yet she also believed she'd been cast in her self-destructive role by her fans. "People, whether they know it or not, like their blues singers miserable," she complained to David Dalton. On another occasion she ventured, "Maybe my audience can enjoy my music more if they think I'm destroying myself." Janis's audience did eat up her flamboyant exploits, but it was Janis herself who had made her life a spectacle. She seemed to feel that her amazing performances weren't enough, that she had to wear her suffering on her sleeve all the time or her fans would turn away. As spring turned to summer, though, Janis began to understand, at least sporadically, that she needn't destroy herself to be successful. She was chipping, but she wasn't strung out. She had so curtailed her drug use that John Cooke thought she had kicked dope entirely. She seemed proud of herself and pleased to be clean, he says. On a trip to Canada in late June, "Janis almost deliberately goaded the customs guy into searching her stuff because she didn't have any dope. She was just so delighted that there was no danger," says Cooke. When the customs official got to Janis's toiletries, Cooke recalls, "he held up a bag of colored powder as if he'd hit pay dirt. 'What is this?' he asked, peering at it. And she said, 'That's douche powder, man.' The man turned beet-red," according to Cooke, "and after a while packed everything back up and sent her on her way. We were there for about forty-five minutes and she was just having a ball. I mean, when we went to Europe she didn't want anyone poking around in her bags."

Janis was also starting to acknowledge, somewhat grudgingly, that she had a drinking problem. At one point that summer when her drinking was way out of hand, she suggested to Myra that maybe she should see a doctor whose specialty was escapism. She couldn't give up her boozing altogether, but on days she performed she did try instituting a regimen of sorts, forgoing alcohol in the afternoons. For a while at least, she'd drink in the morning, pass out in the afternoon, wake up and get sober before show time, when she'd resume drinking. Janis wasn't sober by a long shot, but while her schedule lasted it represented an improvement over going onstage thoroughly bombed, blacking out, and waking up without any memory of the previous night.

The effort to kick junk and cut down on drinking was fueled, more than anything else, by turns in Janis's career. She might have been feeling lonely and used, but by spring 1970 she was finally beginning to take command of her musical development. For more than a year with the Kozmic Blues Band, Janis had fumbled around trying to assert herself as the leader—haughty one minute, self-deprecating the next. Now she had the confidence to front a band. With help from Nick Gravenites and Albert, she'd chosen the band members by early May 1970. Other than the drummer, Clark Pierson, whom Janis discovered playing with Snooky

Flowers at a topless joint in San Francisco, the new guys were seasoned rockers, despite their youth. Ken Pearson, the organist, had played in Jesse Winchester's band before joining Janis; Brad Campbell, the bassist, stayed with Janis from the Kozmic Blues Band, where he'd been from almost the beginning; Richard Bell, the pianist, and John Till, the lead guitarist, had played in Ronnie Hawkins's legendary rock 'n' roll band, the Hawks, although Till had joined Janis earlier, days before Woodstock, replacing Sam Andrew. "These guys were coming in as Janis's boys," says Myra. "And they loved her to death," says Vince Mitchell, her roadie. "I can tell those cats what to do and they'll *do* it!" she enthused. "It's *my* band. Finally it's *my* band," she raved. In contrast to the nameless band that preceded it, this group acquired a name right away. A throwaway remark by Bobby Neuwirth, inviting his friends to a "full-tilt boogie," provided the inspiration and the Full Tilt Boogie Band was born.

Once Bobby Neuwirth convinced John Cooke that Janis was off smack and her new band red-hot, Cooke agreed to return to the fold. As he watched Janis and the guys rehearse, he was immediately struck by her willingness to take charge. There was a huge difference, he says, "between late 1968, when she was trying to put the Kozmic Blues Band together and basically expected it to be done for her by Nick Gravenites, Mike Bloomfield, and Albert, and 1970, when she took a much more active role." At this point, Cooke notes, she was an experienced professional who'd faced all sorts of audiences and cut three records, whereas the Full Tilt Boogie boys were younger and unacquainted with the world of big-time rock 'n' roll. "Janis knew more than they did," he says.

The Full Tilt Boogie Band hit the road in late May 1970, and at last everyone was happy—the critics, the fans, Albert, and Janis herself. When the band played Louisville, Kentucky, on June 12, it stirred a lack-luster crowd into a near riot. The local newspapers couldn't praise her enough. "Howling, screeching, and penetrating the air with . . . brilliance and force," Janis was phenomenal, raved the Louisville *Courier-Journal*. Reporting for *Rolling Stone*, David Dalton thought her new group had "the virtues of spontaneity and freshness without being amateurish." With a solid "wall of sound" behind her, Janis's singing was "more controlled and at the same time more inventive," he wrote. "This band is solid," Janis told him. "Their sound is so heavy you could lean on it." And "it's more of a family thing again." Finally Janis had a band so tight and so committed to her she could improvise onstage without worrying she'd lose them.

With Full Tilt Boogie she began singing country again. She had already performed Kris Kristofferson's "Me and Bobby McGee" back in December. The song had been recorded by the country singer Roger Miller, but given the lack of crossover between genres, it's a safe bet few in the rock 'n' roll audience had ever heard his version. Janis began the song unplugged, accompanying herself on an acoustic guitar, but by the song's end the whole band was in the act, in "Hey Jude" fashion. Janis hadn't sung country since her days in Austin, but now she was ready to explore her musical roots. Her version of "Me and Bobby McGee" was "just the tip of the iceberg, showing a whole untapped source of Texas, country, and blues that she had at her fingertips," says Richard Bell, her pianist. "What we were seeing was how easily she could go back to the old stuff, and with the Full Tilt Boogie she was going to pursue that area down the road." Janis would never abandon soul music, but her new band was discovering what practically no one except her old Austin friends knew—that Janis's repertoire was vast and that she hadn't explored it since making herself over into a rock singer.

She wasn't, however, in the forefront of the country turn. Gram Parsons, the Byrds, Bob Dylan, Tracy Nelson, and the New Riders of the Purple Sage were already experimenting with country music by the time Janis joined their ranks. Like Janis, many of them had played country blues and bluegrass as folkies. Until the late 1960s, though, most rockers viewed country as a hopeless bastion of squareness. Significantly, the country move coincided with the rise of Black Power and a shift by the counterculture from the city to the countryside. Gram Parsons even tried promoting country music as "white soul" music. Although the new interest in country reflected the redrawing of America's color line, for Janis it also had a more positive meaning—the beginning of her journey home, musically speaking, to Texas.

In July, Janis literally returned to her musical roots when she traveled to Austin to help friends celebrate Kenneth Threadgill's birthday. She arrived after a solid month of touring, the highlight of which was the Festival Express, a booze-fueled five-day train trip across Canada that the Full Tilt Boogie Band took with the Grateful Dead, Delaney and Bonnie and Friends, Buddy Guy and his band, and the New Riders of the Purple Sage, among others. They stopped in three cities for gigs, but some of the hottest music was made on the train. It was full-tilt boogie time, with Janis—according to David Dalton—"the presiding spirit of the journey," getting everyone drunk, including those notorious acidheads the Dead.

Once in Austin, Janis assumed a low profile, although she did sing a couple of songs for the crowd of eight thousand that turned out to honor Threadgill. After announcing she couldn't sing rock 'n' roll without her band, she asked for her "gitar." "Will someone tune this thing?" she said, adding she couldn't tune "worth shit." She then launched into two Kristofferson tunes, "Sunday Morning Coming Down" ("Almost as bad as Tuesday morning coming down—or Thursday morning coming down," she joked) and "Me and Bobby McGee." After Threadgill expressed his heartfelt thanks to Janis for attending, she presented him with a gift. "I was in Hawaii and I bought him one thing that I knew he'd like," she said, smiling mischievously. As she placed a wreath of flowers around his neck, she explained: "A good lei."

That month, Janis's musical fortunes took another positive turn when Paul Rothchild reentered her life. It was Rothchild who had tried to lure her to Los Angeles to join a band with Taj Mahal and Stefan Grossman in 1966. Four years later, Rothchild was a big-time producer best known for his work with the Doors. Cooke, who'd kept up with Rothchild for eight years, was keenly aware of Janis's need for a smart, simpatico producer, someone who would both understand her singing and teach her something about how to use and preserve her voice. Rothchild had last seen Janis with the Kozmic Blues Band, when her voice sounded wrecked and she looked wasted from junk. So when Cooke approached him about working on her next album, Rothchild declined. He agreed to catch her San Diego show only when Cooke told him she was doing great, had quit using heroin, and had even cut back on her drinking. Rothchild was "enraptured," and for the first time, Janis, who always agonized about being an imposter, had the chance to work with someone who appreciated her talent.

And not just her talent. After a day spent drinking piña coladas at Janis's home and running around with her to restaurants and bars in Sausalito, Rothchild reported to Cooke, "I learned something very important yesterday. Janis Joplin is a *very* smart woman." At some point during the day, Rothchild had asked her where she wanted to be in twenty or so years' time. "I want to be the greatest blues singer in the world," Janis replied. She could be, he assured her, if she didn't blow out her voice. "Paul could learn how to talk to anybody," says Cooke. "If he could find the key to a musician's language, he could describe what wasn't happening that needed to happen. . . . It's how he could get what he needed in the studio from musicians. Janis had three albums' worth of studio time but had never had a producer who taught her the difference between singing in the studio and singing in a performance."

Janis was ecstatic about the Full Tilt Boogie Band, but despite talking of living for the moment in "superhypermost" mode, she was hardly nonchalant about the future. After the more modest success of her *Kozmic Blues* album—it rose to number five on the charts but didn't yield any hit singles—she was even more anxious about being displaced as rock's leading lady. Bette Midler had just begun performing at the Continental Baths, a gay bathhouse on the Upper West Side, and Janis saw her there several times that summer. She loved Midler's raunchy, campy act but told friends, "That's my next competition." When Janis failed to sell out a few shows, she fretted her star might be fading. "I can't sleep!" she confessed to Myra after a gig in Miami early that summer. "I go to bed worrying and I wake up worrying every morning, worrying that they'll have found out I really can't sing."

In addition, Albert was adopting an increasingly hands-off approach with his clients—leaving most of the day-to-day work to his new partner, Bennett Glotzer—which did nothing to allay Janis's fears. With too many clients in a battle with heroin and his once-close relationship to Dylan gone sour, Albert was growing weary of the business. He spent more and more time away from his Manhattan office, supervising the construction of his recording studio in Bearsville, New York, and tending to his garden in Woodstock. "Albert always said he wanted to be the architect, not the janitor," explains Peter Yarrow of Peter, Paul and Mary. In any case, Myra says Janis understood Albert's flagging interest in the business as desertion, brought on by her own unworthiness. When she was in Brazil she'd cabled him, "I know I'm not the Band or Dylan, but care about me too." Sally Grossman paints a different picture, however, saying Albert continued to answer Janis's phone calls when she'd ring him up at three or four in the morning, distraught about her life. He even flew out to see her and hear the new band several times that spring and summer. And Lyndall Erb remembers the time Albert turned up in San Francisco with a present for Janis—a malamute puppy from his own dog's litter. Albert may have grown tired of managing musicians, but by all accounts he adored Janis. Indeed, Yarrow believes Albert saw something of himself in her. "As powerful as he was, Albert never viewed himself as the massively charismatic person he was." He identified, Yarrow suspects, with Janis's fragility and low self-regard.

Even so, Janis confided her worries about Albert and her career to Myra, who suggested she begin thinking about quitting the business. "This is killing you," she said. Myra's advice must have sounded ominous to Janis, who began crying uncontrollably, much as she had years earlier with Dave McQueen on that road outside of Port Arthur. "I don't have anything else," she kept saying between "horrible, wrenching sobs." There were no counseling programs then for a woman addicted to drugs and alcohol, and Myra surely offered the only advice that came to mind, telling Janis to walk away from her profession. As an unattached twenty-seven-year-old female with a career, Janis was something of an anomaly in 1970. Myra may have inadvertently exacerbated Janis's insecurity by continuing to suggest that she quit the music business whenever she voiced unhappiness with the road or a gig. On one occasion, Janis sat backstage in a crummy theater in Port Chester, New York, waiting to go onstage, and complained that she couldn't take it anymore. Myra was emphatic. "Then *quit*, Janis," she snapped. But Janis made it clear she wanted better bookings and more attentive management. "I wanna know why I'm playing this dump," she said, and "why I'm doing two shows." In fact, Janis had reason to complain that summer, as she was sometimes booked into lousy venues or overbooked in an area. She was certainly still popular: when she appeared in Cambridge at Harvard Stadium she drew forty thousand fans, suggesting that poor planning in Albert's office and inadequate advertising by concert promoters may have caused these problems.

Despite all her worries, there could be no question of quitting. Janis continued to talk about finding one good man and getting married, as she had always done, but sometime that summer a new note of understanding and self-knowledge crept into her statements. She began to talk of herself as a musician first and foremost and to acknowledge more realistically than she had in the past the sacrifices involved. "Women, to be in the music business, give up more than you'd ever know. . . . You give up an old man and friends, you give up every constant in the world except music. . . . So for a woman to sing, she really needs to or wants to," she told a fellow singer, Bonnie Bramlett, during the Festival Express. Janis was weary of the road and all the "people tryin' to get something out of you, tryin' to talk to you. Try to sleep, you can't sleep, nothin' on the tube. At two the bars are closed. It's just *uuuuuugghh!*" But she couldn't walk away from it, she told Bramlett. From the very first time she'd sung with Big Brother, she "never wanted to do anything else. It was better than it had been with any man." Then she added, "Maybe that's the trouble."

Her commitment set Janis even further apart, not only from the conventional society in which she was raised but from her own counter-culture milieu as well: turning her back on marriage and family was about the most radical step a woman could take. Janis had made her choice in 1966 when she threw her lot in with Big Brother; then, however, her decision was driven more by the conviction that she'd never fit in anywhere than by faith in her singing. Now, four years later, Janis was taking herself seriously as a musician. But her choice was never unambivalent; she never made a clean break with the expectations of the straight world. Thus there was always a self-punishing quality to her life as a singer. Janis told herself that real musicians lived recklessly and carelessly and that being a singer gave her license to do the same. In truth, though, Janis's hard living hurt her musicianship: her voice took a beating from the booze and the cigarettes, and when she got really drunk her voice wasn't just raspy, it would break as she tried to hold a note. That summer her concert raps were often sodden and incoherent. On *Joplin in Concert*, Elliot Mazer, its producer, captured just such a moment from a show in Calgary that July. Too drunk to sing "Ball and Chain," Janis talks her way through much of the song, borrowing from raps she'd developed for "Try" and "Get It While You Can," as though the songs have all merged in her brain—one big alcoholic blur. Sounding weary and bitter, she tells the crowd to live in the moment because "tomorrow never comes, man, it's all the same fucking day."

Despite her attempts to straighten out her life, she continued to live on the edge. When Nick Gravenites saw Janis in September he was alarmed and laid into her. "This life is bullshit. Your real life is with people, relationships, cookin' breakfast, takin' out the garbage, dumb things, dumb shit." He made no headway, though. "Aw, man," Janis said, "I don't want to live that way. I want to burn. I want to smolder. I don't want to go through all that crap." At the point that Gravenites ran into Janis, her will to burn, indeed to self-destruct, might well have been magnified by her disastrous trip home to Port Arthur only a month before.

Janis phoned her family from time to time, but she rarely visited. Some of her friends had never even heard mention of the Joplins. "She never talked about her family. Never," says her roommate, Lyndall. Janis might not have spoken to her friends, but she did talk to the press. In June 1970, she told reporters in Louisville, Kentucky, that her mother's efforts to make her behave like a good girl had made her home life a drag. Janis had chosen a life of sex, drugs, and rock 'n' roll; worse still, she made a point of advertising it. Most parents would have been unhappy. Nevertheless, Seth and Dorothy's disapproval cut her deeply. Janis had been devastated when her parents refused to let Michael, who was sixteen and showing signs of following in her rebel footsteps, spend part of the summer in San Francisco with her. "One of you is enough," they'd reportedly said.

As for Port Arthur, everyone knew of Janis's full-on feud with her hometown. So when Myra opened up the invitation to Janis's tenth high school reunion, to be held in August, her first thought was, Oh man, is this fantastic. Let's sock it to 'em! In all probability, the invitation would have gone in the trash had Myra not gleefully shouted, "Janis, look at this! This is too much! You gotta go."

Indeed, the bad blood between Janis and her hometown was so much a part of the Joplin legend that in late June, when she announced on *The Dick Cavett Show* that she'd be attending her high school reunion, the audience burst out laughing at the incongruity of it. Janis Joplin, bad-girl superstar of rock 'n' roll going back to Texas to mingle with a bunch of uptight, redneck Bible bangers? Janis's exuberance was contagious. Anyone who ever had the misfortune of being unpopular could appreciate her sweet revenge—town geek returns home a celebrity. Reaching over excitedly and touching Cavett's knee, Janis asked her somewhat startled host, "Would you like to go, man?" "Well, Janis, I don't have that many friends in your high school class," he quipped. "I don't either, man," she said, smiling. Then, under her breath, but loud enough for the microphone to catch, she muttered, "That's why I'm going." The audience howled. "They laughed me out of class," she added, "out of town, and out of the state, so I'm going *home*."

The Cavett show was hardly the first time Janis had slagged off her hometown to the national media. "I was just 'silly crazy Janis,'" she told the *New York Times*. "Man, those people hurt me. It makes me happy to know I'm making it and they're back there, plumbers just like they were." Her well-publicized animosity toward her hometown did nothing, of course, to endear Janis to Port Arthurans. Karleen Bennett's mother had always supported her, but even she took umbrage at the comment about plumbers. After all, the Bennetts owned a plumbing business. Until the reunion, though, Janis had kept her distance, taking potshots from afar. Now she'd be in their faces, and it was payback time. Janis had no intention of making peace. "She was going home to make them sorry, and she just put people's backs up," recalls Linda Gravenites. Worse, Janis decided to take reinforcements in the form of John Cooke, Bobby Neuwirth, and her limo driver, John Fisher. They'd protect her, she thought, and stand as proof of her sexual desirability. As soon as Myra learned that Janis planned to take them along, she began to have her doubts about the homecoming. "I take full responsibility," she says today of the debacle that followed. The night before Janis flew to Texas, the artist Robert Rauschenberg, a Port Arthur native and a regular at Max's Kansas City, made a last-ditch effort to keep her from going. "I sat up with her the whole night," he recalled. They drank "one tequila after another, but I couldn't convince her not to go."

Janis arrived at the Golden Triangle Airport on August 13 and was greeted by her family and the press. Later that day she went out with her sister, Laura, who was sporting the faux-hippie clothes now sold by department stores—as close to the real thing as most American kids got. Some friends say Janis was growing fonder of her sister, but she had long felt Laura disapproved of her. Shortly before the reunion Janis had given an interview in which she'd described her brother as "really cool" and knocked her sister for being "in a rut." Laura was angry, and she let Janis have it. Janis sat with her head "bowed." Laura claims the tirade cleared the air between them, and maybe it did. Before arriving home, Janis asked her sister whether their parents were proud of her. Sensing the importance of the question, Laura assured Janis that they were but suggested that she didn't "make it easy for them." They were still upset, she revealed, that Janis had told the press they'd kicked her out at fourteen. Janis sighed deeply, "aware of the whole mess," relates Laura. The weekend turned bad quickly. The morning of the reunion, Janis invited Neuwirth, Cooke, and Fisher over for an elaborate breakfast and assumed her parents would stay. She was upset when they left abruptly for the day, claiming a prior obligation—a wedding. Her parents were making a point by absenting themselves; Dorothy and Seth "resented the way she had come home," Laura maintains. They didn't feel like changing their plans for Janis's sake on those rare occasions she deigned to visit.

Janis got back at her parents at the reunion news conference that evening, jokingly complaining that they'd sold her bed, forcing her to sleep on a narrow cot in the den. "You'd think they'd have better accommodations, wouldn't you?" she quipped, quickly adding, "They've been very tolerant. When all my friends came over this morning for breakfast and drinks, they left." Beneath the joking, she was suggesting a lack of generosity and kindness on her parents' part. Asked how Port Arthur seemed to her, she grew more provocative. "There seems to be a lot of long hair and rock, which also means drug use, you know." Would she come back more frequently now? someone asked. "Oh, I come here pretty frequently," Janis replied with a straight face. "I come here every couple of years."

For a while Janis enjoyed the upper hand. The microphones were pointed toward her, not her classmates, and the press hung on her every word. Janis stumbled, though, when a reporter asked her what she remembered most about the town. It was a simple question, but it seemed to transport her back to those dreaded hallways of TJ High. She looked crestfallen, putting her hands up in the air and shaking her head as if to say she'd had enough. "I don't really remem . . ." she said weakly before pausing and giving an uncharacteristic "No comment." Had she entertained at TJ High? she was asked. "Only when I walked down the aisles," Janis volunteered, revealing how vividly painful her school days still felt to her. By the time someone asked how she'd differed from her classmates, Janis had lost her composure. "I don't know. Why don't you ask *them*?" she snapped, her eyes narrowing in a hard stare. "Is it they who made you different?" one reporter pressed her. Janis floundered and seemed on the brink of tears behind her fashionable sunglasses. The reporter rephrased his question, and with a slight stutter Janis answered, "I f-felt apart from them." Asked if she went to the school's football games, she grew even more flustered, claiming she couldn't remember. The press had found its subject and kept at it, lobbing questions about Janis's exclusion at high school. Her visible pain was terrible to see. Perhaps anticipating the next question, she said, "I didn't go to the high school prom. . . ." "Oh, you were *asked*, weren't you?" a reporter interrupted. With a tight smile and her eyes fully open, Janis shot back, "No, I wasn't. They didn't think . . . I don't think they wanted to take me." The relief was palpable when she suddenly joked, "I've been suffering ever since. It's enough to make you want to sing the blues."

The interview continued with questions about her parents. Janis said she got along with them "pretty good, pretty good. Yeah . . ." her voice trailing off, the lack of conviction unmistakable. She brightened considerably when Laura, who was sitting next to her, maintained that their parents had always described their older daughter as "exceptional," but she faltered again as Laura admitted that the family had lost two of her famous sister's three records. The interview, much of which appears in the documentary *Janis: The Way She Was*, is significant for the way it shows—more clearly perhaps than any other document of Janis's life—how very thin her armor was, how close she felt to the hurt and scorn of her high school years. Back among her classmates, Janis found her tough-girl carapace shattering within minutes.

After the reunion dinner, where everyone else's many babies and accomplishments were duly noted, the master of ceremonies said, "Is there anything I've missed?" On cue, someone wearily responded, "Janis Joplin." There was some applause and scattered whistles, Janis took a bow, and she was presented with a gag gift, a tire for having "come the greatest distance." The disappointment was too much. It didn't matter that they were jerks, she still wanted them to love her. In Port Arthur, though, Janis would always remain a despised outsider. As soon as she left, according to one friend, the party was abuzz with stories of how outrageous she'd been.

The Port Arthur weekend went from bad to worse. After the reunion,

Janis and her entourage headed for the Pelican Club, where Jerry Lee Lewis, the fifties rocker turned country artist, was playing. She had tried to visit him backstage in Louisville just two months before; he'd rebuffed her then but she decided to approach him again. Given Lewis's reputation as an irascible good ole boy and Janis's image as a way-out hippie chick (whose star had eclipsed his), it might have occurred to her that this could be a charged encounter. And it was. When Janis introduced him to Laura, the chronically snarky Lewis said, "You wouldn't be bad looking if you weren't trying to look like your sister." As Janis went to hit him, Lewis growled that if she was going to act like a guy he'd treat her like one, then punched her before her friends could intervene. "How could he do that?" Janis kept saying as the group walked out.

They made their way back to the Joplins' house, where they stayed up late talking. Neuwirth and Fisher were sleeping at a motel but got far too drunk to drive back. Janis's parents awoke the next morning to find Fisher stretched out on their living room couch and Neuwirth sleeping outside in a car with its motor running. The Joplins were furious, and not just about the drunken longhairs she'd brought into their home. They'd seen her interview on the local news—or the one minute of it the station had aired, in which Janis had joked about her parents' lack of hospitality. People in Port Arthur would be clucking over Janis's loose talk, trashy getup, and digs about her family for months to come. Appearances were everything, and Janis had blown her family's rickety facade of normalcy. As Myra tells it, Dorothy lashed out at her daughter, saying what parents sometimes think but rarely put into words: "I wish you'd never been born!" The account is Myra's and has not been corroborated. If in her fury Dorothy spoke those words, she was finally confirming what Janis had long suspected: her mother didn't love her. She really was unlovable. Janis was crushed. Dorothy must have felt more ambivalence than her angry remark suggested, but Janis probably couldn't see that. In 1971, Dorothy alluded to their fight in an interview with Myra. She admitted saying things in anger that she hadn't meant, but she didn't elaborate. Dorothy also claimed Janis was contrite. "Mother," she reportedly said, "you were right and I was wrong!" Myra ultimately left out of her book the words Dorothy shouted at her daughter, not wanting to add to the pain and the guilt Dorothy surely felt, especially in the light of what happened only six weeks later.

As she did so often now, Janis took refuge in Pearl. She swept into downtown Port Arthur the next day with her entourage. In a W. C. Fields voice that she liked to adopt when transforming herself into her new persona, Janis said of Port Arthur, "It's f-a-n-t-a-a-a-a-s-t-i-c. I was across the river at the Pelican Club last night and I never had so much fun in my l-i-i-i-i-f-e, except sometimes in California." Would she be returning anytime soon? a reporter wondered. "Uh, I have no immediate plans," she answered, cackling loudly. Bluster was all she had left. Janis had come to get even with her hometown, but her big weekend—touted on national television—had brought a string of humiliations instead.

After the reunion Janis felt she couldn't do anything right, according to Linda Gravenites, who heard about the fiasco through the grapevine. "It was a body blow" whose full impact Janis tried brushing off with what became her standard response. "Well," she'd say with a shrug, "you can't go home again, right?" "I knew that it was going to be a disaster," recalled Robert Rauschenberg, who said she was devastated by the experience. Janis told Lyndall that she'd not had a good time with her family but provided no details. Despite the disastrous trip back home, Janis went ahead with a suggestion her lawyer, Bob Gordon, had first made that July, to change her will. Janis's original will of 1968 had named her brother, Michael, as her sole beneficiary, with a bequest of money to Linda Gravenites. Gordon claims he raised the issue because Janis's estate had grown substantially, she had fallen out with Linda, and she had expressed fonder feelings for her parents and Laura. Even after the terrible fight, Janis proceeded with plans to will half her estate to her parents and a quarter each to Michael and Laura. It's entirely possible she blamed herself for the difficulties with her family. After all, Janis's rebelliousness never entirely overcame her conventionality.

Thumbing her nose at tradition even as she longed for it was Janis's stock in trade and never more in evidence than in the last love of her life. In August, Janis began seeing Seth Morgan, a Berkeley student and cocaine dealer whom she'd met at the notorious tattoo party in May. They'd slept together once in July, but the affair didn't turn serious until she returned to Larkspur from Texas. Within forty-eight hours Janis and Seth were talking marriage. Of course, this was hardly the first time Janis had rushed headlong into a relationship. In a number of ways her new boyfriend resembled her previous fiancé from her North Beach days. Seth, like Michel, was a con artist, claiming he was the grandson of J. P. Morgan, the famous banker. In truth, he was the son of a minor but respected poet, Frederick Morgan, from a prominent New York family, but not the J. P. Morgan dynasty. Nevertheless, Seth always found a way to work his fabled trust fund or his family's inclusion in the social register into a conversation. "It was hard not to be impressed by his name. He kept throwing it in your face," Lyndall recalls. She paid little attention to his endless self-promotion because she herself had grown up in a well-to-do family, but others were more susceptible. In her wildest dreams Janis had never thought she could attract a good-looking, intelligent, wealthy man like Seth. She put great stock in his pedigree and vast fortune because she saw them as proof that he wasn't after her money.

Most of Janis's friends, however, believe Seth was the creepiest of all her boyfriends. Linda Gravenites and Sunshine were not in touch with Janis in the last months of her life and only met Seth later, but Linda sums him up in one word, "awful," while Sunshine calls him "a sleazy mother-fucker." Their harshness has to do less with what Seth was when Janis was alive than with what he became after she died: a junkie who held up women on deserted highways and finally served three years of a five-year sentence for armed robbery. In prison he took up writing and his first novel, *Homeboy*, was published to critical acclaim after his release. In 1990, he and his girlfriend were killed in a motorcycle accident, the result of reckless driving fueled by the booze, cocaine, and Percodan in Seth's system. Moments before the crash, onlookers saw his girlfriend pounding on his back, pleading with him to slow down.

To many, Seth was not a likable character. "Where did you get this Berkeley *punk* in a black leather jacket thinking he's bad on a Harley?" Peggy says she thought when she first saw Seth. But Seth's attractions for Janis are not too hard to fathom. After the misadventure in Port Arthur, she was even more susceptible to any charmer who came along. And Seth wasn't any ordinary charmer. He was smart, he came from money, and he was a bad boy with chutzpah to spare—an irresistible mix.

They were both desperadoes, Janis thought, both from respectable families, and both "very wounded . . . very depressed people," according to Dave Richards, Janis's friend and roadie. There the similarities ended. Janis could be exasperatingly insensitive to others, but she wasn't deliberately unkind. She saved that for herself. Seth, on the other hand, was cruel, and with women he knew how to use cruelty to his advantage, turning on the charm one minute and then becoming abusive the next. Janis may have understood his harshness as brutal honesty at first. She hated all the toadying that went on around her, and Seth's seeming indifference, even hostility, to her celebrity may have convinced her that his affection was genuine. In their first encounter he claims to have said he found Janis's music "mediocre," a comment that seems to have intrigued rather than angered her. Moreover, Seth's meanness and contempt would have resonated only too well with Janis's self-loathing, which was no doubt exacerbated by the reunion.

At least Seth seemed uninterested in turning Janis into a stay-at-home wife; after all, the main reason he'd been drawn to her was her fame. "If she was any old body," he said years later, "I wouldn't have looked at her." Seth would offer the semblance of marriage without the usual constraints. She could continue being Janis Joplin. Her career was more likely to be cut short by riding around on his Harley than by marrying him. When she saw Julie Paul that August, Janis told her all about her new boyfriend, including his penchant for racing around on his bike. "Think of my career!" she joked to Julie Paul. "The short and happy life of Janis Joplin ending crashed on a motorcycle!"

In the beginning, Janis felt she'd finally found a man who wouldn't impinge on her work and was ready and willing to burn with her. But there was a trade-off, which became apparent very quickly: Seth would offer Janis little support, dependability, or love. Two weeks into their affair, Seth moved into the Larkspur house when Janis went off to L.A. to begin recording with Paul Rothchild. She hadn't expected him to be faithful, but neither had she expected him to have sex with other women in her very own bed. Lyndall witnessed the parade of young women in and out of Janis's bedroom throughout September and early October. "He definitely didn't give up any of his other girlfriends," she notes. Nor would he have given them up if he and Janis had married, as he made it clear theirs would be an open marriage. Janis may also have liked the freedom to sleep around, but she didn't necessarily want his disregard demonstrated quite so blatantly. They had a "real genuine flame," Seth said after her death. But if "she hadn't been Janis Joplin, we just would have been rip-roaring friends," he conceded, revealing the limits of his respect and attraction.

Janis remained in L.A. throughout September. She had been clean all August, it seems, and wasn't using when she arrived in L.A. The recording was going well; the chemistry with Paul Rothchild and the band was producing her best studio experience. Yet Seth, who visited on weekends, claimed that Janis declared her desire to have a baby and "wind down" her career. This hardly tallies with the way she was talking to Nick Gravenites and the guys in her group, bragging about a new deal Albert had negotiated with some booking agencies that guaranteed her a half-million dollars a year in performance money. And she was so jazzed about the album she was cutting that she was already thinking about the next one. Still, Janis often contradicted herself when it came to the issue of settling down. One thing is clear: less than a month into their relationship, she and her fiancé were not happy. Janis complained that Seth was always up in San Francisco. He had "emotional problems," she said, and "well, we're just not getting along." She had begun to suspect that Seth was using her, and most of her friends were convinced that was true. "Seth thought marrying Janis would somehow be a step up for him," says Lyndall. "He was out to get what he could from her."

The longer the two were together the less effort Seth put into disguising his motives for wanting to marry her. Janis grew apprehensive; she even asked friends whether he liked her for her money. When they had met with Janis's lawyer, Bob Gordon, Seth had seemed a little too pleased when Gordon confirmed that under California law she wouldn't be entitled to his trust fund money but he would have a claim to half her income. That gave Janis pause. When Gordon later suggested drawing up a prenuptial agreement to protect her money, Janis directed him to do so. In late September she and Seth fought openly about money. During a shopping trip Seth pointed to a shirt he liked and said, "Thanks a lot, that's really nice of you." He claimed to have been joking, but Janis was furious that he assumed she'd just fork over the cash. After raging at him, she went off to her motel room sobbing. According to Seth, she emerged some time later, terrified her outburst might have ended their relationship. "I'd never seen her so scared," he said. Most likely, Janis was scared he was using her, scared to lose him, and scared by the terror she felt about losing him. She might have been aroused by Seth's arrogance and playful ill treatment in the bedroom—as Peggy claims she was—but otherwise Janis began to feel humiliated by his displays of indifference. Increasingly, Seth seemed to want to rub Janis's nose in his lack of romantic feeling, his interest in her as a famous fuck rather than an admired lover.

The shopping trip was to be the last time Janis would see Seth. While he stayed in San Francisco, she continued to hold on to the fiction of their impending marriage. Few people around her, however, believed the relationship would continue much longer. Myra now doubts that Janis was really serious about marrying Seth. Her failing love affair may have led Janis to take up heroin again after six weeks of abstinence, although it was the one reason she didn't offer her friends. What she did say was that her drinking, which had become excessive, was interfering with the recording sessions. And that she was bored with the recording process, which included long periods just waiting to cut the vocals. And that she was just trying it out to see if she "wanted to do it anymore."

Whatever the cause, by mid-September, Janis was back on the needle. Staying at the Landmark, or the Land Mine, as it was known among rock's cognoscenti, was in itself tempting fate. Located on Franklin Avenue in Hollywood, the Landmark, with its fake Polynesian design and tacky shag carpeting, was the motel of choice for those who favored funkiness. But the real draw, according to David Crosby, was the "convenience of being close to the street dealers, who weren't welcome by the sheriff's deputies and Beverly Hills police further west." Janis knew she'd be in a dope element and might run into her former connection, or even Peggy, were she to stay there.

In the second week of September that is precisely what happened. According to Peggy, Janis saw her ex-connection, George, in the Landmark's lobby. "What are you doing here?" she said. "What do you mean, what am I doing here?" he replied. "Didn't you call me?" Peggy, it turned out, was staying at the Landmark that night and had put in an order with George, who had just assumed she was staying with Janis. But Janis hadn't seen Peggy in three months and had no idea she was at the motel. Once the misunderstanding was cleared up, Janis went back to her room and George went off to deliver Peggy's dope. Five minutes later Peggy's phone rang. It was Janis, demanding that Peggy share her heroin. Peggy contends she refused, saying she didn't want to get Janis hooked again. She "made it seem like I wouldn't give it to her because I was cheap," Peggy says. Janis ranted at her, "You motherfucker, all the drugs I gave you!" Peggy relented. "Okay, fine, Janis," she said. "This is really fucked." Others doubt that Peggy had any qualms about ending Janis's abstinence. Why was she staying at the Landmark, they ask, if not to get high with Janis? Today Peggy says, "There's a part of me that goes, 'Come on, what was I doing?' "

Two weeks later Janis was using regularly again and begging Seth to help her stop. But if Janis was trying to mobilize Seth to prove his devotion, it didn't work. "Janis," he reprimanded her, "you jump in a hole and call to someone to show they love you by pulling you out. Then you turn around and jump in another, only deeper this time, and before you know it that person's gonna feel like a sucker and leave you down there." The few friends who knew she was shooting up couldn't understand why; in the last weeks of her life, she seemed in good spirits. "Janis's curve was up," John Cooke maintains. "She had kicked the dope and learned how to pull a band together; she felt in control of it all." He puts it down to the boredom of recording "and the wrong friends coming around. Peggy came around." Kris Kristofferson laid into Janis when he found out she was back on the needle again. Believing everything was swell with Seth, he chided her, "Man, you got everything going for you. You got a man you love; you got a producer you love." Janis's glum response was, "What's it all worth?" It might have looked like Janis was sitting on top of the world, but to Janis she was sitting there all by herself just like she'd always been. More than anyone else, Myra emphasizes Janis's despondency—not so much in the final weeks but in the preceding months. She says Kristofferson told her Janis had even threatened suicide earlier that summer.

Janis's friends' varying accounts of her mood are not surprising. Her relationship with Myra, for example, couldn't have been more different from her friendship with Cooke. Most of Janis's friends—Cooke included—seemed to prefer not knowing too much about her troubled interior. Myra, however, was anxious to know more, sometimes, it seems, almost prying the pain and hurt out of her. Janis grew accustomed to going to Myra when she felt depressed, especially once Linda and Sunshine were out of her life. As a consequence, Myra saw less of her exuberance than most other people. Cooke, on the other hand, heard the same complaints from Janis that everyone else did, but he appears not to have heard her despair. He thought she was having "a rocking good time," as he later put it to *Rolling Stone*.

Whatever she actually felt, there's no evidence that Janis had decided to kill herself. She told her friends that she wanted to stop using and promised them she would as soon as the recording ended. She talked about acquiring some Dolophine to help her kick. But if Janis hadn't resolved to commit suicide, neither was she choosing life. As Fredda Slote points out, "She'd done enough drugs close to the edge. I don't think she ever intended to commit suicide, but I think she was getting very casual about her life, and when you do that, sooner or later you don't have it anymore." Jimi Hendrix had OD'd from barbiturates in mid-September and his death was much on Janis's mind those days. When Myra called to tell her the Associated Press wanted a quote, she said, "How 'bout, 'There but for the grace of Go . . .' " Then she grew contemplative. "I was just thinking . . . I wonder what they'll say about *me* after I die." Seth Morgan claimed Janis said she didn't want to go out the same year as Hendrix, because he was more famous. With Peggy she claimed that two rock 'n' roll stars couldn't die the same year. To others she simply said, "Goddammit, he beat me to it."

There were no traces of little girl blue on October 3, the last day of Janis's life. She was due in the studio that evening and did up—but not a lot. The band recorded the instrumental track for Nick Gravenites's "Buried Alive in the Blues," and Janis was excited about doing the vocals the following day. After the session they all stood around shooting the shit, and Vince Mitchell, her roadie and friend, remembers a "strange look," a "weary look" passing across her face. He put it out of his mind. Some of the band moved on to Barney's Beanery, where Janis and Ken Pearson, the organist, chatted about the album. She asked whether the band loved her as much as she loved them. "If any of you guys ever leave me, I'll kill ya," she said. After some drinks and much talk about the future, they left the bar about twelve-thirty. Back at the Landmark, they headed off to their rooms.

The three-way Janis had set up with Seth and Peggy for that night didn't materialize. Seth had called earlier to say he wouldn't be flying in until Sunday, the next day, and he even sounded noncommittal about that. Janis phoned Larkspur later on from the studio but Seth was nowhere around. As it happened, he was playing strip pool with some waitresses from the Trident. Peggy had flown into L.A. for their tryst, but, loaded on dope and deeply embroiled in a hot affair, she stayed at the Chateau Marmont hotel with her new lover instead of making her way over to the Landmark. She didn't even bother calling Janis, who'd commented on Peggy's desertion to her connection when he'd brought round some dope. Seth and Peggy probably figured she'd be okay—she was busy recording, she had the band, there were plenty of people around.

Once back in her room, Janis shot up. As always, she'd "Janisfied" the place, covering the crummy paintings with an Indian print bedspread, lighting her candles, and putting out her bits of lace and "little weird pictures." Anything to make the room feel less like another faceless motel stop. After fixing, she went back out to the lobby to change a five-dollar bill and buy a pack of cigarettes. Janis wanted to smoke, but she was also looking for company, so she talked with the night clerk for around ten minutes, telling him how her day had been, how excited she was about the recording. He had no idea who she really was but listened to her nonetheless. She returned to the room and sat on the bed, maybe thinking of her band or the album. Maybe the empty motel room provoked lonely thoughts, desolate feelings. Perhaps she sang her favorite ditty, "It's Life," a song about always coming up short. Maybe she thought, Man, it's another Saturday Night Swindle for Janis. Another night in a tacky motel with nothing and nobody, stood up by not just one but two people. But tonight Janis didn't have to suffer the full weight of her loneliness for very long. She put the pack of cigarettes on the bedside table and fell forward, still clutching her change. More powerful than the dope she was used to, the heroin she shot up that night blasted her into unconsciousness.

Epilogue

For a full eighteen hours Janis's body lay wedged between the bedside table and the bed. John Cooke says he thought to look in on her when Seth Morgan called him from the San Francisco airport looking for Janis. After learning from Paul Rothchild that she was late for that evening's session, Cooke says he got the desk key and let himself into her room. Vince Mitchell tells a different story. Late Sunday afternoon he had stopped by Cooke's room, where a small group of people were partying. As the evening wore on, "everybody was asking, 'Seen Janis?'" That no one had seen her all day Mitchell thought odd because in the afternoons Janis usually was by the pool, drink in hand, reading a book. "She was Miss Avid Reader," he says. Mitchell was even more puzzled when he noticed her Porsche in the parking lot. By that time, she should have been in the studio and Janis, he emphasizes, "was never one to shine on a gig, let alone studio time. Hell, she was paying for it. She'd always make some sarcastic remark about paying for the recording."

Mitchell suggested to Cooke that they get the key from the front desk and check her room. "John put the key in the door, I walked in," says Mitchell, "and there she was, laying on the floor." Her nose looked broken. He reached down and touched her. "She was . . . rigor mortis had set in. She was cold, stiff. I said, 'Jesus, John, she's dead.'" Cooke touched her, too. "Oh my God," he said, "I've got to call the police." Mitchell advised him against immediately alerting the cops. "You better call Albert and find out what he wants you to do." Cooke was freaked and Mitchell wasn't in such great shape, either. Albert got hold of a doctor, who arrived shortly to pronounce her dead. "Minutes after that, you would not believe the Landmark Hotel," recalls Mitchell. "There was LAPD, newspaper people, all kinds of people. You couldn't even get through the hall."

The absence of drugs puzzled investigators; they even entertained the possibility that Janis had been murdered. Vince Mitchell was perplexed, too. Janis's room seemed too tidy when he and Cooke arrived. "Well, how the hell did she die?" Mitchell asked as he looked around the room for clues. "There was a little box on top of her dresser and a syringe and a tie, all put away very neatly." There was no dope in the box or anywhere else, as far as he could see. "I didn't search the room," Mitchell admits, "but it was clean, spic and span. My gut feeling ever since has been that somebody else was in that room." Of course, Janis had always been a very tidy junkie, even if not too fastidious in general. Still, questions remain about her death. Someone in Janis's camp did walk off with the evidence—a balloon containing heroin—reportedly to keep the drugs out of the press. After the heroin was returned to her room early the next day, Thomas Noguchi, the Los Angeles County coroner issued his tentative finding: an accidental death caused by the extraordinary purity of the heroin. According to Sunshine, the dope killed eight other people in L.A. that weekend. Reportedly, Janis's connection always had a tester check the dope's strength, but he'd been out of town. However, others who bought from the same connection dispute the idea that the dope was exceptionally strong. In any case, Janis had only been using three weeks so her body was ill-prepared for the blast of smack, and to make matters worse, she was also legally drunk. (In a creepy turn, the drug's purity quickly became its selling point. The week after she died, L.A. dealers hawked the dope by boasting, "It's so strong it OD'd Janis.")

Even those who knew she was using again were hard-hit. Janis had seemed so ebullient those last days in L.A. Janis was the sixth person Paul Rothchild had lost to drugs in as many months, but her death was the most devastating. Dave Getz remembers "crying hysterically for several hours." Jae Whitaker, her lover from North Beach, yelled at the television when she heard the news. "You goddamn stupid bitch!" she shouted. "I was just so angry and hurt." Danny Fields, a scenester and the publicist for Elektra Records, "sort of fainted standing up" when he heard. How could Janis, the very embodiment of "superlife," be reduced to a corpse? To David Dalton, a reporter who had often interviewed her, Janis had always "seemed as solidly situated as Mount Rushmore." What could possibly do her in? he wondered. So many had taken Janis for a boozer, never a hard-core druggie. Indeed, Myra assumed her heroin problem was a thing of the past. Talking to the Joplins that Sunday night, Myra told them she must have died from a cerebral hemorrhage. What else, she thought, could kill Janis at the age of twenty-seven?

Following closely on the heels of Hendrix's OD, Janis's death led to much soul-searching. "Can't we do any better," asked the critic Don Heckman, angry that even the counterculture had failed to create a world with "room enough for the Hendrixes and Joplins." The question haunted many of Janis's friends. "Did we do this?" Kris Kristofferson reportedly whispered as he stared at her body. "Somehow we should have been able to let her know that she did have a home," says Fredda Slote, "that she did have a family, and that we did love her." "To this day," Milan Melvin says, "I can't shake the feeling that some part of her death was my fault. I miss her all the time and it fucks up my whole goddamn day just to hear a recording of hers." Albert was crushed. "I don't know if he ever really recovered," says Sally Grossman. "It seemed to me there was about a year there where you'd see Albert with tears in his eyes."

Of her friends, surely no one felt as guilty as Peggy, whose own addiction deepened after Janis OD'd. She remained a hard-core junkie for years. Peggy's arms still bear those needle tracks—pronounced in some spots, faint in others—history literally written on her body. "Janis died right here," Peggy says, pointing to a hole in her arm. "I know right where she died on my arm." To Peggy, Janis had always seemed the world's most indestructible junkie. Peggy had worried more about her dying in a crack-up in her psychedelic Porsche or on the back of Seth Morgan's motorcycle than about her succumbing to smack. "There are times I think if she hadn't seen George that day . . . Because that's the day she started using again, and then three weeks later she was dead. I think somewhere down the line she would have picked it up again. Her sobriety wasn't strong. It was barely there. Still, maybe it wouldn't have played out the way it did. But it's over. I don't really think about it anymore. If I'm driving and I hear her song . . ." Peggy breaks off.

Some of Janis's friends did manage to kick after years of addiction, but few believe she could have pulled it off, few can imagine her older, quieter, having fulfilled her dream of becoming the world's best blues singer. They can't see her running Pearl's, the blues bar she fantasized about with Linda Gravenites and Sunshine. To Linda, Janis's death was a foregone conclusion. "You know, Janis did it the way she chose. As she said, she preferred doing it full tilt for a little while to lasting a long time. It would have gotten ugly for her had it continued."

Getting Janis clean—of drugs, booze, and self-inflicted pain—could only have been achieved by dislodging her feeling of being deeply unloved and unlovable. Methadone and a month's worth of counseling wouldn't have done it—only great discipline, support, and self-reflection would have. The world she moved in encouraged her addictions, with its commitment to living on the edge and beyond limits—its dedication to recklessness as a matter of principle. And Janis Joplin was that principle writ large. In any case, who could have intervened when there was no concept of intervention? In 1970, drugs still enjoyed real cachet, even as the casualty list was growing. Albert's retreat that summer was probably due in part to the furtive but growing heroin use of his clients and friends. Michael Bloomfield was a junkie, members of the Band were using, and worst of all, Peter Yarrow's younger brother, whom Albert had treated like his own son, had died of an OD in 1969.

Nowhere had drugs been so relentlessly hyped and the casualties greater than in San Francisco. By the fall of 1970, anyone looking around the Haight could see the high price of expanding one's consciousness, not that it served as much of a deterrent. Indeed, local musicians seemed curiously unruffled, even blasé, in their reactions to Janis's death (the first among the city's homegrown stars). The night word of her death hit San Francisco, Big Brother was doing a gig at the Keystone Club, a small bar in North Beach, while the three remaining bands of the original scene—the Grateful Dead, Jefferson Airplane, and Quicksilver Messenger Service—were playing at Bill Graham's Winterland. It was "San Francisco's big night," observed one of Janis's friends, and everyone at Winterland "was done up like it was 1966." Hip San Francisco was determined to party, even as the party was crashing to a halt. The bands played on as news of her death spread. Backstage almost everyone seemed indifferent, except a straight reporter, who burst into tears and was promptly asked to leave because "he was laying his bad trip on everybody."

Most of the musicians who'd come up with Janis in the Haight seemed annoyed by the assumption they should even have a reaction to her death. Admittedly, some people may have resented Janis's "star trip" and grown weary of her relentless self-dramatizing, but at bottom what people most resented was that Janis's death revealed an unwelcome truth: the fun had turned lethal. No one wanted to give the straight world ammunition and, even more, no one was ready to confront the wreckage, the scars of their sweet paradise, to paraphrase Bob Dylan. "When someone gets killed in an auto crash it doesn't make me stop driving," Grace Slick groused. "Why print all that stuff about someone who's dead?" she asked. "She's gone, it's done." Among the "sensitive, far-out, weird people" of the Haight "nobody's really uptight about death," Jerry Garcia explained. "It was the best possible time for her death," he said of Janis. Better that she went out on top like the "skyrocket chick" she was than to have "passed that point into decline, you know, getting messed up, old, senile, done in." Bob Weir of the Dead cited Janis's particular excesses. "I can't bring myself to be in abject misery about it because, like I say, she drank herself to death, she lived up to her image." Janis's alcoholism furnished a comfortable explanation for her death, even when her heroin habit became public knowledge. She had never really been a hippie, some would say, putting distance between Janis and themselves. Her spirit was too dark; she didn't like acid.

Dave Getz believes Garcia and others worried the "whole place would have gone dead" if they'd really tried confronting the meaning of Janis's death. "Maybe it should have." Two days after her OD, in an interview with *Rolling Stone*, Nick Gravenites likened the San Francisco rock sub-culture to a prison. "There's a lot of people using junk in the rock scene, and they're on death row, the rest of them on Tier C." Darby Slick had been among the first San Francisco rockers to experiment with heroin, and years later he'd write, "This was our Vietnam, the Battle of the Brain Cells, and drugs were the weapons and the transport ships, the airplanes, and people were the weapons too." In 1977 the novelist Philip K. Dick, whose own amphetamine addiction seriously damaged his health, wrote of drugs as a "dreadful war," one whose losses he doubted the larger culture would ever fully comprehend or acknowledge.

Throughout the early seventies, Big Brother remained at the center of this war, with James Gurley and Sam Andrew living for a time on Tier C. Sometimes Sam, James, and their new female vocalist didn't even show up for gigs. Dave complained to Peter that maybe the group should call itself Big Brother and the Folding Company. Nevertheless, they managed to release an album in 1970, their first since *Cheap Thrills*. The band wanted to call it *Weird Bummer* and Bob Seidemann designed a suitable cover. "It was a picture of this weird, fucked-up-looking stick figure giving a peace sign," Seidemann recalls. Columbia didn't buy the concept, the cover was scrapped, and the album was renamed *Be a Brother*. Despite good reviews, the record flopped and the group floundered further. "James was falling off the stage because he was so wasted on smack," Seidemann recalls. "Sam couldn't even find his guitar. Big Brother was this wreckage that walked around and barked at people through amplifiers and plucked on strings. Everyone was just destroyed." The whole period was "one great unending, torturous pain. There was such pain and suffering it's almost beyond bearing," Seidemann says. "And thirty years later, I ask myself, what was the attraction this world had for me? Why would I want to go deep into this dark place and take these dangerous drugs and do this thing so intensely and for so long?" The same thoughts haunt James Gurley. "What the hell possessed me to do such stuff? Why would I risk my life and the lives of other people and do these insane things? Didn't I know any better?" Of course James knew better, as did everyone, myself included, who lived through that time. But nothing defines the generation that came of age in the 1960s better than its determination to live outside the bounds of reasonable behavior. After all, where had knowing better gotten our parents? Cautious, reasonable behavior seemed to be the very root of the problem, the cause of "twenty years of marshmallow, plastic, and hopscotch," or what William Burroughs dubbed the "Lie."

America was transformed in the 1960s, but the exhilaration of changing the culture—breaking on through, as Jim Morrison put it—was matched by shattering personal defeat. This is the hidden history of the decade, the underside of the counterculture. Janis didn't live to see the worst of the devastation. Over the years the list of casualties would grow to include Jim Morrison, Ron "Pigpen" McKernan, Michael Bloomfield, Paul Butterfield, Richard Manuel of the Band, and Emmett Grogan of the Diggers, whose OD in a subway car at the end of the line in America's first playground, Coney Island, seemed eerily appropriate. And those are just the famous names. Among Janis's Austin crowd, Tommy Stopher, her painter friend, was just one of several who died of alcoholism. Janis's friend and lover Julie Paul ended her "lifelong struggle with intoxicants of one sort or another" in a car wreck. Acknowledging the casualties, the price of all that high-risk experimenting, isn't to say that the sixties were a mistake. After all, would Janis have been better off had she refused Chet Helms's offer and instead fulfilled her mother's dream by staying in Port Arthur and becoming a schoolteacher? Nevertheless, mistakes were surely made, not the least being the assumption that personal and cultural transformation could be easily achieved—a matter of breaking off and breaking through. It was an assumption that blinded us to how deeply marked we all were by the conventions and expectations of the mainstream, no matter how "counter" we proclaimed ourselves.

In 1971, the rock critic Lillian Roxon argued, half jokingly, that death spared Janis the fate of being eclipsed or upstaged by her imitators. How, she wondered, would Janis have handled "walking into one of those society parties . . . and finding everyone in the room all Joplined up to the nines? . . . Oh the burdens of the innovator," she concluded. In so many ways Janis carried the burden—and suffered the pain—of being an innovator, a maverick, a breakthrough woman in American culture. She refused to knuckle under and become part of the vast vanilla void of America at midcentury. But in this she wasn't alone—tens of thousands of kids, balanced like Janis on the edge of life, were her compatriots. In one area, though, she was a lone pioneer, a single woman making a career in the men's world of rock 'n' roll. She invaded male turf, claiming for herself the prerogatives typically reserved for men—artistic ambition, lust, and the right to live large. Janis made herself a "living nosethumb" to all manner of outmoded customs and conventions. But like too many other talented and tormented women—Sylvia Plath, Anne Sexton, Billie Holiday, Diane Arbus, to name a few—Janis crashed. She would be one of the last famous women whose deaths were in some way linked to the irreconcilability of being an artist and a woman. Feminism spared those who followed. "Sexism killed her," declared one of her lovers, Country Joe McDonald. But had Janis come along just a few years later, feminism might well have dulled her impact. Janis's success had a lot to do with timing; she expressed women's anger and disappointment before feminism legitimized their expression. Her refusal to sound or look pretty prefigured feminism's demolition of good-girl femininity, and much of her music, most notably "Women Is Losers," protests women's powerlessness in matters of the heart. Janis's best-known songs—"Ball and Chain" and "Piece of My Heart," among others—are about the inevitability of being screwed over by men. As she said on *The Dick Cavett Show* a few months before she died, men "just always hold up something more than they're prepared to give."

But if Janis anticipated feminism, she was nonetheless dismayed by it. Like many other women who'd managed to make it on their own, she kept her distance from the fledgling movement. "Gosh, it seemed like they hadn't had a good time in months," she said of radical feminists after reading an issue of *Rat*, a New York underground paper. "They were so crazy about 'They're not giving me this, they're not giving me that.' Well, good heavens, I just say, Rock on out. I mean, I suppose I'm not getting a lot of things. I'm not getting peace of mind, I'm not getting a steady home, I'm not getting a steady old man . . . but I'm having a good time. That's what I think is important."

She kept her distance from radical lesbians as well, although sexuality was another area in which she broke ground; her kick-out-the-jams sexuality is often still seen as freeing America of its hang-ups. In a rousing speech on the occasion of Janis's induction into the Rock and Roll Hall of Fame in 1995, the singer Melissa Etheridge wished Janis were still alive, "making a comeback, doing an *MTV Unplugged*, . . . being a women's-rights advocate or a gay-rights advocate, fighting against AIDS and intolerance." Had she lived, Janis would have benefited from gay liberation's easing of the stigma against same-sex desire, but there's no reason to think she'd have greeted the movement with open arms. Janis hadn't liked being touted as a gay role model, and she almost certainly would have been claimed again. In fact, not long after her death, Jill Johnston outed Janis in her *Village Voice* column, boasting, "We know Janis was gay." Even if Janis had decided she was gay—an unlikely outcome—it's doubtful she would have found Lesbian Nation a particularly congenial place. Not only was Janis deeply ambivalent about her sexuality, she believed in living outside categories rather than enshrining them. In this regard, she was a throwback to an earlier bohemian model of sexual ambiguity. As Peggy says of Janis's proposed union with Seth Morgan, "This wasn't any traditional heterosexual marriage going down here." After all, Janis was looking forward to a three-way with Peggy and Seth the night she died.

Feminist, lesbian, sixties icon—Janis has been claimed as many things, but is probably most remembered as a tragic victim, one of this century's more spectacular "drama queens," as a journalist recently put it in the *New York Times*. Myra Friedman's biography, *Buried Alive,* bears some responsibility for casting Janis in this role. Myra strove to puncture the myth that Janis was the quintessential liberated sixties chick and effectively succeeded, but only at the cost of pathologizing her in the process. The 1979 movie *The Rose*, starring Bette Midler, reinforced this vision of Janis: the central character, a tortured pop singer named Rose, would conjure up Janis to all but the most culturally illiterate. Originally entitled *Pearl*, the film had the support of a number of members of Janis's camp. Paul Rothchild was the musical director and John Cooke introduced the screenwriter to the Full Tilt Boogie Band. In midproject the filmmakers decided to change emphasis and maintained that Rose was a composite figure based on Jimi Hendrix, Jim Morrison, Janis Joplin, James Dean, and Marilyn Monroe. Nevertheless, Janis is the obvious referent. Midler's impersonation of a boozy broad is a good one, but she captures little of Janis's intelligence, strength, or artistry; indeed, Midler's Janis could be any seventies rock star with a habit and a tormented soul. The effect is to make Janis come across as simply a colossally fucked-up woman.

Her musical legacy has been even harder to pin down than her cultural impact. Musically, Janis's influence is both everywhere and nowhere. Writing in 1994, one critic, Karen Schoemer, claimed Janis as the "original influence," the woman who made it possible for white girls to sound something other than pretty. To Melissa Etheridge, Janis paved the way for girls like her to be rock stars rather than secretaries. "Janis made it up," says the singer Chris Williamson. "As far as I know, what she did hadn't existed before." But if Janis made it up, it also ended with her. As Schoemer points out, when Janis OD'd, "pop music pretty much abandoned the prototype." Of course, Janis couldn't be easily cloned, not her emotional intensity or her powerful voice. Several Texas singers—Lou Ann Barton, Marcia Ball, Angela Strehli—bore Janis's influence, as did a number of seventies performers, including Ten Wheel Drive's Genya Ravan and Big Brother's "new Janis," Kathi McDonald. But altogether, there weren't many women singers consciously copying Janis's vocal style. In fact, it was the heavy-metal rock bands who appropriated and kept alive Janis's assaultive way of singing, although for them it was a style, disconnected from her pain and vulnerability. Tellingly, Janis inspired only one actual imitator, a drag queen calling himself Pearl, to whom Janis was "that fat chick from Texas who sounded like me." Rock 'n' roll didn't just scuttle the Janis Joplin prototype, however; it ditched her music as well. *Pearl* was released in early 1971 and was a smash, her biggest album ever. It stayed at the top spot for several weeks and gave Janis her only number-one single, "Me and Bobby McGee." But within a few years, her music faded away. It was as if Janis, once one of rock's biggest superstars, had never mattered musically.

Rock 'n' roll remained a boys' club throughout the eighties, if not longer, but Janis's curious disappearance can't be blamed entirely on sexism. After all, it is the women in rock who have been slow to embrace her. For one thing, some women resented the way she encouraged the audience to eroticize her and thereby reinforced the presumption that they, too, were onstage to turn men on. "I open myself up enough in my songs, for Christ's sake," the singer Bonnie Raitt said. "I make a living making myself depressed every night. I don't think I have to shake my ass too. I wouldn't play that role anyway." Asked what role she meant, she said, "Oh, Janis Joplin." "There was nothing cynical about Janis's sexuality," observes Tracy Nelson, "but it did get her a lot of press."

Until a recent shift, however, the major reason women didn't rush to claim Janis is that the qualities that helped make her famous—her lack of restraint, her palpable vulnerability and pain—seemed too dangerous. Terry Garthwaite of the Joy of Cooking was often called a "more restrained Janis Joplin," but she herself says, "I have a grit I share with Janis, but I don't have her emotional intensity. I guess I don't want to go out to the same edge." To Chrissie Hynde, who was a teenager living in Ohio when she saw Janis perform, she was electrifying but scary. "There you were living your nice little life in the suburbs and suddenly there was this train wreck, and it was Janis." And once she OD'd, Janis stood as a cautionary figure whose path seemed too hazardous to follow. "I didn't go over the edge, because I saw her do it," claims Chris Williamson. No one, including Janis's Chelsea Hotel compatriot, Patti Smith, whose performances were wild and abandoned, projected the emotional extremes that Janis did; no one went to "the outer limits of probability," at least not in the same way. "Janis sang out of her pain," wrote Ellen Willis after her death. More than any other woman in rock, Janis set up the expectation that to be female is to be tortured and miserable—an idea that lots of women were working hard to refute in the seventies. With Helen Reddy singing "I am woman, hear me roar," Chaka Khan declaring "I'm every woman," and Patti Smith and Chrissie Hynde proceeding as if the battle had been won (the culture was, like them, simply beyond sex roles), Janis's insistence on women's pain and victimization was an unwelcome intrusion. To the rock critic Ann Powers, "Janis's thorough explorations of pain's nuances, her devotion to telling it like it was, at first seemed dangerous to take in anything but small doses." Melissa Etheridge was put off, too, when she first saw Janis on TV: "I was 11 years old. She frightened me. She was all hair and she was screaming and I did not understand this at all. I didn't respond to it. . . . I did not get into Joplin until I was 21, and then I just immersed myself because I understood the pain and the singing and the soul." Dangerous, hazardous, scary—these are the words women associated with Janis Joplin.

In 1993, a boxed set of Janis's music was released, finally bringing about a long-needed reappraisal of her work. Critics were forced to reconsider the idea that Janis was a pale imitation or rip-off of the real thing or that her success owed more to her outrageousness than to musical talent. With this collection Robert Christgau wrote, "Janis demolishes the canard that she was some kind of blues imitator or hippie fool." Of course, the idea that Janis was a musical naif, an idiot savant in the world of music, owes a lot to the way she presented herself. Anxious to seem as authentic as her idols, nervous lest she seem pretentious, arty, or ambitious, Janis was a victim of her own publicity. She told unsuspecting interviewers that she simply "felt" things, yet her singing was anything but impromptu. She screeched and screamed and moaned, but all for a purpose. Janis didn't just sing the notes, she sang the meaning, like few other singers have.

The boxed set has helped bring a critical turnabout, but so have changing times. Today everyone from Joan Osborne to Stevie Nicks and Kim Gordon of Sonic Youth cite her influence. Janis is suddenly fashionable again. Of course, rock 'n' roll is nothing like it was even ten years ago. There are so many high-profile female rockers today that women's success verges on the unremarkable, no longer, one hopes, the occasion for yet another special issue on Women in Rock. And after the ferociousness of nineties riot grrrls and the slickly packaged aggro-rock that followed in their wake, Janis's vulnerability and pain can be heard again. Now that women's pain is no longer always in the foreground, now that women like PJ Harvey snarl lyrics like "I'll make you lick my injuries / Till you say, Don't you, Don't you / Wish you'd never, never met her?" Janis may seem safe, maybe even comfortably retro.

Curiously, the way Janis is being remembered has begun to change, too. Younger writers seem interested more in her defiance than in her despair, rediscovering her intelligence, her humor, and her remarkable spirit, which refused to be defeated by a culture that judged her a loser, a nobody. Feel-good celebrations of Janis's daring are an understandable corrective to the portrait of her as a tragic victim, but they are equally wrongheaded. Janis's rebellion and pain were inextricably bound together. Any effort, however well-intentioned, to write off her suffering or construe her recklessness as youthful curiosity distorts. Janis was not a sixties version of Madonna or Courtney Love or PJ Harvey. "When you think of history, you think it was just like now, only then," says James Gurley. "But life was different then." In 1966, when Janis moved to San Francisco and decided to sing rock 'n' roll, there were no role models, no mentors. She took one gamble after another—from the voice she chose to the way she made herself over into a countercultural sex goddess—all the time risking ridicule. In truth, acknowledging Janis's pain only makes her defiance more courageous, more poignant. Perhaps now, some thirty years after her death, we can see that Janis was neither just the ballsy chick who helped throw open the doors of rock 'n' roll nor the little girl lost who longed for the white picket fence.

The 1993 collection includes a previously unreleased outtake of "Cry Baby" from the *Pearl* sessions. As she belts out the first word, soaring higher in that cranked-up Joplin style, holding the note and milking it for all it's worth, she suddenly ditches the script. Instead of finishing the line, she cracks up, as if the whole Janis Joplin thing is one big goof, an elaborate put-on, a gigantic kozmic giggle. Just as quickly, she resumes singing with her customary gutsiness and soulfulness. In a flash, over almost before we can catch it, Janis parodies herself, pokes fun at her image, the spectacularly tormented blues diva. It is a rare moment of self-awareness, made all the more compelling because she sounds so confident, so excited as her voice transports her once again to nirvana.

And in that moment I knew what it was that so grabbed me when I first heard Janis sing. It was the fall of 1968 and I picked up "Piece of My Heart" on a tiny Gaithersburg, Maryland, FM station. I was startled by Janis's voice, which was gritty and expressive in a way I'd never heard from a white woman. But its power to move me eluded me at the time. Later I understood that when Janis sang you could hear her awe and delight at breaking all the rules. In her music, I heard freedom, which was what she longed to communicate. Rock 'n' roll was there to turn on the switch in kids' brains so they'd comprehend that life is more than dreary duty, life is rich with possibility. "You may not end up happy," Janis once said, "but I'm fucked if I'm not going to try. That's like committing suicide the day you're born, if you don't try." Janis refused the compromised, diminished life of her parents' generation by taking a blowtorch to her own. She wasn't always happy, but she went for broke and changed the rules for all of us. In that sense, she won big, bigger than she ever could have hoped.

Where Are They Now?

Not long after the release of their 1971 album, *How Hard It Is*, Big Brother and the Holding Company split up. Sam Andrew moved to New York, where he studied harmony and counterpoint at the New School for Social Research, and Dave Getz, Peter Albin, and James Gurley continued to jam informally with musicians in the Bay Area. By the eighties, James was playing guitar with the Maragu band and Peter was playing bass in the Dinosaurs, a group of Bay Area hippie old-timers that included John Cipollina, Barry Melton, Spencer Dryden, and Merl Sanders. Although Big Brother made a lot of money off *Cheap Thrills*, the band members hadn't earned enough to retire forever to Marin County. James did not develop a second career, but Dave went back to school and earned a teaching certificate, Peter began working as a publicist for a record-distribution company, and Sam eventually moved back to the Bay Area and got into the business of music management. By the time they came together again as Big Brother in 1987, they had become solid musicians.

In 1994, the group began touring actively, playing in Japan, Russia, Mexico, and all over the States. By 1997, however, old tensions resurfaced and James left the group. The band now plays with a new guitarist and is looking for a female vocalist. Although the Big Brother family hasn't stayed intact, all the guys are now partnered and have kids. James's son, Hongo, is a musician, too. Over time, critics have looked more favorably on Big Brother, and the band's 1968 live performance with Janis at Bill Graham's Winterland, which was released by Columbia's Legacy label in the spring of 1998, has pushed the critical pendulum further in the band's favor, with one reviewer calling Big Brother "one of the most unjustifiably maligned bands of that era."

Peggy Caserta's boutique made her a rich hippie, but her heroin addiction eventually cost her Mnasidika and her Stinson Beach home. After getting busted, she got clean and remained off junk for fifteen years. In the early nineties, Peggy opened a coffeehouse in southern California, but she soon developed a coke and heroin habit. After a near-fatal OD in December 1995, she swore off both and has been clean since. She lives in a town south of Los Angeles, where she spends her time meditating and thinking up ways to make a million dollars all over again.

After Janis died, John Cooke walked away from road managing. He now lives in Jackson, Wyoming, where he plays music and writes. He has published three novels and is the creator and writer of the TV documentary series *Outlaws and Lawmen*, which premiered on the Discovery Channel in 1996. He is currently writing a book about his experiences in the sixties and about popular music of the era, from Cambridge to San Francisco, from folk to rock.

Myra Friedman's biography of Janis, *Buried Alive*, was published by William Morrow in 1973 and was nominated for a National Book Award. It was updated and published by Harmony Books in 1992. Myra is currently working on a memoir of "an extraordinary personal experience," as well as on an account of her early experiences in the music business. She lives in Manhattan.

Bill Graham went on to become one of rock's biggest promoters. By the late eighties, however, many top bands, tired of his autocratic style, were snubbing him, and Graham began devoting more of his time to benefit concerts. In 1990, he fulfilled his lifelong dream of being an actor when he snagged the role of the gangster Lucky Luciano in the film *Bugsy*. He died in October 1991 at the age of sixty in a helicopter crash, just months before the movie was released.

Forever mellow, Linda Gravenites lives in northern California, where she makes stained-glass windows, gardens, and enjoys life with her husband.

After Janis's death, Albert Grossman became even more reclusive. Clients who wanted to see him had to drive to Woodstock. By the early seventies when the Band left him to sign with David Geffen, a move that reportedly hurt Albert very deeply, he was no longer a heavy hitter in the music industry. Around this time he became embroiled in a legal battle with a San Francisco insurance company with whom he had taken out $200,000 insurance policies on all fourteen of his artists in 1969, prompted, he said, by Otis Redding's death. Upon investigating Janis's lifestyle and her OD, the company concluded that her death was a suicide and nullified its policy on her. Albert sued and in 1974 won a six-figure settlement out of court. He died in 1986 of a heart attack on a transatlantic flight. He was fifty-nine years old and still married to Sally at the time of his death.

Ever the evangelist, Chet Helms continued to stage happenings and concerts after the closing of the Avalon. When he finally gave that up, he returned to his Dumpster-diving roots, opening Atelier Doré, Inc., a San Francisco art gallery specializing in late-nineteenth- and early-twentieth-century American and European art. He got back into rock promotion long enough, though, to organize a 1997 concert celebrating the thirtieth anniversary of the Summer of Love. Although Chet never amassed a personal fortune, he did have the foresight to copyright the posters advertising the Family Dog dances at the Avalon. His copyright was unsuccessfully challenged in court by the artists who created them.

Seth and Dorothy Joplin moved to Prescott, Arizona, in 1976. Dorothy continues to live there, but Seth died of cancer in 1987. Laura Joplin earned a Ph.D. in education and went on to conduct motivational workshops. Her biography of her sister, *Love, Janis*, was published in 1992 by Villard Books. Married, with children, she lives in Denver, where she devotes much of her time to her sister's estate. Her brother, Michael, a ceramics artist, lives in Arizona and is also involved in managing the estate.

By the end of the Summer of Love, "Haight Street was lined with people with problems…" (Bob Seidemann)

Albert and Sally Grossman at Monterey Pop (Lisa Law)

Big Brother and the Holding Company, McNear's Beach, California, October 1967 (Baron Wolman)

John Cooke (left) and Bob Neuwirth (Betsy Siggins)

Janis and family, Port Arthur, Christmas 1967 (Leonard Duckett)

Big Brother and Janis at the Fillmore West, June 1968. "Those kids out there," she said, "after they see me, maybe they'll have a second thought—that they can be themselves and win." (Bruce Steinberg)

From R. Crumb's *Cheap Thrills* cover

BALL and CHAIN

Vocal: Janis
Lead Guitar: James

"Big Mama" Thornton

Big Brother's last New York performance, Hunter College, November 1968.
Dress by Linda Gravenites (John Cooke)

Janis as Pearl, with the Full Tilt Boogie Band (Jerry Tobias)

Janis and Linda Gravenites on their way to Rio, February 1970 (Richard Hundgen)

Janis at Truchas, New Mexico, in a shoot for a cigar commercial, September 1970 (Lisa Law)

Janis at home in Larkspur, 1970 (AP/Wide World)

Dave McQueen and Patti McQueen split up in the late sixties. After trying to organize a union at a chemical plant just outside Oakland, California, Dave got a job with an alternative radio station, KSAN. He has continued to work in radio, his voice known to thousands of northern Californians who listen to KKSF, the Bay Area's smooth jazz station. Patti McQueen Vickery has worked for many years as an arts administrator. Patti is married and lives in Texas, where she writes a column about life in the backwoods for the *Navasota Examiner* and is part owner of an antiques store.

Milan Melvin's marriage to Mimi Fariña didn't last and in the summer of 1970 he went off to England with a fellow KSANer, Tom Donahue, to work on the concert film *Medicine Ball Caravan*, Warner Brothers' failed attempt to cash in on the youth market. After returning to the States he produced a few records. He now lives in Mexico and is married to a designer and artist. He spends much of his time in water, both as an instructor of scuba diving and as a student of cave diving. When he's not underwater, he's writing a memoir.

When Pat "Sunshine" Nichols kicked her $500-a-day heroin habit once and for all in May 1970, she did it cold turkey. Determined to help others quit, she began working at the Haight-Ashbury Free Medical Clinic Heroin Detoxification Unit. Sunshine was hired there in 1971, the year that the federal government gave Detox its first grant, prompted, she suspects, by all the Vietnam vets coming home with "elephant habits." While working at the clinic she also bartended at the Coffee Gallery. In the late seventies she went to college and earned a B.A. in archaeology at the University of California at Santa Cruz. She works as an administrative assistant in the Silicon Valley area.

Since getting clean in 1983, Tary Owens has been active in the Austin music scene, producing a number of records and documentaries. He has also worked as a drug and alcohol counselor and been involved in AIDS education. He is currently working on a biography of Grey Ghost, a barrelhouse-blues piano player who was reportedly the first black man in Texas to own a car. He and his wife, Maryann Price, a singer, live in Austin.

Travis Rivers managed the singer Tracy Nelson until 1979, when he moved to New York to attend one of the Directors' Guild's training programs, eventually working for five years as an assistant director in film and music videos. In 1987, Travis reinvented himself yet again, as a computer consultant. He was president of Maxcess Inc., a manufacturer of disk drives, for several years and has worked as a product manager for a number of New York–based computer companies.

Powell St. John, like the rest of Mother Earth, chose to stay in the Bay Area after Tracy Nelson left the group. Although he still plays the harmonica, Powell makes a living as a computer consultant. He lives in Berkeley with his kids.

Linda Gottfried Waldron is a trance medium psychic who has been chanelling Janis since November 1970, when she acquired Janis's autoharp. She lives in Hawaii and New York City.

Discography

Big Brother and the Holding Company. Released fall 1967. LP. Mainstream S/6099 (out of print). Producer: Bobby Shad. Side 1: "Bye, Bye Baby" (P. St. John); "Easy Rider" (J. Gurley); "Intruder" (J. Joplin); "Light Is Faster than Sound" (P. Albin); "Call on Me" (S. Andrew); Side 2: "Women Is Losers" (J. Joplin); "Blindman" (P. Albin, S. Andrew, D. Getz, J. Gurley, J. Joplin); "Down on Me" (Arr. J. Joplin); "Caterpillar" (P. Albin); "All Is Loneliness" (Moondog).

Janis is not credited as the writer of "Women Is Losers" in the LP's liner notes. The band discovered "Down on Me" on a John Lomax recording, and Janis "adapted" the lyrics, according to Peter Albin. Columbia Records added two tracks ("Coo-Coo" and "The Last Time") from the Mainstream sessions and reissued the album after Janis's death. That LP (Columbia C30631), too, is now out of print.

Cheap Thrills. Big Brother and the Holding Company. Released Aug. 1968. CD. Columbia CK 9700. Producer: John Simon. "Combination of the Two" (S. Andrew); "I Need a Man to Love" (J. Joplin and S. Andrew); "Summertime" (D. Hayward and G. Gershwin); "Piece of My Heart" (J. Ragovoy and B. Berns);

"Turtle Blues" (J. Joplin); "Oh, Sweet Mary" (J. Joplin); "Ball and Chain" (W. M. Thornton).

Peter Albin, the band's bassist, plays lead guitar on "Turtle Blues" and "Oh, Sweet Mary." John Simon plays piano on "Turtle Blues." James Gurley handles lead on "Ball and Chain" and "Combination of the Two." Sam Andrew plays lead on "I Need a Man to Love" and "Piece of My Heart." On "Summertime," Sam and James trade off playing lead.

I Got Dem Ol' Kozmic Blues Again Mama! Janis Joplin. Released fall 1969. CD. Columbia CK 9913. Producer: Gabriel Mekler. "Try (Just a Little Bit Harder)" (J. Ragovoy and C. Taylor); "Maybe" (R. Barrett); "One Good Man" (J. Joplin); "As Good as You've Been to This World" (N. Gravenites); "To Love Somebody" (B. Gibb and R. Gibb); "Kozmic Blues" (J. Joplin and G. Mekler); "Little Girl Blue" (L. Hart and R. Rodgers); "Work Me, Lord" (N. Gravenites).

Although he is not credited in the liner notes, Michael Bloomfield plays lead guitar on "One Good Man."

Be a Brother. Big Brother and the Holding Company. Released 1970. LP. Columbia C30222. Janis sings backup on "Mr. Natural."

Pearl. Janis Joplin/Full Tilt Boogie Band. Released January 1971. CD. Columbia CK 30322. Producer: Paul Rothchild. "Move Over" (J. Joplin); "Cry Baby" (J. Ragovoy and B. Berns); "A Woman Left Lonely" (D. Penn and S. Oldham); "Half Moon" (J. Hall); "Buried Alive in the Blues" (N. Gravenites); "My Baby" (J. Ragovoy and M. Shuman); "Me and Bobby McGee" (K. Kristofferson and F. Foster); "Mercedes Benz" (J. Joplin and M. McClure); "Trust Me" (B. Womack); "Get It While You Can" (J. Ragovoy and M. Shuman).

In 1971, Columbia Records released a gold-disc, master-sound version of *Pearl.* Legacy 64413.

Pearl/Cheap Thrills. Released 1986. Cassette. Columbia 38219.

Joplin in Concert. July 1972. CD. Columbia CGK 31160. Elliot Mazer collected and assembled these tracks from Janis's performances with Big Brother and with the Full Tilt Boogie Band. With Big Brother and the Holding Company: "Down on Me"; "Bye, Bye Baby"; "All Is Loneliness"; "Piece of My Heart"; "Road Block" (J. Joplin and P. Albin); "Flower in the Sun" (S. Andrew); "Summertime"; "Ego Rock" (N. Gravenites and J. Joplin). With the Full Tilt Boogie Band: "Half Moon"; "Kozmic Blues"; "Move Over"; "Try (Just a Little Bit Harder)"; "Get It While You Can"; "Ball and Chain."

Big Brother's performance at the Grande Ballroom was considered too awful to use on *Cheap Thrills*. Here listeners can hear two songs—"Down on Me" and "Piece of My Heart"—from that gig. (However, at least one of these cuts, "Down on Me," was altered by producer Mazer, who replaced Peter Albin's bass parts with his own. Peter says that Mazer also substituted another drummer's playing for some of Dave Getz's drumming on some of the albums Mazer produced. In fact, it is almost impossible to evaluate any band's performance based upon a "live recordings" release. Mazer himself has said about doctoring: "The first rule is, 'There are no rules.' The second rule is, 'See rule No. 1.' ") Most Big Brother songs were recorded live during the spring and summer of 1968, except for "All Is Loneliness" and "Ego Rock" (sung with Nick Gravenites), which were recorded live in April 1970 when Janis appeared with the band at Bill Graham's Fillmore West.

Janis Joplin's Greatest Hits. Released 1973. CD. Columbia 32168. With Big Brother and the Holding Company: "Piece of My Heart"; "Summertime"; "Down on Me" (recorded live at the Grande Ballroom); "Bye, Bye Baby." With the Kozmic Blues Band: "Try (Just a Little Bit Harder)." With the Full Tilt Boogie Band: "Cry Baby"; "Me and Bobby McGee"; "Get It While You Can"; "Move Over"; "Ball and Chain."

Janis. 1975. LP. Columbia PG 33345 (out of print). From the soundtrack of the motion picture *Janis* (with substituted performances of "Piece of My Heart" and "Cry Baby"). Producer: Paul Rothchild (except for "Piece of My Heart").

Disc 1 (Early Performances). Side 1: "Trouble in Mind" (R. M. Jones); "What Good Can Drinkin' Do" (J. Joplin); "Silver Threads and Golden Needles" (R. Rhodes and D. Reynolds); "Mississippi River" (public domain); "Stealin' " (L. Stock and A. Lewis): "No Reason for Livin' " (J. Joplin); "Black Mountain Blues"° (H. Cole); "Walk Right In"° (G. Cannon and H. Wood). Side 2: "River Jordan"° (public domain); "Mary Jane"° (J. Joplin); "Kansas City Blues" (C. Parker); "Daddy, Daddy, Daddy" (J. Joplin); "C. C. Rider" (M. Rainey); "San Francisco Bay Blues" (J. Fuller); "Winin' Boy" (J. R. Morton); "Careless Love" (H. Ledbetter, A. Lomax, and J. Lomax); "I'll Drown in My Own Tears" (H. Glover).

According to the liner notes, most of the songs on the first disc were recorded in Austin, Texas, in 1963 and 1964. They were more likely recorded in late 1962 and early 1963 with the Waller Creek Boys. The notes claim that those songs I've asterisked were recorded in 1965 with the Dick Oxtot Jazz Band in San Francisco.

Disc 2. Side 1: "Mercedes Benz" (from *Pearl* with the Full Tilt Boogie Band); "Ball and Chain" (from the 1969 Frankfurt concert with the Kozmic Blues Band); "Try (Just a Little Bit Harder)" and Janis's introductory rap (from the 1970 Toronto concert with the Full Tilt Boogie Band); "Summertime" (from the 1969 Frankfurt concert with the Kozmic Blues Band); Albert Hall interview in 1969 (Courtesy of Bavaria Atelier GmbH); "Cry Baby" (from *Pearl* with the Full Tilt Boogie Band). Side 2: "Move Over" (from the soundtrack of the 1970 *Dick Cavett Show* appearance with the Full Tilt Boogie Band); Dick Cavett interview; "Piece of My Heart" (from *Cheap Thrills* with Big Brother and the Holding Company); 1970 Port Arthur high school reunion (Courtesy of KJAC-TV, Port Arthur, Texas); "Maybe" (from the 1969 Frankfurt concert with the Kozmic Blues Band); "Me and Bobby McGee" (from *Pearl* with the Full Tilt Boogie Band).

Farewell Song. Janis Joplin. Released 1982. CD. Columbia CK 37569. Producer Elliot Mazer (on asterisked tracks), liner notes by Country Joe McDonald. "Tell Mama"° (M. Daniel, W. Terrell, and C. Carter) with the Full Tilt Boogie Band, Toronto, June 28, 1970; "Magic of Love" (M. Spoelstra) with Big Brother, Detroit, Mar. 1, 1968; "Misery 'N'"° (P. Albin, S. Andrew, D. Getz, J. Gurley, and J. Joplin) with Big Brother, *Cheap Thrills* sessions, Apr. 1, 1968; "One Night Stand" (B. Flast and S. Gordon) with the Paul Butterfield Blues Band, Mar. 28, 1970; "Harry" (P. Albin, S. Andrew, D. Getz, J. Gurley, and J. Joplin) with Big Brother, *Cheap Thrills* sessions, Apr. 1, 1968; "Raise Your Hand"° (E. Floyd, S. Cropper, and A. Isbell), with the Kozmic Blues Band, Frankfurt, Apr. 12, 1969; "Farewell Song" (S. Andrew) with Big Brother, live at Winterland, Apr. 13, 1968; Medley°: "Amazing Grace" (trad. arr. P. Albin, S. Andrew, D. Getz, J. Gurley, and J. Joplin)/"Hi-Heel Sneakers" (R. Higginbottom) with Big Brother, live at the Matrix, Jan. 31, 1967; "Catch Me Daddy" (P. Albin, S. Andrew, D. Getz, J. Gurley, and J. Joplin) with Big Brother, *Cheap Thrills* sessions, Apr. 1, 1968.

Peter Albin says that Mazer replaced some of his bass parts and Dave Getz's drum parts. However, Mazer denies doctoring "Magic of Love" from Big Brother's Grande Ballroom performance although he did replace Peter's bass with his own on "Farewell Song." "One Night Stand" was originally produced by Todd Rundgren. On Rundgren's version, which can be heard on the 1993 boxed set, Janis's vocal sounds as if it's been sped up. Her vocal on this CD sounds like Janis Joplin, not one of the Chipmunks.

Cheaper Thrills. Big Brother and the Holding Company. Released 1983. LP. Edsel Records 135 (out of print). "Let the Good Times Roll" (L. Lee); "I Know You Rider" (trad. arr. Big Brother and the Holding Company); "Moanin' at Midnight" (C. Burnett [Howlin' Wolf]); "Hey Baby" (Big Brother and the Holding Company); "Down on Me" (trad. arr. Big Brother and the Holding Company); "Whisperman" (Big Brother and the Holding Company); "Women Is Losers" (J. Joplin); "Blow My Mind" (J. McCracklin); "Ball and Chain" (W. M. Thornton); "Coo-Coo" (trad. arr. Big Brother and the Holding Company); "Gutra's Garden" (Big Brother and the Holding Company); "Harry" (D. Getz).

Dave Getz produced this LP of Big Brother's July 28, 1966, performance at San Francisco's California Hall. Rhino Records reissued it as *Big Brother and the Holding Company Live* with one additional cut, "Oh My Soul," as Rhino RNLP 121. It's now out of print.

Janis. Released 1993. 3-CD boxed set. Columbia Records C3K48845. Compilation producer: Bob Irwin. Liner notes: separate essays by Ellen Willis and Ann Powers.

Disc 1: "What Good Can Drinkin' Do," recorded live by John Riney in his home in Austin, Texas, Dec. 1962; "Trouble in Mind"; "Hesitation Blues" (public domain); "Easy Rider"; "Coo-Coo"; "Down on Me"; "The Last Time" (J. Joplin); "All Is Loneliness"; "Call on Me," recorded live by Bob Cohen at the Avalon Ballroom, Mar. 17, 1967; "Women Is Losers," recorded live by Bob Cohen at the Avalon Ballroom, Dec. 9, 1966; "Intruder"; "Light Is Faster than Sound"; "Bye, Bye Baby"; "Farewell Song," previously unissued from the *Cheap Thrills* sessions; "Flower in the Sun," recorded by Dan Healey and Owsley at San Francisco's Carousel Ballroom, June 23, 1968; "Misery 'N," previously unissued alternate version from the *Cheap Thrills* sessions; "Road Block," recorded live at 1967 Monterey Pop Festival; "Ball and Chain," recorded live at 1967 Monterey Pop Festival.

Unless otherwise noted, the cuts on this disc are from the Mainstream album *Big Brother and the Holding Company*.

Disc 2: "Combination of the Two"; "I Need a Man to Love"; "Piece of My Heart"; "Turtle Blues"; "Oh, Sweet Mary"; "Catch Me Daddy," previously unissued from the *Cheap Thrills* sessions; "Summertime," previously unissued alternate take from the *Cheap Thrills* sessions; "Kozmic Blues"; "Try (Just a Little Bit Harder)"; "One Good Man"; "Dear Landlord" (B. Dylan), previously unissued from the *Kozmic Blues* sessions; "To Love Somebody"; "As Good as You've Been to This World"; "Little Girl Blue"; "Work Me, Lord"; "Raise Your Hand," recorded live, *The Ed Sullivan Show*, Mar. 16, 1969; "Maybe," recorded live, *The Ed Sullivan Show*, Mar. 16, 1969.

The first five tracks appear on the *Cheap Thrills* album. The remaining cuts, except as noted, are from the *Kozmic Blues* album.

Disc 3: "Me and Bobby McGee," previously unissued, alternate version (this was Janis's solo acoustic demo for Paul Rothchild); "One Night Stand," previously unissued, alternate take from Janis's Mar. 28, 1970, session with the Paul Butterfield Blues Band; "Tell Mama" with the Full Tilt Boogie Band in Calgary on July 4, 1970; "Try (Just a Little Bit Harder)" with the Full Tilt Boogie Band in Calgary on July 4, 1970; "Cry Baby," previously unissued, recorded on Sept. 5, 1970, during the rehearsals for *Pearl*; "Move Over"; "A Woman Left Lonely"; "Half Moon"; "Happy Birthday, John (Happy Trails)" (On Sept. 26, 1970, Janis and the Full Tilt Boogie Band took a break and recorded this as a birthday greeting to John Lennon); "My

Baby"; "Mercedes Benz" (includes a longer spoken intro by Janis); "Trust Me"; "Get It While You Can"; "Me and Bobby McGee."

Unless otherwise noted, all cuts appear on the *Pearl* album.

Woodstock Diary. Released 1994. CD. Atlantic 82634-2. The performances on this disc appear in the film *Woodstock Diary*. Janis is represented by two cuts, "Try (Just a Little Bit Harder)" and "Ball and Chain."

Texas International Pop Festival. Janis Joplin. Released 1995. CD. Oh Boy 1–1969 Tex 4. Recorded live with the Kozmic Blues Band in Dallas, Texas, Aug. 30, 1969. "Raise Your Hand"; "As Good as You've Been to This World"; "Try (Just a Little Bit Harder)"; "Maybe"; "To Love Somebody"; "Summertime."

18 Essential Songs. Janis Joplin. Released 1995. CD. Columbia CK67005. "Trouble in Mind"; "Down on Me"; "Bye, Bye Baby"; "Ball and Chain"; "Piece of My Heart"; "I Need a Man to Love"; "Summertime" (alternate version); "Try (Just a Little Bit Harder)"; "One Good Man"; "Kozmic Blues"; "Raise Your Hand" (live); "Tell Mama" (live); "Move Over"; "Mercedes Benz"; "Get It While You Can"; "Half Moon"; "Trust Me"; "Me and Bobby McGee" (acoustic demo).

Cheap Thrills/I Got Dem Ol' Kozmic Blues Again Mama!/Pearl. Released 1997. 3-CD boxed set. Columbia 64804.

Live at Winterland '68. Janis Joplin with Big Brother and the Holding Company. Released March 1998. CD. Columbia CK 64869. "Down on Me"; "Flower in the Sun"; "I Need a Man to Love"; "Bye, Bye Baby"; "Easy Rider"; "Combination of the Two"; "Farewell Song"; "Piece of My Heart"; "Catch Me Daddy"; "Magic of Love"; "Summertime"; "Light Is Faster than Sound"; "Ball and Chain"; "Down on Me."

Columbia Records denies that its engineers enhanced this disc, although music critic Fred Goodman argues that with digital technology alterations can be easily made "and no one—including perhaps the musicians—would be the wiser."

COMPILATIONS AND SOUNDTRACKS

"Ball and Chain" and "Combination of the Two" in *Fear and Loathing in Las Vegas*.
"Ball and Chain" in *Legends of Guitar*, vol. 1.
"Combination of the Two" in *Rock Goes to the Movies*, vol. 1.
"Down on Me" in *Baby Boomer Classics: More '60s*.

"Me and Bobby McGee" in *Rock Classics of the '70s*.

"Summertime" in *The War*.

"Piece of My Heart" in *Rock Classics of the '60s*, *China Beach*, and *Baby Boomer Classics: Electric '60s*.

JOPLIN CLASSICS BY THE ORIGINAL ARTISTS

Janis Joplin Classics. Various artists. 1992. CD. Blues Interactions (Japan) PCD 25316. Hideyo Itoh compiled the tracks on this disc. "Walk Right In," Rooftop Singers with Eric Darling; "San Francisco Bay Blues," Jesse Fuller; "Careless Love," Blind Boy Fuller; "C. C Rider," Leadbelly; "Coo-Coo," Jean Ritchie; "Moanin' at Midnight," Howlin' Wolf; "Amazing Grace," the Weavers; "Hi-Heel Sneakers," Tommy Tucker; "Let the Good Times Roll," Shirley and Lee; "Oh My Soul," Little Richard; "Summertime," Billie Holiday; "Piece of My Heart," Erma Franklin; "Ball and Chain," Big Mama Thornton; "Raise Your Hand," Eddie Floyd; "Maybe," the Chantels; "To Love Somebody," the Bee Gees; "Little Girl Blue," Nina Simone; "Tell Mama," Etta James; "Cry Baby," Garnet Mimms and the Enchanters; "A Woman Left Lonely," Ella Brown; "My Baby," Garnet Mimms; "Get It While You Can," Howard Tate; "Trust Me," Roscoe Robinson.

TRIBUTE ALBUM

Blues Down Deep: Songs of Janis Joplin. Various artists. CD. House of Blues 51416 1251 2. "What Good Can Drinkin' Do," Tracy Nelson; "Move Over," Tad Robinson; "Ball and Chain," Etta James; "Piece of My Heart," Otis Clay; "Maybe," Lonnie Brooks; "One Good Man," Lou Ann Barton; "Down on Me," Paul Black; "Get It While You Can," Koko Taylor; "Trouble in Mind," Willie Kent; "Turtle Blues," Lynne Jordan; "Try (Just a Little Bit Harder)," Cathy Richardson with Sugar Blue; "Me and Bobby McGee," Syl Johnson; "Mercedes Benz," Taj Mahal.

May 20 and June 25, 1995; Barry Feinstein, June 25, 1997; B. J. Fernea, May 27, 1996; Martine Fiero, Aug. 1998; Sallie Fiske, May 15, 1996; Snooky Flowers, June 27, 1995; Jim Fouratt, Aug. 1994; Myra Friedman, Apr. 1 and 2, 1995; Jeanie Gallyot, Nov. 14, 1997; Terry Garthwaite, July 10, 1997; Dave Getz, June 23, 1995; Bernard Giarratano, Sept. 16, 1997; Bennett Glotzer, Aug. 1998; Judy Goldhaft, June 25, 1995; Carl Gottlieb, July 30, 1996; Linda Gravenites, Aug. 26, 1994, and June 21, 1996; Mike Gray, Feb. 1997; Sally Grossman, Oct. 7, 1996; Ed Guinn, June 6, 1996; James Gurley, Aug. 13, 1997; Tommy Hall, Oct. 18, 1997; Bill Ham, June 14, 1995; Jim Haynie, Sept. 15, 1994; Chet Helms, Oct. 5, 1994, June 22 and 24, 1995; Lee Housekeeper, Jan. 1998; Richard Hundgen, June 30, 1995; George Hunter, June 20, 1996; Fredda Slote Hutchinson, Oct. 12, 1996; Diane Ihley, Nov. 14, 1997; Jack Jackson, June 8, 1996; Billy James, Nov. 17, 1997; John Jennings, June 20, 1995; Annie Johnson, June 1995; Laura Joplin, Jan. 17, 1997; Lenore Kandel, June 19, 1996; Alton Kelley, May 18, 1995; Lisa Kindred, May 20, 1995; Frances Kirkpatrick, Aug. 1997; Edward Knoll, Nov. 12, 1997; Janice Knoll, Nov. 17, 1997; Michael Kondray, Jan. 12, 1998; Mary Anne Kramer, Nov. 16, 1997; Jim Langdon, Oct. 1, 1997; Lisa Law, Jan. 13, 1998; Sally Lee, Sept. 21, 1997; Grant Lyons, Aug. 26, 1997; Glenn McKay, Sept. 29, 1994; Dave McQueen, June 16, 1996; Elliot Mazer, May 25, 1995, and Mar. 26, 1997; Milan Melvin, Oct. 9, 1996; Vince Mitchell, Sept. 9 and 10, 1997; Alice Molloy, June 14, 1996; Dave Moriaty, May 22 and Nov. 3, 1996; Etta Moriaty, Nov. 23, 1996; John Morris, Sept. 8, 1994; Robert Morrison, Aug. 19, 1997; Stanley Mouse, Aug. 24, 1997; Mark Naftalin, June 1995; Paul Nelson, Jan. 15, 1998; Tracy Nelson, May 7, 1997; Pat "Sunshine" Nichols, June 1995 and June 1997; Michael Ochs, Nov. 17, 1997; Odetta, Jan. 2, 1997; Tary Owens, May 21, 1996, and Jan. 28, 1997; Richard Oxtot, May 30, 1996; Deanie Parker, Dec. 15, 1997; Mary Sue Plank, June 22, 1995; Pepi Plowman, July 26 and 31, 1996; Linda Poole, June 30, 1998; Maryanne Price, May 21, 1996; Michael Pritchard, July 16, 1996; Nancy Quam-Wickham, Mar. 13, 1998; Hillel Resner, June 29, 1995; Andy Rice, Feb. 4, 1997; Travis Rivers, June 8, 1997; Trish Robbins, June 19, 1996; Bob Roberts, Oct. 1995; Karen Roberts, Oct. 1995; Rhonda Saboff, Oct. 1995; Powell St. John, June 13, 1996; Don Sanders, Nov. 21, 1997; Todd Schiffman, Feb. 1996; Bari Scott, Aug. 1995; Bob Seidemann, May 31 and June 6, 1996; Pat Sharpe, July 3, 1997; Roy Siegal, June 1995; Bob Simmons, May 28, 1996; John Simon, May 6, 1995; Darby Slick, Jan. 1996; Jack Smith, Aug. 30, 1997; Bruce Steinberg, Jan. 14, 1998; Chris Strachwitz, June 21, 1996; Wali Stopher, Dec. 8, 1996; Randy Tennant, Nov. 24, 1997; John Till, Aug. 15, 1998; Linda Tillery, June 30, 1995; Patti McQueen Vickery, July 29, 1996; Frances Vincent, Aug. 19, 1997; Linda Waldron, April 22 and Sept. 4, 1997; Malcolm Waldron, Nov. 1 and 5, 1997; Jae Whitaker, Aug. 16, 1997; Burton White, June 9, 1996; Joshua White, Aug. 14, 1994; Vickie Wickham, Sept. 1998; Ramsey Wiggins, Feb. 1997; Chris Williamson, Oct. 1995; Mary Works, June 1995; Peter Yarrow, June 19, 1998.

INTRODUCTION

page

xi   "Janis, what are you doing?": Interview with Patti McQueen Vickery.

xii   "the most obvious": Interview with Fredda Slote.

"went through all the changes": David Dalton, *Piece of My Heart: A Portrait of Janis Joplin,* rev. ed. (New York: Da Capo, 1991), p. 107.

"sailing like gypsies": Tom Wolfe, *The Electric Kool-Aid Acid Test* (New York: Bantam Books, 1969), p. 16.

"came to the ghetto fleeing America": Osha Neumann, "Motherfuckers Then and Now: My Sixties Problem," in Marcy Darnovsky, Barbara Epstein, and Richard Flacks, eds., *Cultural Politics and Social Movements* (Philadelphia: Temple University Press, 1995), p. 55.

"Money doesn't talk": Bob Dylan, "It's Alright Ma (I'm Only Bleeding)," on *Bringing It All Back Home*, Columbia Records.

xiii   "first white-black person," Laura Joplin, *Love, Janis* (New York: Villard Books, 1992), p. 124.

"no guy ever made me feel as good": Dalton, p. 59.

xiv   "dynamic of reversal": Ann Douglas, *Terrible Honesty: Mongrel Manhattan in the 1920s* (New York: Farrar, Straus and Giroux, 1995), p. 414.

"what strange, weird events": Dalton, p. 188.

"female Elvis": Bob Allen, liner notes to *Janis Martin: The Female Elvis, Complete Recordings,"* RCA, May 1987. In Australia, Alis Lesley was billed the "female Elvis," and rockabilly singer Wanda Jackson was called the "female Gene Vincent." Selling women musicians as analogues to male stars was a well-established practice, even into the seventies, when Patti Smith was called the "female Bob Dylan."

xv   Fifties girls: For a fuller discussion of sexuality, gender, and race in early rock 'n' roll see Alice Echols, "Smooth Sass and Raw Power: R&B's Ruth Brown and Etta James," in Barbara O'Dair, ed., *Trouble Girls: The* Rolling Stone *Book of Women in Rock* (New York: Random House, 1997), pp. 35–39.

"Folk music was so easy": Alice Echols, "30 Years with a Portable Lover: Alice Echols talks to Joni Mitchell," *LA Weekly,* Nov. 25–Dec. 1, 1994, p. 27.

"music for the neck downwards": Simon Frith, *Sound Effects: Youth, Leisure, and the Politics of Rock* (London: Constable, 1980), p. 163.

"Janis was *so* powerful": Bill Graham and Robert Greenfield, *Bill Graham Presents: My Life inside Rock and Out* (New York: Doubleday, 1992), p. 165.

xvi   "erect under her knit pantsuit": Robert Christgau, *Any Old Way You Choose It: Rock and Other Pop Music, 1967–1973* (Baltimore: Penguin Books, 1973), p. 24.

her style was absorbed: In the last few years, musicians—mostly women—

have begun citing her. But even Steven Tyler, the lead singer of Aerosmith, has said, "I can tell you one thing, I wouldn't care how she does it or what she looks or smells like, but I would cut this interview off right now if Janis Joplin were playing across the street. I'd be right there" (David Fricke, "Talk This Way: The *Rolling Stone* Interview with Steven Tyler," *Rolling Stone*, Nov. 3, 1994, p. 60).

"people do": Cree McCree, "Janis Lives," *High Times*, Sept. 1993, p. 58.

xvii "You could walk around a concert": Lillian Roxon, "A Moment Too Soon," in Robert Somma, ed., *No One Waved Good-bye* (New York: Outerbridge & Dienstfrey, 1971), p. 93.

black style: White musicians' appropriation of black style is a lamentable fact of American life, one that has angered many black performers, including the soft-spoken jazz stylist Billy Eckstine, who complained, "Tom Jones openly declared that he got his style from Otis Redding, from Jackie Wilson, from Chuck Berry, and that he started in learning to sing ballads by listening to my records. Now all four of us—where's our compensation? Where are we? Where's ours?" Particularly outspoken were black R & B artists, many of whom felt rock 'n' roll was R & B in whiteface. Louis Jordan, whose "Caldonia" has been cited as the first rock 'n' roll record, argued, "Rock 'n' roll was not a marriage of rhythm and blues and country and western. That's white publicity. Rock 'n' roll was just a white imitation, a white adaptation of rhythm and blues" (Arnold Shaw, *Honkers and Shouters: The Golden Years of Rhythm and Blues* [New York: Macmillan, 1978], p. 73). Bo Diddley said that R & B stood for "ripoff and bullshit. It was to keep me from getting my hands on any money. . . . So rock and roll was for the Caucasians and R & B was for the black cats" (*Rolling Stone*, Feb. 12, 1987, p. 12).

"like an angel who came": Etta James and David Ritz, *Rage to Survive* (New York: Villard Books, 1995), p. 192. This is a wonderfully evocative memoir, particularly of James's hometown, postwar south-central L.A.

While Elvis reportedly said: In the course of researching *A Turn in the South*, V. S. Naipaul interviewed an elderly black man who claimed Elvis said, "All I want from blacks is for them to buy my records and shine my shoes." Eric Lott recounts Naipaul's anecdote in a book review ("Loving You," *Nation*, June 1, 1992, p. 761), which is where I first learned of it. Those who challenge the shoe-shine story point to the absence of corroborating evidence and to other stories that suggest Elvis was free of racial prejudice. We will never know if Elvis actually uttered these words. The rumor was reported in the popular black magazine *Jet*, however, and Elvis never denied the story, despite its impact on his popularity with African Americans. Venise

Berry of the University of Iowa says Elvis was very popular in the black community in which she was raised until the shoe-shine story reached her neighborhood. Greil Marcus, who has defended Elvis against the charge that he was a bigot, suspects the story may be true, despite the lack of supporting evidence. Certainly, he argues, "a lot of people believe it. Believe me, Vernon Reid [of Living Colour] has heard that story. Spike Lee has heard that story. Chuck D [of Public Enemy] has heard that story." Indeed, the story was so much "in the air," it seems reasonable to conclude, as Eric Lott does, that Elvis did say something of the sort. (Telephone conversation with Eric Lott, Mar. 23, 1998). Both Berry's story and the Marcus quotation are from Gilbert B. Rodman, *Elvis after Elvis: The Posthumous Career of a Living Legend* (New York: Routledge, 1996), pp. 36–37.

"showed me the air and taught me": Douglas, p. 414. For more about the classic blues singers of the 1920s, see Hazel Carby, "It Jus Be's Dat Way Sometime," in Ellen DuBois and Vicki Ruiz, eds., *Unequal Sisters* (New York: Routledge, 1990), pp. 238–49; Francis Davis, *The History of the Blues: The Roots, the Music, the People from Charley Patton to Robert Cray* (New York: Hyperion, 1995), pp. 57–85; Douglas; Daphne Harrison, *Black Pearls: Blues Queens of the 1920s* (New Brunswick: Rutgers University Press, 1990). Even the founders of the Black Panther Party: Greil Marcus, "Sly Stone: The Myth of Staggerlee," in *Mystery Train*, rev. ed. (New York: Dutton, 1982), p. 108.

xviii   "lay life": Peter Coyote, quoted in Nicholas von Hoffman, *We Are the People Our Parents Warned Us Against* (Chicago: Quadrangle, 1968), p. 131. Peter Coyote is identified here as Peter Cohon, his given name.

"If you can remember the sixties": Charles Shaar Murray, *Crosstown Traffic: Jimi Hendrix and the Post-War Rock 'n' Roll Revolution* (New York: St. Martin's Press, 1989), p. 11.

"like a flying saucer landed": James Miller, *Democracy Is in the Streets: From Port Huron to the Siege of Chicago* (New York: Simon and Schuster, 1987), p. 315.

"post-Beat, bohemian": Paul Buhle, "Looking Forward to Looking Backward," *Radical America*, vol. 21, no. 6 (1987), p. 26.

xix   "the emotional dust bowl": Neumann, p. 55.

"It wasn't a party": Interview with Bob Seidemann.

"There's a time when the operation": Mario Savio, "An End to History," reprinted in Alexander Bloom and Wini Breines, eds., *Takin' It to the Streets* (New York: Oxford University Press, 1995), p. 111.

"the feeling then was": Interview with Carl Gottlieb.

page

xx   "I'd rather have 10 years": Michael Lydon, "Every Moment She Is What She Feels," *New York Times Magazine*, Feb. 23, 1969, p. 39.

less than respectful: Here I am referring to Ellis Amburn's *Pearl: The Obsessions and Passions of Janis Joplin* (New York: Warner Books, 1992) and Peggy Caserta's *Going Down with Janis*, as told to Dan Knapp (Secaucus: Lyle Stuart, 1973). Caserta claims she didn't write the more sensationalistic parts of her book.

"trepidation about walking": Interview with Milan Melvin. All subsequent quotations are from this interview unless otherwise noted.

xxii   "You forget you have acne": Neil Louison, "Priming the Pump," in Somma, p. 39.

1 · THE GREAT NOWHERE

page

3   "What's happening never happens there": Laura Joplin, *Love, Janis* (New York: Villard Books, 1992), p. 71. Once she became famous, Janis made a point of knocking her hometown. Her Port Arthur friend Jack Smith didn't like it and, on one of her trips back to Texas, confronted her. He claims she said she had fabricated her feud with Port Arthur because it made such good copy. So many other close friends, however, attest to Janis's long-standing animosity toward Port Arthur that I can only conclude Janis was telling Smith what she knew he wanted to hear. Even her father said, "she never had many local friends. People were kind of afraid of her. . . . Apparently, since her death, more people here were her friends than she knew." Chet Flippo, "An Interview with Janis' Father," *Rolling Stone*, Nov. 12, 1970, p. 18.

"an eerie doomsday red" Jim Langdon, "A Firefly Trapped in Amber," *Houston Chronicle*, Jan. 19, 1988, p. 1.

" 'the smell of money' ": Ibid.

"you'd end up feeling": Interview with Herman Bennett.

4   "foot fungus": Molly Ivins, "Ezra Pound in East Texas," review of *The Liars' Club*, by Mary Karr, *Nation*, July 3, 1995, p. 21.

"oiled the world": Langdon, p. 1.

"all drive-in movies": Joplin, p. 71.

"There was simply nowhere to go": Interview with Dave Moriaty. All subsequent quotations are from this interview unless otherwise noted.

page

"didn't really have much of an idea": Interview with Patti Skaff. All subsequent quotations are from this interview.

"Port Arthur is not a Janis Joplin town": Interview with Harry Britt.

5   "wide-open town": Interview with Dave McQueen. All subsequent quotations are from this interview.

"phoniness:" Interviews with Dave Moriaty and Dave McQueen.

"those envelopes of cash": Interview with Dave McQueen.

6   "nigger knocking": Janis quoted in *Time*, Aug. 9, 1968, p. 71.

Rock 'n' roll concerts: For a discussion of the racist view of rock, see Linda Martin and Kerry Segrave, *Anti-Rock: The Opposition to Rock 'n' Roll* (Hamden, CT: Archon Books, 1988), pp. 31–41. Asa Carter was the secret author of the famous 1963 speech in which George Wallace declared, "Segregation now, segregation tomorrow, segregation forever." Under the pseudonym Forrest Carter, he would later write the best-selling *Education of Little Tree*. The book was praised by critics and Indians alike for its authentic depiction of Native American culture, until historian Dan T. Carter revealed the author's true identity.

"down to the level of the Negro": Martin and Segrave, p. 41. Recently, Lloyd Price, a black rock 'n' roller who scored a national hit in 1952 with "Lawdy, Miss Clawdy," has said that when he was drafted in 1953 to serve in the Korean War a member of his draft board told him, "Washington wants you in the service. They don't like what you're doing, integrating the music (Quoted in Jon Pareles, "It's a California Jam Session for the Rock-and-Roll Hall of Fame," *New York Times,* Jan. 14, 1998, sec. B, p. 3.

7   "Malled out of existence": Interview with Dave McQueen.

8   "make things work": Joplin, p. 24.

"playboy": Joplin, p. 23.

9   "real tame": Interview with Jack Smith. All subsequent quotations are from this interview unless otherwise noted.

10   "The biggest thing": David Dalton, *Piece of My Heart: A Portrait of Janis Joplin,* rev. ed. (New York: Da Capo, 1991), p. 184.

"a secret intellectual": Ibid.

"best teacher": Joplin, p. 37.

"last gasp of 'traditional' family life": Elaine Tyler May, *Homeward Bound: American Families in the Cold War Era* (New York: Basic Books, 1988), p. 11.

"Well, she got her share": Interview with Myra Friedman, who notes Dorothy Joplin did not make this comment during their formal interview.

"half-bitterly": Joplin, p. 37.

11   "very straight": Interview with Bernard Giarratano. All subsequent quotations are from this interview unless otherwise noted.

"very straitlaced": Ellis Amburn, *Pearl: The Obsessions and Passions of Janis Joplin* (New York: Warner Books, 1992), p. 17.

very forceful: The speaker prefers to remain anonymous.

"kind of in the background": Interview with Karleen Bennett, who confirmed a rumor I had heard about Seth's drinking.

nonbeliever: On Seth Joplin's atheism, see Joplin, p. 36.

"The Great Saturday Night Swindle": Dalton, p. 185. Seth's best friend, "the only other intellectual in town," according to Janis, introduced Seth to this expression.

12   "geologic fault": Dalton, p. 94. Dalton is making a different but related point here.

"Then the whole world turned": Myra Friedman, *Buried Alive: The Biography of Janis Joplin* (New York: Harmony, 1992), p. 12.

"She'd been cute": Amburn, p. 17.

"didn't have any tits at fourteen": Joplin, p. 48.

"a never-ending series": Ibid.

"once you turned fourteen": Interview with Grant Lyons. All subsequent quotations are from this interview unless otherwise noted.

13   "Was it loud enough, Karleen?": Joplin, p. 57.

"Our parents were in a sad situation," Donald Katz, *Home Fires: An Intimate Portrait of One Middle-Class Family in Postwar America* (New York: HarperCollins, 1992), p. 150.

"She just changed totally": Joplin, p. 58.

"I even worried about it": Friedman, 11.

"Think before you speak": Nat Hentoff, "We Look at Our Parents and . . ." *New York Times*, Apr. 21, 1968, p. 19.

"emotionally terrorized": Joplin, p. 58.

"You're ruining your life": Joplin, p. 69.

"We had to look it up": Interview with Karleen Bennett. All subsequent quotations are from this interview.

14   "drag, a big drag": Interview broadcast on a Louisville, Kentucky, radio station, summer 1970. Tape courtesy of Myra Friedman.

"He was very important": Dalton, p. 184.

"be like everybody else": Hentoff, p. 19.

15   "She could never win": The speaker wishes to remain anonymous.

page

"Don't you ever leave her at home?": Joplin, p. 67.

16 "your greatest weakness": Quoted in Ivins, p. 21.

"absolute poison": Amburn, p. 22.

17 "every guy down there": Interview with Tary Owens. All subsequent quotations are from this interview unless otherwise noted.

"Sometimes they think": Dalton, p. 115.

18 "any friends at all": Amburn, p. 24.

"We were saboteurs": Amburn, p. 28.

19 "Port Arthur people thought": Michael Lydon, "Every Moment She Is What She Feels," *New York Times Magazine,* Feb. 23, 1969, p. 94.

"but as somebody who'd be there": Interview with Grant Lyons.

"wore pretty much what we wore": Amburn, p. 23.

"extremely expressive": Interview with Grant Lyons.

"Beaumont socialite": Amburn, p. 28.

"weirdness by association": J. David Moriaty, "Come On, Take Another Little Piece of My Corpse, Now Baby," *Austin Sun,* June 27, 1975, p. 22.

20 "inappropriate": Joplin, p. 63.

"exposed to such visions": Ibid.

"The rumor was": Amburn, p. 17.

21 "It seemed so shallow": "Rebirth of the Blues," *Newsweek,* May 26, 1969, p. 84.

"making the triangle": Dave Harmon, "Janis Joplin: At the University and Beyond," *Daily Texan,* Apr. 27, 1989, p. 10.

"This is the thing": Robert Shelton, *No Direction Home: The Life and Music of Bob Dylan* (New York: Penguin, 1986), p. 55.

"like a flash": "Rebirth of the Blues," p. 84.

"the force of a sledgehammer": Charles Wolfe and Kip Lornell, *The Life and Legend of Leadbelly* (New York: HarperCollins, 1992), p. 139. On Leadbelly's MLA appearance, see Francis Davis, *The History of the Blues* (New York: Hyperion, 1995), p. 168.

22 "if you were old enough": Interview with Dave McQueen.

"great Jimmy Reed": Chet Flippo, "Janis Reunes at Jefferson High," *Rolling Stone,* Sept. 17, 1970, p. 8.

23 "prestige from below": The phrase was apparently coined by Stuart Hall and is quoted in George Lipsitz, *Time Passages: Collective Memory and American Popular Culture* (Minneapolis: University of Minnesota Press, 1990), p. 283.

"drawing its juice": Todd Gitlin, *The Sixties: Years of Hope, Days of Rage* (New York: Bantam, 1987), p. 38.

"another realm": Interview with Michael Bloomfield by Tom Wheeler, in Jas Obrecht, ed., *Blues Guitar: The Men Who Made the Music* (San Francisco: Miller Freeman Books, 1993), p. 265.

a "black" speaking style: "The funny thing was that a lot of people, including black people, thought those disc jockeys were black, talking all this smooth jive" (James Brown with Ken Tucker, *James Brown: The Godfather of Soul* [New York: Thunder's Mouth Press, 1986], p. 53).

24 "black by persuasion": Lipsitz, p. 141.

"the Negro": Norman Mailer, "The White Negro," reprinted in Judith Albert and Stewart Albert, *The Sixties Papers* (New York: Praeger, 1984), p. 97.

"the 'Daddy-O' ": Linda Hamalian, *A Life of Kenneth Rexroth* (New York: Norton, 1991), pp. 271, 284.

"a kind of walking phallic symbol": James Baldwin, *Nobody Knows My Name* (New York: Dell, 1961), p. 172. The essay was originally published in the May 1961 issue of *Esquire*.

"even though her family": Interview with Dave Getz.

25 "They were talking the Mann Act": Joplin, p. 68.

"was so bad": Ibid.

"drinking and improper behavior": Joplin, p. 69.

26 "I've been this chick": Dalton, p. 100.

"Port Arthur was hostile": Joplin, p. 57.

"laughed out of class": Janis made this remark on *The Dick Cavett Show* in the summer of 1970.

"It just seemed like every time": Dalton, p. 53.

"Anyone with ambitions": Joplin, p. 71.

"the great Nowhere": Mary Karr, *The Liars' Club* (New York: Viking, 1995), p. 138. It's actually Karr's mother who utters these words.

27 "You take all those high schools": Amburn, pp. 29–30.

"hurried us out": Joplin, p. 74.

28 "the fine art of hanging out": Eric von Schmidt and Jim Rooney, *Baby, Let Me Follow You Down: The Illustrated Story of the Cambridge Folk Years,* 2nd ed. (Amherst: University of Massachusetts Press, 1994), p. 185.

"kids seeking engineering degrees": Interview with Tary Owens.

"the country boys with slide rules": Interview with Wali Stopher.

"dank and lonely": Interview with Dave McQueen.

29 "kind of family": Ibid.

"prodigious amounts": Ibid.

30 "I had one of the good roles": Interview with Frances Vincent.

page

"keep tabs": Interview with Jim Langdon. All subsequent quotations are from this interview unless otherwise noted.

felt "as if she were being banished": Interview with Randy Tennant.

"Mother insisted": Joplin, p. 80.

"artist shack": Joplin, p. 81.

"a lot of mileage": Interview with Ramsey Wiggins.

32   "dried-up pot": Joplin, p. 83.

"I don't want your money": Joplin, p. 84.

33   "an invisible line between Janis" and "adopt her ways": Joplin, p. 86.

"This wasn't supposed to happen": Joplin, p. 88.

34   "Why is everyone a pair except me?": Ibid.

35   "There's Jack and Nova": Friedman, p. 40.

"Janis wanted": Interview with Frank Davis.

36   "be a beatnik": Dalton, p. 241.

"I knew I had a good voice": Ibid.

"in those days": Interview with Ramsey Wiggins.

37   "I hope we'll all be killed": Friedman, p. 33.

"None of us planned": Langdon, p. 1.

2 · MAGNETIZED INTO MUSIC

page

38   "the best-kept secret": Dave Harmon, "Janis Joplin: At the University and Beyond," *Daily Texan,* Apr. 27, 1989, p. 10.

"oddballs, weirdos": Interview with Dave McQueen. Of course, college towns such as Berkeley, Ann Arbor, and Madison also became havens for kids who felt out of step, but Austin seems to have attracted more rebels than other southern college towns. The changing face of America's university and college towns reflects, of course, the enormous expansion of higher education and the sheer numbers of college-age baby boomers.

"racist, redneck, and somnolent": Clifford Endres, "Homeless with the Armadillo," in Daryl Janes, ed., *No Apologies: Texas Radicals Celebrate the '60s* (Austin: Eakin Press, 1992), p. 241.

"like being granted sanctuary": Endres, p. 240.

39   "I think you're right": Harmon, p. 10.

"straight hair": Interview with Fredda Slote. All subsequent quotations are from this interview.

page

40   "monoliths of conventionality": Endres, p. 240.

a resurgence of conservatism: "We must assume that the conservative revival is the youth movement of the sixties," wrote the journalist Murray Kempton after a big Young Americans for Freedom rally in Madison Square Garden in 1962. See Dan Wakefield, *New York in the Fifties* (New York: Houghton Mifflin, 1992), p. 270.

"generation gap": Barry Shank, *Dissonant Identities: The Rock 'n' Roll Scene in Austin, Texas* (Hanover, NH: Wesleyan University Press, 1994), p. 41. The 1962 manifesto of Students for a Democratic Society, the leading New Left group in the sixties, characterized the typical college campus as "a place of mass affirmation of the Twist, but mass reluctance toward the controversial stance." See the "Port Huron Statement," reprinted in Alexander Bloom and Wini Breines, eds., *"Takin' It to the Streets": A Sixties Reader* (New York: Oxford University Press, 1995), p. 68.

dormitory visitation rules: Pat Rusch, "Dorm Coeds Hear UT Housing Segregation Restrictions," *Daily Texan*, Sept. 27, 1961, p. 1; Mariann Garner-Wizard, "The Lie," in Janes, p. 84; interview with Bari Scott. By 1964, UT began desegregating its women's dorms.

"more afraid": Interview with Pepi Plowman. All subsequent quotations are from this interview.

41   "a great lacquered helmet": Dave Moriaty, quoted in Harmon, p. 10.

"most women never left": Interview with Ramsey Wiggins. All subsequent quotations are from this interview.

"She goes barefooted": Pat Sharpe, "She Dares to Be Different!" *Summer Texan*, July 27, 1962; interview with Pat Sharpe.

"Everybody had an attitude": Interview with Jack Jackson.

42   "the stronghold": Interview with Bob Brown.

"a living as well as counterculture fame": Interview with Bob Brown.

"skinny kid": Interview with Powell St. John.

"battered paperback copy": Stephanie Chernikowski, "Greetings from the Underground," *Austin Chronicle*, Mar. 12, 1993, p. 37.

"vast repertoire": Interview with Ramsey Wiggins.

43   "ballsy but insecure": Interview with Pat "Sunshine" Nichols.

"set the standard": Interview with Ramsey Wiggins. All quotations in this paragraph are from this interview.

"Between the folksing people": Interview with Bob Brown. All subsequent quotations are from this interview.

"this amazing group of disaffiliates": Endres, p. 240.

"like a fraternity": Interview with Jack Smith.

"It was a crash pad": Interview with Jack Jackson. All subsequent quotations are from this interview.

44 "party central": Interview with Dave McQueen.

"a commonly held place of assignation": Interview with Ramsey Wiggins.

"We were all experimenting": Harmon, p. 10.

"Shit, man": Interview with Bob Simmons. All subsequent quotations are from this interview.

45 "She didn't know": Interview with David Martinez. All subsequent quotations are from this interview, unless otherwise noted.

"Wait a minute, Jack": Interview with Robert Morrison. All subsequent quotations are from this interview.

"foundering on the reefs": Eric von Schmidt and Jim Rooney, *Baby, Let Me Follow You Down: The Illustrated Story of the Cambridge Folk Years,* 2nd ed. (Amherst: University of Massachusetts Press, 1994), p. 210.

"magnetized into music": Von Schmidt and Rooney, p. 183.

Art students: British Invasion rockers like John Lennon, Pete Townshend, Keith Richards, and David Bowie and seventies New Wave musicians like the Talking Heads all attended art school rather than college. In Britain, as opposed to the United States, art school was "somewhere they put you if they [couldn't] put you anywhere else," says Keith Richards (Simon Frith, *Sound Effects: Youth, Leisure, and the Politics of Rock* [London: Constable, 1980], p. 76). But the prominence of art students in the folk music scene suggests these rockers weren't the first musicians who were refugees from art school.

46 Jim Hershberger, the UT student who recorded Janis that day, would record her informally in the future, too. Some of the recordings are included in the Janis Joplin boxed set.

"blown away": Interview with Wali Stopher. All subsequent quotations are from this interview.

Waller Creek Boys Plus One: Interview with Ramsey Wiggins.

"hang out and get drunk a lot": Quoted in David Dalton, *Piece of My Heart: A Portrait of Janis Joplin,* rev. ed. (New York: Da Capo, 1991), p. 95.

"displaced persons": Interview with Michael Bloomfield by Tom Wheeler, in Jas Obrecht, ed., *Blues Guitar: The Men Who Made the Music* (San Francisco: Miller Freeman Books, 1993), p. 262.

University of Chicago: For more on the hoots there, see Ed Ward, *Michael Bloomfield: The Rise and Fall of an American Guitar Hero* (New York: Cherry Lane Books, 1983), p. 23.

47   thirty to forty . . . a hundred: Interviews with Stephanie Chernikowski, Wali Stopher, and Bob Brown.

"It took a couple of weeks": Interview with Stephanie Chernikowski. All subsequent quotations are from this interview.

48   "Almost everyone knew": Interview with David Martinez.

"real scholar": Interview with Powell St. John. All subsequent quotations are from this interview unless otherwise noted.

"They'd only want me": Interview with Fran Kirkpatrick. Shirley Dimmick, a white blues singer from Austin who performed in the forties and fifties with all-black bands, claims to have given Janis voice lessons. Although it's a great story and may even be true, I have been unable to corroborate it (Glyn Alyn, *I Say Me for a Parable: The Oral Autobiography of Mance Lipscomb, Texas Bluesman* [New York: Da Capo, 1994], p. 183; interview with Alyn).

49   Janis didn't have much competition: Interviews with Wali Stopher and Roger Baker.

"She could barely play": Interview with Frank Davis.

"hillbilly" and "race" records: On the lumping together of the two, see Arnold Shaw, *Honkers and Shouters: The Golden Years of Rhythm & Blues* (New York: Macmillan, 1978), p. 127.

debut at Gerde's Folk City: Bob Spitz, *Dylan: A Biography* (New York: McGraw-Hill, 1989), pp. 144–45. According to his friend Mark Spoelstra, Dylan had nothing to wear for his debut and prevailed on Hooker to loan him a pair of pants.

"thing was to exhume": Spitz, p. 155.

50   "a lot of one-upmanship": Interview with Peter Albin. All subsequent quotations are from this interview unless otherwise noted.

once the preserve of the left: Critical to the mainstreaming of folk music was the postwar red scare, which destroyed America's best-selling folk group, the Weavers. The group recorded a string of hits, including "Goodnight, Irene"—the most popular song of 1950—until an FBI informant testified before the House Un-American Activities Committee that Pete Seeger, Ronnie Gilbert, and Fred Hellerman—three of the four Weavers—were party members. The informant was later convicted of perjury, but his 1952 testimony ruined the Weavers. Unable to find a hall in which to perform, the group disbanded a year later. They reunited in 1955. See Robert Cantwell, *When We Were Good: The Folk Revival* (Cambridge, MA: Harvard University Press, 1996), p. 181, and Barbara Tishler, "Folk Music," in Mari Jo Buhle, Paul Buhle, and Dan Georgakas, eds., *Encyclopedia of the American Left* (New York: Garland, 1990), p. 231.

page

On the commercialization of folk, see Spitz; Cantwell; Robert Shelton, *No Direction Home: The Life and Music of Bob Dylan* (New York: Penguin, 1986); and Fred Goodman, *The Mansion on the Hill* (New York: Times Books, 1997).

51   "every available nook and cranny": Spitz, p. 120.

ABC's *Hootenanny*: The show became embroiled in controversy when its producers blacklisted Pete Seeger and the Weavers, who had re-formed. Carolyn Hester and Judy Collins initiated a performers' boycott. Even before the protest, though, many performers refused to appear on the show. Albert Grossman kept his artists off the program on the grounds that TV exposure would hurt attendance at college concerts (Shelton, p. 168).

"The American public": Shelton, p. 88.

"some 'pure' folk singers": Ibid.

"You *had* to hate": Spitz, p. 140.

Popular Front: For more on folk music in this period, see Robbie Lieberman, *"My Song Is My Weapon": People's Songs, American Communism, and the Politics of Culture, 1930–1950* (Urbana: University of Illinois Press, 1989); Shelton; and Cantwell.

the hootenanny came into being: See Shelton, p. 168.

52   Woody Guthrie clones: "There were hundreds of little Woody Guthries running around," says Rolf Cahn, who opened the Cabal coffeehouse in Berkeley (von Schmidt and Rooney, p. 76).

"stand-ins": See Endres, p. 239. Austin's movie theaters were segregated: blacks sat in the balcony and whites downstairs. At the ticket window, white protesters would ask, "May I sit in the balcony?" and black protesters if they could sit downstairs. When told they couldn't, they would rejoin the line, making for long waits for everyone who actually wanted to pay to see a movie.

"alienated and rebel groups": Shank, p. 44.

"We were outsiders": Eric von Schmidt, a Cambridge folksinger, is even more emphatic than Chernikowski, claiming, "Believe me, politics were not on our mind" (personal communication with author, Aug. 11, 1996). Greenwich Village folkies were more politically oriented than their Cambridge counterparts. According to John Boyd, the production manager of the 1965 Newport Folk Festival, New York folksingers "sang union songs, wrote political songs and delved into the roots of folk music in order to show the universal brotherhood of mankind," whereas Boston folkies "delved into the roots in order to learn how to play clawhammer banjo perfectly, like Dock Boggs." (see his letter to the editor, *New York Observer*, May 11, 1998). Bob Dylan's case is more complicated. Dylan dismissed his message songs, claiming he'd written them only to gain attention. As Todd Gitlin argues, however, it's unlikely Dylan's political songs were a matter of rank opportunism. After all, Dylan wasn't going to win lots of new fans by showing up at SDS's December 1963 National Council meeting or by visiting with organizers in a mining area of east Kentucky. He also performed at a voter registration rally sponsored by SNCC (Student Nonviolent Coordinating Committee) outside of Greenwood, Mississippi, where he hung out with movement activists for several days. His girlfriend, Suze Rotolo, worked with another civil rights organization, CORE. Gitlin maintains that if Dylan's "political commitment was a put-on phase to catapult him to stardom . . . he was probably putting himself on as well" (Gitlin, *The Sixties: Years of Hope, Days of Rage* [New York: Bantam, 1987], p. 198). In 1964, Dylan told Nat Hentoff, "I'm no part of no Movement. I just can't sit around and have people make rules for me. . . . I just can't make it with any organization" (Shelton, p. 202). Dylan's repudiation of politics may be related to the escalating demands of movement involvement: simply showing up for a meeting or a concert wasn't enough as the decade wore on. Of course, at this point few knew how extraordinarily mercurial Dylan could be. Commenting on Dylan's abrupt transformation a few years later from a rolling stone to a "dedicated family man," a friend said, "There's so many sides to Bob Dylan, he's round" (Shelton, p. 383).

The divide: For a view that differs from mine, see Doug Rossinow, "The Break-through to New Life: Christianity and the Emergence of the New Left in Austin, Texas, 1956–64," *American Quarterly*, vol. 46, no. 3 (1994), pp. 309–400.

their interracialism: Often townspeople and family were put off by the group's interracialism. Bob Simmons, another folk music maven, remembers going to a local pool hall with Ed Guinn, a biracial UT student, and being told by the manager, "You can get outta here if you're gonna come with him." As a consequence, their crowd would sometimes seek out "neutral territory," especially Mexican restaurants, which weren't segregated (interview with Bob Simmons).

53   "I used to say": Quoted in Robert Draper, "O Janis," *Texas Monthly*, Oct. 1993, p. 182. UT dropouts and high school students were also listed. Many believe that UT was in communication with the Austin police and maybe even the local FBI.

jukebox: Interview with Tary Owens.

Jimmie Rodgers: For background on Rodgers, see Francis Davis, *The History of the Blues: The Roots, the Music, the People from Charley Patton* to *Robert Cray* (New York: Hyperion, 1995), p. 88. On Threadgill, see Shank, p. 39.

54   "a microphone and a small, old amplifier": Shank, p. 42.

"the musicians had to move": Stan Alexander, "Janis and the Austin Music Scene," *Houston Chronicle,* Dec. 13, 1981.

"Her range and power": Ibid.

55   "That girl's really good": Interview with Powell St. John.

her voice: Interviews with Ramsey Wiggins and Tary Owens.

"a kind of hick-genteel admiration": Alexander.

"He surpassed them all": Dalton, p. 95.

Mr. Threadgill . . . would sing: Shank, p. 42.

"Someone would say": Dalton, p. 95.

56   "bunch of weird kids": Interview with Tary Owens.

a "pretty tame bunch": Interview with Ramsey Wiggins. Travis Rivers agrees: "I did not once hear a discouraging word there" (interview with Rivers).

"too disruptive": Shank, p. 45. Guinn, whose father was the third African American to graduate from UT's medical school, came to UT with the intention of playing in the Longhorn band. His dream died when the school barred him from joining. Although a letter-writing campaign forced the school's hand, Guinn left the band almost as soon as he was allowed to join. Forced to play "Dixie" as his first song with the Longhorns, he could see the struggle was far from over. He quit the band and began hanging out with the folkies. About Threadgill's, Guinn says, "I felt no need to blow up their bucolic scene. They were all my friends, anyway. I was already playing with them all" (Shank, p. 45). Moreover, he adds, "you have to choose the battles you fight. The right to be in a bar with bad music wasn't one I chose. I was into Hank Williams, not Jimmie Rodgers. I was interested in a little more complicated and, frankly, more elegant musical delivery than what I took to be happening there" (interview with Guinn).

57   A halfhearted protest: Interview with Tary Owens.

"There's a black man coming": Interview with Powell St. John. No one can say for sure when Mance Lipscomb integrated Threadgill's, although the best guess is 1966.

"a consummate musician": Interview with Powell St. John. Lipscomb could outplay many better-known musicians and knew more songs than just about anyone else. Pepi Plowman recalls hearing him at a gig in Boston where "Lightnin' Hopkins was trying to show off. Mance just played circles around him."

58   "Black players didn't come": Interview with Toni Brown. Recalling the great folk music parties hosted by the Huffmans and the Fredricksons—the two reigning doyens of Berkeley folk music—Brown notes there was little in the way of meaningful interaction between anyone—white or black. Music, not talk, was the purpose of the parties.

"were *still* living": von Schmidt and Rooney, p. 198. Spiro and his friends found House in Rochester, New York. Spiro cites Dick Waterman and Chris Strachwitz as important exceptions to the rule.

"If I had yo voice": Quoted in Alyn, p. 469.

59   "a horse's ass": Interview with Roger Baker.

60   "For some reason Janis": Interview with Travis Rivers. All subsequent quotations are from this interview unless otherwise noted.

"Man, we were lucky": Michael Lydon, "Every Moment She Is What She Feels," *New York Times Magazine,* Feb. 23, 1969, p. 95.

61   "Janis was her own worst enemy": Interview with Frances Vincent.

Janis's sexuality: David Moriaty says Janis was "AC/DC" and made no effort to hide it. Tary Owens describes Janis as "bisexual" but says she preferred men. Stephanie Chernikowski believes Janis was "heterosexual if she was anything; she just really liked to fuck."

62   "she went through men": Interview with Ramsey Wiggins.

"It ended when": Ellis Amburn, *Pearl: The Obsessions and Passions of Janis Joplin* (New York: Warner Books, 1992), p. 37.

"kept her in line": Laura Joplin, *Love, Janis* (New York: Villard Books, 1992), p. 109.

63   " 'Hi ya, boys' style": Dalton, p. 101.

"Janis *was* easy with guys": Interview with Peggy Caserta.

64   "Janis was constantly searching": Myra Friedman, *Buried Alive: The Biography of Janis Joplin* (New York: Harmony, 1992), pp. 333–34.

"She'd walk": Amburn, p. 38.

frat-sponsored contest: On the Ugly Man contest, see Harmon, p. 10.

Jack Jackson doubts: Jack Smith agrees: "Janis wasn't damaged by anything that happened in Austin."

65   There were barely two hundred rebels: This is Jeff Shero Nightbyrd's assessment (Shank, p. 44).

66   "By that time, the Waller Creek Boys": Powell agrees. "Janis knew she had to leave Austin to make it," he says.

not a "career move": Interview with Ramsey Wiggins.

"the cross-country party": von Schmidt and Rooney, p. 123.

page

when Muldaur and the band came to town: The jam took place either at a private party or at Threadgill's.

67 "living on the outer limits": Lydon, p. 88.

"A lot of people challenge you": Dalton, p. 92.

"So Sad to Be Alone": My account is drawn from my interview with Stephanie Chernikowski. I first heard the tape at Tary Owens's home in Austin.

3 • ON THE EDGES OF AMERICA

page

68 The "sixties": Since the mideighties, scholars have moved away from the idea that the sixties were an utterly distinctive, exceptional decade. The social movements of the sixties didn't emerge full-blown out of nowhere, they say, but rather had their roots in the activism of the postwar period. The argument against sixties exceptionalism is an important corrective, especially to the depiction of the fifties as an era totally devoid of dissent. Certainly the civil rights movement, which took off in the years immediately following World War II, in many ways marks the beginning of the sixties. And the work of fifties leftists, homophile activists, and feminists certainly helped create a climate in which other kinds of injustice could be challenged as well. But while it's critical to view the sixties within the context of the postwar years, the period is not a seamless whole. After all, it was called the *New* Left for a reason. The fifties were more complicated than previously thought, but there is no getting around the chilling influence on American culture of the Cold War and the politics of containment.

occurred in the midfifties: One can make a case for the first stirrings of change occurring even earlier, the late forties or early fifties. After all, civil rights activism heated up in the late forties, and many would argue that the first rock 'n' roll records appeared in the late forties or early fifties. Critics often cite Wynonie Harris's "Good Rockin' Tonight" (1949) or "Rocket 88" (1951) by Ike Turner's sideman, Jackie Brenston, as the earliest rock records. I choose 1955 as the watershed year because that's when these changes began to register on the nation's consciousness.

Jim Crow music industry: In 1945, for example, Leadbelly was prevented from recording with white musicians in San Francisco when the local musicians union opposed it. In the Bay Area, "there was a long-standing rule" at Musicians Local Union 6 barring black and white musicians from playing together in public (see Charles Wolfe and Kip Lornell, *The Life and Legend of Leadbelly* [New York: HarperCollins, 1992], p. 234). Black artists recorded either for small, independent labels or for the separate "race record" divisions maintained by the majors. And as Richard Greener, a white programmer at black radio stations, notes, "race records" were not sold in record stores alongside music by white artists. One had to "hunt them down in beauty shops, barber shops, small grocery stores and even from street-corner vendors" (letter, *New York Times*, Sept. 17, 1993, p. A12).

69   "its glorification of madness, drugs, and homosexuality": Quoted in Dan Wakefield, *New York in the Fifties* (New York: Houghton Mifflin, 1992), p. 179.

"none of us wanted": Quoted in Michael Schumacher, *Dharma Lion* (New York: St. Martin's Press, 1992), p. 215.

"hidden and skulked": Diane Di Prima, *Memoirs of a Beatnik*, 1969 (San Francisco: Last Gasp, 1988), p. 127.

70   "communists, beatniks and eggheads": Schumacher, p. 339.

"as solid as the Empire State Building": Schumacher, p. 532.

"aversion to movements": Carl Solomon, *Emergency Messages: An Autobiographical Miscellany* (New York: Paragon, 1989), p. 43.

"who knew what we knew": Di Prima, p. 126.

"way-out people": Maria Damon, "The Jewish Entertainer as Cultural Lightning Rod: The Case of Lenny Bruce," *Postmodern Culture*, v. 7, no. 2 (1997). Kaufman, not Herb Caen of the *San Francisco Chronicle*, coined the term *beatnik*. His "Abomunist Manifesto" can be found in Bob Kaufman, *Solitudes Crowded with Loneliness* (New York: New Directions, 1965). Details of his life are drawn from his son Parker Kaufman's remembrance in Daniel Pinchbeck, "Children of the Beats," *New York Times Magazine*, Nov. 5, 1995, p. 38, and Mona Lisa Saloy, "Black Beats and Black Issues," in Lisa Phillips, ed., *Beat Culture and the New America, 1950–1965* (New York: Whitney Museum of Art, 1996), p. 163.

71   "a very depressing scene": Interview with Linda Gravenites. All subsequent quotations are from this interview unless otherwise noted.

"to be part of the Beat Generation": Ellis Amburn, *Pearl: The Obsessions and Passions of Janis Joplin* (New York: Warner Books, 1992), p. 50.

"only thing to do": Jack Kerouac, *The Dharma Bums* (New York: Signet Books, 1958), p. 95.

"to stay out of the mainstream": Interview with Pat "Sunshine" Nichols. All subsequent quotations are from this interview unless otherwise noted.

72 "seemed like the 1950s": Interview with Linda Gottfried Waldron. All subsequent quotations are from this interview unless otherwise noted.

"swearing like a trooper": Amburn, p. 44. Other details of this trip are from my interview with Chet Helms.

73 Janis was clear: Interviews with Powell St. John, Chet Helms, Linda Gottfried Waldron, Jae Whitaker, and Edward Knoll.

74 "on the dole": Myra Friedman, *Buried Alive: The Biography of Janis Joplin* (New York: Harmony, 1992), p. 47.

"No one in those days": Di Prima, p. 97. Further details come from my interviews with Linda Gravenites, Linda Gottfried Waldron, Janice Knoll, Mary Anne Kramer, Malcolm Waldron, and Bob Clark.

"We all stole steaks": Amburn, p. 47.

the Salvation Army: Interview with Sally Lee.

"she *still* kept a schedule": Friedman, p. 334.

75 "is nuts": Ibid.

"I'm gonna make it!": Interview with Jae Whitaker. All subsequent quotations are from this interview.

"She was incredibly strong": Interview with Toni Brown. Her friend Sally Lee and Philip Elwood, a music critic for the *San Francisco Examiner*, recall Janis hanging out with Sonny Terry and Brownie McGhee one night at the home of Barbara Dane, a folksinger. Dane has no memory of the evening but says lots of kids stopped by and Janis may well have been one of them (interviews with Sally Lee, Philip Elwood, and Barbara Dane).

"incredible": Interview with James Gurley.

76 "She was hungry": Interview with Edward Knoll. All subsequent quotations are from this interview. Jorma Kaukonen did back up Janis on a few occasions, and a recording of them can be heard on the 1993 boxed set.

"I used to tell Janis": Interview with Linda Poole.

"hit the street with Chet": Friedman, p. 48.

One night, she crashed the motorcycle: Interview with Malcolm Waldron. All subsequent quotations are from this interview.

"Are you kidding, man?": Amburn, p. 46.

77 "they beat the shit": Amburn, p. 53.

"walked right into a speed crowd": Friedman, p. 48.

"My aunt used to bring": Interview with Diane Di Prima. All subsequent quotations are from this interview.

"eating Benzedrine": Solomon, p. 35. On Ginsberg's drug use, see Schumacher, p. 348. For more on the Beats' drug experimentation, see Steven Watson, *The Birth of the Beat Generation: Visionaries, Rebels, and Hipsters, 1944–1960* (New York: Pantheon, 1995).

"The amount of liquor": Brad Gooch, *City Poet: The Life and Times of Frank O'Hara* (New York: HarperCollins, 1994), p. 203.

"We thought we were growing": Laura Joplin, *Love, Janis* (New York: Villard Books, 1992), p. 126.

78   "A lot of artists": Joplin, p. 126.

"Somewhere deep inside": Interview with Sally Lee.

"She felt she had to pay": Bill Graham and Robert Greenfield, *Bill Graham Presents: My Life inside Rock and Out* (New York: Doubleday, 1992), p. 204.

"I could play the blues": Interview with Michael Pritchard.

79   "I have a recording": Interview with Frank Davis.

"pretty heavy": Friedman, p. 82.

"She was playing the autoharp": Interview with Guy Clark.

New York: Janis told Poole she wanted to go to New York to make it because no one there knew her. In Poole's view, Janis was embarrassed by the attention she got in San Francisco. "If she made it where people didn't know her, that would be okay," according to Poole. However, Chet Helms maintains, as do others, that Janis loved the attention; she was "a glory hound." She may have wanted to go where no one knew her, but only because she had developed a reputation as irascible and unreliable in San Francisco (interviews with Linda Poole and Chet Helms).

80   "We basically partied": Interview with Andy Rice.

Old Reliable: See John Gruen, *The New Bohemia* (Pennington, NJ: A Cappella Books, 1996), p. 23.

"Man, I've lived": Interview with Janice Knoll. All subsequent quotations are from this interview unless otherwise noted. Laura Joplin has disputed Knoll's account that Janis was shooting speed in New York; her sister, she argues, wasn't close to Knoll. Others, however, have corroborated that they were good friends and that Janis was indeed shooting speed in New York in the summer of 1964.

81   "She'd go up to guys": Interview with Mary Anne Kramer.

"too flashy": Friedman, p. 51.

"wowed": Joplin, p. 122.

"strung out on speed": Friedman, p. 53.

82   "Is this all there's gonna be?": Ibid. When he was interviewed by Myra

Friedman, Seth Joplin remembered Janis's sending him several letters. Janis herself told David Dalton she had written her father a "big long letter" (Dalton, p. 184).

"I had a couple": Dalton, p. 96.

83   "just looked at each other": Joplin, p. 126.

"I wanted to smoke dope": Friedman, p. 48.

"There were no windows": Interview with John Jennings. All subsequent quotations are from this interview.

watermelon juice: Interview with Janice Knoll.

84   Hunter's initial success: Eric Jacobsen, a record producer, recorded the Charlatans in the fall of 1965 largely on the basis of their publicity still.

"I had no idea": Interview with George Hunter. All subsequent quotations are from this interview.

"tough-looking gal": Interview with Richard Oxtot. Malcolm Waldron was with Janis that night and corroborates Oxtot's account of the audience's reaction. "The whole place just went dead silent," he says.

85   Beat and gay worlds: Maria Damon writes that in bars like the San Remo in Greenwich Village or the Anxious Asp in North Beach, Beat and gay subcultures "overlapped in sometimes uneasy, sometimes supportive proximity" ("Victors of Catastrophe: Beat Occlusions," in Phillips, ed., *Beat Culture*). Brad Gooch calls the San Remo, a fictional version of which appears in Kerouac's *The Subterraneans*, a "mixed talky bar to which all genres of poets, writers, intellectuals, and bohemians were drawn" (p. 201).

"You needed apostles": Solomon, p. 13.

"twenty-four hours a day": Amburn, p. 49.

86   For most of 1963 and 1964: The dates I give for Janis's relationship with Jae (and later with Michel Raymond) are approximate. They have proven impossible to establish with any precision because those who claim to remember have all given me different dates.

88   "I think he kind of": The speaker prefers to remain anonymous.

"When he was with you": The speaker prefers to remain anonymous.

"saw his pain": The speaker prefers to remain anonymous.

"Janis would change her mind": Friedman, p. 57.

90   "The only thing": Amburn, p. 57.

4 · THE BEAUTIFUL PEOPLE

page

91   Laura took her sister: My account of Janis's shopping trip is drawn from Laura Joplin, *Love, Janis* (New York: Villard Books, 1992), p. 131.

92   "She told me she'd been shooting methedrine": Interview with Frances Vincent. All subsequent quotations are from this interview.

      "poison in the social system": Anne Parsons, quoted in Wini Breines, *Young, White, and Miserable: Growing Up Female in the Fifties* (Boston: Beacon Press, 1992), p. 178. The daughter of the prominent sociologist Talcott Parsons, she used the phrase in a letter to Betty Friedan, whose book, *The Feminine Mystique*, she had just read.

      "Michel said he'd come": Interview with Debbie Boutellier. All subsequent quotations are from this interview.

93   "terribly proper": Joplin, p. 132. My account of Michel's visit is drawn from Joplin, 132–33, and interviews with Linda Gottfried Waldron and Debbie Boutellier.

      "jumped up and down": Joplin, p. 133.

95   "She had her hair": Ellis Amburn, *Pearl: The Obsessions and Passions of Janis Joplin* (New York: Warner Books, 1992), pp. 58–59; interview with Grant Lyons.

      "very thin but enthusiastic": Amburn, p. 59.

      "life as a nun": Joplin, p. 135.

      "I mean she got so straight": Friedman, p. 60.

      acoustic folk music had run its course: Jerry Garcia describes the folkie scene in 1965 as "bankrupt" (Philip Ennis, *The Seventh Stream: The Emergence of Rock Rocknroll in American Popular Music* [Hanover, NH: Wesleyan University Press (University Press of New England)], 1992, p. 334).

96   Haight-Ashbury: The best book about Haight-Ashbury remains Tom Wolfe, *The Electric Kool-Aid Acid Test* (New York: Bantam Books, 1969). Also useful are Charles Perry, *The Haight-Ashbury: A History* (New York: Random House, 1984); Joan Didion, "Slouching towards Bethlehem," in *Slouching towards Bethlehem* (New York: Dell, 1968); Peter Coyote, *Sleeping Where I Fall* (New York: Counterpoint, 1998); Emmett Grogan, *Ringolevio: A Life Played for Keeps* (New York: Citadel Press, 1990); Warren Hinckle, "A Social History of the Hippies," *Ramparts,* Mar. 1967, reprinted in Gerald Howard, ed., *The Sixties: The Art, Attitudes, Politics, and Media of Our Most Explosive Decade* (New York: Pocket Books, 1982), pp. 207–32; the prefatory essay in Allen Cohen, *The San Francisco Oracle,* facsimile ed. (San Francisco: Regent Press, 1994). On the San Francisco bands, see Joel

page

Selvin, *Summer of Love* (New York: Penguin, 1994). For a compelling fictional treatment, see Jennifer Egan, *The Invisible Circus* (New York: Picador, 1995).

"Peggy, *what* is going on here?": Interview with Peggy Caserta. All subsequent quotations are from this interview unless otherwise noted.

Within a year: Peggy bought the barbershop and installed Bobby Bowles, a leather crafter who had been working in a corner of her boutique, Mnasidika. They left two of the barbershop's chairs and its glass cabinets in their new store, the Boot Hook.

"come off the leash": Todd Gitlin, *The Sixties: Years of Hope, Days of Rage* (New York: Bantam, 1987), p. 242.

"Would you believe": Interview with Bob Seidemann. All subsequent quotations are from this interview.

"I won't bore you": Wolfe, p. 121.

97 "a system pouring its junk": Quoted in Gitlin, p. 9.

an almost forgotten part: Cohen, p. xxiii, and Perry, p. 6. I have also drawn on interviews with Peter Albin, Peter Berg, Bill Belmont, and Pat "Sunshine" Nichols.

"Everything was designed": Bill Graham and Robert Greenfield, *Bill Graham Presents: My Life inside Rock and Out* (New York: Doubleday, 1992), p. 184.

98 "anonymous good guys": Didion, p. 99. This is most decidedly not Didion's view of the Diggers.

"hip Salvation Army": The phrase was coined by Ralph Gleason, the music critic for the *San Francisco Chronicle*. Although Peter Coyote felt it obscured the group's true radicalism, Peter Berg, another Digger, thinks Gleason was trying to take the heat off the Diggers by making them seem like selfless do-gooders.

Free Store: My account is drawn from an interview with Peter Berg; Coyote's account in Graham and Greenfield, p. 184; and Emmett Grogan's *Ringolevio*. According to Grogan, "only a fraction of the goods used and accepted were secondhand and they were made available and displayed to affect a Salvation-Goodwill-salvage cover to conceal the fact that the rest of the stuff was new and fresh and had been stolen" (p. 249). According to Peter Berg, the Diggers also suggested to Bobby Seale that the Black Panther Party establish a free-food program (interview with Berg).

"families": Interview with Richard Hundgen. All subsequent quotations are from this interview.

99 "twenty years of marshmallow": Quoted in Nicholas von Hoffman, *We Are*

page

the People Our Parents Warned Us Against (Chicago: Quadrangle, 1968), p. 131.

"tired of the gray life": Interview with Jim Haynie.

"destroy your now": Nat Hentoff, "We Look at Our Parents and . . ." *New York Times*, Apr. 21, 1968, p. 19.

A UC Berkeley dropout: On Owsley, see Wolfe, p. 188, and Perry, p. 4.

"orgasm behind the eyeballs": Wolfe, p. 36

"adventure shortage": Perry, p. 7.

"bummer": Wolfe, p. 159.

"like being addicted": Graham and Greenfield, p. 295.

psychodelics: Wolfe, p. 40.

"always thought existed": Bill Barich, "Dead Reckoning," *Rolling Stone,* Sept. 21, 1995, p. 78.

100 "you can hear it all": Hank Harrison, *The Dead: Volume 1* (San Francisco: Archives Press, 1990), p. 42.

squeaky clean: For the resistance early rock 'n' roll encountered, see Linda Martin and Kerry Segrave, *Anti-Rock: The Opposition to Rock 'n' Roll* (Hamden, CT: Archon Books, 1988).

"The most exciting thing": Ray Gosling, quoted in Andrew Ross, *No Respect: Intellectuals and Popular Culture* (New York: Routledge, 1989), p. 148.

"The first books": Graham and Greenfield, p. 216.

101 "substitute": Clinton Heylin, *Bob Dylan: Behind the Shades* (New York: Summit, 1991), p. 102.

"taken": David Crosby and Carl Gottlieb, *Long Time Gone: The Autobiography of David Crosby* (New York: Dell, 1988), p. 92.

"Beatle struck": Crosby and Gottlieb, p. 83.

"It was great": Crosby and Gottlieb, p. 93.

"Wow, man": Robert Shelton, *No Direction Home: The Life and Music of Bob Dylan* (New York: Penguin, 1986), p. 309.

102 "plastic man": Bob Spitz, *Dylan: A Biography* (New York: McGraw-Hill, 1989), p. 210.

"in the lap of outrageous luxury": Eric von Schmidt and Jim Rooney, *Baby, Let Me Follow You Down: The Illustrated Story of the Cambridge Folk Years,* 2nd ed. (Amherst: University of Massachusetts Press, 1994), p. 240.

"If I had an axe": Fred Goodman, *The Mansion on the Hill* (New York: Times Books, 1997), p. 9. My account of Newport 1965 is drawn from Shelton, Goodman, Heylin, Michael Bloomfield's account in Ed Ward, *Michael Bloomfield: The Rise and Fall of an American Guitar Hero* (New York:

Cherry Lane Books, 1983), and my interview with Peter Yarrow. For a behind-the-scenes account from the production manager of the festival, see John Boyd's letter to the editor in the *New York Observer*, May 11, 1998. Although the *Observer* identifies him as "John" Boyd, the production manager at Newport was Joe Boyd (see Goodman, p. 8).

"capitulation to the enemy": Goodman, p. 9.

"grinning like a couple of cats": Spitz, p. 299.

103   "how you write a hit song": Shelton, p. 333.

"Dylan has sold out to God": Heylin, p. 147.

"major poet": Shelton, p. 333.

"When Dylan went electric": Interview with Bill Belmont. All subsequent quotations are from this interview.

the Jabberwalk: Interview with Terry Garthwaite.

104   "one big piece": Wolfe, p. 95. Details of Kesey and the Pranksters are taken from Wolfe, Perry, and Graham and Greenfield.

"huge party circuit": Interview with Chet Helms. All subsequent quotations are from this interview unless otherwise noted.

"camaraderie there already": Darby Slick makes the same point in *Don't You Want Somebody to Love: Reflections on the San Francisco Sound* (Berkeley: SLG Books, 1991), p. 53.

"In its heyday": Interview with Bob Cohen. All subsequent quotations are from this interview.

big bashes: Interviews with George Hunter and Chet Helms.

105   "way ahead of its time": Interview with Dave Getz. All subsequent quotes are from this interview unless otherwise noted.

avant-garde: See Richard Cándida Smith, *Utopia and Dissent: Art, Poetry, and Politics in California* (Berkeley: University of California Press, 1995). On the San Francisco Mime Troupe, see Graham and Greenfield; R. G. Davis, *The San Francisco Mime Troupe* (Palo Alto: Ramparts, 1975).

106   "what Andy Warhol is doing": Wolfe, p. 8.

"real Johnny Appleseed": Perry, p. 67.

"What the fuck's a light show?": Interview with Alton Kelley. All subsequent quotations are from this interview unless otherwise noted.

"hippies were the people": Interview with Carl Gottlieb. All subsequent quotations are from this interview.

107   "Love Hoax": Grogan, p. 238.

when *hippie* first appeared: Michael Fallon, "A New Paradise for Beatniks," *San Francisco Examiner*, Sept. 5, 1965. The article was the first in a series on the Haight. In the underground press, *beatnik* continued to be used, too. For example, in early 1967, before the so-called Summer of Love made *hippie* a household term, New York's *East Village Other* published "What Is a Beatnik?" in which sixth graders in a Lower East Side public school were asked to respond to the question. The article was reprinted in the *Austin Rag*, Mar. 27, 1967, p. 8.

108   "reject any kinship": Hunter S. Thompson, "The 'Hashbury' Is the Capital of the Hippies," *New York Times Magazine,* May 14, 1967, p. 29.

"The media portrait": Graham and Greenfield, p. 195. The article by Warren Hinckle cited earlier was more discerning than most, although it was printed in the radical magazine *Ramparts*. Hinckle criticized hippies' "unrelenting quietism" on the grounds that it undermined continued activism. Noting that dropping out could be fun, Hinckle also warned, "but when that is done, you leave the driving to the Hell's Angels" (p. 232).

"apocalyptic edge": Susan Gordon Lydon, *Take the Long Way Home: Memoirs of a Survivor* (New York: HarperCollins, 1993), p. 74.

109   "For us this show": Interview with Joshua White. All subsequent quotations are from this interview. White exempts the Airplane's Marty Balin from this characterization.

"darker side": Slick, p. 44.

Kerouac walked out: Details of the encounter are taken from Michael Schumacher, *Dharma Lion* (New York: St. Martin's Press, 1992), p. 414.

110   "something wilder and weirder": Wolfe, p. 90.

"very high and very up": Ennis, p. 334.

"outniggered": Wolfe, p. 23.

"a swinging group of American men": Jack Kerouac, "The Origins of the Beat Generation," *Playboy,* June 1959, p. 32. For an interesting account of the Beats, see the interview with Neal Cassady's widow, Carolyn Cassady, in Gina Berriault, "Neal's Ashes," *Rolling Stone,* Oct. 12, 1972, p. 32. Speaking of all the men "enamored of the Neal myth," she says, they "never knew and don't know how miserable these men were, they think they were having marvelous times—joy, joy, joy—and they weren't at all." See also Carolyn Cassady, *Off the Road* (New York: William Morrow, 1990); Hettie Jones, *How I Became Hettie Jones* (New York: Penguin, 1990); and the chapter on the Beats in Barbara Ehrenreich, *The Hearts of Men* (New York: Anchor, 1983).

"Hippies treat their women": Interview with Bob Seidemann. As a lefty, Rifkin's mother was aware of male chauvinism.

111   "hippie folk music": Barry Shank, *Dissonant Identities: The Rock 'n' Roll Scene in Austin, Texas* (Hanover, NH: Wesleyan University Press, 1994), p. 46.

page

"it basically worked": Shank, p. 47.

niggardly: Ibid.

"proto-hippie": Tary Owens, quoted in Shank, p. 48.

"far superior": Stephanie Chernikowski, "The 13th Floor Elevators: Visions of Ecstasy," *Austin Chronicle*, Mar. 12, 1993, p. 37.

"she *still* looked different": Myra Friedman, *Buried Alive: The Biography of Janis Joplin* (New York: Harmony, 1992), p. 58.

112   "I was down there": David Dalton, *Piece of My Heart: A Portrait of Janis Joplin*, rev. ed. (New York: Da Capo, 1991), p. 98.

"burning": Friedman, p. 64.

113   "Dorothy": Friedman, p. 63.

"Stop encouraging her": Amburn, p. 61.

"back to school": Amburn, p. 62.

"women's business suits": Ibid.

114   "didn't know what the hell": Interview with Don Sanders.

"Jean Ritchie falsetto": Amburn, p. 61.

"She had a true chameleon's voice": Dave Harmon, "Janis Joplin: At the University and Beyond," *Daily Texan*, Apr. 27, 1989, p. 10.

115   Red Dog Saloon: My account is drawn from Travus T. Hipp, "Legend of the Red Dog Saloon," *Edging West*, June/July 1995, p. 20; Mike Sion, "Capturing the Life and Times of the Red Dog Saloon," *Reno Gazette-Journal*, Mar. 17, 1994, 1E; Perry; Selvin; and interviews with Bob Cohen, George Hunter, and Alton Kelley.

116   "playing their tambourines": Interview with Ray Anderson.

"managed to appear": Slick, p. 54.

"Red Dog was to be modeled": Hipp, p. 20. Laughlin goes by the name Travus T. Hipp.

117   "was kind of poetic": Interview with Jim Haynie. All subsequent quotations are from this interview.

"master of the mystic arts": Perry, p. 29.

"astonished": Perry, p. 30.

"They can't bust us all": Selvin, p. 28. John Cipollina's reaction is noted in Selvin, p. 27.

"certainty of the birth": Slick, p. 56.

Ralph Gleason raved: Perry, p. 31.

118   "the American Liverpool": John Glatt, *Rage and Roll: Bill Graham and the Selling of Rock* (New York: Carol Publishing Group, 1993), p. 31.

"blew us right out of the water": Glatt, 32. Kelley confirmed this account in his interview with me, and Chet Helms backs up Kelley's claim. How

Graham came to hear about the Fillmore Auditorium is a matter of some dispute. Ronny Davis of the Mime Troupe claims he told Graham about the Fillmore, but Graham says Ralph Gleason told him about it (see Graham and Greenfield, pp. 128–29).

"towering cultural events": Graham and Greenfield, p. 125.

"cultural revolution": Graham and Greenfield, p. 124.

119   "this fucking line": Graham and Greenfield, p. 123.

"absolute art serfs": Peter Coyote, quoted in Graham and Greenfield, p. 118.

"stealing and swindling": Glatt, p. 25.

"gleam": Graham and Greenfield, p. 199.

"Look, I get up early": Glatt, p. 44. My account of the ill-fated partnership is also based on Graham and Greenfield, pp. 144–49 and my interview with Helms.

"Fuck It Academy of Dance": Graham and Greenfield, p. 148.

120   "pop plebes": Graham and Greenfield, p. 237.

"taking the ticket money": Graham and Greenfield, p. 190.

"like doing business": Graham and Greenfield, p. 200.

121   "I never understood": Glatt, p. 50.

"Bill's profits were enormous": Glatt, p. 49.

"Money": Graham and Greenfield, p. 199.

"all these airheads": Graham and Greenfield, p. 190.

"It *would* take": Interview with Alton Kelley. The artist in question prefers to remain anonymous.

"Just for the sake": Didion, pp. 103–04.

122   complimentary passes: Perry, p. 62.

"work off the top": Interview with Bob Simmons.

jam sessions: Details of the jams are drawn from my interviews with Peter Albin and Chet Helms. Albin recalls the price of admission as seventy-five cents; Chet remembers it as fifty.

123   Big Brother and the Holding Company: My account of the band's earliest days relies heavily on my interview with Peter Albin, the "memory" of Big Brother.

"1984, monopoly capitalism": Perry, p. 37.

"Oh wow, could you get busted": Ibid.

"all very amateurish": Interview with Sam Andrew. All subsequent quotations are from this interview unless otherwise noted.

124   "with a stethoscope taped": Selvin, p. 36.

"sort of walking down the street": Interview with Richard Hundgen.

"script doctor": James Gurley denies Nancy ever worked for such a doctor.

page

125   "a bunch of choppy bits": Selvin, p. 37.

     "had been hyping the group": The account is from Slick, pp. 88–89.

126   "a vibe of success": Slick, p. 55.

127   "sheets of sound": Joe Goldberg, liner notes to *Lush Life*, by John Coltrane, Prestige, 1987. The album was recorded live in 1957 and 1958.

     "logicless exploration": Perry, p. 71.

     "prime characteristics": Slick, p. 52.

128   "right off": Interview with James Gurley. All subsequent quotations are from this interview unless otherwise noted.

     "give too strange an aura": Amburn, p. 65.

     "she was strange": Amburn, p. 72.

129   Tommy Hall: For Hall's reluctance to include Janis, I have drawn on my interview with him.

     "didn't simply sing": Bill Bentley, liner notes, *Where the Pyramid Meets the Eye*, Sire Records, 1990. See also Chernikowski's *Austin Chronicle* article.

     "That's what I wanna do": Interview with Travis Rivers.

130   "been fucked into being": Dalton, p. 98.

     "beautiful": Friedman, p. 68, and Amburn, p. 68.

     "making Janis think": Interview with Jim Langdon.

     "Without your influence": Joplin, p. 142.

     "Mr. Big": Joplin, p. 146.

5 · BIG BROTHERIZED

page

132   "He was joking": Seidemann's comment was taken literally by another writer, but he says he was making a joke.

     Chet Helms: For Helms's reaction and that of Stanley Mouse, see Ellis Amburn, *Pearl: The Obsessions and Passions of Janis Joplin* (New York: Warner Books, 1992), p. 73.

133   "We knew we were going": Les Kippel and Robert Bromberg, "Big Brother Speaks: An Interview with Peter Albin," *Relix*, vol. 19, no. 5.

     "in space city": David Dalton, *Piece of My Heart: A Portrait of Janis Joplin*, rev. ed. (New York: Da Capo, 1991), p. 99.

     She had never been: Sam Andrew, "Recollections of Janis," *Blues Revue*, no. 17, p. 35.

     "I sang blues": Dalton, p. 99.

page

It's no accident: On the receptiveness of Austinites to Dylan's electric set, see the account in Levon Helm with Stephen Davis, *This Wheel's on Fire: The Story of Levon Helm and the Band* (New York: William Morrow, 1993), p. 137. Stephanie Chernikowski alerted me to this passage.

"I can't exaggerate": Andrew, p. 35.

"a tape on fast forward": Amburn, pp. 72–73.

134   Janis and the band rehearsed: Kippel and Bromberg.

"insane, free-jazz": Andrew, p. 35.

"I didn't have any hip clothes": Dalton, p. 99.

"It was nearly impossible": Darby Slick, *Don't You Want Somebody to Love: Reflections on the San Francisco Sound* (Berkeley: SLG Books, 1991), p. 97.

135   "stood still": Myra Friedman, *Buried Alive: The Biography of Janis Joplin* (New York: Harmony, 1992), p. 74.

"big open notes": Richard Goldstein, *Goldstein's Greatest Hits* (Englewood Cliffs, NJ: Prentice-Hall, 1970), p. 55.

"You can't sing like that": Friedman, p. 74.

She saw a dermatologist: Janis refers to this in a letter home to her family in the fall of 1966 (Laura Joplin, *Love, Janis* [New York: Villard Books, 1992], p. 175).

136   When Redding played the Fillmore: Bill Graham and Robert Greenfield, *Bill Graham Presents: My Life inside Rock and Out* (New York: Doubleday, 1992), p. 174.

"absorbed Redding's every syllable": Andrew, p. 38.

"visible": Janis, quoted in Dalton, p. 117.

"I started singing rhythmically": Goldstein, p. 55.

"It was the hippie version": Amburn, p. 84.

"for hours into the night": Andrew, p. 34.

137   "The Big Brother scene began with speed": Chet Helms insists that speed entered the band a bit later, through Sam Andrew's girlfriend, Rita.

"a maniac with needles": Amburn, p. 87.

139   sharing an apartment: Details of Janis's relationship with Travis Rivers are drawn from my interview with him.

140   "a couple of desperadoes": Amburn, p. 72.

"What an embarrassing situation": Amburn, p. 80.

141   "the hippie ethic of freedom": Amburn, p. 87.

"Boy, am I turned on": Amburn, p. 78. Dave identifies Jae as the woman in question.

"dirty, faded, frayed jeans": Peggy Caserta (as told to Dan Knapp), *Going Down with Janis* (Secaucus: Lyle Stuart, 1973), p. 43.

page

"as if they were made": Ibid.

142   "What is it": Ibid.

Altogether, Peggy was not: Details of Peggy's life are taken from my interview with her and from her book.

"super-straight little": Caserta, p. 102.

143   "buddies": Joan Baez, *And a Voice to Sing With: A Memoir* (New York: New American Library, 1987), p. 78.

"Well, Peggy's lover": Amburn, p. 103.

Joe scrupulously avoided it: For Joe's sharing songwriting credit and his preference for anonymity, I have drawn on my interview with Bill Belmont.

145   "what everybody wanted": Amburn, p. 85.

"Janis would carry": Interview with John Morris. All subsequent quotations are from this interview.

146   "for its nerve calming properties": Slick, p. 97.

"alcydelic": Joel Selvin, *Summer of Love* (New York: Penguin, 1994), p. 102.

"needed a couple of shots": Amburn, p. 94.

"I could've had two zithers": Fred Goodman, *The Mansion on the Hill* (New York: Times Books), 1997, p. 30.

147   A year later: On the light-show artists' strike, see Charles Perry, *The Haight-Ashbury: A History* (New York: Random House, 1984), p. 287.

"The musicians barely did anything": Interview with Joshua White. All subsequent quotations are from this interview unless otherwise noted.

"took the heat off": Interview with Glenn McKay. All subsequent quotations are from this interview.

148   "You were lucky": Interview with Lyndall Erb.

"some of my friends": Allen Katzman, ed., *Our Time: Interviews from the East Village Other* (New York: Dial Press, 1972), p. 208.

149   "Fuck that": Bill Graham and Robert Greenfield, *Bill Graham Presents: My Life inside Rock and Out* (New York: Doubleday, 1992), p. 168.

"lock this band down": Chet Helms, quoted in Amburn, p. 91.

Outraged, Chet declared: Peter Albin, and Selvin, p. 73. Details of the band's relationship to Chet are drawn from my interviews with Helms, Albin, and Getz.

"farther and farther out": Joplin, p. 162.

150   "He's gonna make me a star!": Friedman, p. 79.

"Cadillac and a house": Interview with Peter Albin. My account is drawn from interviews with Albin and Getz, as well as from Janis's letters home, quoted in Laura Joplin's book.

"schoolmarmish quality": Amburn, p. 90.

151   "poor black farmhand": Bob Spitz, *Dylan: A Biography* (McGraw-Hill, 1989), p. 301. According to Joe Boyd, the production manager at the 1965 Newport Folk Festival, Lomax was against "white boys doing the blues" (Clinton Heylin, *Bob Dylan: Behind the Shades* [New York: Summit, 1991], p. 138).

"could barely play": Steve Hochman, "Steve Miller," *Rolling Stone*, Sept. 2, 1993, p. 22.

"full frontal assault": Interview with Sam Andrew.

"This chick had this hair": Friedman, p. 79.

152   "this half-naked chick": Joplin, p. 166.

"the master": Andrew, p. 36.

"ample opportunity": Ibid.

153   "was afraid of the needle": Amburn, p. 96.

the most marketable part: In a letter to her parents, Janis bragged of Shad's opinion (Joplin, p. 168).

154   The Fish's David Cohen: Interview with Bill Belmont.

"Fuck you, man": Amburn, p. 97.

"whole life": Joplin, p. 202.

155   Journalists were used to covering: This is Dave Getz's observation.

"we share everything": Joplin, p. 190.

156   Although the poster: According to popular legend, Big Brother did play, but Peter Albin insists all those accounts are false.

157   "life" drugs: On the distinction between "life" drugs and "death" drugs, see Hunter Thompson's "The 'Hashbury' Is the Capital of the Hippies," *New York Times Magazine*, May 14, 1967, p. 29 and pp. 120–24, and Warren Hinckle's "A Social History of the Hippies," *Ramparts*, Mar. 1967, reprinted in Gerald Howard, ed., *The Sixties: The Art, Attitudes, Politics, and Media of Our Most Explosive Decade* (New York: Pocket Books, 1982), pp. 207–32. These two influential essays claim hippies made a different distinction: between "head" drugs and "body" drugs. Both writers categorize speed as a "head" drug, as opposed to a bad "body" drug (Thompson, p. 122; Hinckle, p. 217). Chet Helms maintains, though, that both Thompson and Hinckle were outsiders whose knowledge of the scene was superficial. Speed, Helms insists, was not regarded as a benign drug.

"We're in the same business": Hinckle, p. 213.

Janis insisted that the cover: Correspondence, Robert Crumb.

"She could handle them": Amburn, p. 110.

158   The poet Michael McClure: Interview with Michael McClure conducted

page

by Richard Ogar in 1968–69, Manuscript Collection, Bancroft Library, University of California, Berkeley.

"Their method of clearing": Interview with Bruce Barthol.

159   "to be the unconscious": Didion, "Slouching towards Bethlehem," in *Slouching towards Bethlehem* (New York: Dell, 1968), p. 113.

160   "That's when we were all together": Amburn, p. 81.

"real show biz": Joplin, p. 158.

"celebrity": Joplin, p. 192.

6 · HOPE AND HYPE IN MONTEREY

page

161   "Monterey is very groovy": *The History of Rock 'n' Roll: Plugging In*, Warner Brothers video, 13853. My account of Monterey Pop is drawn primarily from Ed Ward, Geoffrey Stokes, and Ken Tucker, *Rock of Ages: The* Rolling Stone *History of Rock & Roll* (New York: Simon & Schuster, 1986); Robert Christgau, *Any Old Way You Choose It: Rock and Other Pop Music, 1967–1973* (Baltimore: Penguin Books, 1973); Bill Graham and Robert Greenfield, *Bill Graham Presents: My Life inside Rock and Out* (New York: Doubleday, 1992).

"Hippie heaven": Ward et al., p. 375.

"There are no hippies": Christgau, p. 14.

"You could get food": Graham and Greenfield, p. 189.

162   "Everywhere you looked": Robert and Joanalee Hurwitt, "Pops Groove, Cry for More," *Berkeley Barb,* June 23–29, 1967, p. 3.

"Oh, these fucking hippies": Graham and Greenfield, p. 176.

"cultural revolution": Redding's manager, Phil Walden, the speaker here, was describing the experience of Redding and other "black guys from the South" who hadn't spent any time around hippies.

"on the far fringes": Christgau, p. 15.

"music mart": Ward et al., p. 374.

"L.A. hurts our eyes": Richard Goldstein, *Goldstein's Greatest Hits* (Englewood Cliffs, NJ: Prentice-Hall, 1970), p. 118.

"Hollywood sharpies": The phrase is used by Michelle Phillips in her autobiography, *California Dreamin': The True Story of the Mamas and the Papas* (New York: Warner Books, 1986), p. 141.

163 "to hijack and market": John Glatt, *Rage and Roll: Bill Graham and the Selling of Rock* (New York: Carol Publishing Group, 1993), p. 68.

"were coattailing a bunch of L.A. acts": Graham and Greenfield, p. 193.

"act like hippies": Christgau, p. 19.

"the scum of Hollywood": Derek Taylor, quoted in Graham and Greenfield, p. 188.

164 "vengeance": Charles Shaar Murray, *Crosstown Traffic: Jimi Hendrix and the Post-War Rock 'n' Roll Revolution* (New York: St. Martin's, 1989), p. 91.

"You've taken this": Ibid.

"revenge of the R & B sideman": Nelson George, *The Death of Rhythm and Blues* (New York: Plume, 1988), p. 109.

"out-Visigoth": Murray, p. 1.

"love crowd": Phil Walden, Redding's manager, suggested that Redding come up with a rap about the "love crowd," as the audience at Monterey was known that weekend. Together they wrote the "recitation" Redding delivered (see Graham and Greenfield, p. 191).

"Otis was king": Hurwitt, p. 10.

"the phrase 'almost as bad as Laura Nyro' ": Fred Goodman, *The Mansion on the Hill* (New York: Times Books, 1997), p. 123. Despite a recent article (Deborah Sontag, "An Enigma Wrapped in Songs," *New York Times,* Oct. 26, 1997) suggesting that the uncut film of Monterey Pop proves Nyro was a hit at the festival, other evidence doesn't support the claim. Nyro may not have been booed off the stage as some have alleged, but neither was she embraced by the crowd. According to Fred Goodman, Nyro's manager, Artie Mogull, was "enraged that Nyro had embarrassed him" in front of so many industry heavyweights. Clive Davis of Columbia Records considered her performance "amateurish and overdramatic" (Clive Davis with James Willwerth, *Clive: Inside the Record Business* [New York: William Morrow, 1975], p. 98). Michelle Phillips of the Mamas and the Papas felt so bad for Nyro that she whisked her away in her limo for some weed and beer (M. Phillips, p. 147). Peter Albin says Nyro turned in not a bad performance but, rather, a "pretentious" one. Nyro went on to make some of the most adventurous and infectious pop music of the period.

165 they were not yet one of the city's top draws: Michael Lydon, "Every Moment She Is What She Feels," *New York Times Magazine,* Feb. 23, 1969, p. 43.

Janis appeared onstage: Charles Perry, *The Haight-Ashbury: A History* (New York: Random House, 1984), p. 208.

page

"Janis was so nervous": John Phillips, liner notes, Monterey Pop boxed set, Rhino Records, 1997.

"Where did she come from?": Quoted in Sam Andrew, "Recollections of Janis," *Blues Revue,* no. 17, p. 36.

"the scene-stealer": John Phillips, *An Autobiography* (New York: Dolphin Books, 1986), p. 178.

"terrible energy": Lydon, p. 39.

"her voice and body hurled": Nat Hentoff, "We Look at Our Parents and . . ." *New York Times,* Apr. 21, 1968, p. 17.

"get back": Quoted in Simon Frith, *Performing Rites: On the Value of Popular Music* (Cambridge: Harvard University Press, 1996), p. 203.

"it's about feeling things": Goldstein, p. 56.

166 "When I sing": Lydon, p. 43.

"the fierceness of joy": Lydon, p. 39.

"got a reaction": Christgau, p. 24.

"choked up": Davis, p. 77.

"By marshalling an array": Quoted in Frith, p. 203.

"It's real": *Janis: The Way She Was,* MCA Home Video, 1975.

167 "Listen, you guys": Ellis Amburn, *Pearl: The Obsessions and Passions of Janis Joplin* (New York: Warner Books, 1992), p. 127.

"Green Julius": Ibid, p. 99.

motorcycle accident: At the time, Dylan's accident was characterized by the press as serious. Several people who were close to Dylan now claim it was minor (see Goodman, p. 102).

"totally frantic": Interview with Sally Grossman. All subsequent quotations are from this interview.

"Julius Karpen doesn't know it": Joel Selvin, *Summer of Love* (New York: Penguin, 1994), p. 134.

"She pronounced it 'lame' ": Andrew, p. 36.

168 "Big Brother's Boobs": R. E. Maxon, *L.A. Free Press,* July 19, 1968, p. 32.

"To hear Janis sing": Goldstein, p. 57.

"to keep them down": Hentoff, p. 19.

"be like everybody else": Ibid.

"one of the highest points": Laura Joplin, *Love, Janis* (New York: Villard Books, 1992), p. 241.

169 "sanguine goofiness": Christgau, p. 25.

"Those were real flower children": Joplin, p. 241.

"there was truly an absence": Joplin, p. 195.

"it wasn't about money": Art Garfunkel, liner notes, Monterey Pop boxed set, Rhino Records, 1997.

"check-book A&R": Goodman, p. 77.

"the band with the incredible chick singer": Lydon, p. 96.

"two-thirds Willie Mae Thornton": Christgau, p. 24.

170 "berserk with ecstasy": Interview with Myra Friedman. All subsequent quotations are from this interview unless otherwise noted.

"the creative turning point": Fredric Dannen, *Hit Men* (New York: Vintage Books, 1991), p. 75. My account of Clive Davis and Columbia Records draws on both Dannen and Goodman.

"smells but sells": Goodman, p. 52.

"the label of Robert Goulet": Dannen, p. 98.

"Let me read": Dannen p. 66.

171 "I'll leave you the books": Joplin, p. 205.

"a real businessman": According to John Morris, who would manage Bill Graham's Fillmore East in New York sometime during the summer or fall of 1967, Janis tried to convince Graham to manage Big Brother, but he declined. He could see, he explained to John, that managing Janis would be a full-time proposition (interview with John Morris).

"were just so jazzed": Myra Friedman, *Buried Alive: The Biography of Janis Joplin* (New York: Harmony, 1992), p. 91.

172 the power manager: My account of Grossman draws on interviews with Elliot Mazer, John Simon, and Peter Yarrow; Fred Goodman's wonderful chapter on him; and Robert Shelton, *No Direction Home: The Life and Music of Bob Dylan* (New York: Penguin, 1986).

"native": Goodman, p. 96.

"the best grass": Goodman, p. 97.

"If it hadn't been for Albert": Goodman, p. 102.

"The Bear": Shelton, p. 142.

"son of a bitch": Levon Helm with Stephen Davis, *This Wheel's on Fire: The Story of Levon Helm and the Band* (New York: William Morrow, 1993), p. 293.

"seemed to enjoy saying no": Shelton, p. 144.

"You could see it": Goodman, p. 94.

173 "It was the most intimidating experience": Ibid.

"He had a loud air conditioner": Interview with Elliot Mazer. All subsequent quotations are from this interview unless otherwise noted.

"He could wait anyone out": Bob Krasnow, quoted in Goodman, p. 93.

page

"He'd enter into some kind": Ibid.

"a king-size cigarette": Shelton, p. 106.

There were only two managers: On Grossman's position in the world of folk music, see Shelton, pp. 142–44, and Bob Spitz, *Dylan: A Biography* (New York: McGraw-Hill, 1989), p. 176.

174   Albert was left-leaning, too: Interview with Mike Gray.

"a Cheshire cat": Shelton, 106.

"the show business principle": Eric von Schmidt and Jim Rooney, *Baby Let Me Follow You Down: The Illustrated Story of the Cambridge Folk Years*, 2nd ed. (Amherst: University of Massachusetts Press, 1994), p. 280.

"Because every time you talk": Goodman, p. 89.

"Albert was the first guy": Goodman, p. 86.

"would take as long": Stan Cornyn, quoted in Goodman, p. 89.

"greatest achievement": Goodman, p. 89.

Mary Travers: Shelton, p. 144.

Publishing royalties: Goodman, pp. 103–05.

"marvelous, wonderful": Interview with Odetta. All subsequent quotations are from this interview.

"a strong one-way street": Goodman, p. 86.

"isolate the star": Helm, p. 210.

"brutally honest": Shelton, p. 144.

176   "There would never have been": Clinton Heylin, *Bob Dylan: Behind the Shades* (New York: Summit, 1991), p. 72.

"had to swallow the rest": Davis, p. 79.

When the band asked: Amburn, p. 153, and interview with Dave Getz.

177    $2,500 a night: Joplin, p. 197.

"Make it a hundred thousand": Selvin, p. 137.

"If I can't make you that": Joplin, 209.

"so low-key": Amburn, p. 153.

"Don't ever trust me": Friedman, p. 92.

"One thing": Selvin, p. 138.

"I've seen terrible things": Friedman, p. 92.

Albert never revealed: On his wife's death from an OD, see Goodman, p. 105.

178   "Oh, I need a mother": Interview with Linda Gravenites.

"did everything Janis didn't": Amburn, p. 146.

"We'd walk down Haight Street": Amburn, p. 147.

"And because she was a singer": Interview with Stanley Mouse. All subsequent quotations are from this interview.

page

179   Supposedly, Janis had sex: Both Linda Gravenites and Sunshine insist Janis didn't go to bed with Hendrix, but Peter Albin says she did.

       "She hated Jim Morrison": Interview with Todd Schiffman.

       "A piece of work": Interview with Linda Bacon.

180   "I used to ask guys": Dalton, p. 161.

181   "I don't ever remember hurting": Amburn, p. 173.

       Janis had an abortion: Interviews with Linda Gravenites and Todd Schiffman; Joplin, p. 213.

       "in terrible, agonizing pain": Interview with Todd Schiffman. All subsequent quotations are from this interview.

182   "so insecure": Joplin, p. 191.

       "I'm on an audience trip": Joplin, p. 179.

       "Like most girls": Dalton, pp. 119–20.

183   "It hardly shows, Mother": Joplin, p. 203. When Big Brother appeared on San Francisco TV station KQED in the spring of 1967, Janis signed off provocatively by saying, "Hi, Mom," in a sullen, fuck-you way.

       "Isn't it wonderful?": My account of the family's visit is drawn from Joplin, p. 204.

184   "happy accident": Christgau, p. 121.

       In 1962, record sales totaled $500 million: Goodman, p. xi.

185   "asshole": Frank Barsalona, quoted in Glatt, p. 98.

       "I just want to say": Goodman, p. 43.

       "But the Man Can't Bust Our Music": See Abe Peck, *Uncovering the Sixties: The Life and Times of the Underground Press* (New York: Pantheon, 1985), p. 164.

       "as a person": Dannen, p. 75.

       " 'I went to the Monterey Pop Festival' ": Dannen, p. 77.

186   " 'a highly commercial rock allegory' ": Christgau, p. 52.

       "It looked psychedelic": Cynthia Heimel, *If You Can't Live without Me, Why Aren't You Dead Yet?* (New York: HarperCollins, 1992), p. 187.

       "If the industry is gonna want us": Goldstein, p. 119.

       "turned into who can buy": Ben Fong-Torres with Nick Gravenites, "The Saddest Story in the World," *Rolling Stone*, Oct. 29, 1970, p. 12.

187   "a lot of the bands": Jack McDonough, *San Francisco Rock* (San Francisco: Chronicle Books, 1985), p. 22.

       "everyone had their own fiefdoms": Ibid.

       "tragedy . . . that the musicians": Ibid.

       "the high priests of our culture": Lipsitz, "Who'll Stop the Rain," unpublished ms., p. 36.

page

among the first rock 'n' roll stars: This is Raechel Donahue's somewhat tongue-in-cheek observation (interview).

"Oh man, that was the best hustle": Lydon, p. 43. As for the corporate suits at Southern Comfort, she wondered, "How could anybody in their right mind want *me* for their image?" It was Grossman who thought "it looked a lot better for Janis to have some kind of 'gift' other than a check," says Myra Friedman. She thinks Grossman arranged for Janis to purchase her famous lynx coat from his cousin, who was in the fur business in Chicago.

"swallowed by the voracious maw": Heimel, p. 188.

"The girls were in ruffled dresses": Graham and Greenfield, p. 166.

188 "Kids from the Midwest": Dalton, p. 164.

"People aren't supposed": Lydon, p. 94.

Council for the Summer of Love: For details, see Charles Perry, *The Haight-Ashbury: A History* (New York: Random House, 1984), p. 171.

189 In a one-month period: Jeff Jassen, "What Price Love?" *Berkeley Barb*, May 5–11, 1967, p. 5.

Hippie Hop Tour: Perry, p. 171.

Pete Townshend visited the Haight: Graham and Greenfield, p. 190.

"Some of the musicians": R. G. Davis, *The San Francisco Mime Troupe* (Palo Alto: Ramparts, 1975), 80.

"tighter and stranger": Graham and Greenfield, p. 207.

"Haight Street was lined": Don McNeil, *Moving through Here* (New York: Knopf, 1970), p. 136.

"griseous and filthy": Ed Sanders, *The Family* (New York: Avon Books, 1972), p. 40.

"There was a six month period": Quoted in Heimel, p. 187.

190 710 Ashbury Street: For the Dead bust, see Perry, p. 242.

"Uh oh, the street people": Interview with Raechel Donahue.

"outpost of Nirvana": Christgau, p. 254.

"Ain't nothing": Joplin, p. 241.

"I've always believed": Ibid.

7 · BYE, BYE BABY

page

191 "How do you want us": Myra Friedman, *Buried Alive: The Biography of Janis Joplin* (New York: Harmony, 1992), p. 104.

"awful silence": Friedman, p. 105.

"We didn't know": Ellis Amburn, *Pearl: The Obsessions and Passions of Janis Joplin* (New York: Warner Books, 1992), p. 160.

"I mean, what kind of image": Friedman, p. 105.

"bunch of beaded musicians": Friedman, p. 106.

192   "What they were trying": Amburn, p. 160.

change in billing: The change didn't happen overnight or consistently throughout the country. In their hometown of San Francisco, the band continued to be called Big Brother, but elsewhere theater marquees and newspaper ads began singling out Janis.

Myra Friedman vigorously denies: Interview with Myra Friedman.

From this point on: Interviews with Dave Getz and John Cooke.

"Can you dig it?": Amburn, p. 162.

"New York in that era": Interview with Bruce Barthol. All subsequent quotations are from this interview.

193   "She gave him an earful": Amburn, p. 169.

"ambition, pressure, and pushiness": Friedman, p. xiv.

"seemed to have made us": Nat Hentoff, "We Look at Our Parents and . . ." *New York Times,* Apr. 21, 1968, p. 19.

"Nobody had road managers": Interview with John Cooke. All subsequent quotations are from this interview unless otherwise noted. Cooke is joking here, but it is true that road managing was an alien concept in the world of folk music until Albert introduced the practice.

194   the band members' weekly draw: Within six months Cooke's weekly salary would be bumped up to two hundred dollars. Of course, band members earned money over and beyond the weekly draw. By the end of 1968, Big Brother's account held roughly fifty thousand dollars, which was split five ways, according to Dave Getz.

"Man, can you imagine": Friedman, p. 275.

195   "magnetism": Friedman, p. 106.

"just about the phoniest front": This characterization and the others of Janis and herself are from Friedman, pp. 123–24.

"Vatican": Friedman, p. 99.

"groans": The various expressions of exasperation appear in Friedman, on pp. 120, 135, 139, 141, 191, 253, and 261.

196   "big time": Phil Baratta, quoted in Bill Graham and Robert Greenfield, *Bill Graham Presents: My Life inside Rock and Out* (New York: Doubleday, 1992), p. 226.

"Do I look old?": Friedman, p. 107.

page

"We're just a sloppy group": Ibid.

"I go whoooosh": David Dalton, *Piece of My Heart: A Portrait of Janis Joplin*, rev. ed. (New York: Da Capo, 1991), p. 187.

"Never before": Friedman, p. 108.

197   "the click in his eyes": Graham and Greenfield, p. 229.

"like a big kid squealing": Neil Louison, "Priming the Pump," in Robert Somma, ed., *No One Waved Good-bye* (New York: Outerbridge & Dienstfrey, 1971), p. 39.

"If I turn out": Friedman, p. 124.

"her sitting at a bar alone": Louison, p. 39.

198   "What is this crap?" Amburn, p. 158.

"She's fantastic!": Friedman, p. 109.

"as remarkable a new pop-music talent": Robert Shelton, "Janis Joplin Is Climbing Fast in the Heady Rock Firmament," *New York Times,* Feb. 19, 1968, p. 51.

"Ahhh! Gettin' drunk": All the quotations regarding the press party are from Friedman, pp. 113–14.

199   "very intent": Interview with Myra Friedman.

"Listen": Interview with Myra Friedman.

"Had I *wanted* to 'hype' her": Friedman, p. 118.

she had thanked Ralph Gleason: On Janis's positive reaction to his pan, see Ralph Gleason, "Perspectives: Another Candle Blown Out," *Rolling Stone,* Oct. 29, 1970, p. 16. Shortly after the publication of Gleason's review criticizing the Mainstream record as a "bad representation" of the band's sound, Janis told him, "Hey, man, thanks for what you said about our shitty record."

200   "Singers usually had": Interview with John Simon. All subsequent quotations are from this interview unless otherwise noted.

"on the other side of society": "Janis Joplin, New Shout," *Vogue,* May 2, 1968, p. 210.

"social phenomonemone": Linda Gravenites, quoted in Laura Joplin, *Love, Janis* (New York: Villard Books, 1992), p. 234.

"wizard with words": Friedman, p. 115.

"At that time to say": Interview with Myra Friedman.

falling in love twenty times": Friedman, p. 136.

"little resentments stewed": Joplin, p. 241.

"in some ways": Friedman, p. 120.

"Maybe you don't like the story": Ibid.

201   "Tell him Janis": Interview with Richard Hundgen.

page

"A wonderful producer": Interview with Fred Catero. All subsequent quotations are from this interview.

202   "most of the bands we signed": Levon Helm with Stephen Davis, *This Wheel's on Fire: The Story of Levon Helm and the Band* (New York: William Morrow, 1993), p. 162.

"two-sevenths of your royalties": Simon says he signed for a standard 3 percent.

"with its flaming guitars": Helm, p. 166.

If the strength of San Francisco's sound was "live": Richard Goldstein, *Goldstein's Greatest Hits* (Englewood Cliffs, NJ: Prentice-Hall, 1970), p. 117.

205   Simon insisted: Legend has it that, in an effort to obtain usable takes, Simon recorded over two hundred tapes, but both Simon and Catero deny that they recorded anywhere near that number. Maybe twenty-five reels, ventures Catero.

"What you hear": *Janis: The Way She Was,* MCA Home Video, 1975. The footage was Pennebaker's, but he did not make this documentary.

"John has more skill": Friedman, p. 120.

"We're passionate": Nat Hentoff, p. 19.

206   In April: According to the liner notes for the 1993 Janis Joplin boxed set, the band was recording in L.A. on April 12, the day of their Winterland show in San Francisco. In June, however, Janis told her parents that the band had just finished a month's worth of recording in L.A. According to the band's itinerary, the L.A. recording began on April 29 (see John Cooke, *Janis Joplin: A Performance Diary* [Petaluma, CA: Acid Tests Productions, 1997]).

"they couldn't make music": Friedman, p. 119.

"branded as an undesirable group": Joe Smith of Warner Brothers, quoted in Joel Selvin, *Summer of Love* (New York: Penguin, 1994), p. 155.

"endless jams": Interview with Bruce Barthol.

"Most people didn't really": Jack McDonough, *San Francisco Rock* (San Francisco: Chronicle Books, 1985), p. 24.

207   "amplify her coarseness": Friedman, p. 131.

"She was planning out": Friedman, pp. 130–31.

208   "feels things": Hentoff, p. 19.

The *Cheap Thrills* version of "Ball and Chain": Peter Albin and Dave Getz think this live version is from the band's Fillmore and Winterland shows during the weekend of April 11, 1968. If so, John Simon may have added some "live effects" to the one truly live song on the album. The two screams that follow James's opening guitar solo, for example, are not audible on the tapes from those shows. Alternatively, the engineers who worked on these tapes for the 1998 Columbia CD *Janis Joplin with Big Brother and the Holding Company Live at Winterland 1968* may have deleted the shouts.

209   Simon's version included "Harry": Interview with Dave Getz.

"Frank Zappa–like song": Interview with Dave Getz.

"mopping up": Interview with Elliot Mazer.

"trying to figure out": Friedman, p. 131.

210   "had something": Amburn, p. 169.

He knew all along: Fred Catero, by contrast, had no idea how the album would do and thinks that most of those working on the album were also uncertain. He speculates that Simon might have kept his name off the album because he was worried that such a rough-sounding album might tarnish his reputation.

"was as good as the band": Review of *Cheap Thrills*, *Rolling Stone*, Sept. 14, 1968, p. 21.

For Big Brother the kicker: Interview with Dave Getz.

"work hard enough": Joplin, p. 162.

211   "passionate and sloppy": "Singers: Passionate and Sloppy," *Time,* Aug. 9, 1968.

"learning to control success": Hentoff, p. 19.

"hot shit": Friedman, p. 116. Janis used this phrase in a letter to Linda Gravenites.

"The reviews were relentless": Clive Davis with James Willwerth, *Clive: Inside the Record Business* (New York: William Morrow, 1975), p. 86.

212   "dog shit": Ben Fong-Torres with Nick Gravenites, "The Saddest Story in the World," *Rolling Stone,* Oct. 29, 1970, p. 12.

"too full of soul": Larry Kopp, "Janis Joplin Too Full of Soul for Holding Company Partners," *L.A. Free Press,* Sept. 29–Oct. 5, 1967.

"messy and a general musical disgrace": Friedman, p. 129.

"lots of disparaging comments": Interview with Lee Housekeeper.

"Big Brother is just a wretched": "The *Rolling Stone* Interview: Michael Bloomfield, Part II," Apr. 27, 1968, p. 11.

"that Big Brother could grow": Davis, p. 87.

213   "some time away from the band": Selvin, p. 164.

"charitable": Jon Landau, "The Newport Folk Festival," *Rolling Stone,* Aug. 24, 1968, p. 17.

Landau had never taken to Big Brother: Fred Goodman, *The Mansion on the Hill* (New York: Times Books, 1997), p. 19.

page

214 "band in back of Janis": Vince Aletti, "Janis," *Rat,* Aug. 9–22, 1968, p. 19.

"at least Joplin": Vince Aletti, "Hendrix/Joplin at the Bowl," *Rat,* Sept. 6–19, 1968, p. 18.

"you gonna play the wrong chord": *Joplin in Concert,* CD, Sony Music, 1972.

"goony": Dalton, p. 234.

"What drove me crazy": Lydon, p. 48. The subsequent quotations of Janis in this paragraph are from here as well.

215 "Janis was the best musician": Lydon, p. 49.

"I wasn't doing anything": Dalton, p. 135.

Her decision to quit: On Janis's difficulty in leaving Big Brother, I've also relied on interviews with Milan Melvin and Peggy Caserta.

"It was a very sad thing": Lydon, p. 48.

"I want to play with horns": Amburn, p. 164. Amburn gives the impression that Janis made this declaration in March or April, but Sam says it occurred in September when the band appeared on the TV show *Hollywood Palace.* Sam can't remember for sure when Janis first suggested she might leave the group, but he thinks it was probably that June.

216 "I don't think it's possible": Dalton, p. 174.

Albert had upped their weekly draw: The money began kicking in for the guys, too, beginning in early 1969. "We got about $30,000 each in the first quarter of 1969," Dave recalls. "And we made good money—between $25,000 and $40,000—through 1972. I thought I'd never have to work again." Still, once Janis left Big Brother, her income skyrocketed. Whereas Janis and Big Brother typically earned $7,000 to $10,000—split five ways—for two nights at one of Graham's venues, a single gig less than one year later would bring Janis, as a solo artist, between $25,000 and $30,000 (interviews with Dave Getz and Peter Albin, Friedman, p. 152).

217 "a whole new life for the band": Amburn, p. 182.

Janis had vacillated: Janis told David Dalton, "Sam and I sang very well together. And I thought we could really do well together" (Dalton, p. 174). Sam suspects Janis wanted some continuity, as well.

Peggy Caserta echoes the feelings: In the Bay Area it was widely assumed that Janis left the band because she was being pressured by Albert and by Clive Davis. The gossip column of the September 28, 1968, issue of *Rolling Stone* includes the following item: "Last week we incorrectly attributed the possibility of Janis leaving the band to the current plans of her manager and her record company. According to Janis and all others involved, this is incorrect. We stand corrected."

page

"Albert would say": Joplin, p. 236.

Indeed, Janis bragged: Joplin, p. 237.

218   "I could tell": Davis, p. 86.

"amicable": Friedman, p. 131.

"Even being in the same room": Lydon, p. 49.

"Man, he called me a dog": Selvin, p. 192.

219   "solidest guy": Dalton, p. 171.

"I was just trying to be nice": Selvin, 193.

"You were just trying": Joplin, p. 240.

With the Hell's Angels' stamp of approval: According to Peter Albin, the San Francisco Angels got into trouble with other Angels for allowing the group to use their logo and the words "Approved by Hell's Angels Frisco" on the front cover of *Cheap Thrills*.

"Let's trash it, boys": Joplin, p. 228.

"always underrated": Robert Christgau, *Any Old Way You Choose It: Rock and Other Pop Music, 1967–1973* (Baltimore: Penguin Books, 1973), p. 76.

"one of the greats": Bill Fibben, "Reviews and Previews, *Great Speckled Bird*, Aug. 16–19, 1968, p. 10.

220   "does sound just like": Annie Fisher, "Riffs," *Village Voice*, Sept. 19, 1968, p. 44.

"a fair approximation": Review of *Cheap Thrills*, *Rolling Stone*, Sept. 14, 1968, p. 21.

"Janis Joplin has a good voice": Wilson Lindsey, "Sounds," *Fifth Estate*, Sept. 19–Oct. 2, 1968, p. 15.

"Every cut on the album": Bill Kloman, "The 50s Come Back," *New York Times*, Sept. 1, 1968, sec. 2, p. 18.

"star-maker machinery": Joni Mitchell, "Free Man in Paris," on *Court and Spark*, CD, Reprise Records, 1974.

221   "was a good foil": Ellen Willis, "Rock, Etc.," *New Yorker*, Mar. 15, 1969, p. 173.

In his 1972 review: Lester Bangs, "Try (Just a Little Bit Harder)," *Rolling Stone*, June 8, 1972, pp. 62, 64.

"rough anything-goes": Robert Christgau, "Consumer Guide," *Village Voice*, Dec. 21, 1993, p. 32.

222   "errant energy": Bangs, "Try (Just A Little Bit Harder)," *Rolling Stone*, August 27, 1987, p. 115.

Chet and his partners: Charles Perry, *The Haight-Ashbury: A History* (New York: Random House, 1984), p. 287.

page

"Janis, please": Bruce Steinberg, a photographer, recalled this detail in an interview with David Dalton shortly after Janis's death.

"seemed a failure": Michael Lydon, "Every Moment She Is What She Feels," *New York Times Magazine,* Feb. 23, 1969, p. 39. p. 48.

223   "rock and roll was a shitty place": Robert Christgau, "Are You Experienced? Bette Midler Sings Everything," *Village Voice,* Oct. 5, 1993, p. 71.

"very primitive attitudes": Interview with Tracy Nelson.

"That's the man": Interview with Bob Simmons.

"They sure laid a lot of shit": Dalton, p. 174.

"having our noses rubbed": Bangs, p. 62.

224   "That stuff made me famous!": Friedman, p. 121.

"bordering on brilliant": Friedman, p. 178. Danny Fields called her a "whizzer" (Danny Fields and Jeff Nesin, "Conversation," in Somma, p. 57).

"If you practice long enough": Joplin, p. 231.

225   "pizzazz and amplification": Friedman, p. 128.

"about me trying": Dalton, p. 175.

"unsettled mix": Lydon, p. 39.

"ballsy, funky": Dalton, p. 85.

"I can't relate to that": Dalton, pp. 120–21.

she was still complaining: Friedman, p. 138.

"the couple laughing": Dalton, p. 58.

226   "If so, please send": Joplin, p. 226.

227   "she couldn't sing at all": Friedman, p. 137. Peggy Caserta confirms Janis's insecurity about her singing.

"She looked too lonely": Lillian Roxon, "A Moment Too Soon," in Somma, p. 96.

228   "pay for everything": Robert Hilburn, "Joy for Janis Was Onstage Rush," reprinted in *Austin American Statesman,* Nov. 8, 1970.

"You don't see anything": "Rebirth of the Blues," *Newsweek,* May 26, 1969, p. 84.

"a chick laying": Friedman, p. 157.

"ludicrous": Kathleen Orloff, *Rock 'n' Roll Woman* (Los Angeles: Nash Publishing, 1974), p. 101.

"She was a little loaded": Graham and Greenfield, p. 205.

8 · LITTLE GIRL BLUE

page

229   "where it's at!": Stanley Booth, "The Memphis Debut of the Janis Joplin Revue," *Rolling Stone,* Feb. 1, 1969, p. 4.

Like Jimi Hendrix: For Stax's decision to invite Janis, I have drawn on my interview with Deanie Parker, the national publicity director for the label. For a loving and detailed account of southern soul music, including the history of Stax Records, see Peter Guralnick, *Sweet Soul Music: Rhythm and Blues and the Southern Dream of Freedom* (New York: Harper and Row, 1986). See also Nelson George's important book, *The Death of Rhythm and Blues* (New York: Plume, 1988).

230   "It was her constant fear": Myra Friedman, *Buried Alive: The Biography of Janis Joplin* (New York: Harmony, 1992, rev. ed.), p. 145.

"zebra-striped flannel jumpsuits": Booth, p. 4. The two surviving members of the Bar-Kays re-formed the group.

"It was the first sign": Ibid.

231   "At least they didn't throw things": Booth, p. 1.

"the significance of the military-industrial complex": David Dalton, *Piece of My Heart: A Portrait of Janis Joplin,* rev. ed. (New York: Da Capo, 1991), p. 22.

"Janis Joplin died in Memphis": Booth, p. 1.

"was sheer insanity": Ellis Amburn, *Pearl: The Obsessions and Passions of Janis Joplin* (New York: Warner Books, 1992), p. 190.

232   "traded off the black": Lou Reed, "Fallen Knights and Fallen Ladies," in Robert Somma, ed., *No One Waved Good-bye* (New York: Outerbridge & Dienstfrey, 1971), p. 88.

"big warm blanket": David Crosby and Carl Gottlieb, *Long Time Gone: The Autobiography of David Crosby* (New York: Dell, 1988), p. 120.

"I just want some fucking peace": Interview with Linda Gravenites.

"somethin' new": Friedman, p. 93.

233   "had to do was look": Amburn, p. 176.

"none of us were strung out": Laura Joplin, *Love, Janis* (New York: Villard Books, 1992), p. 233.

"adrenaline-raising": Joplin, p. 232.

"It didn't seem insane": Joplin, p. 233.

234   "abject boredom": Dalton, p. 134.

"it was the blues-singer mystique": Joplin, p. 233.

"Chemical soul": Interview with Tracy Nelson. All subsequent quotations are from this interview.

page

235   "Blues has something to do": "Rebirth of the Blues," *Newsweek,* May 26, 1969, p. 85.

Muddy Waters claimed: Interview with Tracy Nelson.

"I will always be indebted": Interview with Bill Belmont.

White audiences: Reflecting on the greater popularity of white musicians, Michael Bloomfield speculated that white teenaged record buyers "more readily identify sexually and personally with a white person than like with Otis [Redding]" ("The *Rolling Stone* Interview: Michael Bloomfield," *Rolling Stone,* Apr. 6, 1968, p. 14).

"a note-for-note cop": John Swenson, "Albert King: 1923–1992," *Rolling Stone,* Feb. 4, 1993, p. 12. In this same article, Jimmie Vaughan admits that King taught "the secret of his seemingly indecipherable tuning" to Vaughan's famous brother Stevie Ray. Bill Belmont worked with King at Fantasy Records and got to know him fairly well. "King would start rambling about white kid guitar players. They just bugged him because they'd steal his licks and they'd get to play and be famous, while he was struggling. Stevie Ray Vaughan was supposed to produce a record for Albert King, but it never happened, because Vaughan's management company felt he was making too much money from touring to work on it. Albert would say to me, 'But I taught him everything he knows. Why ain't he producing my record?' "

Remarkably, black players: Interviews with Mark Naftalin, Sam Andrew, Peter Albin, James Gurley.

when Howlin' Wolf snubbed him: Tracy Nelson remembers the night one well-known white guitarist (not Michael Bloomfield) climbed onstage to sit in with Wolf at Silvio's, a Chicago blues joint. As he went up to join the band Wolf "literally whacked him off the stage," she says. Nelson hung out in Chicago blues bars and suspects Wolf was amused by all the adulation, despite his sometimes fierce growl. "Friends of mine who know him say he was a perfectly nice guy, but he just loved mau-mauing all these little white kids. And we just ate it up."

236   "that carefree blues lifestyle": Nick Gravenites, "Bad Talkin' Bluesman," *Blues Revue,* June/July 1996, p. 15.

"I keep trying to tell people": Nat Hentoff, "We Look at Our Parents and . . ." *New York Times,* Apr. 21, 1968, p. 19.

237   "Janis Joplin sings the blues": Dalton, p. 38.

"She had been sucking on": Charles White, *The Life and Times of Little Richard: The Quasar of Rock* (New York: Harmony, 1984), p. 141.

"That girl feels like I do": Interview with Chris Strachwitz.

"She gave me respect": Etta James and David Ritz, *Rage to Survive* (New York: Villard Books, 1995), p. 192.

Mickey Hart: On Hart's attempt to lure Janis into a supergroup, see Joel Selvin, *Summer of Love* (New York: Penguin, 1994), p. 194.

"Everything changed at Stax": Guralnick, p. 355.

"an undercurrent of racial division:" Guralnick, p. 364. My own view differs somewhat from that of Guralnick, who writes that his "direct involvement" with soul music ended after King's assassination: "the climate had changed, a new note of hostility had entered the air" (p. 354). While I, too, mourn the loss of interracialism in the wake of King's murder, I think black power accomplished some good by encouraging racial pride and provoking a much-needed appraisal of institutionalized racism. Guralnick may also, but he seems more critical of the way black power affected southern soul music than of the unequal power relations that obtained before King's murder.

238   "blacks made the music": Guralnick, p. 384.

"All of a sudden": Guralnick, p. 387.

By the early seventies: Guralnick, p. 379. In 1972, Jim Stewart, who founded Stax Records with his sister, was bought out by his partner, Al Bell.

"We did Dylan's": Harry Shapiro and Caesar Glebeek, *Jimi Hendrix Electric Gypsy* (New York: St. Martin's Press, 1990), p. 156. For more on Hendrix's response to the changing political landscape, see Charles Shaar Murray's wonderful book *Crosstown Traffic: Jimi Hendrix and the Post-War Rock 'n' Roll Revolution* (New York: St. Martin's Press, 1989), especially chapter 4. Murray contends that Hendrix's manager and his record label were keenly aware that Hendrix's fans viewed him as an "honorary white." Janis's friend the blues guitarist Johnny Winter, an albino Texan, frequently jammed with Hendrix and says that, after Hendrix formed the all-black Band of Gypsies in 1969, the "white guys and managers would say [to Jimi], 'Don't play with these niggers, man; the fourteen-year-olds can't relate to all that space stuff. Get the cute English guys back." And then, says Winter, "the black guys would tell him he was selling out to whitey. Jimi was a pretty sensitive person, plus he was pretty loaded all the time, and he didn't know what to do" (Murray, p. 84).

"They can *play*": "Rebirth of the Blues," p. 83. A few years later, Muddy Waters would hire white sidemen in his band, and he actually helped mentor Butterfield, Bloomfield, Gravenites, Clapton, and Johnny Winter. Bob Margolin, a white guitarist, played in the Muddy Waters Blues Band for seven years and contends, "None of the black players EVER brought up the subject of race. They felt that if you can play, you can play and if you can't, you can't" ("Down at the Crossroads, There's a Devil of a Debate," *New York Times,* Mar. 5, 1995, 16).

While much recent writing: Here I am thinking of Francis Davis, *The History of the Blues: The Roots, the Music, the People from Charley Patton to Robert Cray* (New York: Hyperion, 1995); Ann Douglas, *Terrible Honesty: Mongrel Manhattan in the 1920s* (New York: Farrar, Straus and Giroux, 1995); Stanley Crouch, *Notes of a Hanging Judge: Essays and Reviews, 1979–89* (New York: Oxford University Press, 1990); Eric Lott, *Love and Theft: Black-face Minstrelsy and the American Working Class* (New York: Oxford University Press, 1993); Andrew Ross, "Hip and the Long Front of Color," in *No Respect: Intellectuals and Popular Culture* (New York: Routledge, 1989). Long before it was fashionable, Albert Murray insisted on the mulatto character of American culture. See *Stomping the Blues* (New York: McGraw-Hill, 1976) and *The Omni-Americans: Black Experience and American Culture* (New York: Vintage, 1983, first published in 1970.)

twenty-something: Of course, there were a number of rock critics who weren't young, such as Phil Elwood and Ralph Gleason, who started out reviewing jazz and folk music.

239 "Tom travesties": Quoted in Simon Frith, *Sound Effects: Youth, Leisure, and the Politics of Rock* (London: Constable, 1980), p. 22.

"the misguided notion that a black": Mary Wilson, *Dreamgirl: My Life as a Supreme* (New York: St. Martin's Press, 1986), p. 210.

"What happened to the days": Quoted in Frith, p. 22.

"has the authenticity": "Lady Soul: Singing It Like It Is," *Time,* June 28, 1968, p. 62.

In one of the earliest attacks: "Stop This Shuck, Mike Bloomfield" was published in the May 11, 1968, issue of *Rolling Stone,* p. 10. Nick Gravenites defended Bloomfield in the next issue with "Stop This Shuck, Ralph Gleason," *Rolling Stone,* May 25, 1968, p. 17.

Erma Franklin's version: Jon Landau, "The Newport Folk Festival," *Rolling Stone,* Aug. 24, 1968, p. 17.

"stereophonic minstrel show": Bill Kloman, "The 50s Come Back," *New York Times,* Sept. 1, 1968, sec. 2, p. 18. Janis was generally attacked by white critics, although, according to the *Village Voice*, one black magazine did accuse her of ransacking black music.

"How much more authentic": Richard Goldstein, *Goldstein's Greatest Hits* (Englewood Cliffs: Prentice-Hall, 1970), p. 183.

page

240   "when you're making $10,000": "Rebirth of the Blues," p. 83. Similarly, Peter Guralnick pronounced the death of soul music—"Soul is over"—when a record by Solomon Burke, a gritty southern soul singer, scored a Top 40 hit. See Guralnick's review of Burke's LP, *Rolling Stone*, Aug. 9, 1969, p. 34.

"This is where Janis": Quoted in "Random Notes," *Rolling Stone*, Sept. 28, 1968, p. 6.

"too down and lonely": Dalton, p. 181.

"waking up": Amburn, p. 213.

"One day, I realized": Dalton, p. 182.

241   "Michael was so headstrong": Ben Fong-Torres with Nick Gravenites, "The Saddest Story in the World," *Rolling Stone*, Oct. 29, 1970, p. 12.

"She's doing the hardest thing": Michael Lydon, "Every Moment She Is What She Feels," *New York Times Magazine*, Feb. 23, 1969, p. 39.

"sound test" . . . "preview": Paul Nelson, "Janis Joplin: The Judy Garland of Rock?" *Rolling Stone*, Mar. 15, 1969, p. 6.

"Janis kept walking": Ellen Willis, "Changes," *New Yorker*, Mar. 15, 1969, p. 173.

242   "the new tunes on a record": Nelson, p. 8.

The *New York Times*: Mike Jahn, "New Band Liberates Joplin Blues Sound," *New York Times*, Feb. 12, 1969.

"stop killing herself": Willis, p. 173.

"the band made all local stops": Nelson, p. 6.

243   "drag": *Rolling Stone* reprinted parts of Gleason's review in a summary of Janis's career after she died (*Rolling Stone*, Oct. 29, 1970, p. 10).

"she's-gettin'-too-big": Amburn, p. 207.

"Janis came": Jonathan Cott and David Dalton, "Janis and London Come Together," *Rolling Stone*, May 31, 1969, p. 6.

"Soul": The raves from the British press are reprinted in Cott and Dalton, p. 6.

"Hey man": Randy, "Pearl or Memories of a Stone Soldier," *Rag*, Feb. 22, 1971.

244   the band's personnel: For the numerous changes, I've relied on "John Cooke Tells How It Was," *Rolling Stone*, Nov. 12, 1970, p. 19.

245   "Everyone felt as if tomorrow": Amburn, p. 215.

"very friendly": Interview with Maury Baker. All subsequent quotations are from this interview.

"would talk shit": Interview with Vince Mitchell. All subsequent quotations are from this interview.

page

"When he did arrive": Sam Andrew, "Recollections of Janis," *Blues Revue,* no. 17, p. 10.

"We were musicians": Interview with Snooky Flowers. All subsequent quotations are from this interview unless otherwise noted.

"band was better": Joplin, p. 262.

246   "Everybody was putting down": Friedman, p. 161.

"saying more": Interview with Sye Mitchell.

"the brass in her second group": Chet Flippo, "An Interview with Janis' Father," *Rolling Stone,* Nov. 2, 1970, p. 18.

Michael Bloomfield's scorching guitar: Bloomfield's solo on "One Good Man" went uncredited on the album. One wonders if John Burks of *Rolling Stone* would have characterized this solo as "a tolerable bottleneck introduction and obbligato" had he known that it was the paper's favorite son, Bloomfield, and not Big Brother's "lone survivor," Sam Andrew, on that cut. Review of *Kozmic Blues, Rolling Stone,* Nov. 1, 1969, p. 40.

Jumbo: For more on this musical, see William G. Hyland, *Richard Rodgers* (New Haven: Yale University Press, 1998), pp. 103–04.

247   "lumpier than a beer hall accordion band": Burks, p. 40.

"They didn't get me off": Dalton, p. 89.

248   "in the back": Interview with Toni Brown. All subsequent quotations are from this interview.

"Laura wanted to tell her": Clive Davis with James Willwerth, *Clive: Inside the Record Business* (New York: William Morrow, 1975), p. 86.

"was not exactly friendly": "Joni Mitchell Missed Woodstock," *Interview,* July 1994, p. 59.

"life without anxiety": John Colapinto, "Heroin," *Rolling Stone,* May 30, 1996, p. 16.

"good pioneer stock": Amburn, p. 216.

"Well, some people die": Friedman, p. 174.

249   "A junkie's life": Tom Wheeler, interview with Michael Bloomfield, in Jas Obrecht, ed., *Blues Guitar: The Men Who Made the Music* (San Francisco: Miller Freeman Books, 1993), p. 266.

"Junk is not a kick": Steven Watson, *The Birth of the Beat Generation: Visionaries, Rebels, and Hipsters, 1944–1960* (New York: Pantheon, 1995), p. 57.

"gray" and "defeated": Dalton, p. 188.

"her talismanic bottle": "Rebirth of the Blues," p. 84.

"float in and out": Friedman, p. 135.

page

Yet, in Myra's view: Myra argues that Janis's behavior was self-contradictory, but she stresses Janis's indiscretions and further argues that "heroin users are notorious for wallowing in the role of outlaw." As evidence, Myra cites an incident in Cincinnati in which members of Big Brother shot up with strangers, Janis's carelessness with a *Playboy* reporter, her asides to Elliot Mazer about "getting high," her many hints to Myra herself, and her "confessions" to doctors. I don't doubt these reports, but I think the picture is somewhat fuzzier than Myra's account suggests.

Curiously, others claim: Janis's last lover, Seth Morgan, maintains that Janis cleaned her own motel room rather than let maids enter it. On extended stays, she'd permit maid service once a week. "She was paranoid about her heroin and paraphernalia being discovered," he writes. (Seth Morgan, " 'Pink Cocaine': A True Account ... of the Last Days of Janis Joplin," *Fortune News,* July/Aug. 1978, p. 5.)

250   "Joe, where are you, Joe?": Friedman, p. 182.

251   "sexual preferences": Friedman, p. 5.

       "She was terrified that people": Friedman, p. 127.

252   gays expecting to find: Others have commented on homophobia in the Haight. "No one was gay in the hippie scene," claims Richard Hundgen. To Bob Seidemann the scene was "overwhelmingly heterosexual." Nor were the Diggers, despite their political engagement, any more enlightened when it came to gays and lesbians. When Emmett Grogan broke up an SDS meeting he shouted at the startled group, "Faggots! You haven't got the balls to go mad" (Jonah Raskin, *For the Hell of It: The Life and Times of Abbie Hoffman* [Berkeley: University of California Press], 1996, p. 104). Timothy Leary, meanwhile, proclaimed acid "a specific *cure* for homosexuality" (Warren Hinckle, "A Social History of the Hippies," *Ramparts,* Mar. 1967, reprinted in Gerald Howard, ed., *The Sixties: The Art, Attitudes, Politics, and Media of Our Most Explosive Decade* [New York: Pocket Books, 1982], p. 225.

253   "I was stark naked": Peggy Caserta (as told to Dan Knapp), *Going Down with Janis* (Secaucus: Lyle Stuart, 1973), p. 7.

254   The evidence is that Janis was taken with Peggy: Interviews with Lyndall Erb, Milan Melvin, and Linda Gravenites. Janis's last boyfriend, Seth Morgan, told Myra Friedman that Peggy was "the girlfriend Janis most admired" (Friedman, p. 304).

255   "This is my life now": Amburn, p. 206.

       "She was flirting in a way": Milan goes on to say, "The view of a lesbian at that time was really short-haired women wearing suits and ties, smoking cigars in clubs." Neither Janis nor her friends were like that, he contends. "This was a new thing. This wasn't a lesbian thing." Milan may be right, but Peggy and Kimmie were part of San Francisco's lesbian community. I am not so sure that Peggy's affairs with men were so unusual among lesbians in the mid- to late sixties. The assumption that lesbians sleep only with women may owe more to seventies lesbian feminism, which proscribed sex with men, than to actual behavior.

257 "I was so furious with her": Amburn, p. 175.
With friends whose habits: Interview with Peggy Caserta. Peggy was not among these unlucky friends but remembers witnessing this behavior.

258 "sitting astride him": Amburn, p. 210.

260 "She had a thing about fixing": Amburn, p. 203.
"gotten all that satisfaction": Friedman, p. 188.
"The saddest part": Kathy Dobie, "Midnight Train: A Teenage Story," in Barbara O'Dair, ed. *Trouble Girls: The* Rolling Stone *Book of Women in Rock* (New York: Random House, 1997), p. 234.
"Who can you talk to": Reed, p. 90.

261 "stood back there": "Riffs," *Village Voice*, Aug. 8, 1968, p. 18.
"Onstage I make love": Ellen Willis, "Musical Events," *New Yorker*, Aug. 14, 1971, p. 81.

9 · TRADING HER TOMORROWS

page

263 "The only . . . real surprise": Ellen Willis, quoted in Stacey D'Erasmo, "Woodshlock Nation," *Village Voice*, July 19, 1994, p. 25.
"What kind of culture": The underground paper *Rat* reprinted the *New York Times* editorial (see *Rat*, Aug. 27–Sept. 9, 1969, p. 12). Abe Peck quotes from it as well in *Uncovering the Sixties: The Life and Times of the Underground Press* (New York: Pantheon, 1985), p. 179.
"I can always tell": Bill Graham and Robert Greenfield, *Bill Graham Presents: My Life inside Rock and Out* (New York: Doubleday, 1992), p. 288.
"Instead of the widespread notion": David Clurman, letter to the editor, *New York Times*, Aug. 10, 1994, p. A14.
"Woodstock was horrible": Graham and Greenfield, p. 287.

264 "They expected the audience": Graham and Greenfield, p. 283.

page

"beautiful, transcendent acceptance": D'Erasmo, p. 25.

"Woodstock was a bunch": Graham and Greenfield, p. 297.

"First Annual Charlie Manson": Graham and Greenfield, p. 294.

"whether the youth culture": Peck, p. 226.

265   She had the misfortune: Here I am relying on information provided in Bob Spitz, *Barefoot in Babylon* (New York: Norton, 1979). My account of her performance is based on the recently released director's cut of the film *Woodstock* (Janis wasn't in the 1970 version)—which includes "Work Me, Lord"—as well as on the compact disc *Woodstock Diary*, which features "Try (Just a Little Bit Harder)" and "Ball and Chain."

266   "tortured and crying": Joel Makower, *Woodstock: The Oral History* (New York: Doubleday, 1989), p. 234.

"I'm not fucking talking": Ibid.

"I wrote the part": Laura Joplin, *Love, Janis* (New York: Villard Books, 1992), p. 289.

"the underlying bleakness": Myra Friedman, *Buried Alive: The Biography of Janis Joplin* (New York: Harmony, 1992), p. 115.

"the real secret": Susan Cheever, *Home before Dark: A Biographical Memoir of John Cheever by His Daughter* (New York: Pocket Books, 1984), p. 165.

"Success gets in your way": "Rebirth of the Blues," *Newsweek,* May 26, 1969, p. 84.

"Oh, this is no kind of life": Interview with Pepi Plowman.

267   "Well, you've really done it": J. David Moriaty, "Come On, Take Another Little Piece of My Corpse, Now Baby," *Austin Sun,* June 27, 1975, p. 27.

"It just got worse and worse": David Dalton, *Piece of My Heart: A Portrait of Janis Joplin,* rev. ed. (New York: Da Capo, 1991), p. 172.

"audiences had to be swarming": Friedman, p. 174.

"It was like Janis": Friedman, p. 175.

"Listen, Mister": "Janis Busted for Naughty Words," *Rolling Stone,* Dec. 13, 1969, p. 8.

268   "I say anything I want": Joplin, p. 263.

"It would be illegal": Johanna Schier, "Riffs," *Village Voice,* Dec. 25, 1969.

"for her attitude in general": Friedman, p. 307.

"She might as well": Friedman, p. 174.

"Janis was pretty down": Interview with Myra Friedman.

269   "other way": Friedman, p. 171.

"failed to take real command": Fred Goodman, *The Mansion on the Hill* (New York: Times Books, 1997), p. 108.

"never would have discussed": Sally Grossman says that Albert arranged for Janis to see at least two doctors about her heroin addiction.

270   "He was not a sycophantic": Interview with Peter Yarrow. All subsequent quotations are from this interview unless otherwise noted.

"I can do this": Friedman, p. 177.

"edgy": Friedman, p. 182.

"a green-white glow": Friedman, p. 184.

"Gee, am I glad": Joplin, p. 266.

"I'm going to be clean": Friedman, p. 185.

271   "act supportive" . . . "I don't know": Joplin, p. 270.

"You know, you look": Joplin, p. 275.

"going off into the jungle": Dalton, p. 280.

She told Myra: Friedman, p. 189.

"You're a cunt": Joplin, p. 273.

272   "Every time we went out": Joplin, p. 275.

"He's determined to turn me": Ellis Amburn, *Pearl: The Obsessions and Passions of Janis Joplin* (New York: Warner Books, 1992), p. 248.

"out on the road": The rap can be found on the 1993 Janis Joplin boxed set.

"motion, motion, motion": Friedman, p. 264.

273   There was the time: Interview with Peggy Caserta. Pat "Sunshine" Nichols says that Bloomfield OD'd alarmingly often because he had a bad heart, a condition he was unaware of.

"He makes too much money": Linda Gravenites reports Janis's saying this.

274   gross annual earnings: Testifying in an insurance trial after Janis's death, Harold Davis, Albert Grossman's lawyer, said that in the last year of her life Janis grossed $750,000 ("Another Look at Janis's Death," *Rolling Stone*, Apr. 25, 1974).

"What's the fucking idea": Peggy Caserta (as told to Dan Knapp), *Going Down with Janis* (Secaucus: Lyle Stuart, 1973), p. 232. Although parts of the book are inaccurate, Peggy Caserta confirms this story.

Sometimes Peggy cackles: Interview with Peggy Caserta.

275   She started chipping: Interviews with Linda Gottfried Waldron and Sam Andrew.

Travis Rivers contends: Amburn, p. 251.

276   "Janis was real good": Interview with Lyndall Erb. All subsequent quotations are from this interview.

She fretted: Interview with Stanley Mouse.

"and then bitch": Friedman, p. 203.

page

277   "It's true!": Friedman, p. 240.

"separate stage persona": Joplin, p. 279. While Janis undoubtedly had such conversations with Bobby Neuwirth, her friend and former roadie Dave Richards claims that the name itself grew out of a conversation she had with him. "I was in a health food store," Richards says, "and I saw the name pearl barley. I made a joke about pearl barley and that's where the Pearl thing started" (Amburn, p. 156).

feathers in her hair: George Ebbe, a friend and onetime lover, says that Janis started wearing feathers in her hair to give it a fuller look and to disguise all her split ends. He says Janis attributed her scraggly hair to her heroin use (interview with George Ebbe).

"If you call drinking": Friedman, p. 201.

278   "Fuck you": Friedman, p. 209.

"People, whether they know it": Dalton, p. 190.

"Maybe my audience": Dalton, p. 58.

279   At one point: Friedman, p. 210.

280   "I can tell those cats": Friedman, p. 197.

Full Tilt Boogie Band: For information on the makeup of the band, see Dalton, pp. 87–88.

"Howling, screeching": Quoted in David Dalton, "Janis Joplin's Full-Tilt Boogie Ride," *Rolling Stone,* Aug. 6, 1970, p. 10.

"the virtues of spontaneity" . . . "This band": Dalton, "Janis," pp. 10–11.

"it's more of a family thing again": Dalton, *Piece,* p. 88.

281   "just the tip of the iceberg": Amburn, pp. 291–92.

"white soul": Iian Chambers, *Urban Rhythms* (New York: Macmillan, 1985), p. 120.

282   "the presiding spirit of the journey": Dalton, *Piece,* p. 197.

"Will someone tune": The anecdote is in Friedman, pp. 234–35. Wali Stopher spoke briefly with Janis and thought she seemed "jet-lagged and drug-lagged." This would jibe with Linda Gottfried Waldron's account of Janis's visit to Hawaii, which preceded her trip to Austin. Linda says Janis later admitted that she'd been using in Hawaii.

"I learned something": John Cooke reports Rothchild's saying this.

283   "I want to be the greatest": Joplin, p. 292.

"That's my next competition": Amburn, p. 270; interview with Pat "Sunshine" Nichols.

"I can't sleep!": Friedman, p. 218.

"Albert always said": Goodman, p. 106.

"I know I'm not the Band": Friedman, p. 219.

284   "This is killing you": Friedman, p. 219.

"Then *quit*, Janis": Friedman, p. 269.

But Janis made it clear: Myra claims that Janis's provocative behavior had "severe repercussions" on her bookings (Friedman, p. 176). Yet neither Sally Grossman nor Albert's partner, Bennett Glotzer, remembers any problems. John Till, her lead guitarist, doesn't recall "any concert that wasn't well attended from my point of view, which was looking out from the stage." He felt "her popularity was on the rise, not declining" (interviews with Sally Grossman and Bennett Glotzer; personal communication from John Till).

285   "Women, to be": Dalton, *Piece*, pp. 239–40.

"people tryin' to get something": Dalton, *Piece,* p. 131.

"never wanted to do anything else": Dalton, *Piece,* p. 241.

Too drunk to sing "Ball and Chain": In the middle of the song Janis sings the word "Tryyyyy," over and over, but her voice betrays her. Then she starts talking about living in the present, echoing her rap for "Get It While You Can."

286   "This life is bullshit": Amburn, pp. 292–93.

Some of her friends: Interview with Myra Friedman. Myra knew of Janis's parents, but she learned that other friends didn't when she was researching her book.

"One of you is enough": Interview with Linda Gravenites.

The Dick Cavett Show: My account of her appearance on the show is drawn from *Janis: The Way She Was*, MCA Home Video, 1974.

287   "I was just 'silly crazy Janis' ": Michael Lydon, "Every Moment She Is What She Feels," *New York Times Magazine*, Feb. 23, 1969, p. 40.

Karleen Bennett's mother: Interview with Herman Bennett.

"I sat up with her": "Buddy and Janis," *Magazine of the Houston Post*, Jan. 19, 1986, p. 9.

"really cool": The account of Janis's visit is in Joplin, pp. 296–98.

288   "You'd think they'd have": Chet Flippo, "Janis Reunes at Jefferson High," *Rolling Stone,* Sept. 17, 1970, p. 8.

"There seems to be": The account of the interview is drawn from the footage in *Janis: The Way She Was*.

289   "Is there anything": Joplin, p. 301.

As soon as she left: Friedman, p. 288.

290   "You wouldn't be bad looking": Joplin, p. 302.

Janis's parents awoke: My account of the morning after the reunion is drawn from Laura Joplin's book and my interview with Myra Friedman.

page

"I wish you'd never been born!": Myra says that Janis told her of the fight immediately after returning to California. No one I interviewed was able to corroborate Myra's story, although Lyndall Erb says that Janis had not had a good time with her family (Michael excepted) and felt they didn't like her. Neither Linda nor Sunshine, the two friends Janis was most likely to have told of the fight, were in contact with her then. This is the first time Myra has gone on record with this account.

"Mother": Friedman, p. 291.

291   "It's f-a-n-t-a-a-a-a-s-t-i-c": *Janis: The Way She Was.* See also Flippo, p. 8.

"Well": Friedman, p. 291.

"I knew that it was going": "Buddy and Janis," p. 9.

292   "a sleazy motherfucker": Amburn, p. 279.

In 1990, he and his girlfriend: Joplin, p. 306.

"very wounded": Amburn, p. 289.

293   "mediocre": Seth Morgan, "Pink Cocaine," *Fortune News,* July-Aug. 1978.

"If she was any old body": Joplin, p. 305.

"Think of my career!": Friedman, p. 297.

294   "real genuine flame": Joplin, 305.

"wind down": Friedman, p. 306.

bragging about a new deal: On Albert's deal and her talk of the next album, see Amburn, pp. 291–92.

"emotional problems": Amburn, p. 290.

When they had met: On the meeting with Bob Gordon, see Friedman, p. 306. In his memoir, "Pink Cocaine," Seth Morgan mentions the prenuptial agreement but denies he and Janis were about to be married. He claims that the day after Janis died, Grossman's office "promulgated" the story of their impending marriage to *Newsweek* because Thomas Noguchi, the Los Angeles County coroner, was doing a "psychological autopsy" on Janis to determine if her OD was accidental or intentional. "Plans to marry," wrote Seth, "constituted convenient prima facie evidence of happiness," and not incidentally would allow Grossman to collect on the insurance policy he had on Janis.

"Thanks a lot": Friedman, p. 315. For Janis's growing apprehensiveness about Seth, I have drawn on my interview with Peggy Caserta.

295   "wanted to do it anymore": Friedman, p. 314. On Janis's other reasons for taking up heroin again, see Joplin, p. 307.

"convenience of being close": David Crosby and Carl Gottlieb, *Long Time Gone: The Autobiography of David Crosby* (New York: Dell, 1988), p. 198.

page

296   "Janis . . . you jump": Morgan, p. 4.

"Man, you got everything": Friedman, p. 314.

She says Kristofferson: Friedman, p. 253. Today, Kristofferson's manager, Vernon White, says the actor's comments were exaggerated. My requests to speak with Kristofferson on this matter were declined.

297   "a rocking good time": "John Cooke Tells It Like It Was," *Rolling Stone*, Nov. 12, 1979, p. 19.

Whatever she actually felt: With the exception of Myra Friedman, who doesn't rule out the possibility of suicide and characterizes Janis's life as "chronic suicide," none of Janis's friends—or none of the ones with whom I spoke—believe she set out to take her own life.

"How 'bout": Friedman, p. 313.

"Goddammit, he beat me": Dalton, p. 107.

"If any of you guys": Friedman, p. 319.

298   "Janisfied": The term is Linda Gottfried Waldron's, quoted in Friedman, p. 334.

"It's Life": Dalton, p. 91.

EPILOGUE

page

299   John Cooke says: This is the account Cooke gave *Rolling Stone* after her death and the story he told me as well.

300   Still, questions remain: For one, people have wondered why so much time elapsed—maybe ten or fifteen minutes—between the time of injection and her death. Laura Joplin suggests that the delay occurred because Janis skin-popped that night instead of shooting directly into her vein. Perhaps, but Janis's friends insist she never skin-popped but always went for the rush. Others including Scott Carrier, spokesman for the L.A. County coroner's office, and Joe Lucky of the Orange County coroner's office, say that even when used intravenously, heroin doesn't always kill instantaneously. Curiously, the heroin's strength seems not to have come up in the 1974 insurance inquiry into her death. Vince Mitchell is by no means the only person who thinks Janis wasn't alone the night she died. There are some things we simply cannot know, and what exactly happened the night she died is one of them.

"It's so strong it OD'd Janis": Interview with Richard Hundgen.

page

Janis was the sixth person: Laura Joplin, *Love, Janis* (New York: Villard Books, 1992), p. 311.

301   "sort of fainted": Danny Fields and Jeff Nesin, "Conversation," in Robert Somma, ed., *No One Waved Good-bye* (New York: Outerbridge & Dienstfrey, 1971), pp. 60–61.

"seemed as solidly situated": David Dalton, *Piece of My Heart: A Portrait of Janis Joplin*, rev. ed. (New York: Da Capo, 1991), p. 106.

"Can't we do any better": Don Heckman, "Janis Joplin, 1943–1970," *New York Times*, Oct. 6, 1970.

302   growing heroin use of his clients and friends: Bloomfield spoke openly of his addiction when he was clean in the eighties; Levon Helm discussed heroin use in the Band in *This Wheel's on Fire: The Story of Levon Helm and the Band* (New York: William Morrow, 1993); and Fred Goodman writes of the OD of Peter Yarrow's younger brother in *The Mansion on the Hill* (New York: Times Books, 1997).

303   "San Francisco's big night": Fields and Nesin, p. 59.

"he was laying his bad trip": Charles Perry, "The News Reaches San Francisco," *Rolling Stone*, Oct. 29, 1970, p. 14.

"When someone gets killed": "Janis Joplin," *Rolling Stone*, Oct. 29, 1970, p. 7.

"sensitive, far-out, weird people": Perry, p. 14. Recently, the Dead's former comanager, Rock Scully, claimed that Garcia was "blown away" that night at Winterland when he heard of Janis's death (Rock Scully with David Dalton, "Chronicles of the Dead," *Playboy*, 1996, p. 192).

"I can't bring myself": Perry, p. 14.

304   "There's a lot of people": Ben Fong-Torres with Nick Gravenites, "The Saddest Story in the World," *Rolling Stone*, Oct. 29, 1970, p. 12.

"This was our Vietnam": Darby Slick, *Don't You Want Somebody to Love: Reflections on the San Francisco Sound* (Berkeley: SLG Books, 1991), p. 63.

"dreadful war": Philip K. Dick, *A Scanner Darkly*, 1977 (New York: Vintage, 1991), p. 259.

Dave complained to Peter: Susan Gordon Lydon, *Take the Long Way Home: Memoirs of a Survivor* (New York: HarperCollins, 1993), p. 119. Susan Lydon, who was once married to the rock critic Michael Lydon, was involved with Dave Getz in this period.

305   "twenty years of marshmallow": Peter Cohon (Coyote). Quoted in Nicholas von Hoffman, *We Are the People Our Parents Warned Us Against* (Chicago: Quadrangle, 1968), p. 131.

"lifelong struggle with intoxicants": Interview with Ramsey Wiggins.

page

      "walking into one of those society parties": Lillian Roxon, "A Moment Too Soon," in Somma, p. 96.

306   "living nosethumb": Roxon, p. 95.

      "Sexism killed her": Gillian Gaar, *She's a Rebel: The History of Women in Rock and Roll* (Seattle: Seal Press, 1992), p. 107.

      "just always hold up something": *Janis: The Way She Was*, MCA Home Video, 1974.

      "Gosh, it seemed like": Interview on Louisville, Kentucky, radio station, summer 1970. Tape courtesy of Myra Friedman.

307   "making a comeback": "Melissa Etheridge on Janis Joplin," *Rolling Stone*, Feb. 23, 1995, p. 50.

      "We know Janis was gay": Johnston's November 1971 column was reprinted in *Lesbian Nation* (New York: Simon & Schuster, 1973), p. 231. Her claims were reported in "Random Notes," *Rolling Stone*'s gossip column, on January 20, 1972.

      "drama queens": Daniel Mendelsohn, "The Drama Queens," *New York Times Magazine*, Nov. 24, 1996, p. 72.

      Midler's impersonation: By contrast, Jennifer Jason Leigh's performance in *Georgia* (1995), in which she plays a junkie singer who "can't sing," seems informed by Janis's edginess, emotional skittishness, and overwhelming neediness. The character even utters a line Janis used with Dick Cavett: "I don't write songs, I make them up."

308   "original influence": Karen Schoemer, "Heaven Sent," *Mirabella*, Mar. 1994, p. 64.

      "Janis made it up": Interview with Chris Williamson.

      Lou Ann Barton, Marsha Ball, Angela Strehli: "All three of them told me they were inspired by Janis," says Tary Owens.

      "that fat chick from Texas": Charles Perry, "Pearl: The Voice is Janis', but He Shaves," *Rolling Stone*, May 10, 1973, p. 12.

      "I open myself up enough": "Bonnie Raitt: The *Real Paper* Interview," *Real Paper*, Oct. 24, 1973, p. 28.

309   "more restrained Janis": Interview with Terry Garthwaite.

      "There you were living": Chrissie Hynde, liner notes to *Janis Joplin with Big Brother and the Holding Company Live at Winterland*, Sony, 1998.

      "Janis sang out of her pain": Ellen Willis, "Musical Events," *New Yorker*, Aug. 14, 1971, p. 81.

      "Janis's thorough explorations": Ann Powers, "Janis without Tears," July 1993, p. 31, liner notes to the 1993 Sony boxed set.

page

      "I was 11 years old": Karen Ocamb, "Melissa Etheridge," *Lesbian News,* Sept. 1993, p. 44.

310 "Janis demolishes the canard": Robert Christgau, "Consumer Guide," *Village Voice,* Dec. 21, 1993, p. 97.

311 "You may not end up happy": Dalton, p. 164.

Acknowledgments

In the five years I was at work on this project, I incurred many more debts than I can ever repay. Although I can't thank every person who took the time to talk with me, I do want to single out a few people. I could never have written this book without the help of Peter Albin, Sam Andrew, Dave Getz, and James Gurley—Janis's band mates in Big Brother and the Holding Company. Peter, Sam, and Dave were especially helpful and always gracious, even when I prodded them to think about those difficult times after Janis left the band. Of Janis's San Francisco friends, I want to thank Peggy Caserta, Linda Gravenites, Milan Melvin, Pat "Sunshine" Nichols, and Jae Whitaker, whose memories, insights, and hard-earned knowledge enrich this book. I am also grateful to Bob Seidemann for trusting me enough to drop his hipster act and talk honestly with me about life in the Haight. Bill Belmont, John Morris, and Jim Haynie taught me a lot about Bill Graham and San Francisco rock 'n' roll. Elliot Mazer, John Simon, and Fred Catero shared their thoughts about recording technology and their experiences working on Big Brother's break-out album, *Cheap Thrills*. The droll observations of Sally Grossman were priceless, even if they were off the record; she also put me in touch with many people. So did Casey Monahan, director of the Texas Music Office for the State of Texas. Janis's Texas friends were great storytellers, and they were remarkably forthright and committed to my "getting it right." I am especially grateful to Chet Helms, Dave McQueen, Dave Moriaty, Pepi Plowman, Travis Rivers, Powell St. John, Bob Simmons, Fredda Slote, Jack Smith, Wali Stopher, Patti McQueen Vickery, Frances Vincent, and Ramsey Wiggins. Myra Friedman freely shared with me her opinions about Janis—and much more. Although we disagree on a number of key issues, I benefitted greatly from her compelling biography of Janis, *Buried Alive*. The photographers Bill Brach, John Cooke, Leonard Duckett, Herb Greene, Lisa Law, Steve Rahn, Bob Seidemann, Betsy Siggins, Bob Simmons, Bruce Steinberg, Burton Wilson, and Baron Wolman were a pleasure to deal with as was Richard Hundgen, who graciously allowed me to use several photographs from his collection.

Lois Banner, Wini Breines, Ellen DuBois, Tania Modleski, Connie Samaras, and Alice Wexler read the manuscript and commented on it extensively. Both demanding critics and supportive friends, they were always there when I needed advice. Susan Harris, Adriene Jenek, Vivien Rothstein, and Devra Weber also read the manuscript and made many useful suggestions. Conversations with M. J. Echols, Janis Butler Holm, Peg Lourie, Karen Merrill, Charlotte Nekola, Paula Rabinowitz, Torrey Reade, Hilary Schor, Katie Stewart, and Lydia Szamraj helped clarify a number of ideas. Joseph Styles made me an all-important audiotape that included earlier recordings of songs made famous by Janis. I have no idea how he found six versions of "Little Girl Blue" by other singers, but his excavation proved critical to me. Patty McCarthy and Jim Welch provided me with incomparable research assistance. Kate Arnold and Kay Trimberger put me up when I was interviewing people in the Bay Area.

My editor, Sara Bershtel, has been absolutely indefatigable in her support of this book. Both she and Riva Hocherman did a stellar job turning a somewhat unwieldy manuscript into a coherent narrative. Roslyn Schloss's copyediting was truly full-tilt. Much thanks to my agent, Geri Thoma, who expertly guided me through this whole process from beginning to end.